THE ELEMENT ENCYCLOPEDIA OF THE CELTS

D1157324

THE ELEMENT ENCYCLOPEDIA OF THE CELTS

the ultimate a–z
of the symbols, history,
and spirituality of the
legendary celts

Rodney Castleden

HarperCollins*Publishers*
77–85 Fulham Palace Road
Hammersmith, London W6 8JB
www.harpercollins.co.uk

First published by HarperCollins*Publishers* 2012

10 9 8 7 6 5 4 3 2 1

A catalogue record of this book is
available from the British Library

ISBN 978-0-00-792979-5

Printed and bound in China

DEDICATION

This book is dedicated to a people who, over many centuries, have been misunderstood and frequently misrepresented.

> *The harp that once through Tara's halls*
> *The soul of music shed,*
> *Now hangs as mute on Tara's walls*
> *As if that soul were fled.*
> *So sleeps the pride of former days,*
> *So glory's thrill is o'er,*
> *And hearts, that once beat high for praise,*
> *Now feel that pulse no more.*

The Irish poet Thomas Moore (1779–1852)

CONTENTS

PREFACE

"SO SLEEPS THE PRIDE OF FORMER DAYS"

This book is an attempt to explore the entire spectrum of Celtic culture. Each of us carries, sometimes consciously, sometimes unconsciously, a particular image of the Celts and their culture. It is like a distinctive and familiar smell or flavor that we recognize as soon as we encounter it.

To some "Celtic" means the soulful, echoing music of harps or bagpipes, or a particularly plaintive style of singing, while to others it means a political movement striving to create—or restore—a regional identity. To some it means modern team games, while to others it means clans and tartans. To some it is a wild, rocky landscape with mist, sea spray, and the roar of breaking waves, while to others it is dissent, tribal warfare, and the world of

Braveheart. To some it means ancient legends about dragons, King Arthur, and the Lady of the Lake, while to others it means a lost empire that more than 2,000 years ago spanned Iron Age Europe.

With so many different contemporary takes on Celticness, it will be useful to explore where these ideas have come from. Those who are Celts may want to relive what Thomas Moore called "the pride of former days" and bring that pride into the present, but to do that honorably there is a need to be honest about the past.

One important idea that will emerge from this book is that the nature of Celticness has changed through time, and that means that we need to look at the Celts of 2,000 years ago, look again at the Celts of the Middle Ages, and look yet again at the Celts of today. In order to reach the true nature of Celticness, we have to establish who the Celts were—and who they are.

The Element Encyclopedia of the Celts

INTRODUCTION

WHO WERE THE CELTS?

For many people, the word "Celt" conjures two different images; two quite different personalities. One is hot-blooded, fiery, passionate, quick to take offense, volatile, and argumentative. The other is quiet, nostalgic, thoughtful, contemplative, mystical, and in tune with the natural world and also with the world of the spirit. These are two quite different personalities, but they complement each other. They are the two sides of an ancient Celtic coin: the Janus faces of Celticness.

The Celts have tended to dwell on their past, forever looking back to days of former glories and brooding over past defeats. The ancient and medieval Celts loved to tell stories about their tribes, their leaders, their heroes, and their gods. Sometimes there was

a practical value in this. Kings and princes needed to justify their positions of privilege, and their ancestry was an integral part of their title. "I am your king because my father was your king and his father before him..." They needed bards to recite their genealogies so that their subjects were regularly reminded of their lords' pedigrees. Sometimes these genealogies included glamorous imaginary heroes and the recitation of the family tree developed into entertainment.

Storytelling has always been an important element in the Celtic psyche, and the edge between story and history has always been blurred. But a story, or the complex web of interlocking stories that made up the tribal myth, was what held Celtic society together. Every community needs an idea of itself in order to survive, a clear self-image that makes it possible to tell the difference between itself and other communities. This was why one tribe adopted one totem animal and another tribe adopted a different animal, and why one tribe adopted one species of tree, and another tribe a different species. "We are the elm people." "We are the oak people. We are different." That sense of special identity has always been important.

An important theme in this book is that the key to that sense of identity has changed through time. The basis, the foundation, of Celticness is not the same now as it was. What I hope to show is that in spite of this the roots of Celticness are deep; they are thousands of years old, much older than most modern-day Celts realize.

PEOPLE WE KNOW

Sometimes we think of that early world of the Celts as being an anonymous tribal world, a place where we know no one. In fact we know a surprisingly large number of people who lived in that world and we

will be meeting some of them in the first section of this book.

There were several kings in Britain whose names are known: Cassivellaunus (or Caswallawn), Cunobelin (or Cymbeline), Caratacus, Cogidumnus, Cartimandua the client queen of the Brigantes, Boudicca the warrior queen of the Iceni, Diviciacus the Druid king who visited Rome and befriended Cicero, and Vercingetorix the heroic Gaulish king who surrendered to Caesar rather than see his horses, or any more of his companions, killed. A few centuries later we stumble upon St. Patrick, St. Columba, and the ever-mysterious, ever-elusive figure of King Arthur.

Arthur has somehow moved across from history to myth, acquiring the character of a Celtic god along the way, and some of the mystification surrounding his life may reflect the religious beliefs of the time. Another section of this book is devoted to these beliefs.

The spirit world was integrated into the everyday Celtic world in a way that it no longer is today. There was no separation between the people and the spirits: the gods and goddesses who inhabited and controlled everything. The spirits were seen as residing within the natural features of the landscape. Every hill and headland, and every stream and spring, every forest and marsh had its own in-dwelling spirit. Worship was a matter of communing with the spirits in the places where they lived. People went to riverbanks to commune with the spirits of the river. They went to springs to commune with the sprites who looked after those magic places where life-giving water seeped out from the Underworld. There were temples and shrines, but a great deal of the mediation between the everyday world and the spirit world went on out in the landscape, in the open air.

Another section of this book looks at places that have special associations with the Celts: their settlements and strongholds, the scenes of their famous victories and defeats in battle, their sanctuaries and cult places.

There is also a section about the symbols and archetypes that underpin the culture of the Celts and another looking at a selection of their myths, legends, and folktales; the Celts have always been great storytellers.

The final section is a brief overview of the last thousand years or so of Celtic history, which falls

into two halves. One is a phase of suppression and eclipse which I call the "Celtic twilight." The second is a phase of rediscovery and re-emergence—the "Celtic revival"—which brings this review of the Celts up to the present day.

To go back to the beginning, the origin of the people first named the Celts by classical writers has long been the subject of speculation and discussion. The Celts of the Iron Age have an aura of mystery about them because, like the Minoans, they did not leave us any written literature of their own. There are some inscriptions and a fragmentary calendar, but there is no literature as such. The ancient Celts, either deliberately or inadvertently, surrounded themselves with mystery, like the hero Caswallawn with his magic plaid of invisibility.

Who were they? It is a question we are going to come back to again and again, and it is not an easy one to answer. BBC Wales has posted a Celts "factfile" on its educational website aimed at children. The first question is: "Who are the Celts?" It is answered by a simple timeline showing five blocks of time: "STONE AGE" (to 2000 BC), "BRONZE AGE" (to 600 BC), "IRON AGE CELTS" (to AD

50), "ROMANO-BRITISH" (to AD 400), followed by "CELTS OF TODAY." There are two cartoon Celts: one wearing a helmet and waving a sword, for the Iron Age, and one wearing a yellow shirt and blue tracksuit bottoms for today. So, according to BBC Wales, "Celt" has two senses, describing a group of people today and another group of people 2,000 years ago. Then a link between them is made: "Their culture lives on in language, music, song, and literature."

One of the questions this book needs to address is how far that is true. Is the Celticness of today really the same as that of 2,000 years ago?

BARBARIANS?

The earliest documented reference to the Celts comes from about 450 BC. Herodotus, long known as "the father of history," mentions the "Keltoi" briefly:

The River Ister [Danube] begins in the country of the Celts and the city of Pyrene [perhaps Girona, near Barcelona] and flows through the middle of Europe, bisecting it. The Celts are outside the Pillars of Heracles, bordering the Kynesians, who dwell at the edge, farther toward the setting sun than all other inhabitants of Europe.

Herodotus was well traveled, but he admitted to knowing little about northern and western Europe. His Celts are located in relation to the source of the Danube, which he wrongly believed to be near the Pyrenees, but he emphasized that the Celts lived further west in Europe than any other race. This implies that he was thinking of them as being the people of the Atlantic fringe, not of central Europe, but the misplacing of the Danube source confuses the issue. Herodotus had perhaps heard that the Kynesians and Keltoi lived in the far west (the Bay of Biscay coast of northern Spain), not far from the Pyrenees, and that was true. It was also true that those people lived further west than the Pillars of Heracles, which were the Straits of Gibraltar (longitude 5° 21'W). The longitude of La Coruña in Galicia is 8° 25'W, three degrees further west. Herodotus was just mistaken about the course of the Danube. Nineteenth-century scholars chose to correct him regarding the river's source, which is in the Black Forest, and accordingly moved the homeland of the Celts to southern Germany as well.

Other fragmentary references to the Keltoi suggest that some Greeks may have used the name loosely to apply to all the tribes of northern and western Europe.

The ancient Greeks thought their own language was the hallmark of civilization and that people who gabbled away in foreign languages were automatically uncivilized—the meaningless "barbar" of their speech defined them as barbarians. So the Greeks tended to lump together all the indigenous peoples of northern, central, and western Europe—non-Mediterranean Europe—and treat them as if they were all the same, even though they were not.

By the fourth century BC, the Celts were regarded as one of the four peripheral peoples of the known world. To the south were the Ethiopians, to the east were the Scythians, and a long way farther off were the Indians. It was a simple, generalized view: only the Mediterranean world was in sharp focus.

The Roman writers of 2,000 years ago took the same view as their Greek predecessors, regarding all the non-Latin-speaking peoples who lived to the north as "barbarians." The word was not used with any anthropological accuracy—even then—and covered a multitude of peoples with a range of customs and traditions. Roman writers had little interest in the ethnic differences among these peoples. The word *Galli* was used in the same negative way as the label "barbarian"—the Galli, Gauls, or Celts were all the uncivilized people on the other side of the Alps, and the Romans were doing them a tremendous favor by conquering and civilizing them.

The Romans stereotyped these people, denigrating them in standard clichés. The Celts wore trousers (a very primitive garment compared with Roman tunics and togas) and let their hair grow long and tousled. They were tattooed, foolhardy, and aggressive. They were childish, quarrelsome, and inconstant. They went in for bloodthirsty rituals including human sacrifice. They were headhunters and drunkards, and led scandalous sex lives. In Britain, most amazingly of all, their warriors tore about in chariots—an outmoded style of warfare that in the Mediterranean world had gone out with Homer's *Iliad*. (The Romans used chariots only for racing and for sport, not for warfare.)

The Romans liked to portray the Celts as backward and primitive. When Roman legionaries were posted along Hadrian's Wall, they referred disparagingly to the native Celts as *Brittunculi*—"wretched little Brits." It was typical colonial army talk.

The mindset of the Romans was not so very different than that of the British imperialists who 1,700 years later denigrated a wide range of native peoples all around the world, labeling them "pagans," "heathens," or even "cannibals." Bringing such unfortunates under the umbrella of British rule and converting them to Christianity was seen as the right thing to do. The British genuinely believed they were doing these modern barbarians a favor by conquering them, imposing British law, and forcing on them a Victorian version of Christianity.

Having said this, the Roman commentators were partially right, at least in grouping together the peoples who lived north of the Alps. In the period 500–200 BC, north of the Alps from France across Europe to the Black Sea, there was a family of peoples who shared a number of common elements.

A surge in population growth seems to have driven the central European group to become expansionist. In about 400 BC, Celtic tribes moved south into Italy. In 387 BC, they defeated the Romans in battle and sacked Rome itself. In 279 BC, another group of Celts moved into Greece, attacking and plundering the rich, sacred site of Delphi. The following year, 278 BC, three tribes crossed into Asia Minor. Together these three tribes were known as the *Galatae*, which may be the ultimate origin of the name *Keltoi* (in Greek) or *Celtae* (in Latin). They established colonies in what is still known as Galatia.

These things happened. But nineteenth-century historians believed that there was an aggressive expansion in all directions.

The Element Encyclopedia of the Celts

THE NINETEENTH-CENTURY VIEW

There is a familiar and often-repeated classic nineteenth-century view of the Celts, which survives in some serious academic work written as late as the 1970s, and in more popular writings since then that are based on the older books. It is still being promoted in some quarters. As recently as the 1990s, a book was published in Ireland, in Irish, and therefore presumably for Irish consumption, which gave the view in outline:

Before Rome became a power, the people we call Celts dominated much of Europe. Their influence ranged from Britain and Ireland in the north to France and Spain in the south and east as far as Turkey. They were united not by a common ruler but by a common language and culture... Their power declined, the influence of their language and culture remains.

This persuasively expressed view gives us an Iron Age race of people bonded by language and culture, with a heartland in central Europe in the first millennium BC. These people migrated outward from their heartland in all directions to invade and colonize most of Europe, taking their culture with them (roughly 800–100 BC). The objects unearthed by antiquarians and archeologists were identified as being in more than one style, so three successive invasions or waves of migrants were inferred, representing three different cultures: Hallstatt, La Tène, and Belgic.

A key element in this approach is the idea that almost everywhere the old pan-European Celtic culture has died out. Only a few refuges are left in the far west—Galicia, Brittany, Cornwall, Wales, Scotland, and Ireland.

Interestingly, however, the Greek and Roman writers who used the word "Celts" applied it only to the barbarian people who were their northern neighbors, not to the people living on the Atlantic fringes to the far northwest. There is a certain irony in this, as these are just the people who are usually thought of as Celts today.

THE NEW VIEW

By the 1960s, the nineteenth-century view was being seriously challenged. There was no real archeological evidence for three major invasions; in fact there seemed to be no evidence of any invasions.

Now we come to an important archeological reality: there was no Iron Age Celtic explosion in the center of Europe spinning migrant Celts off in all directions. This will make an enormous difference to the way we view the modern Celts of the Atlantic coastlands. If those territories on the western fringe of Europe were *not* invaded by waves of Celtic invaders or migrants in the first millennium BC, the people who live there now are unlikely to be descendants of the central European Celts. This is an idea we will come back to later.

The modern view may perhaps be disappointing to some people. There was not, after all, a pan-European Celtic civilization that was uniform in language, culture, and race: there was no golden age of the Celts. Instead there were many separate autonomous communities—tribes—who exchanged goods, styles, and ideas but remained quite diverse and independent, and their relationships with one another shifted through time. This modern view is based on greater archeological and anthropological knowledge.

The new view is that the prehistoric Celts were essentially two distinct groups: the Iron Age peoples of central Europe and the Iron Age peoples of the Atlantic coastline of western Europe. The Atlantic Celts were more or less stationary, although there was a good deal of trading and other communication among them. The central European Celts, on the other hand, were on the move, migrating south into Italy and east toward Romania and Greece.

A fascinating and exciting aspect of this new approach is the realization that the Atlantic Celts did not arrive in the west as a result of an Iron Age migration in the first millennium BC. They were there already and they had been there for a very long time. Their culture had been evolving over thousands of years. They borrowed or acquired some fashions from the central European Celts, but as a result of contact and trade, not invasion or mass migration. The book will focus mainly on the Atlantic Celts, whose enduring culture was a very long time evolving, though there will be entries about the central European Celts too.

THE PAST IN BOOKS

The Celts had their roots in several pasts. We are perhaps too accustomed to reading about peoples in books, where the neatness and clarity of chapter headings can give too sharp a focus.

In nineteenth-century school history books, centuries, periods, and reigns were separated off from one another in just this way; it made history simpler for pupils to learn, simpler for teachers to test.

There was a leftover of this approach in a recent TV history program. The writer and presenter, a distinguished historian, compellingly described the Battle of Hastings and its climax with the death of the last Saxon king of England, King Harold. "That was the end of Saxon England" made a dramatic and memorable conclusion to the program. The battle was certainly a major landmark in English history. The Saxon king was dead, hacked to pieces on the battlefield, and there would never be another Saxon monarch, but 99 percent of the "Anglo-Saxon" population of England lived on, and they passed on their genes, their language, and many of their customs to their children and grandchildren, whereas only a small number of Norman French people arrived in England in 1066. In a very real way, England went on being as "Saxon" as it was before, in spite of being ruled by Normans.

But this raises another question: were the people living in England Anglo-Saxon when Duke William conquered it in 1066? Had the Celtic population of England really been wiped out and replaced by the Anglo-Saxon colonists who had arrived in the fifth, sixth, and seventh centuries?

To take one area as an example, when the Jutes arrived from Jutland on the European mainland, they landed in Kent and established a base on the Isle of Thanet in 449. From there they were able to take over the old kingdom of Kent by military force. They did this by murdering or driving out British (Celtic) ruling class. The conquering Jutish chief, Hengist, ruled Kent from about 455 to 488.

The Element Encyclopedia of the Celts

Hengist was succeeded by Aesc, who reigned from 488 to 512. His family and descendants, the new Kentish ruling class, became known as Aescings. This was to distinguish them from all the other people living in Kent, the Kentings, who were descendants of the Cantii, the Iron Age tribe living there before both the Jutish and Roman occupations. The Kentings were the Britons who were doing the manual work and producing the food. They were the the slave class. They were Celts. In the nineteenth century there was an assumption that the invaders had massacred all the existing inhabitants, but this would not have been pragmatic. It was more useful to keep the Kentings, who knew the land and how to work it.

Throughout the country, the Anglo-Saxon conquest was a process of replacing the ruling class, but underneath that there was continuity of community: continuity of bloodline, continuity of genetic material, and continuity of custom. Again, as far as the nineteenth-century historians are concerned, it is a case of a chapter boundary that has been drawn too sharply.

Many people living in southeast England today are less English than they imagine. In terms of ancestry, they are more Celt than Saxon. According to Professor Stephen Oppenheimer, a leading DNA expert, as few as 5 percent of the people now living in England are of Anglo-Saxon stock; most people who think of themselves as English are genetically of a much more ancient native stock—not Germanic incomers at all.

This discovery, a result of the DNA revolution, raises many questions about ethnic identity. Often when the issue of devolution has been discussed in relation to Wales or Scotland, journalists and politicians have spoken of the views of "the Welsh" or "the Scots," as if the Welsh and the Scots are distinct and recognizable populations. But, in the terms envisaged in any referendum that has been conducted or planned, they are simply those with Welsh or Scottish addresses who are entitled to vote. Many people of Welsh and Scottish origin have moved to England in search of work; are they no longer Welsh or Scottish? There are also many people raised in England who have gone to Wales or Scotland to live; have they ceased to be English? Did they become Welsh or Scottish by moving house? Defining the Welsh and the Scots turns out to be much harder than anyone imagined.

Professor Norman Davies dedicated his excellent 1999 book *The Isles: A History* to "the memory of Richard Samson Davies: English by birth, Welsh by conviction, Lancastrian by choice, British by chance."

Simon James, who wrote *The Atlantic Celts* (also 1999), makes the interesting point that each of us possesses more than one ethnic identity, because several identities nest inside one another. Simon James himself is a Westerner, a European, a British citizen, an Englishman, a Southerner, and a Londoner. He also has more than one ethnic identity because of his mixed ancestry. Among his recent forebears (he is not specific, but by implication his grandparents and great-grandparents) he can identify Welsh or Cornish, Norman-French, and English people, which gives him the mixed genes of Celtic, Latin, and Germanic bloodlines.

I worked for three years in London, but that did not make me a Londoner. I lived for 12 years in Northamptonshire, but that did not turn me into a Mercian. I was born in Sussex of Kentish parents, Kentish grandparents, and Kentish great-grandparents: Kentish farm laborer stock. That ought to make me thoroughly English. I was brought up to believe that I was English and I feel as though I am English, yet my bone structure tells a different story: I am of pre-Anglo-Saxon British stock—Celtic. That unique British expert on the archeology of feet, Phyllis Jackson, tells me I have trademark Celtic feet. And if you are wondering what Celtic feet look like, they are long and narrow, with toes almost in a straight line, and a long longitudinal arch. My descent is therefore (probably) from that necessary Kenting slave class kept on by the Jutes when they colonized Kent in the fifth century. In fact a great many people born and bred in England are Celtic, as Professor Oppenheimer's research has shown.

It works the other way too. A great many people living in Scotland and Wales are Anglo-Saxon in origin. It is not what one might have expected. DNA test results turn up more and more problems for claimed or perceived ethnicity.

The words "Celts" and "Celtic" have themselves been used differently over time, especially over the last 200 years, as perceptions of the past and perceptions of the present have shifted. The Celtic revival of the eighteenth and nineteenth centuries identified two kinds of Celt (the Celt according to race or language), and the twentieth century produced three further kinds (the Celt according to culture, politics, or preference). We tend to use the name "Celts" to include people from a continent-wide area, right across Europe, and across quite a long period too, from the Iron Age to the present day. But a lot of those people would never have thought have calling themselves by that name. A monk living on Iona in the eighth century AD would probably have thought of himself as an Irishman in exile. A man in a plaid driving cattle down a Scottish glen in the sixteenth century would have seen himself as a Highlander and a Campbell. A woman living at the Maiden Castle hillfort in the fourth century BC would have thought of herself as a member of the Durotriges tribe, possibly with kin across the water in Brittany. Each of these people would have been startled to hear themselves called Celts: as far as they were concerned, that was not their identity.

THE ATLANTIC CELTS

We have to set aside the long-held assumption that the Celts were a pan-European Iron Age race. This means rethinking European prehistory. Modern archeological and anthropological evidence is pointing toward a reality that is far more exciting.

Instead of the Celts of the west being relative newcomers, arriving in the Atlantic coastlands between 2,000 and 3,000 years ago, they are emerging as an indigenous people with a very ancient ancestry indeed. Ten thousand years ago, the last cold stage of the Ice Age was ending and the ice that had covered much of Britain and Ireland was melting back. After the long glacial episode, the islands were becoming habitable again. What happened then was that people living in refuges in northern Spain began to migrate northward, bay-hopping along the coast, to colonize the lands that were thawing out. These early migrants spread through exactly the areas that we now think of as Celtic—Galicia, Brittany, Cornwall, Wales, and Scotland—plus a margin along their eastern edges—northern Spain, the Bay of Biscay coast of France, Normandy, and the whole of England. *This* is where the Celtic ancestry of Britain (England included) came from—this ancient migration from the south.

The people we call Celts were the descendants of these Middle Stone Age hunters, gatherers, and fishermen, and of the New Stone Age farmers, pastoralists, and stone circle builders who succeeded them.

One of the stone circles, Stonehenge, has become an emblem of Celtic Britain. Modern Druids have claimed it as theirs, and we could question this entitlement, but this process of claiming and adopting has probably been repeated over and over again through time. Stonehenge was once thought to be the work of a Mycenaean architect, partly because of the similarity between the stone trilithons and the architecture of the great Lion Gate at Mycenae, built in 1250 BC, and there are carvings on the stones that seem to show a Mycenaean dagger. But now radiocarbon dates show that they were raised long before that, in 2500 BC. The earth circle round them dates from 3100 BC, and the totem poles that stood close by were raised in 8000–7000 BC. Stonehenge turns out to be a monument that was modified and developed repeatedly, by indigenous people, during the course of the long evolution of the Atlantic Celtic culture. The site witnessed and expressed the whole span of the Atlantic Celts' prehistory.

Most of the big standing stones in the lands of the Atlantic Celts were raised in the Neolithic (3000–2000 BC), some in the Bronze Age (2000–600 BC), and a small number in the Iron Age. They clearly speak of the bond the Atlantic Celts had developed with standing stones.

The megaliths that are known to belong to the Iron Age tend to be relatively small—man-height—and single monoliths only. Some are simple, tapering, and rounded pillars, others are fluted like Doric columns. Another group is low and rounded, almost cushion-shaped, like the Turoe Stone in County Galway.

The Christian Celts of later centuries remained interested in the earlier megaliths. They Christianized some of the old pagan stones, converting them by carving their tops into crude crosses. They even raised a brand-new family of megaliths: magnificently carved massive Celtic crosses such as Muireadach's Cross at Monasterboice in Ireland.

Big standing stones were a part of the Atlantic Celtic consciousness all the way through.

Another link across this long span of time was made in 1996, when the remains of Cheddar Man were subjected to DNA analysis. Cheddar Man is the complete skeleton of a man who lived in Somerset in 7150 BC and when he died was buried in Gough's Cave at Cheddar. It was found that this Stone Age man's DNA was a close match with that of a local teacher, Adrian Targett. So, a man living and working at the Community School in Cheddar in the late twentieth century turned out to be a direct descendant of someone living in the same place more than 9,000 years before.

THE CELTS AND THE OCEAN

The Celts and their culture are also deeply embedded in their windswept, wave-washed, and rocky landscape. The Atlantic coastline has played a major role in shaping the coastal communities and producing a convergence of mindset. The smell of the sea saturated the lives and histories of these communities. They depended on the richly stocked waters for fish, and for the trade that they made possible. Tribes on opposite sides of the English Channel traded with each other, and trade led to other contacts, including treaties of mutual defense and intermarriage; kinship bonds developed. On the British side of the Channel, the Durotriges, the Iron Age tribe of Dorset, traded with the Coriosolites, who lived on the north coast

of Brittany around what is now St. Malo. Coins minted by the Coriosolites have been found at Hengistbury, the Durotrigians' main port in Christchurch Harbor. The trade route ran by way of the Channel Islands, immediately off the coast and directly between the Coriosolites' territory and Dorset; coins of the Coriosolites tribe have been found on Jersey. There were lively cross-Channel contacts between 100 and 50 BC; trade that had been going on for 2,000 years. In 80 BC the Durotriges looked across to Gaul when they adopted not only coinage but the simple designs they put on their coins.

After 50 BC there was a downturn in cross-Channel trade, which narrowed the horizons of the Durotriges and left them in a backwater. This was partly a result of piecemeal Roman conquests in Gaul generally and political settlements that left the Hengistbury merchants high and dry. It was probably largely due to an embargo imposed on the Durotriges by Julius Caesar as a punishment for supporting the Armorican rising against him in 56 BC. The people of Iron Age Dorset had felt sufficiently strong kinship with their trading partners across the sea to send warriors in an attempt to stem the Roman invasion of Gaul.

The resistance to Rome was a failure in the end, but it shows the determination of the Durotriges to resist the might of Rome. When the armies of Claudius arrived in Britain 90 years later, the fiercely independent Durotriges were once more among those offering the most aggressive resistance. Even though they were conquered by Vespasian in AD 44, they were still able, 20 years later, during the revolt of another fiercely independent tribe, the Iceni under Boudicca, to offer a potential threat to Rome's hold on southern Britain.

This snapshot of one tribe's activities during the first centuries BC and AD shows how a community of Atlantic Celts functioned in relation to other tribes—and not just near neighbors. There were networks of relationships that spread far and wide, thanks to the all-embracing ocean.

The relationship between peoples and the sea helps us to understand what has been called the *longue durée*: the underlying consistencies that bind communities together and the persistent rhythms that influence their development across long periods of time. The peoples of the Atlantic façade shared common values and beliefs over thousands of years, and this sharing was conditioned to a great extent by their unique habitat on rocky coastlines looking out across the ocean.

A simple Breton verse sums it up:

At sea, all is anguish.
At sea, all is prayer.

To this day, some of the islanders living on the small islands off the Irish coast depend on boats to get them about, yet they do not learn to swim. They surrender to fatalism when they see someone in difficulties in the sea because the sea is claiming its own. "But," as an Aran islander once said, "we do only be drownded now and again."

TWO KINDS OF IRON AGE CELTS

In 500 BC, there were two communities of Celts, the central European Celts and the Atlantic Celts, leading parallel lives. How much contact was there between the two?

The arrival in Britain of distinct artistic styles that can be related to the styles prevailing in central Europe shows that there was contact. The similarities of style are so strong that they formed the basis of the idea of migration. Now it is thought more likely that only small numbers of people were on the move, perhaps traders and a small number of migrants, yet these movements were enough to take stylistic ideas from one area to the other.

The western Celts interacted with successive European cultures: the Hallstatt, La Tène, and Belgic cultures within the Iron Age, then the Roman civilization, and then the cultures of the Jutes, Angles, Saxons, and Vikings. On the Atlantic fringe, sometimes the culture of the western Celts spread far and wide, making a continuously identifiable Atlantic culture. On occasions this culture was continuous with the central European culture, so that a very extensive culture area was formed. At other times it shrank to relatively small pockets, cells, or refuges.

The waxing and waning of other cultures have sometimes inhibited the development of Celtic culture; at other times they have stimulated it. There was a long period of stasis and conservatism in Europe in the Bronze Age. Much of what happened was a response to the more dynamic and aggressive cultures of south-eastern Europe. In Anatolia (modern Turkey) there was the great Hittite Empire, and adjacent to that were the thriving Minoan and Mycenaean civilizations of the Aegean region. In about 1200 BC the Hittite Empire collapsed. The Minoan civilization was already weakened and subsumed by the Mycenaean civilization, then that too collapsed. Whether these collapses were to do with fundamental inherent weaknesses—time-bombs embedded within the cultures—or were precipitated by invasions or raids from outside, perhaps by the mysterious Sea Peoples, archeologists continue to debate. What is certain is that the pace of cultural development in Europe was suddenly no longer wholly governed from its south-eastern threshold.

The collapse of the Hittite Empire meant that the secrets of iron-working, which had until then been a Hittite monopoly, spread across Europe. The "barbarians" of Europe learned a new technology, which involved beating bronze into thin sheets that could be made into cups, shields, and helmets. They also acquired a taste for wine, which led to an opening of trade routes south to the Mediterranean so that wine could be acquired. Finally, the opening of contact between northern and southern Europe led to a fruitful interchange of ideas between the two regions.

The Bronze Age Europeans who underwent these major changes were the Urnfielders: the people who were the central European (Iron Age) Celts' immediate precursors.

Even within the Iron Age, what happened in central Europe was affected by what was happening in, and to, Greece. In 540 BC the Phocaean Greeks were in conflict with Carthage, and the two forces fought for supremacy in the western Mediterranean region in a sea battle off the Italian coast. The Carthaginians won and blockaded Greek trade in the Mediterranean.

The Element Encyclopedia of the Celts

This in turn meant that the Celtic communities developing north of the Alps were cut off from Greek goods, and therefore from Greek models and standards. Those trading relationships were not recovered for 50 years. When they were, developments in Iron Age Celtic culture had taken it elsewhere. A new and more advanced Celtic culture was evolving, the La Tène culture, with a focus on the Rhône and middle Marne valleys.

Later, in the first century BC, came the major inhibiting force of Rome, as the Roman Empire spread northward and westward into the territories of the Celts, conquering, subduing, and Romanizing.

REAL PEOPLE

When the Romans left Britain in the fifth century AD, the Dark Age Celts (the Romanized Britons left behind) had a new battle for sur-vival on their hands, this time against an incursion of Anglo-Saxon invaders.

This was the time of Arthur, the legendary Arthur, the Dark Age Celtic king who rallied the Britons and led them into battle, halting the westward advance of the Saxons across Britain for a quarter of a century, until he too fell in battle at Camlann in 547—if indeed he existed. There are some who believe that he really did. If so, how many of the stories about him are true?

There is a wide spectrum of views about Arthur. Some people believe that he was everything the legends of the high Middle Ages say he was—a noble, true, and Christian king who rallied the na-tive Britons at a time when they were being overwhelmed by the westward march of the Saxons. Others believe that he never ex-isted at all, that there was no such king, and that he was invented in retrospect long after the British struggle for survival had been lost. Was he perhaps a typically Celtic keening for a lost might-have-been history?

King Arthur does seem to rep-resent the essence of Celticness in the same way as a bagpipe lament.

Complex and enigmatic, resonant with visionary ideals, noble failure, and a wistful nostalgia for what might have been, his story represents a dark, vibrant, inspiring, and wonderful past that we desperately want to believe in.

For centuries, myth, mystery, magic, and mysticism have been associated with the Celts. I hope this book will satisfy any curiosity regarding that spiritual side of the Celtic personality. But it is also important to remind ourselves that the Celts ate and drank and lived in houses, worked for their living, played music, told stories, and liked playing games. This everyday side needs to be sketched in, however lightly, to round out the picture of a remarkable, inventive, and long-enduring people—a real people, as real as we are.

PART 1

Celtic People and Lifestyle

ADDEDOMARUS

A king of the **Trinovantes tribe** at the end of the first century BC. His territory consisted of what is now Essex and south Suffolk. Although this area is now part of England, Addedomarus and his **people** were not English but native Celtic Britons. He was the first British king north of the Thames **River** to mint inscribed **coins**.

Addedomarus moved the Trinovantes' tribal capital from Braughing in Hertfordshire to **Camulodunum** (Colchester) in Essex. In about 30 BC, **Tasciovanus**, king of the neighboring **Catuvellauni** tribe to the west, seized his territory from him and began issuing his own coins from Camulodunum. The two kingdoms were apparently then run jointly from the Trinovantian capital by the Catuvellaunian king.

Addedomarus somehow regained control in about 20 BC and reigned over the Trinovantes until his death in 10 BC (approximate dates). He is thought to be the king who was buried in the **Lexden Tumulus** in Camulodunum. On his death, he was succeeded by Dubnovellaunus.

In the Welsh Triads, Addedomarus is remembered as one of the founders of Britain.

ADOMNÁN

Abbot of Iona 686–704. He was the main northern Irish advocate of support for the Roman Easter. With others, in 697, he was responsible for setting up the *Cain Adomnain*, a code of war designed to protect non-combatants. He went to Northumbria in 686 to negotiate the release of 60 Irish prisoners abducted by the Northumbrians in a raid.

AED

Sixth-century Irishman, brought up in Meath without any education. His brothers divided their father's inheritance, giving him nothing. To force their hand, he abducted a young woman. He was rebuked by Bishop Illand for his action and promised something better if he entered the Church, which he did.

Aed was consecrated bishop in Meath, where he founded monasteries and performed miracles. He also secured the release of many slaves and prisoners who wanted to enter monasteries: it was a recruitment drive.

AEDAN

Aedan was a sixth-century monk sent from Iona to Lindisfarne as bishop. He was abbot of the Columban house of Lindisfarne (north of Bamburgh) and bishop of the Northumbrians. The chronicler Bede emphasized the single-minded simplicity of his life.

AEDAN MAC GABRAIN

Aedan mac Gabrain was King of Dal Riada in south-western Scotland. He was probably born about 550 and became king in 574. He named his firstborn son Arthur (Artorius), probably after the great **Arthur**, the overking who had recently died.

According to the *Life of Columba*, Aedan was unsure which of his three sons—Arthur, Eochaid Find, or Domingart—would be his successor. St. **Columba** chillingly prophesied that "none of these three shall be king, for they shall fall in battle, slain by their enemies; if you have any younger sons let them come to me, and the one the Lord has chosen will at once rush into my lap." Fortunately, Aedan did have more sons. It was Eochaid Buide who ran straight to Columba.

Arthur and Eochaid Find were killed shortly afterward in the Battle of the Miathi in about 575–80. Domingart was defeated and killed in battle in "Saxonia," which was presumably what is now eastern England. Eochaid Buide did indeed become king, 608–29. Aedan himself lived on until 609.

AEDUI

A Gaulish **tribe**, with its main center at Bibracte. According to the Roman historian Livy, the Aedui joined the expedition of Bellovesus into Italy in the sixth century BC. Around 90 BC they became allies of Rome. When they were invaded and defeated by their neighbors the Sequani, they sent **Diviciacus** the **Druid** to Rome to appeal to the senate on their behalf.

When **Julius Caesar** arrived in Gaul in 58 BC, he restored their independence. Even so, the Aedui joined the coalition of Gaulish tribes against Caesar. After **Vercingetorix** surrendered at **Alesia**, however, they were glad to go back to supporting Rome. Augustus ordered Bibracte, their native capital on Mont Beuvray, destroyed; it was replaced by a new town, Augustodunum (Autun).

AGRICOLA

See **Aircol**.

AILLEL MOLT

The High King of Ireland in the late fifth century. There were several major kings in Ireland, of Leinster, Munster, Connacht, Ui Neill, and Uliad, with many petty kings and sub-kings beneath them. Aillel Molt was their overking. He was killed by an alliance of Irish kings in the Battle of Ocha in 482. Then the High Kingship fell to King Loegaire's son Lugid.

AIRCOL

A Dark Age king of Demetia (south-west Wales), Aircol was also known by the Latin form of his name, Agricola. His father's personal name was forgotten by the chroniclers, who referred to him only as "The Tribune."

Dark Age Celtic leaders valued what was to them a precious Roman legacy; in their minds, using Latin gave them higher status, and they invariably used it on their memorial stones, sometimes alongside their native Celtic names. For example, a sixth-century memorial stone near Chesterholm is inscribed: "Brigomaglos, who is also Briocus, [lies] here."

Aircol was one of the two Dark Age kings **Gildas** praised. He was also mentioned as an exemplary warrior hero by **Taliesin**. Cynan Garwyn of **Powys** was described in battle in Aircol's own kingdom, as "like Aircol himself on the rampage."

Aircol died in 515 and was succeeded by his son Gordebar, or **Vortipor** the Protector.

AMBIANI

A Celtic **tribe** in Gaul, with its main center at Samarobriva (later Amiens). In 57 BC, the year of **Julius Caesar**'s campaign against the Belgae, the Ambiani were said to be able to raise 10,000 armed men to fight. They joined the great Gaulish rebellion against Rome.

AMBIORIX

The chief of the Eburones **tribe** in Gaul at the time of the Battle of **Alesia** (see Places: **Alesia**).

AMBROSIUS AURELIANUS

The battle leader, or *dux bellorum*, of the British in their struggle against the Anglo-Saxons. He was the leader who succeeded **Vortigern** (and may have been responsible for ousting him from power) and immediately preceded **Arthur**. It is odd that he is mentioned by the sixth-century historian **Gildas**, then in the eighth century by Nennius, but by no other historian until the Middle Ages. He nevertheless existed. Gildas describes him as a modest man, which is a surprising quality in a battle leader.

He appears to have been a Celtic nobleman and it has been suggested that the "Ambros" place-names may represent the stations of the units that he raised and led, styled Ambrosiaci. This is an attractive idea, but it is unclear how Amberley, deep in West Sussex and very close to the south Saxon heartland, could possibly have functioned as such a base for Celtic troops.

The Latinized form, Ambrosius, of the Celtic name Ambros or Emrys may have been given by a chronicler, or adopted by Emrys himself as a badge of formal respectability, something that many other British noblemen did (see **Aircol**). It does not prove, as some have proposed, that he was a member of a Roman family who stayed on after the Roman troops left. He represents a class of post-Roman native British aristocrats who clung to an older order of things and disapproved of Vortigern's reckless politicking with the untrustworthy Germanic colonists.

It is likely that Ambrosius was a focus for dissent among the Britons over the way Vortigern was leading the confederation to disaster.

Gildas describes how Ambrosius' leadership marked the beginning of a more successful phase for the British:

When the cruel plunderers [the Saxons attacking the British in about 460] had gone back to their settlements, God gave strength to the survivors [the British]. Wretched people flocked to them from all directions, as eagerly as bees when a storm threatens, begging burdening heaven with unnumbered prayers that they should not be destroyed. Their leader was Ambrosius Aurelianus, a gentleman who, perhaps alone of the Romanized Britons, had survived the shock of this great storm [the Saxon invasion of Britain]; certainly his parents, who may have worn the purple, were slain in it. Under him our people regained their strength and challenged the victors to battle.

After this the British started to win battles, and they were eventually rewarded with the overwhelming victory at **Badon**.

Another view of Ambrosius comes from Nennius' *Miscellany.* There Ambrosius is "the great king among all the kings of the British nation." This may mean only that his reputation grew steadily after his death, that he was promoted by history, rather as Arthur would be a little later. It may alternatively be a genuine reflection of Ambrosius' status as *dux bellorum.*

Interestingly Cynan of **Powys** was later to be called Aurelianus, which may have been another title of the *dux bellorum.*

Although it is not known where Ambrosius came from or where he lived, Amesbury in Wiltshire is possible. Amesbury was spelt "Ambresbyrig" in a charter dated 880 and may derive its name directly from Ambrosius himself. If he held Salisbury Plain as his estate, or at any rate this part of it, he would have controlled the critical north-eastern corner of **Dumnonia**. The frontier of Dumnonia was marked by an earthwork called the **Wansdyke**, and it lies 7 miles (12km) north-east of Amesbury. Where Ambrosius' stronghold was is not known, but it may have been the Iron Age hillfort known as Vespasian's Camp, just 1 mile (1.6km) to the east of **Stonehenge**. This spacious fort would have made an excellent rallying-point for the forces Ambrosius gathered; it would also make sense of the otherwise inexplicable association that Geoffrey of Monmouth made between Ambrosius and Stonehenge.

From about 460 Ambrosius is said to have organized an island-wide resistance of the British to the Anglo-Saxon invasion. His campaign prospered. *The Anglo-Saxon Chronicle* is silent about this period, suggesting that the British were in the ascendancy; there is no boasting of a Saxon victory until 473. Gildas enthused about Ambrosius: "though brave on foot, he was braver still on horseback." This implies a preference for cavalry action, which his successor, Arthur, would share. "The Britons fled to him like swarms of bees who fear a coming storm. They fought the war with Ambrosius as their leader."

Fanciful legends were later embroidered round this heroic figure. It was said that in Ambrosius' reign **Merlin** the **magician** brought the stones of Stonehenge over from Ireland and set them up in Wiltshire. This does not square with the geology or archeology of Stonehenge. The sarsen stones came from the chalk downs near Avebury; the bluestones came from Pembrokeshire. Both arrived on Salisbury Plain in the middle of the third millennium BC—and that was long, long before the time of Ambrosius Aurelianus.

AMMINIUS

One of three sons of **Cunobelin**. The Catuvellaunian kings enlarged their sphere of influence to include Kent, which became Amminius's fiefdom, with Canterbury as his capital. There was some kind of family quarrel, as a result of which in AD 40 Amminius fled to Rome—the Rome of the emperor Caligula. His arrival with some sort of complaint about the way he had been treated gave Caligula a welcome pretext to reopen the question of Britain.

Julius Caesar had failed to annex Britain for the Roman Empire, but it was still on the wish list for conquest. The strength of Catuvellaunian control in south-eastern Britain was such that an invasion could not be undertaken lightly. If the divine Julius could not conquer Britain, could Caligula conquer it? In AD 40 he got as far as the Channel coast at Boulogne before losing his nerve and returning to Rome.

In AD 43, after the assassination of Caligula, his successor, Claudius, determined to invade, and he succeeded.

ANEIRIN

*See **The Gododdin**.*

ART

Celtic art has often been compared with classical art, the art of Iron Age Greece and Rome, and been found wanting. European and North American artists of the eighteenth and nineteenth centuries tended to look to classical models.

Celtic art comes closer in spirit to some of the art movements of the twentieth century. The Celtic artist looked at a model, whether human or animal or part of the physical landscape, and tried to reduce it to its raw essentials. The aim was to simplify and so draw attention to certain raw qualities or characteristics. The carving might be done with care, without necessarily producing a "realistic" representation of the model. The same is true of the bronzes, many of which have survived in good condition. The Matisse-like figurine of a naked woman dancing is a superb piece of Celtic art: rhythmic, free, and uninhibited.

As for the images, reduced to their essentials, they could appear rough, crude, and massive. These works can be visually reminiscent of Henry Moore's sculptures, and they have a similar presence.

Sometimes there was a desire to make images ambiguous. It is difficult to be sure whether the legs of **Cernunnos** have actually turned into writhing **serpents** or if he is simply standing behind the snakes. It is as if the artist was deliberately setting up a visual riddle. The pairing of Cernunnos, the antlered **god**, with his companion, the **stag**, in itself suggests a bond between them. But to give both stag and god identical antlers is taking the statement a step further, toward **shapeshifting**. Can the stag and the god actually transform into one another? Are they in fact two manifestations of the same being?

The weirdness of some images is intentional; this is the weirdness of the **Otherworld**—the dream world where **people** and gods can mingle, and where the living can meet the dead. It is the strange world we inhabit, or migrate to, when we fall asleep.

One of the finest pieces of artwork from Britain in the first century AD is the Battersea shield—if judged by classical standards. This piece of Romano-Celtic bronze parade armor was deposited in the Thames River at Battersea, and probably left there deliberately.

The bronze-covered iron **helmet** found at Agris in Charente must have been made for ceremonial use. It is covered in fine detail in low relief, with gold and coral inlays added: an astonishingly sophisticated piece of metalwork, more crown than helmet.

The distinctive art style that we generally recognize as Celtic is really the linear art that began with the **La Tène culture**. It consists of a decorative line that curves sinuously in an S-shape, often repeatedly and rhythmically, sometimes symmetrically, and sometimes not. The S-shape was often developed with eddies and circles to make very elaborate patterns. The style reached its peak long after the La Tène culture was over, indeed long after the Celts generally had lost their political and cultural dominance in Europe, when even their religious beliefs had been overwhelmed and supplanted. The peak was reached in the illuminated gospels drawn and painted by monks in the eighth and ninth centuries AD, works such as *The Book of Kells* and *The Lindisfarne Gospels.*

The minutely elaborate detailing of *The Book of Kells* was described by a visitor in 1185 as "the work of an angel," and so it still seems. It is so ornate, so exuberant, so controlled, and so perfect that it can scarcely be the work of human hand. The intricate design was not a sudden late invention, but part of a long tradition that went back to the fourth century BC.

It is hard to single out specific artworks as representing the pinnacle of a culture, but there is general agreement that the illustrated manuscripts of the eighth and ninth centuries AD are the finest productions of Celtic art. There is a certain irony in this. The Celts of pre-Christian, pre-Roman Europe were reluctant writers; the miraculous fusion of elements in the early medieval *The Book of Kells* is really a masterpiece of calligraphy, the most elaborately decorated **writing** ever conceived.

ARTHMAEL

St. Arthmael was the son of a noble in **Glevissig** (Glamorgan), who was probably educated at **Illtud**'s school. He took holy orders on leaving school. He was a pioneering, crusading Christian and is thought by some to be one of the prototypes for an otherwise fictional **Arthur**. He decided to give up his property and emigrate to Brittany. When Conomorus killed Jonas of Domnonie, Arthmael withdrew for safety with Judwal of Domnonie along with St. **Samson** and others. They took refuge for a time with Childebert in Paris. When Arthmael returned to Brittany, he settled at St. Armel near Rennes.

ARTHUR

Possibly the best-known and least-known figure of the Celtic Dark Ages. Everyone knows the name of Arthur, but there are many different views about his historicity. Some scholars think he was a real British king, though not the king of all Britain, while others think he is a complete fiction. My own view is that he was real.

DID HE REALLY EXIST?

There are two certain dated references to Arthur in the Easter Annals, which show that he existed as a prominent historical figure:

516: Battle of Badon, in which Arthur carried the cross of our lord Jesus Christ on his shoulders for three days and three nights, and the British were victors.

537: Strife of Camlann, in which Arthur and Medraut perished [or fell].

There are various scraps of evidence of his celebrity as warrior and war leader, for instance in **The Gododdin** (a series of elegies) a warrior is compared unfavorably with Arthur—he fought well, though "he was no Arthur."

The inscriptions on scattered stone memorials created in the sixth century are consistent in content and date with **genealogies** and other documents that we only have in copies written down much later. In other words, some of the later documents are corroborated by evidence dating from Arthur's time. A pedigree from Pembrokeshire running to 31 generations mentions a prince named Arthur who lived in the later sixth century

and was probably born around 550, just about the time of Arthur's death according to the Easter Annals. It is possible that the child was named in memory of the king who had recently died.

An argument against Arthur's existence is that he is not mentioned in *The Ruin of Britain* by the monk **Gildas**, written in about 540. "The silence of Gildas" can be explained fairly easily. First, Arthur was so well known by Britons living in the mid-sixth century that they didn't need Gildas to explain who he was. Secondly, Gildas refers to kings obliquely, by nickname. Contemporary readers would have known exactly who he meant, even if we don't, and it was his contemporaries Gildas was addressing. But Gildas describes a king called Cuneglasus as "the Bear's charioteer." The identity of the **Bear** is not immediately obvious to us, but Gildas played word games with the names of other kings, referring, for example, to Cynan or Conan as Caninus, the **Dog**. "The Bear" in Welsh is Arth, which brings us equally close to the name of Arthur. King Cuneglasus might as a young princeling 20 years earlier have served in Arthur's army, and he might have been given the privileged position of driving Arthur's **chariot**. So, Arthur does appear to be mentioned by Gildas after all, even if in disguise.

Some of those scholars who believe that Arthur did not exist argue their case on something very close to conspiracy theory. They begin from the presupposition that he never existed, therefore all the references to him, even in otherwise authentic documents, must be unhistorical, later interpolations, anachronistic intrusions, and corruptions of the text. Once a decision is made that Arthur cannot have existed, any evidence that he did exist must be fake. This is not so far from the conspiracy theory about the Apollo moon landings, which some **people** like to see as an elaborate hoax. The more evidence that is brought forward to show that the flights to the moon really happened, the more elaborate and cunning it proves the hoax to be.

We could contrast the historic Arthur and the mythic Fionn. Fionn is alleged to have fought with Vikings, but he died in AD 283, which is too early for him to have encountered them. Conversely, the Easter Annals strongly imply that Arthur fought his major campaign against the Saxons in the sixth century, between the Battle of **Badon** in 516 and the Battle of Camlann in 537, which is exactly the right time—according to the archeology—for him to have been doing that on the eastern boundary of **Dumnonia**.

WHO WAS ARTHUR?

This scenario converges on the idea that Arthur was primarily the King of Dumnonia. This ancient kingdom is now the English West Country, consisting of Cornwall, Devon, Somerset, and Dorset. Gildas's peculiar account of the state of Britain, *The Ruin of Britain*, is really a tortured lament about the poor leadership shown by the Dark Age kingdoms that occupied the English West Country and Wales in the first half of the sixth century. This region coincides exactly with the fourth-century Roman administrative province of Britannia Prima, and it implies that after the Romans abandoned Britain some vestiges of the Roman administrative structure remained.

Certainly by AD 314, when the names appear in the Verona List, Britain was formally divided into four provinces: Prima, Secunda, Maxima Caesariensis, and Flavia

Caesariensis. It is possible to visualize a loose confederation of Dark Age kingdoms still functioning in the sixth century within the boundaries of Britannia Prima.

Perhaps the kings of this province went their separate ways most of the time and came together only when there was a common danger. That common danger was the approach of the Saxon colonists, so the many small war-bands of the separate kingdoms needed to be coordinated. In Gail, the Bibracte council in 52 BC agreed on a common strategy: to join forces and resist Rome under the war leadership of one of their kings. In exactly the same way the kings of Britannia Prima agreed to resist the encroachment by the Saxons; and their choice of war leader was Arthur. He was to be *dux bellorum,* the leader of battles, while that threat existed.

The dates for Arthur's first and last battles, 516 and 537, give us the span of his later military career, and they imply that he was born in about 475. This would have made him 41, a mature and accomplished commander at the time of Badon, and 62 at the time of Camlann.

A pedigree of unknown reliability exists in the Welsh tradition.

Here Arthur was the son of Uther and Ygraine (or Eigr). Ygraine was the daughter of Amlawdd Wledig, who married Gwenn, daughter of Cunedda Wledig. *Wledig* or *gwledig* means "king" or "overking," so Arthur's maternal line at least was royal. Ygraine had a sister Reiengulid, who was the mother of St. **Illtud**, which is how Illtud comes to be Arthur's cousin.

The lack of a well-authenticated (paternal) pedigree for Arthur can be interpreted in many ways. Some say it shows he never existed, while others see it as evidence that he was not of royal blood and others as evidence that he was a usurper. Whatever his origins, Arthur became a king, then overking, and probably through prowess more than birth.

WHERE WAS CAMELOT?

Elsewhere, I have argued that Arthur was initially the sub-king of a small north Cornish territory called Trigg (meaning "three warbands"), with his home at Castle Killibury, not far from the modern town of Wadebridge. Killibury was a small and discreetly defended hideaway that had a superb view down the Camel estuary, which Arthur probably used as his harbor. In fact imported Dark Age pottery wares have recently been discovered near the seaward end of the estuary.

It is highly significant that early Welsh tradition gives Kelliwic as the name of Arthur's favorite residence; even the Welsh saw Arthur's principal home as Castle Killibury. A Welsh Triad lists the places where Arthur held court in *Three Tribal Thrones of the Island of Britain*. The northern one was at Pen Rhionydd—a place that has not been identified, but thought to near Stranraer in Galloway. The Welsh throne was at St. David's and the Cornish tribal throne was at Kelliwic. Kelliwic was firmly recognized as Arthur's base long before any idea of Camelot came up. The poem *Culhwch and Olwen* mentions five times that Kelli Wic was Arthur's port. An old name for Castle Killibury is Kelly Rounds and an Anglo-Saxon charter mentions a place called "Caellwic."

Not far away is **Tintagel** Island. A significant amount of very high status and very expensive pottery imported from the Mediterranean confirms it as a royal focus of some kind. It was not a permanent settlement but a place for special occasions. The footprint carved into the living rock at the island's summit marks it as the coronation place: the spot where kings of Trigg (north Cornwall), and perhaps kings of all Dumnonia, came to take their oath and assume the mantle of kingship. This was where Arthur drew his power from the stone (see Places: **Tintagel**).

Like other Dark Age and medieval kings, Arthur was always on the move. Kings had to peregrinate around their kingdoms in order to be seen by their subjects and maintain the bond of loyalty between king and subject.

Arthur had various muster points where the Dumnonian warbands could gather before being marched east to engage the Saxons: Warbstow Bury and Lydford were two in the center of Dumnonia; **South Cadbury** was the major one close to the eastern border, the "war zone."

One of the many mysteries surrounding Arthur is the location of Camelot, that place of special mystique. It is unlikely to be Castle Killibury. The name "Camelot" strongly suggests a connection with the Celtic **war god**, Camulos, and if Camelot was named for the war god it is likely to be associated with fighting and with gatherings of the war-bands. Camelot is elusive, for the simplest of reasons: it was not one place, but several. It was mobile; it was wherever Arthur was encamped with his warriors.

THE LAST BATTLE

The site of the last battle, Camlann, has been discussed endlessly. Every author who has written about Arthur has their own favored site. I have discussed elsewhere the reasons for thinking that the likeliest place is Pont ar Gamlan: a boulder-strewn fording-place at the confluence of the Eden and Mawddach **rivers** a few miles north of Dolgellau in North Wales. A third river, the Gamlan, flows down the steep mountainside from the west to join the Mawddach close by. It flows down through an **oak** forest and over some impressive waterfalls: the Black Falls, just above Ganllwyd. The name "Gamlan" is very close to the traditional name of the last battle, and in Welsh a *cadgamlan* is an utter rout, a complete massacre, and this is likely to be the original meaning of the battle's name, now commemorated in the name of the river.

This may seem an odd place for Arthur to be fighting a battle in that the threat from the Saxons was from the east. But the various traditions about the last battle have in common the idea that it was a fight amongst the British. Arthur was betrayed by a relative, perhaps a nephew, called Modred or Medraut. With that in mind, the final battle might have been fought well inside the frontiers of Britannia Prima, in Devon, Cornwall, or anywhere in Wales.

The North Wales location suggests that Arthur was making his way north into the kingdom of **Gwynedd** along the major south–north Roman **road** known as Sarn Helen. The King of Gwynedd was **Maelgwn**, and his fortress was Castell Degannwy, perched on a rocky, twin-peaked hilltop overlooking the Conwy estuary. Like many other Dark Age strongholds, this was a refortified Iron Age fort. The site has yielded sixth-century pottery and there is a tradition that it was the seat of Maelgwn, though, like Arthur, Maelgwn had a less conspicuous refuge residence, at Aberffraw on the west coast of Anglesey. Degannwy was Maelgwn's frontline fortress, and this was where Arthur was heading.

The Element Encyclopedia of the Celts

The last battle took place in an atmosphere of distrust and civil war, and Arthur was probably hoping to deal with Maelgwn's disloyalty.

Maelgwn had a reputation for ruthlessness. We know from the outright condemnation of him by Gildas that he murdered his own uncle in order to become King of Gwynedd; now he was envious of Arthur's High Kingship and determined to get it for himself. Maelgwn was Arthur's enemy; the king who was destabilizing the British confederation and who wanted him dead so that he could be *dux bellorum* himself.

Whether Arthur and his warband rode into Gwynedd to quell an overt rebellion and open and anticipated hostility or were lured there by some guile of Maelgwn's and fell unsuspecting into a trap at Ganllwyd cannot be determined from the existing evidence. Certainly the site, confined by steep valley sides and dense forests, is ideal for an ambush.

Two things are known for certain: Maelgwn did gain the High Kingship shortly after the Battle of Camlann and Arthur's disappearance—in 546, according to one version—and gained it by deception. There is also the tradition that Arthur was in the end the victim of treachery at Camlann: perhaps the treachery was Maelgwn's, not Modred's. And just possibly Arthur was the murdered "uncle" mentioned by Gildas.

If Maelgwn was indeed responsible for the death of Arthur and for bringing the Arthurian peace to an end, Gildas's extraordinary hatred and condemnation of Maelgwn's many-sided wickedness becomes understandable. Arthur was behind the golden years of relative stability and justice between the Battles of Badon and Camlann, and those years came to an end with his final defeat. Gildas mentions specifically that Maelgwn removed and killed many tyrants (meaning kings, not necessarily tyrants in the modern sense), that Maelgwn was "last in my list but first in evil," and that Maegwn "cruelly despatched the king your uncle." Here, too, is the uncle-slaying regicide motif that would later be attributed, by Geoffrey of Monmouth, and possibly mistakenly, to Modred.

THE DISAPPEARANCE

OF ARTHUR

What happened to Arthur after the Battle of Camlann is shrouded in mystery. One version of the story is that he was carried from the battlefield mortally wounded and either died elsewhere or simply disappeared. One explanation is that locally the truth of the matter was known—that Arthur had died on or near the battlefield—and this tradition was preserved and passed on through Welsh families, like the details about the few fellow warriors who survived the battle. Meanwhile, Arthur's subjects in Cornwall had less detailed information about what had happened to the king. All they really knew was that he had not returned. In the days and weeks following the Battle of Camlann, all kinds of misinformation and rumor may have circulated.

Writing in the Middle Ages, Geoffrey of Monmouth was aware of the uncertainties. In his version of Arthur's disappearance he describes him as "mortally wounded" on the battlefield, yet moved to **Avalon** "to have his wounds healed." Some scholars have argued persuasively that Geoffrey was deliberately ambiguous about what had happened because he had on his desk two different versions of the king's fate: one originating in Wales and giving Arthur as killed in battle; the other from Cornish or Breton sources and giving Arthur as surviving the battle and being transported elsewhere to recover or die.

This is persuasive and goes a long way toward explaining the post-Camlann confusion, but it may be that the contradictory stories carried a different clash of scenarios. It may have been known, to a privileged few in Wales, that Arthur had been wounded, rescued from the battlefield, and taken north to a place of safety; meanwhile, in Cornwall, the story was that Arthur was "missing presumed dead."

Great play has been made of the absence of a grave for Arthur. The sixth or seventh-century poem *Songs of the Graves* gives the locations of many Dark Age heroes, for instance:

The grave of Owain ap Urien in a secluded part of the world,
Under the grass at Llan Morvad;
In Aberech, that of Rhydderch Hael.
(Stanza 13)...
The wonder of the world, a grave
for Arthur. (Stanza 44)

The missing grave became a major element in the mystique surrounding the vanished king. If Arthur was the great overking, chief of the kings of Britain and *dux bellorum*, we might expect to find an impressive monument of some kind raised over his grave, or at any rate for its location to have been remembered, but there is nothing. On the other hand, where is the grave of Aelle, the first Saxon *bretwalda*? Where is **Vortigern**'s mausoleum? Even the whereabouts of the tombs of King Alfred and King Harold are uncertain. So perhaps we should not be surprised that we have no grave for Arthur.

There is a tradition that he was buried secretly. The *Life of St. Illtud* credits Illtud with being the priest who conducted the secret funeral. Probably only those who were actually present—perhaps only ten people altogether—ever knew where the king was buried, and as likely as not those ten took the secret with them to their own separate graves.

One question naturally arises: why should those close to Arthur have wished to bury him in secret? Obviously his death was disastrous to the British cause. If he had succeeded only recently in re-cementing the loyalty of the kings of southern and central Wales to a common cause, the news of his death could have precipitated immediate fragmentation, laying Wales open to attack from the east; alternatively, and equally dangerously, it could have exposed **Powys** and the southern kingdoms to attack from Gwynedd first, rendering them powerless to resist Saxon incursion from the east. The continuing expansion of Gwynedd a century or two later seems to show that this was an ever-present danger. If news of Arthur's death had reached the Saxons, who had been held at bay by his power for 20 years, they would have pushed westward with confidence and ease; if it had spread widely among the Britons, they would have been demoralized and given in under the renewed Saxon onslaught. In every

The Element Encyclopedia of the Celts

way and for every reason it was important to conceal the death of Arthur, and those close to him may have hoped to hide the catastrophic truth long enough for a successor to be found and for him to establish his position as overking before too many people realized what had happened.

It may be that an alternative fate was concealed, but for the same reasons. If Arthur was not killed at Camlann but so badly wounded that he was going to be unfit to fight or even ride for a long time, he would have been forced to retire. It was common for Dark Age kings to retire when they became physically incapable of fighting through age or infirmity. They withdrew from public life completely by entering monasteries.

Several examples are known from these times. In around 580 Tewdrig or **Theodoric**, King of **Glevissig** (Glamorgan) abdicated in favor of his son **Meurig** and retired to a religious house at Tintern. He made the mistake of coming out of retirement in about 584, when his son engaged the Saxons in battle nearby, and was mortally wounded in the battle. Pabo Pillar of Britain, King of the Pennines, similarly abdicated in fa-

vor of his sons and went to live in seclusion in a remote monastery in Gwynedd, far from his own kingdom; he later died and was buried there, in the church at Llanbabo in Anglesey. A link between the Pennine kingdom and Gwynedd is suggested by another example. In the church at Llanaelhaearn on the Lleyn Peninsula is a fifth or sixth-century memorial stone inscribed with the words "Aliortus, a man from Elmet, lies here."

There are hints in the medieval genealogies that a much earlier Dumnonian king, **Coel Godebog**, also retired a long way from home: he died and was buried in the far north, in York, in 300.

Did Arthur, now aged 62 and badly wounded, decide to abdicate and retire immediately after Camlann? *The Legend of St. Goeznovius*, a Breton saint, includes some information that is corroborated in other sources, such as the migration of British saints to Brittany in the fifth and sixth centuries. It may overstate Arthur's achievement, in boasting that the Saxons were largely cleared from Britain by "the great Arthur, King of the Britons" but, in a telling phrase, it relates how Arthur's career ended when he "was summoned from human activity." This is equivocal, in that it holds back from saying that Arthur died, even if most of us reading the story would infer that that was meant. The expression might equally be taken to mean that Arthur withdrew from secular, worldly affairs in order to lead a purely religious life.

If Arthur's reign ended at Camlann but he lived on in retirement, it could explain the discrepancy between the date of 537 or 539 given in the Welsh Annals for Arthur's fall at Camlann and the date of 542 given by Geoffrey of Monmouth. Perhaps Geoffrey had access to a tradition of Arthur living on for another five years after the battle (*see* Places: **Avalon**).

The idea that Arthur did not die but somehow lived on and will one day return may seem to remove Arthur completely from history and place him safely in the world of myth and mysticism. Yet Arthur is but one of many great charismatic leaders, many of them kings, who were believed to have lived on after their "official" deaths. The last Saxon King of England, Harold Godwinson, officially died at the Battle of Hastings close to the site of the high **altar** of Battle Abbey and his remains were buried at the same spot. The Bayeux Tapestry is unambiguous—"*Harold interfectus est*"—but even in 1066 doubts were circulated about the official story. The Norman chronicler William of Poitiers reported that the Conqueror contemptuously ordered Harold's body to be buried on the beach. More uncertainty arose because of the mutilation of the corpse, so even a burial in Battle Abbey might have been that of another battle victim. By the thirteenth century an Icelandic story was told of Harold being found alive on the battlefield by two peasants who were looting corpses the night after the battle. They took him home with them and it was suggested that he should rally the English once more, but Harold knew that many would have sworn fealty to William and he did not want to compromise them. He would retire to a hermitage at Canterbury. Three years later, when Harold died, William was told and he saw that Harold was given a royal burial. Gerald of Wales, writing in 1191, also affirmed that the Saxons clung to the belief that Harold was alive; as a hermit, deeply scarred and blinded in the left eye, he is said to have lived for a long time in a cell at Chester, where he was visited by Henry I.

Similar survival stories have been told about other historical figures: the Norwegian King Olaf Tryggvason, Richard II, the Grand Duchess Anastasia, Alexander I of Russia, Holger Danske, Sebastian of Portugal. These were real people, yet elaborate stories adding layers of mystery to their deaths are still told. The mystery elements added to Arthur's life do not mean that he never existed at all.

THE SYMBOLIC VALUE OF ARTHUR

Why did this particular king so fascinate his contemporaries and those who came after? The most immediate reason is that his military prowess halted the westward progress of the Anglo-Saxon colonization of southern Britain for 20 years. His time would afterward be remembered as the sunset of Celtic England. A distinctive feature of the Celts is dwelling on defeats; there is wailing, keening, lamentation, and nostalgia. A. L. Rouse commented, "It was the hero of the losing side, King Arthur, who imposed himself on the imagination." Arthur became a symbol of the glory of Britain as it once was

and might yet have been, but for its destruction by the Saxon invaders. He was the perfect symbol of a kingdom and a **culture** lost.

The image of the king hung over the aristocracy of the Middle Ages like a faded, tattered, war-torn battle standard hanging in a royal chapel, redolent of past greatness and signifying virtues that could never be matched by the living. The idea of Arthur became a force in politics. Henry II wanted to prove that Arthur was dead in order to remove any hopes the Celts may have nursed that he would rise again to do battle against the Plantagenets. It was probably for this reason that in 1190 Henry II arranged for Arthur's coffin to be "discovered" at **Glastonbury** and exhumed. We know that, when Henry II visited Pembrokeshire in 1179 and met the **bard** who told him where Arthur's grave was, he was also told of the tradition that Arthur would ride once more. If Henry could produce Arthur's bones, even the most superstitious would be able to see that there was no chance of Arthur riding again.

King Edward III identified himself as Arthur's successor when he contemplated re-establishing the Round Table as an order of chivalry. In the end, in 1348, he founded the Order of the Garter instead, but still in imitation of King Arthur's order of Round Table knights.

ARVERNI

An Iron Age Gaulish **tribe**, with its main center at Gergovia: a hillfort on a plateau in the Puy-de-Dome. In the second century BC, under King Luernios, they were the most powerful tribe in Gaul. Luernios was known for scattering **gold** and silver coins to his followers from his **chariot**. When his son Bituitus was defeated by the Romans in 121 BC, the power of the Arverni was diminished and the **Aedui** and Sequani became the leading tribes in Gaul. The Arverni were able to negotiate a peace treaty with the Romans that preserved their independence, though in the end they lost territory. No more kings are mentioned.

ATREBATES

An Iron Age British **tribe** in central southern England. Their territory occupied the modern counties of West Sussex, West Surrey, Hampshire, Berkshire, and north-east Wiltshire.

The Atrebates in England had strong ties with the Atrebates of north-west Gaul, where Commius was king under **Julius Caesar**. When Commius fled from Gaul, he went across the Channel to join the British Atrebates; and it was there that he had his new **coins** struck.

B

BARDS

A class of poets, like the minstrels of the Middle Ages, specializing in popular and non-religious subjects. They were distinct from ovates or *vates*, a class of **priest** with a focus on composing and performing prophetic poetry. Bards had a particular and recognized place in **society**.

Posidonius describes an incident involving a bard:

When at length he fixed a day for the ending of the feast, one of their barbarian poets arrived too late. The poet met Luernius [or Luernios, King of the Arverni] and composed a song magnifying his greatness and deploring his own late arrival. Luernius was delighted and asked for a bag of gold and threw it to the poet who ran beside his chariot. The poet picked it up and sang another song saying that the very tracks made by his chariot on the ground gave gold and blessings to mankind.

The bards also had a public role in disseminating myths and **genealogies** amongst the ordinary **people**. There were different grades of bard, the lowest of which was the novice, or Mabinog.

BARINTHUS

The Navigator, also known as Barrfind and Barrindus, who guided **Merlin** and **Taliesin** on their voyage to the **Otherworld** with the wounded **Arthur**; Barinthus was the ferryman of the dead.

Barinthus also accompanied Ternoc on a voyage to the Land of Promise and reported his experience to **Brendan**.

BARRFIND

See **Barinthus**.

BARRINDUS

See **Barinthus**.

BATTERSEA SHIELD

See **Art**.

BELLOVACI

An Iron Age Gaulish **tribe** with its capital at Beauvais. The Bellovaci intended to expand their territory and **Julius Caesar** saw this as a threat to his plan to control the whole of Gaul. He confronted the Bellovaci under their leader

Correus. They were taken by surprise, but Caesar was intimidated by the size of the enemy force. At first there were only skirmishes and the Bellovaci retreated into their camp. When Correus attempted an ambush of Roman troops, the Bellovaci were defeated and Correus himself was killed. Caesar treated the Bellovaci leniently, as a result of the intercession of **Diviciacus**.

BENIGNUS OF ARMAGH

Pupil and successor of St. **Patrick** in 468.

BERACHUS

Berachus of Kilbarry in Roscommon was a pupil of Dagaeus and lived in the sixth century. He acquired Kilberry from a "minister" by a miracle, and was prosecuted by a royal wizard who claimed inheritance by hereditary law (*see* **Magicians**). The case was referred to **Aedan**, King of Dal Riada, who passed it on to Aed Dubh of Brefni and Aedh of Tethba. The wizard was struck dumb and fled; he was later killed. An attempt by the wizard's heirs to set fire to the monastery was thwarted by a miracle.

Aedan granted Berachus a fort to use as a monastery at Aberfoyle, commanding the northern road from Loch Lomond to the upper Forth: the only route usable by Dal Riada armies to reach the southern **Picts** without violating **Alcluith** territory. The site was of enormous strategic value to the kings of Dal Riada, so granting it implies a great favor from Aedan, who must have thought highly of Berachus.

BERNACUS

See **Brynach**.

BEUNO

Welsh saint, son of Bugi, and born in the kingdom of **Powys**. He studied under Tangusius at Caerwent during the old age of King Ynyr Gwent and was granted Berriew near Welshpool by Mawn, son of Brochmail, King of Powys. He heard Saxons shouting "Ker Gia," apparently calling to their hunting **dogs**, but perhaps abusing the Welsh. After this, he withdrew westward, staying with Tyssilio at Meifod. He founded a church, but was later expelled by the sons of Selyf, son of Kynan.

One of his miracles was replacing the **head** of Teuyth's daughter Wenefred, after it was severed by a nobleman whose advances she had spurned. Wenefred lived to a great age as an abbess, patroness of Holywell, Flint.

Beuno also brought back to life the daughter of Ynyr Gwent, who had been murdered by her husband, an artisan from Aberffraw who had been employed at the court of Caerwent. Her brother Idon came to Caernarvon to reclaim her dowry. He also decapitated the murderous husband, but Beuno again replaced the head.

BITUITUS

See **Arverni**.

BITURIGES

An Iron Age Celtic **tribe** in Gaul, with its main center at Avaricum (Bourges). When the Romans arrived to conquer Gaul, the Bituriges were politically one of the main tribes; their **Druids** in particular held great power. As **Julius Caesar** reduced the power of the Druids, the power of the Bituriges also declined.

Vercingetorix pursued a scorched earth policy, burning Gaulish towns as the Roman legions advanced. But Avaricum was not burned—an indication of the importance of the Bituriges. The Romans destroyed it instead (*see* **Redones**).

BOATS

See **Ships and Boats**; Symbols: **Boat**.

BOECIUS

Boecius of Monasterboice, a great monastic center which he founded, was Irish by birth, but studied in Italy under Abbot Tilianus. From there he sailed to the land of the **Picts** with what are described as 60 "German" saints (presumably Saxons).

Boecius resuscitated King Nectan (ruled 462–86), who gave him a *castellum*. Then he crossed to Irish Dal Riada and resuscitated the daughter of the king. Boecius died in 521.

THE BOOK OF KELLS

See **Art**.

BOUDICCA

Queen of the **Iceni tribe**. Boudicca was born in about AD 25 and lived at **Thetford** in Norfolk at the time of the Roman invasion of Britain. She married **Prasutagus** in AD 48, when she was about 23 and he was perhaps ten years older. He was King of the Iceni, one of three Celtic tribes to have treaty arrangements with Rome; the others were the Regnenses and the **Brigantes**. Boudicca gave birth to

two daughters: one in AD 49 and one in 50. On the death of Prasutagus, in AD 60, she became regent.

Prasutagus bequeathed half his kingdom to Nero, reserving the rest for his widow and daughters. The Roman governor **Suetonius Paulinus** was away on campaign in Wales when Prasutagus died, and the procurator, Decianus Catus, decided to swoop in and take the whole of Prasutagus' estates for Rome. Decianus Catus was ruthless and acquisitive, and his officials were backed by undisciplined troops. The operation was bungled and army discipline broke down. The soldiers raped Boudicca's daughters, who can only have been 11 or 12 years old, and flogged the queen herself.

The Iceni rose against Rome behind their humiliated queen, joined by their neighbors to the south, the **Trinovantes**, who had also been roughly handled by greedy legionaries at **Camulodunum** (Colchester). Together, the Iceni and Trinovantes attacked and burned down the new town. Then Boudicca and her army moved on to sack Verulamium (St. Albans) and London. Paulinus brought 10,000 legionaries back from Wales to confront her somewhere to the north-west of London. At an unidentified location somewhere along Watling Street, Boudicca's army was slaughtered. The queen herself escaped from the battlefield but died shortly afterward of some illness, perhaps after taking poison; according to Dio Cassius she was given a rich burial. Boudicca's **treasure**-laden grave has never been discovered.

Boudicca was famously described in Rome: "She was huge of form and terrifying of aspect and with a harsh voice. A great mass of red hair fell to her knees and she wore a great twisted gold necklace, and a tunic of many colours."

Dio Cassius makes a point of describing her as invariably wearing a "great twisted golden necklace." The marvelous **gold** torc found at Snettisham was made in about 50 BC, which at first sight makes it too early to have belonged to Boudicca. But royal regalia is often several generations old—its antiquity is part of its ceremonial value—and it is possible that this torc, and the rest of the Snettisham hoard, did belong to the queen.

BOYA

See **David**.

BRENDAN OF CLONFERT

Brendan (486–578) was a pupil of Bishop Erc of Kerry. He was a navigator and sailed to Iceland. From there he sailed **west** to a "beautiful land beyond the fogs." He also sailed to the Fortunate Islands (assumed to be the Canary Islands). The ocean voyages took place in the years before 560.

Exactly where Brendan went is the subject of endless speculation. Some believe he discovered North America long before Columbus. What is certain is that he traveled to Wales, to Iona, and then to Ireland, where he founded a monastery at Annaghdown. There he spent the rest of his days, dying there in about 578 while visiting his sister Briga. Before his death, he arranged for his body to be taken secretly back to the monastery he had founded at Clonfert; it was transported hidden in a luggage cart. What he feared was that his followers might dismantle his body for relics. He was buried, intact, in Clonfert cathedral.

BRENNUS

There were two Gaulish chiefs of this name, both leaders of invasions. It is possible that "Brennus" was a title, meaning *dux bellorum* or "commander-in-chief" rather than a personal name.

Diodorus Siculus tells us about the second Gaulish King Brennus, who lived in the third century BC:

Brennus the King of the Gauls, on entering a temple [at Delphi in Greece] found no dedications of gold or silver, and when he came only upon images of stone and wood, he laughed at them [the Greeks], to think that men, believing that gods have human form, should set up their images in wood and stone.

The implication is that the more sophisticated Gauls did not think of the **gods** in anthropomorphic terms and this tallies with their **art**, much of which at that time did not feature humanoid forms.

It was an earlier Gaulish King Brennus, who was the King of the Senones **tribe**, who led the Celtic warriors in the sack of Rome in 387 BC. He caused more havoc there than would be seen again until Alaric the Goth descended on the city in the fifth century AD. Brennus demanded his own weight in **gold**, with the cry, *"Vae Victis!"* ("Woe to the defeated!") He was interested in loot rather than conquest, which was perhaps unfortunate in the longer term, though the Celts remained a force to reckon with in Italy until 295 BC.

BRIDEI

King of the **Picts**, who reigned from 555 to 584. He is the only British king from the fifth or sixth centuries to be mentioned in a chronicle on the European mainland. Bede describes him as *rex potentissimus*, "most powerful king," which suggests that the Picts had their own overking. Bridei, or Brudeus, was a son of **Maelgwn**, King of **Gwynedd**, and he was elected king. The Picts would not have chosen an obscure or low-ranking person as their king, and Maelgwn, we know, was an overking. Pictish succession passed through the female line, so it is likely that for him to be eligible for the

Pictish throne; Bridei's mother or grandmother was a Pict. In fact Welsh tradition has it that Maelgwn's mother was a Pict.

Bridei's high reputation among the Picts rests on a great military victory won in 560. Gabran, King of Dal Riada, had taken a large area of Pictland and, by defeating him in 560, Bridei won most or all of this land back and once more united the northern and southern Picts.

St. **Columba** visited him and asked **Broichan**, his chief **magician**, to set free his Irish slave girl.

Bridei was eventually killed in 584 during a rebellion of the southern Picts.

BRIGANTES

An Iron Age **tribe** in the north of England. At the time of the Roman invasion, Queen **Cartimandua** was their ruler; she had a treaty arrangement with Rome.

BRIGHID

See Religion: **Brighid**.

BRIOC

St. Brioc was born in 468 in the West Wales kingdom of Ceretigan (or in Latin Coriticiana, modern Cardigan). He was the son of Cerpus and Eldruda. He performed various miracles, including rescuing a **stag** from a king in Ceretigan.

In about 510 he sailed away with 168 companions to a port in Cornwall and converted King Conan (or Kynan) and his people to Christianity. Later he crossed the Channel to Brittany, but went back to Ceretigan again to comfort his people when plague struck them in 547.

The Cornish port was probably on the Camel estuary: St. Brioc's (now St. Breock's) parish is very large, covering the area south of Padstow. Recently a Dark Age port has been uncovered on the Camel estuary near Padstow.

BROICHAN

The wizard of the Pictish King **Bridei**. Broichan covered Loch Ness with darkness and raised a storm so that for a time St. **Columba** was unable to set sail on the lake (*see* **Magicians**).

BRUDEUS

See **Bridei**.

BRYCHAN

See **Nectan, Theodoric**.

BRYNACH

Brynach or Bernacus was of noble birth, and probably Welsh rather than Irish. He visited Rome and killed a **dragon**. He returned by way of Brittany to Milford Haven in south-west Wales. There he resisted attempts at seduction and founded many churches. He resisted a demand from **Maelgwn** for food and managed to secure a grant from him exempting him from future royal exactions.

CADFAN

A king of **Gwynedd** who died in about 620 or 630. The Llangadwaladr Stone on the island of **Anglesey** is his memorial. Translated from some oddly laid-out Latin, the inscription reads "Cadfan, wisest king, most renowned of all kings." The lettering suggests a date around 620, which fits with the information in the Welsh Annals, to the effect that Cadfan's father died in 616 and his son **Cadwallon** was killed in 633 by Oswald of Northumbria. This is his **genealogy**: Cadfan, son of Iago, son of Beli, son of **Rhun**, son of **Maelgwn** of Gwynedd.

CADO

See **Geraint**.

Cadoc of Lancarfan

Son of Gwynnliw of **Glevissig**, educated at Caerwent, Cadoc refused the royal scepter of Penychen because of his commitment to the Church and was granted Llancarfen by Paul Penychen; there he built Castil Kadoci, perhaps to be identified as Castle Ditches near Llancarfen. Much later he left Llancarfen to Elli of Llanelli and moved to Beneventum (possibly Abergavenny), where he was visited annually by Elli and became bishop under the name Sophias.

He visited Rome in the time of Pope John III (560–72). He also visited Jerusalem, Cornwall, and Brittany. He acquired **Gildas'** bell, though Gildas refused to surrender it to Cadoc until he was ordered to do so by Pope Alexander; he also acquired the Gospel book that Gildas wrote while studying at Nantcarvan for a year while Cadoc was away in Scotland.

He was finally martyred "by the soldiers of a cruel king."

Cadoc has more church dedications than any other Welsh saint except **David** and he is very prominent in both Welsh and Breton fable.

Cadwallon

A Dark Age king of **Gwynedd**. He fought alongside Penda of Mercia in the Battle of Meicen in which King Edwin of Northumbria was killed. The battle was noted by a British scribe as *gueith meicen*, 'the strife of Meicen." The battle in which the great King of Northumbria was slain justified a longer-than-usual entry in the annals.

Caledonii

A major **tribe** living in the Grampians in Scotland at the time of the Roman occupation. The incredibly hardy Caledonii were described by Dio Cassio:

The Maeatae live near the wall [Hadrian's Wall] that divides the island [of Britain] in two, the Caledonii beyond them. Both inhabit

rough mountains with marshy ground [the Scottish Lowlands] between them, neither have walled places or towns or cultivated lands. They live by pasture, hunting, and on a kind of fruit with a hard shell [hazelnuts?]

They eat no fish, though their waters are full of many species. They live in tents, unclothed and barefoot. They have their women in common, and raise all their children. Their government is democratic, and they delight in raids and plunder. They fight from chariots and have small, fast horses. Their infantry move fast, and have great stamina. Their weapons are a shield and a short spear with a bronze knob at the butt end.

They can stand hunger, thirst, and all other hardship. They dive into the marshes and can hold out there for several days with only their heads above water. In the forest they live on bark and roots.

CALETI

A Gaulish **tribe** with its main center at Harfleur. Its territory was in what is now Normandy.

CANTII

The Iron Age British **tribe** who lived in Kent. The Cantii probably went into a state of shock when they saw **Julius Caesar** landing with his troops in their territory. **Cassivellaunus** was disappointed with the poor support they gave to his resistance to the Roman invasion.

But there was one useful attack by the Cantii. Four Kentish kings—Cingetorix, Carvilius, Taximagulus, and Segovax—organized a surprise attack on Caesar's ships, where they were drawn up on a Kentish beach. The Roman troops managed to beat this attack off by capturing Lugotorix, a British noble. Caesar does not make much of the incident, though he was present when it happened.

At least it was not the case that the Cantii did nothing.

CARADOC VREICHVRAS

Caradoc Vreichvras, "Strong-Arm," was the king of lands in both south Dorset and Brittany in around 550. South Dorset, between Chesil Beach and Lulworth Cove, is the likeliest location for Caradoc's British territory, as this was the only area on the central south coast of England that was not in Saxon hands in 550.

CARADOG

See **Caratacus**.

CARATACUS

A king of the **Catuvellauni tribe**, who led the British resistance to the Roman invasion in the first century AD.

Caratacus (Caradog in Welsh) was a son of King **Cunobelin** of the Catuvellauni and a warrior chief already experienced in **warfare** before the Roman conquest began. He was actively involved in the expansion of his tribe's territory, fighting battles to achieve this.

He was the *protégé* of his uncle Epaticcus, who was responsible for extending the power of the Catuvellauni westward into the territory of the **Atrebates**. Epaticcus died in about AD 35, and after that the Atrebates, under their leader, King Verica, were successful in regaining some of their lost territory. But Caratacus regained the upper hand, completed the Catuvellaunian conquest of the Atrebates, and Verica was deposed.

Success for Caratacus meant defeat for his enemies, and defeated kings went to Rome with their grievances. Verica went and appealed to Claudius to have his kingdom restored to him. This gave Claudius the pretext he was looking for to invade and conquer Britain in AD 43. By now, the powerful Cunobelin was dead and the defense of his Southern Kingdom was in the hands of two of his sons, Caratacus and **Togodumnus**. The smaller kingdoms in Britain were relatively powerless and disorganized, so it was left to Caratacus and Togodumnus to provide the leadership.

Rome meanwhile pitted four legions against Britain, under Aulus Plautius: around 40,000 men. In his resistance to Rome, Caratacus used a combination of guerrilla warfare and set-piece formal battles. He was more successful in guerrilla fighting and kept to this whenever he could.

The Catuvellauni were defeated in two crucial battles, on the Medway and Thames, and this led to the loss of most of the south-east to the Romans. According to one reading of the Roman accounts, Togodumnus was killed and the Catuvellauni territory was overrun by Rome. Another reading suggests that Togodumnus may have been on the side of Rome against his brother, survived the two battles and later continued to collaborate with the Romans.

Claudius arrived in Britain in time to witness his legions marching in triumph into the town of **Camulodunum**.

Caratacus survived this final defeat, retreating to the **west**, where he continued the resistance against the spread of Roman control in Wales, leading the Silures and Ordovices tribes. He was now fighting Plautius' successor as governor, Publius Ostorius Scapula. Scapula defeated Caratacus in the Battle of Caer Caradoc, captured Caratacus' wife and daughter, and received the surrender of his brothers. Carata-

cus himself somehow escaped capture and fled northward into the territory of the **Brigantes**. There Queen **Cartimandua** captured him and handed him over to the Romans.

Once Caratacus had been captured, the Romans were in control of most of what is now England and Wales. He was sent to Rome as a prize of war, and would, according to normal Roman practice, have been executed after a triumphal procession. In spite of being a captive, he was allowed to make a speech to the senate:

If the degree of my nobility and fortune had been matched by moderation in success, I would have come to this City as a friend rather than a captive, nor would you have disdained to receive with a treaty of peace one sprung from brilliant ancestors and commanding a great many nations. But my present lot, disfiguring as it is for me, is magnificent for you. I had horses, men, arms, and wealth: what wonder if I was unwilling to lose them? If you wish to command everyone, does it really follow that everyone should accept your slavery? If I were now being handed over as one who had surrendered immediately, neither my fortune nor your glory would have achieved brilliance. It is also true that in my case any reprisal will be followed by oblivion. On the other hand, if you preserve me safe and sound, I shall be an eternal example of your clemency.

This speech was so impressive and effective that Claudius pardoned Caratacus. He was granted a pension and he and his family were permitted to live in Rome. Caratacus in his turn was so overwhelmed by the majesty of the city that he was bewildered that the Romans could be interested in conquering Britain. He said, "And can you, then, who have such possessions and so many of them, covet our poor tents?"

CARTIMANDUA

Queen of the **Brigantes** in the first century AD. Her kingdom was in northern England and she ruled from about AD 43 until 69.

Little is known about her, though she was clearly influential in Roman Britain. Unlike **Boudicca**, who opposed the Romans, Cartimandua was an ally of Rome. In fact she formed a large tribal alliance that was loyal to Rome. The inscription on the triumphal arch of the emperor Claudius declared that 11 "kings" of Britain surrendered to Rome without fighting, and Cartimandua may have been one of them. She was of noble birth and probably ruled by hereditary right rather than by marriage. Her husband was Venutius. The couple were seen by Rome as loyal and, in return, they were "defended by our [Roman] arms."

In AD 51, when **Caratacus** sought refuge with Cartimandua after he had been defeated by Ostorius Scapula in Wales, she put him in chains and handed him over to the Romans. In return for supplying Claudius with the prize exhibit for his triumph, she was rewarded with enormous wealth.

Eventually Cartimandua divorced Venutius and married his armor-bearer, a common soldier called Vellocatus. She took the precaution of holding Venutius' brother and other relatives hostage, but Venutius still made war against her, building alliances against her. In about 55, he invaded her kingdom, but the Romans anticipated this and supplied Cartimandua with troops for her defense. There was some inconclusive fighting until Caesius Nasica appeared with a legion to defeat Venutius and the rebels. Rome recognized its debt to Cartimandua and helped her to keep her kingdom.

In 69, the year of four emperors, she was less lucky. During the instability Venutius mounted another revolt, aided by other **tribes**. Cartimandua asked the Romans for help, but this time they sent only auxiliaries. Cartimandua was evacuated and Venutius took over the kingdom of the Brigantes.

From this moment, Cartimandua vanishes from history.

CASSIVELLAUNUS

A great Celtic chief, and the earliest British Celt whose name we know. He was known as Caswallawn by his fellow Britons; the Romans knew him by the Latin form of his name, Cassivellaunus. He was king of the powerful **Catuvellauni tribe** and led the British resistance to **Julius Caesar**'s invasion of 55 and 54 BC. Caesar mentions him by name in his reminiscences. Cassivellaunus killed the King of the **Trinovantes**, whose son Mandubracius fled for his life to the European mainland to seek Caesar's protection. At that time, Caesar was engaged in the conquest of Gaul and some of the British tribes had been supporting Gaulish tribes in resisting him, which explains his interest in invading Britain.

The Roman legions landed in Cantium (Kent) and their focus of attention was on the Thames estuary. Cassivellaunus's strategy was to draw the Roman columns into the interior, with a view to mounting an attack on their landing-site, perhaps to cut off their retreat. His difficulty was in persuading his fellow kings to collaborate with his strategy. His ancestral tribal base was at St. Albans, but he had an ongoing feud with his neighbors to the east, the Trinovantes, who gave in to Caesar without a fight. Cassivellaunus also failed to rally the **Cantii**. Alone, the Catuvellauni were no match for the heavily armed legionaries of the Roman army. On the other hand, Cassivellaunus's 4,000 **chariots** were able to harry the Romans very effectively as they tried to ford the Thames **River**, and the Catuvellauni put up a good fight in pitched battle.

Cassivellaunus and his soldiers fled north, perhaps first to St. Albans and then to **Camulodunum**, hoping for an attack on the

Romans' rear from Cantium. When he saw that it was not going to happen, Cassivellaunus surrendered hostages to Caesar, who made him promise to leave the Trinovantes in peace and agree to pay Rome an annual tribute. Caesar also allowed the Trinovantes to appoint Mandubracius as their king.

After Cassivellaunus's submission, Caesar considered that as far as Rome was concerned Britain had been conquered, and sailed away.

Cassivellaunus was the grandfather or great-grandfather of **Cunobelin**.

CASWALLAWN

See **Cassivellaunus**; Myths: **Branwen**.

CATHBAD OF ULSTER

See Religion: **Druids**.

CATUVELLAUNI

A very powerful British **tribe** in the first centuries BC and AD. Its territory extended across the modern counties of Hertfordshire, south Bedfordshire, and Buckinghamshire, but the Catuvellauni reached out to control their neighbors. Their kings were very strong and the lack of hillforts within their borders shows that they had their petty kings and local chiefs firmly under control.

There was a long-term power struggle between the Catuvellauni and their neighbors to the east, the **Trinovantes**. It was probably pressure from the Catuvellauni that led to the expulsion of the Trinovantian prince Mandubracius. He went to appeal to **Julius Caesar** in Gaul. Rome found political refugees like Mandubracius useful, especially when they were looking for an excuse to intervene; disaffected princes must also have been a useful fund of intelligence.

Other British tribes who feared the Catuvellauni joined the Trinovantes, including the **Iceni**. This was a great bonus for Caesar, because they brought with them exactly the information he needed—the whereabouts of **Cassivellaunus**'s headquarters. Cassivellaunus was King of the Catuvellauni, but he had adopted the Trinovantian capital, **Camulodunum**, as his base. It speaks highly of the loyalty that he inspired that he was able to keep this secret for so long. Caesar marched on Camulodunum at once.

The defenders ran away and it seems that Cassivellaunus escaped. He appealed for peace through Commius, King of the **Atrebates**, and the resistance to Caesar was over. Surprisingly, Caesar had already decided to withdraw from Britain to Gaul for the winter, because he had intelligence of an imminent uprising there. Perhaps Cassivellaunus should have gone on fighting; Caesar could scarcely have coped with a continuing British insurrection and the large-scale **Vercingetorix** rising that was about to erupt.

At the pinnacle of their power, the Catuvellauni achieved the confederation of south-eastern England in an informal Southern Kingdom (*see* **Tasciovanus, Trinovantes**).

CAUUS

Cauus or Caw of Alclud (see Places: **Alcluith**) was the father of **Gildas**. He lived in the upper Forth valley, perhaps 20 miles (30km) north of Glasgow. In about 495, he and his family moved to Wales. Legend gives him a second son, Cuil, who stayed in Scotland and died fighting against **Arthur**, but legend also makes Cauus a **giant**, because the word "cawr" in Welsh means "giant" (*see* **Funeral Odes**).

CAW

See **Cauus; Funeral Odes**.

CELTOMANIA

There has been a surge of renewed enthusiasm for all things Celtic in modern times. It began in the early eighteenth century with the awareness that there were links between the ancient **languages** of the Atlantic Celts, and intensified with the growing awareness that these languages were in retreat.

The surge of interest in **tartan** and Celtic **art** in the nineteenth century and Celtic **music** in the twentieth century were further symptoms of Celtomania. There has recently been a political dimension too, as people have become aware that peripheral regions of Europe could lose their cultural identity as the hub of the European Union develops and strengthens (*see* Part 6: Celtic Twilight and Revival).

CENOMANI

A Celtic **tribe** in Gaul; its main center was at Le Mans.

CERDIC

See **Natan-Leod**.

CERETIC GULETIC

The King of **Alcluith** (Clyde) at the end of the fifth century. He appears in the story of St. **Patrick** as King Coroticus; Patrick claimed to have turned him into a fox.

Ceretic's fleet went across to raid the Irish in the middle of the fifth century.

He died in 500 and was succeeded by his son **Dyfnwal**.

CHARIOTS

Chariots were used for showing off before battle. Queen Medb of Connaught, for example, was driven in her chariot around her camp as a prelude to battle.

Here is what **Julius Caesar** had to say about the British Celts on the battlefield:

In chariot fighting the Britons begin by driving all over the field hurling javelins, and generally the terror inspired by the horses and the noise of the wheels are sufficient to throw the opponents' ranks into disorder. Then, after making their way between the squadrons of their own cavalry, they jump down from the chariots and engage on foot. In the meantime their charioteers retire a short distance from the battle and place the chariots in such a position that their masters, if hard pressed by numbers, have an easy means of retreat to their own lines. Thus they combine the mobility of cavalry with the staying-power of infantry; and by daily training and practice they are able to control the horse at full gallop, and to check and turn them in a moment. They can run along the chariot pole, stand on the yoke, and get back into the chariot as quick as lightning.

Caesar saw all this first hand and he was impressed by what he saw.

Chariots could also acquire cult status. Two Gaulish cult vehicles were imported, dismantled, and buried in a mound with a cremation burial at Dejbjerg in Denmark in the first century BC. There was a throne at the center of each wagon, and the bodies buried at the site are believed to have been female. Were they perhaps warrior queens?

No British Iron Age chariots have survived, though a chariot **wheel** was found in a second-century rubbish pit. It was a single piece of **ash** bent in a circle, fixed to an elm hub, with **willow** spokes.

Early Irish folk-tales, such as *The Wooing of Emer,* from the **Ulster Cycle**, offer descriptions of working chariots:

I see a chariot of fine wood with wickerwork, moving on wheels of white bronze. Its frame very high, of creaking copper, rounded and firm. A strong curved yoke of gold; two firm-plaited yellow reins; the shafts hard and straight as sword blades.

CHILDHOOD

Very young children had low status in Celtic **society**, counting as extensions of the family. Individual identity was allowed only as a child grew. Among the nobility, the education of children took place away from the parents. There was a widespread practice of sending children away to be brought up by another family, often with the intention of creating new kinship ties with a group far away. This fostering practice was carried through into the Middle Ages. The **Druids** took charge of the education of many children.

Julius Caesar mentions that in Gaul boys were not allowed to appear in public until they were old enough to bear arms. It was considered a disgrace to the father if a son who was still a child stood beside him in public. The change in status marked by bearing arms suggests a rite of passage of some kind, and it is likely that there were complex initiation rites associated with status changes at different ages. In the Irish tales about **Cú Chulainn**, we hear about the rites of passage he has to undergo with other boys to acquire manly status. In one ritual, he is attacked by 159 boys throwing their hurley sticks at him. The young hero manages to dodge all of them.

Probably **headhunting** marked a later rite of passage. In Ireland, killing a foe and taking his **head** was the signal that a youth's military instruction was complete.

A further rite of passage was marriage, which had, in Irish folktales at least, to be preceded by an adventure. Cú Chulainn has to undertake a long journey, during the course of which he has to undergo various ordeals. When he returns to take his bride-prize, he finds he has to force his way into her house and abduct her. This is no doubt a heightened version of some real trial by adversity that real-life grooms had to undergo.

CIARAN OF SAIGAR

An Irish saint, born in Ossory, Ciaran lived for 30 years in Ireland, unbaptized because the community he lived in was pagan. He went to Rome in the time of Pope Hilary (461–68) and was consecrated bishop. He founded a double monastery, for men and women, with his mother in charge of the women.

Ciaran, Ailbe, Declan, and Ibar were the four bishops of southern Ireland who preached before **Patrick**.

Ciaran was abused by **Aillel**, King of **Munster**, and stopped a war between Aillel and Loegaire, the Irish High King. He visited Tours and died in Cornwall.

CIVILIS

See Religion: **Druids**.

CLEMENS

See **Petroc**.

CLYTO

See **Fingar of Gwinnear**.

COEL GODEBOG

"Coel the Magnificent," according to one tradition, was a prince of Cornwall, son of Tegvan ap Dehevraint. The tradition is that he took upon himself the kingdom of Britain in 272 and held it for 28 years. The Romans were in power at that time, so it is scarcely possible for Coel to have been in any real sense "King of Britain." There may, even so, have been some sort of agreement among the native kings and chieftains as to seniority.

Another tradition has Coel as Lord of Colchester, a local ruler who was allowed to rule under Rome with status of a municipal senator or Decurion.

COEL HEN

"Coel the Old" lived around 350–430. According to one tradition he was **Coel Godebog**'s successor as Lord of Colchester, and was the last ruler there, under Rome, at the time when the Romans left. He earned his nickname because he was long-lived.

But there was an early tradition, which therefore may be more authentic, that Coel Hen was a powerful king in the north of England. According to this version, he ruled the kingdom of York and perhaps the whole of the north, south of Hadrian's Wall.

Coel's mother went by the extraordinary name of Stradwawl, "Street Wall." He named his daughter simply Wawl, "Wall."

Apart from this, we know very little about the real Coel. He lives on, just, in a children's nursery rhyme:

Old King Cole was a merry old soul,
and a merry old soul was he;
he called for his pipe,
and called for his bowl
and he called for his fiddlers three.

This is a reminder that the Celtic inheritance is a strange one, sometimes more colorful than its origin, but sometimes a paler and weaker wraith. The nursery rhyme really tells us nothing about the flesh-and-blood King Coel.

COGIDUMNUS

Tiberius Claudius Cogidumnus was the king of the Regnenses **tribe** (West Sussex and Hampshire) in the first century AD. He was a tribal chief in the years before the Roman conquest of Britain in AD 43, then a British client king under Rome.

The Regnenses were a group within the **Atrebates** tribe, and Cogidumnus may have been king over all of the Atrebates. In one Roman document he is said to have governed several civitates as a client ruler after the conquest and to have been loyal to Rome "down to our own times" (in the 70s). His name is on a damaged inscription found in the Roman city of Chichester, a few miles from Fishbourne, which reads, "To Neptune and Minerva, for the welfare of the Divine House, by the authority of Tiberius Claudius Cogidumnus, great King of the Britons, the guild of smiths and those in it gave this temple at

their own expense." This indicates that he was given Roman citizenship by the emperor Claudius.

Cogidumnus's collaboration with Rome ensured the success of Vespasian's conquest of central-southern Britain, not least because Vespasian was able to utilize Chichester Harbor, which the Romans called "The Great Harbor," for their fleet.

Sir Barry Cunliffe, the principal excavator of the Roman palace at Fishbourne, at the head of Chichester Harbor, believes that Fishbourne was the palace of Cogidumnus.

COINAGE

The Celts on the European mainland began minting coins in the fourth century BC, with designs based on Greek originals. Many of these found their way into Britain during the course of trading and eventually, in the first century BC, British kings began minting their own coins. This started in Cantium (Kent), with cast imitations of bronze coins of the Ambiana tribe across the Channel in northern Gaul.

Coins were made in surprisingly

large numbers. It is said that from the middle of the **La Tène** period, they were minted by the million.

Pre-Roman Celtic coins sometimes have figurative images on them: representations of animals or **people**. These are evidently heavily symbolic. Some coins show a **boar**, and this is a motif on other objects too, such as the Witham shield made in the second century BC. It is also thought that coins had a special role as largesse and as an indicator of wealth, which would have made the imagery more potent.

A Gaulish coin found near Maidstone shows a **stag** and a boar running together. The stag has a huge eye and over-large antlers. The boar has over-large bristles. There are three different circular symbols, one of which may represent a rayed **sun**.

Coins of the Aulerci Eburovices **tribe**, who lived in the Evreux region in Gaul, show a boar image superimposed on the neck of a manlike image. This has a link with a similar pairing on a stone carved from Euffigneix: a human figure wearing a torc, with a boar carved along its torso.

By AD 10, the **Camulodunum** mint was turning out magnifi-cent **gold** coins inscribed in full with name of the king, CVNO-BELINVS. More often, kings contented themselves with an abbreviated form of their names and the names of their mints, so some coins had CVN and CAM (or CAMV) on them or CVN REX TASCIO F, "King Cunobelin, son of **Tasciovanus**."

A British coin bearing King **Cunobelin** has the short form of his name on one side, CVNO, and the abbreviated name of his capital on the other, CAM for Camulodunum. The designs are admirably simple, compared with the fussy designs on modern coins.

The imagery on these coins sometimes tells us a lot about the tribal mindset. Cunobelin was setting out to be as Roman as could be. Other **tribes** portrayed totem images. Others went on imitating Gaulish coins, in ever-freer styles, so that the images became totally abstract. The **head** of Apollo was transformed into a swirl of hair. The image of a **horse** became more and more stylized until it was reduced to a few sweeping lines. The exploded horse image was already in existence in Britain, drawn on the chalk hillside at Uffington, and that had been there since the very beginning of the Iron Age, so the image was already available, and it is possible that the coin image was copied from it.

On the other hand, some northern tribes, such as the Parisii and the **Brigantes**, seem to have held back from engaging in the money **econom**y and never struck any coins of their own.

COLUMBA OF IONA

Columba was born a prince of the northern Ui Neill in 521. Two of his first cousins became kings during his lifetime, and he himself was eligible for kingship. When he was in his twenties, he was hostile to the overriding influence of the (non-aristocratic) Ciaran of Clonmacnoise.

Columba is said to have founded around 40 monastic houses in Ireland: the first at Derry, close to the dynastic home of his family at Ailech.

Without permission, he copied the *Gospel Book of Finnian* belonging to Moville, who sought judgment against him from King Diarmait. Diarmait had executed the King of Connacht's son, who had killed a youth while playing games and who had sought sanctuary with Columba. Columba rallied the monks and the regional kings of Ireland against Diarmait's centralized and tyrannical rule. He also won a military victory against him at the bloody battle of Cuil Dremhne in 563.

The consequence was exile, imposed on Columba by a monastic synod that deplored the involvement of monks in political **warfare**. This is how Columba arrived at Iona.

Once there, Columba converted Brudeus or **Bridei**, King of the **Picts**, and consecrated **Aedan**, King of the Scots, at Dal Riada. He appointed monks as bishops to communities in Britain; as monks, they remained under Columba's authority. He visited Ireland several times, and also the Irish colonists in Dal Riada in Britain; he made at least two journeys to visit the northern Picts, where Bridei had enormous respect for him.

Overall, Columba had enormous influence over the development of the Church in northern Britain and Ireland. He also wielded considerable political power, and it was probably his influence that kept the northern kingdoms at peace with one another.

CONAN

See **Brioc**.

CONCHOBAR MAC NESSA

See Myths: **The Ulster Cycle**; Symbols: **Sky Falling Down**.

CONOMORUS

See **Gildas**, **Leonorus**.

CORIOSOLITES

An Iron Age Celtic **tribe** living on the north coast of Brittany, around St. Malo. The main tribal center was at Corseul.

CORMAC MACAIRT

See Symbols: **Magic**.

COROTICUS

See **Ceretic Guletic**.

CORREUS

See **Bellovaci**.

CULTURES

The central European Celts of the Iron Age had their origins in the Urnfield culture of the late Bronze Age. This had its beginnings in about 1300 BC, just 50 years before the Trojan War. It flourished at the same time as the great warrior-hero culture of the Mycenaeans and its growth may be connected with the decline of Mycenaean power.

As the name suggests, Urnfield was associated with a distinctive type of cemetery: large-scale cremation burials laid out in flat cemeteries, without burial mounds. These cemeteries were widespread over such a large area that archeologists have been confident in identifying the Urnfield **people** as proto-Celts, the immediate predecessors of the Celts.

The introduction of cremation (instead of the burial of the unburned body) suggests a change in beliefs regarding death and the afterlife. The use of large quantities of sheet bronze implies industrial-scale production of metal and reliable, well-organized trade routes to supply that industry. The sheet-bronze was used to make a variety of objects, including large vessels and shields. Sometimes the vessels were mounted on wagons for religious ritual.

The development of religious paraphernalia shows an increasingly complex religious symbolism and more integrated and uniform ways of expressing religious ideas.

Other changes were under way as well. By about 800 BC **horses** were used not just as draft animals but for riding. The horse became a symbol of the warrior elite, just as the horse-drawn **chariot** had been the symbol of the Mycenaean warrior heroes.

By 700 BC the Hallstatt culture had emerged out of Urnfield. This is the first of the classically recognized Celtic cultures. It was at Hallstatt, a picture-postcard lakeside village in Austria, that archeologists first identified new types of metal horse harness. The salt mines in the mountains were the basis of the prosperity and fame of this area between 700 and 400 BC. For the first time iron-working appears on a big scale. Hundreds of years before, the Mycenaeans evidently knew about iron, but they did not think of using it for tools or for weapon-making. The practice of iron-making was quickly copied at site after site. By 600 BC, the Atlantic Celts were making iron in Britain and Ireland.

The Hallstatt culture in central Europe has distinctive hallmarks. One is the rich burial of a warrior-prince or king in a timber mortuary-house, often with a four-wheeled wagon (sometimes in dismantled kit form), covered by a burial mound made of earth. Often in these burials there are three sets of horse-harness. The wagon-team would have comprised a pair of horses, just like a Mycenaean chariot, so what is the third set of trappings for? It is possible that it represented the prince's or king's personal steed: his charger.

The elite men, and sometimes women, buried in these opulent graves were rich enough to import wine from the Mediterranean lands.

By 500 BC the power centers had moved away from Austria, north and west toward the Rhineland and the Marne Valley in northern France. Changes in burial custom at the same time led archeologists to identify this development as a new culture: **La Tène**. The culture was named after a site in Switzerland, on the shore of Lake Neuchatel. La Tène means "The Shallows" and it was a location along the lakeshore that was seen as sacred: a fit place to leave offerings to please the **gods**. When the site was excavated in 1906–17, it yielded a rich haul of objects that were of new types, including iron **swords** and everyday ironwork.

There was still a warrior aristocracy and it still went in for burials with funerary carts, but now the carts were a more elegant two-wheeled type rather than the heavier four-wheeled type: a chariot more on the lines of the Mycenaean chariot; a two-wheeled vehicle was far more maneuverable. The old four-wheeled wagons were more the vehicles of fighting farmers; the new two-wheeled chariots were skillfully designed, showing collaboration between carpenters, blacksmiths, and wheelwrights to produce a professional fighting machine.

More arresting still, the accoutrements of the warrior-princes were elaborately decorated with what we now see as typical Celtic designs. The La Tène style is familiar to us: it is the root of all the later artwork that we recognize as Celtic. The S-shaped line that endlessly repeats suggests a variety of things, including rippling **water** and plant tendrils. But there are also surprises. In the middle of a swirl of lines we sometimes recognize an animal **head**, so stylized that we cannot be sure whether it is really there, intended by the artist-craftsman, or we ourselves are projecting it—like the **giants** or mountain landscapes we sometimes see in cloud formations. And here is a hint of the Celtic love of **shapeshifting** legends.

According to the threefold model for Iron Age Britain, a third wave of innovation came with a third lot of migrants, the Belgae, who arrived in south-east England late in the first century BC. The Belgic culture area extended from Belgium across northern France into south-east England. Distinctive objects associated with the Belgae in Britain were wheel-made pottery and Gallo-Belgic **coins**.

But this threefold model has been shaken by the general acceptance that there were no mass movements of people into Britain in the first millennium BC. There were no invasions, apart from **Julius Caesar**'s; instead we should think rather of a complex evolution of an indigenous culture.

CUNOBELIN

King of the **Catuvellauni tribe**, son of **Tasciovanus**, and grandson or great-grandson of **Cassivellaunus**. He was the successor of Dubnovellaunus, King of the **Trinovantes**, the Catuvellauni's eastern neighbors, when he died in about AD 10. Dubnovellaunus had fled to Rome, taking refuge at the court of Augustus when the Catuvellauni had annexed his territory and had no doubt been hoping that the emperor would intervene on his behalf. Cunobelin anticipated trouble from Rome and prudently became a Roman ally. As a client king he could expect favorable treatment from Augustus.

Cunobelin was a strong ruler and under his leadership the old imposed alliance between the Catuvellauni and the Trinovantes was re-asserted. This expanded kingdom was undoubtedly the strongest political entity in Britain on the eve of the invasion by the emperor Claudius in AD 43, and the Roman historian Suetonius described Cunobelin as "King of Britain."

Cunobelin ruled the large joint kingdom from **Camulodunum**, near modern Colchester, which was previously the chief settlement of the Trinovantes. This move appears to have been made in order to tap into the European trading network more easily.

Camulodunum was a large urban complex covering 12 square miles (30 square km) and marked out by flanking **rivers** and big earth ramparts. It was a major industrial focus that included a mint. At Gosbecks there was a massive concentration of expensive imported pottery in one area, which was probably Cunobelin's palace. Nearby there was a royal burial ground.

Cunobelin and his court were Romanized Celts. They were native Britons, but they were also keen to acquire all the luxury goods they could from Rome. They may have adopted Latin; some Latin graffiti have been found, though they could have been inscribed by Roman visitors. The Catuvellaunian aristocrats were in effect being bought or groomed by Rome in advance of the Claudian invasion. Having some client kings in Britain made invasion and annexation much easier.

Strabo observed that certain British kings "procured the friendship of Caesar Augustus by sending embassies and paying court to him."

Cunobelin is the original of Shakespeare's Cymbeline, and the only pre-Roman chief to be remembered in later times. Shakespeare's portrayal of Cymbeline bears little relation to history, except for the idea that a client king was expected to pay annual tribute to Rome and that he found this hard to suffer:

…Britain is.
A world by itself, and we will nothing pay
For wearing our own noses.

The **Lexden Tumulus** in Colchester may be the grave of **Addedomarus** or of Cunobelin. It is about the right date to be Cunobelin's, and of the right status. It contained chain-mail armor, Roman bronzes, furniture, and 15 wine *amphorae*. The bronze ornaments in the grave date from the eve of the invasion by Claudius. One of the grave goods is a pendant made out of a silver coin with a fine portrait bust of the young Augustus on it (see Places: **Lexden Tumulus**).

Cunobelin may have worn the pendant: he saw himself as the British Augustus. On his own coins he had the portrait of Augustus imitated and labelled *CVNO*.

After Cunobelinus's death, his two sons, **Togodumnus** and **Caratacus**, expanded Catuvellaunian power even more aggressively than their father. They seemed to be fearless of the Romans hesitating to invade on the other side of the Channel.

CURSE TABLETS

Romano-Celtic curses inscribed informally on sheets of lead are known by the Latin name *defixiones*, because of the form of words often used: somebody's name followed by *defictus est* ("is cursed.") They were deposited with other offerings in shrines. In effect the curse was offered up to the gods just like any other prayer.

In 1930 only four curse tablets were known, but subsequent excavations, at places such as **Bath**, and Uley in Gloucestershire, have revealed many more of them. They are difficult to read because they have been hastily scratched.

Curse tablets are of interest in their intensely personal character. A fine example was found at the Romano-Celtic sanctuary at Uley. It was written on both sides of a rectangular lead sheet 3.5 inches

(9cm) across and then rolled up tightly, presumably so that no one except the **god** would be able to read it. When it was found, it had to be unrolled very carefully under laboratory conditions, to make sure that it did not break up. The conservation was successful, and this is how the inscription runs:

A reminder to the God Mercury from Saturnina, a woman, concerning the linen cloth she has lost. Let him who has stolen it have no rest until he brings the aforesaid things to the aforesaid temple, whether this is a man or a woman, slave or free. She gives a third part to the aforesaid god on condition that he exacts those things which have been written above. A third part of what has been lost is given to the god Silvanus on condition that he exact this whether [the culprit?] is a man or woman, slave or free.

This curse was left at the shrine, where a fine stone statue of **Mercury** presided; its **head** has survived. Where Saturnina wrote the name of the god Mercury, the name of another god, **Mars-Silvanus**, has been erased. The later reference to Silvanus confirms that the woman was depositing her curse with two gods, not just one, as an insurance. It also looks as if she had left a curse with Mercury before: this is "a reminder." Whether Saturnina ever got her linen back we shall never know.

Some tablets sound more legalistic. One from Bath reads: "I have given the goddess Sulis six silver pieces which I have lost. It is for the goddess to extract it from the debtors Senicianus, Saturninus, and Anniola. This document has been copied."

Some are difficult to translate because they have been written informally and ungrammatically, apparently in a rage. One of these, again from Bath, reads: "I curse whoever has stolen, whoever has robbed Deomorix from his house. Whoever is guilty may the god find him. Let him recover it with his blood and his life." Deomorix was a Celt.

A tablet from Moorgate in London was written in a towering rage: "I curse Tretia Maria and her life and mind and memory and liver and lungs all mixed up together, her words, thoughts and memory, thus may she be unable to speak of things concealed…"

One from Harlow, addressed to Mercury, is not about theft—

which most are—but about a love triangle: "I entrust to you my affair with Eterna and her own self, and may Timotneus feel no jealousy of me at risk of his life blood."

CYNLAS

See **Ewein Whitetooth**.

DAVID

David or Dewi of Menevia (St. David's) was probably born in 523. He died in 589. He was the son of "Sanctus," King of Cardigan, and Nonnita, daughter of Cynyr, "in the time of King Triphunus and his sons." He was baptized by Ailbe and educated at Vetus Rubus (Henllwyn) under **Illtud**. After a time he established Vallis Rosina (Hodnant, now called Merry Vale). David was harassed by an Irish chief called Boya, who paraded naked women in front of his monks in order to tempt them. He established an austere monastic rule, living on vegetables and **water**, which earned him the nickname David Aquaticus. **Gildas** denounced his extremism.

At the Synod of Brefi, in about 545, called to discuss Pelagianism, David addressed the assembly and his oratory persuaded them, much to the anger of **Cadoc**, who was then overseas. But this synod was a decisive victory for David. New monastic houses were founded all over the country and David was informally acclaimed archbishop or even "head" of all Britain.

One notable disciple was Aedan of Ferns, and through him up to one third of Ireland followed David's rule. David's name recurs frequently in the *Lives of Irish Saints*.

The cult of David spread widely in Demetia (Pembrokeshire), Brecon, and the Wye Valley. It was more scattered in Cornwall and Brittany, was never established in Glamorgan, where Cadoc and Illtud held sway, and was absent from Scotland.

DECEANGLI

A British **tribe** living in North Wales, in what is now Clwyd.

DECIANUS CATUS

See **Boudicca**.

DEWI

See **David**.

DIARMAIT

See **Columba of Iona**, **Ruadan**.

DICUL

An Irish abbot who set up a small monastic house at Bosham, in Sussex, in around 650. He had with him five or six monks and they apparently had no effect at all on the local (pagan Saxon) population. St. Wilfrid found them there when he arrived in 680.

DIODORUS
SICULUS

A Greek historian who lived in the first century BC. He was born in Sicily and later lived in Rome, where he collected the materials for his huge history of the world in 40 books. Some of our most reliable information about the state of Europe in the late Iron Age, not least about the Celts, comes from Diodorus.

DIVICIACUS

A **Druid** of whom **Julius Caesar** had personal knowledge. As well as being a Druid, Diviciacus was chief of the **Aedui tribe** and brother of **Dumnorix**. He went on a diplomatic mission to Rome, where he got to know Cicero, who described how Diviciacus would predict the future by augury. Cicero referred to him as a Druid.

Diviciacus helped Caesar enormously in his conquest of Gaul by persuading some of the tribes to collaborate with Rome. Caesar depended on him to form alliances that enabled him to conquer Gaul

more smoothly and rapidly.

Caesar must have known that Diviciacus was a Druid, yet he does not mention it. But he did remember him as "the greatest man in Gaul"—a leader who had held sway among Gallic tribes and was also influential in Britain.

DOCCO

Also known as Kyngar of Congresbury, Docco was the son of Luciria and the emperor Constatinus III. He was born in 400–10. He was a cleric who traveled from Italy to found several major early monastic houses in Britain, including Congresbury in Somerset. The site was on the estate of a Roman villa, though the villa itself had by then gone.

Docco also crossed the Severn Sea to Glamorgan to found a monastery in the territory of Paulentus Penychen and visited Ireland, Aran, Rome, and Jerusalem. His monastery at St. Kew is the earliest known Cornish monastery—it was already well-established when St. **Samson** visited it in 540.

Docco died in Jerusalem in 473 and his body was buried at Congresbury.

Docco, **David**, and **Gildas** are the only British churchmen to be mentioned in the Irish Annals.

DRESS

In the first century BC, **Posidonius** wrote this colorful description of the Celts:

To the frankness and high-spiritedness of their temperament must be added the traits of childish boastfulness and love of decoration. They wear ornaments of gold, torcs on their necks, and bracelets on their arms and wrists, whilst people of high rank wear dyed garments besprinkled with gold.

The torc was a neck ring that was a mark of status of freeborn Celtic men (and sometimes women). Rich people wore **gold** torcs, which were flexible enough to be bent and sprung back around the wearer's neck. Poorer **people** wore torcs of iron or bronze, which had movable sections that could be pegged into place. The huge difference in wealth between rich and poor is clear from the finds of torcs.

The Snettisham hoard, found in Norfolk between 1948 and 1968, includes a rich array of gold torcs dating from perhaps AD 50, and it shows how incredibly rich the **Iceni** nobility were compared with the ordinary people. The magnificent Snettisham torc is fine enough to have been a piece of royal regalia, and it may have been worn by the kings and queens of the Iceni: Snettisham was in their territory (*see* **Boudicca**).

Torcs were worn by the aristocracy throughout the world of the Celtic **west**, even in Galicia.

DRUIDS

See Religion: **Druids**.

DUBNOVELLAUNUS
See **Addedomarus**, **Cunobelin**.

DUBRICIUS

Dyfrig, also known by his Latinized name, Dubricius, was a Dark Age saint. According to Geoffrey of Monmouth's glamorized version of King **Arthur**, after Uther's death, Britons gathered "from their various provinces in the town of Silchester and suggested to Dubricius, the Archbishop of the City of the Legions [Caerleon], that he should crown Arthur, the son of Uther, as their king."

Dubricius was a real historical figure living in sixth-century post-Roman Britain, and the only bishop to be attached to a city. Today that is normal, but in the Dark Ages bishops were more often unattached. Bishops were usually creatures of their kings, and very much personal appointments. Dubricius consecrated **Samson** as bishop, apparently as his successor.

DUMNORIX

A chief of the **Aedui tribe** in Gaul in the first century BC. He fought vigorously against any Gaulish alliance with **Julius Caesar**. In 54 BC, Caesar chose him as one of the hostages he would take with him on his expedition to Britain, fearing that he would cause trouble if left behind in Gaul. When he failed to argue his way out of this, on the grounds that he suffered from seasickness, Dumnorix tried to escape from Caesar's camp. Caesar sent cavalry after him. Dumnorix was killed, shouting that he was "a free man and a citizen of a free state" (*see also* **Diviciacus**).

DUNAWT

See **Pabo Post Prydain**.

DURATIOS

See **Pictones**.

DUROTRIGES

A fiercely independent Celtic **tribe** who resisted the Roman conquest. Their territory coincided with the modern English county of Dorset. Their capital was the magnificent hillfort of **Maiden Castle**, which was attacked by the Romans and then replaced by a new open town (Dorchester) on lower ground nearby.

Dwellings

The standard dwelling in the Iron Age was a stoutly built round wooden hut with a conical thatched roof and a porch opening to the south-east.

Chysauster in Cornwall, inhabited from about 50 BC to AD 300, was built in a much more ancient tradition. The irregular, fetus-shaped houses with thick, stone-built walls were much more like the stone houses built in Neolithic Orkney hundreds of years earlier. The design was probably partly remembered from an earlier age, and partly a response to a windy, maritime environment.

At **Jarlshof** in Shetland, the communal **memory** linking the centuries is made visible. Jarlshof was first inhabited in the Neolithic and continued as a village through the Bronze Age and into the Iron

Age, with interruptions when it was engulfed by sand.

Like the Jarlshof houses, the houses at Chysauster were in effect stoutly walled courtyards designed to keep out the wind, with rooms opening out of them. Once there were walled fields round Chysauster, the walls dating from the same time as the village. Thanks to an insane EU subsidy policy, these were plowed up some time ago to make a rocky landscape that is no use for arable or pasture, and its archeology has been destroyed too.

The *brochs* of Orkney, Shetland, and the Western Isles of Scotland represent a similar design approach—rooms ranged around a courtyard—but carried up into the air to make imposing towers. The finest is the **Broch of Mousa**, which has survived almost intact because of its inaccessibility on an uninhabited island off the east coast of Shetland. Built in the first century BC and inhabited until about AD 150, it soars 40 feet (10m) above the shore in a graceful drum shape. Timber ranges once lined the interior walls, with galleries at various levels, reached by stone staircases built within the thickness of the outer wall. There was

The Element Encyclopedia of the Celts

a single door and no windows; it must have been very dark and dank inside.

The hearth was the centerpiece of every dwelling and it had the status of an **altar** in domestic cult. This custom may have had its roots in the Neolithic; the layout of the stone houses at Skara Brae in Orkney, with large central square hearths, treats the domestic fire almost theatrically.

The *Laws of Hywel Dda* supply inventories of the objects to be seen in a typical household in early medieval Celtic Britain. They include boilers, blankets, bolsters, coulters, fuel axes (axes for chopping firewood), broad axes, augers, gimlets, firedogs, sickles, baking griddles, trivets, pans, and sieves.

DYFNWAL

Dyfnwal Hen was a king of **Alcluith** (Clyde), whose fortress was the formidable Dumbarton Rock below Glasgow. His father or grandfather was **Ceretic Guletic**.

Dyfnwal lived at the end of the fifth century. His grandson was Tutagual Tutclit, and his great-grandson was Riderch, mentioned by St. **Adomnán** as ruler of the Rock of Clyde. From another son of Dyfnwal descends a long line of recorded kings of Strathclyde, right down to the end of the kingdom in the tenth century.

DYFRIG

See **Dubricius**.

ECONOMY

The Celtic economy was strongly rural in character, with some arable farming and a great many livestock. The Iron Age landscape was a patchwork of small irregular fields and meadows, with scattered round huts separated by substantial areas of dense forest.

By the end of the Bronze Age a particularly hardy form of wheat called spelt and a new hardy type of barley (hulled instead of naked barley) were introduced into Britain. These innovations meant that in the Iron Age a crop could be sown in the autumn and harvested in the spring—before the spring-sowing. The Greek writer Hecateus observed that as early as the sixth century BC the people of Britain reaped two harvests a year.

The fields were irregular in shape, but on average roughly 1 acre (0.4 hectares) in area. It was the size of field that could be plowed in a day by two oxen ambling along at 2 miles (3km) per hour.

The farming year was marked by four major quarter-day festivals, **Imbolg**, **Beltane**, **Lugnasad**, and **Samhain**.

he was not only Maelgwn's son but a cousin of Egferth, King of the Bernicians. A kinship alliance of this kind between Gwynedd and Pictland was something of a threat to the security of the Celtic kingdoms in between, Clyde and Rheged.

But Rhydderch's raid on Gwynedd was unsuccessful and he had to withdraw. Rhun, King of Gwynedd, responded by gathering an army and marching it north, probably by way of York. It was a march of legendary length and duration and the warriors returned to Gwynedd in triumph.

ELIDYR

A king of South **Rheged** (Lancashire and Cheshire) who was the son-in-law of King **Maelgwn** of **Gwynedd**.

Elidyr landed near Caernarvon in an attempt to take Gwynedd from **Rhun, son of Maelgwn**, but was killed on the beach. He was apparently not supported by the York or Pennine kings. Instead it was Rhydderch and other northern allies who sailed south to Gwynedd to avenge his death.

Rhun's half-brother **Bridei** had become King of the **Picts** in 555;

ELISEG

A king of **Powys**, commemorated on the Pillar of Eliseg. The inscription, as read by Edward Lhuyd in 1696, is as follows:

Concenn, son of Cattell, Cattell son of Brohcmail, Brohcmail son of Eliseg, Eliseg son of Guoilliac. Concenn, who is therefore great-grandson of Eliseg, erected this stone to his great-grand-father Eliseg. Eliseg annexed the inheritance of Powys throughout nine years from the power of the English.

The inscription also mentioned that "Britu moreover was the son of Vortigern whom Germanus blessed," which seems to tell us the name of King **Vortigern**'s successor.

The inscription has deteriorated as a result of weathering and is no longer legible (*see* Symbols: **Phallus**).

ELOQUENCE

The Celts have always admired eloquence, believing it to be more powerful than brute strength.

ETAIN

Etain of the **Tuatha dé Danann** was the heroine of the Irish love story ***Midhir and Etain***. This tale has been the inspiration of poems and plays, and is probably best known through Fiona McLeod's play *The Immortal Hour* and Rutland Boughton's opera, which in turn is based on the McLeod play (*see* Part 6: Celtic Twilight and Revival).

EWEIN WHITETOOTH

King of **Powys** in the early sixth century. He was murdered by **Maelgwn**, the notorious King of **Gwynedd**, and succeeded by his (Ewein's) son Cynlas. Cynlas was nicknamed, possibly privately by **Gildas**, Cuneglasus, which meant "Pale Dog" in Brittonic.

Fannell

See Religion: **Headhunting**.

Farannan

An Irish monk from Sligo who went with **Columba** when he left for Iona.

Feic

See **Fiacc of Sletty**.

Fergna Brit

An abbot of Iona, 608–624.

Fiacc of Sletty

A magus or wizard of Loegaire, High King of Ireland. Fiacc or Feic was a student under Dubthach Maccu Lugir. He was the only one of Loegaire's magi to accept **Patrick** (*see* **Magicians**).

Filidh

See **Learning**.

Fingar of Gwinnear

A Cornish saint. He was the son of an Irish king called Clyto. When **Patrick** visited Clyto's court in Ireland, Fingar alone honored him. Fingar was apparently disinherited and emigrated to Brittany (via Cornwall) where he founded monasteries with his sister Piala and 770 companions and seven bishops. They were accompanied by St. Hia, who traveled by herself on a leaf. This odd convoy landed at Hayle, where it was attacked by the local King **Theodoric**, a pagan who was afraid the missionaries would convert his subjects. He had been warned by Clyto that his son had sailed and fell on the rear of one party and killed them. According to one account, Fingar's party then surrendered and were massacred. Fingar himself was beheaded, but he replaced his **head** and went on to perform several miracles.

FINNIAN OF CLONARD

Finnian was the "teacher of the saints of Ireland." He founded Clonard, where he encountered the magus Fraychan.

Finnian's mother founded a monastic house for women, together with the mother of Ciaran of Clonmacnoise.

Finnian lived on a simple diet of bread, vegetables, and **water**, and a little fish on feast days. He slept on the ground with a stone pillow. He died in 551.

His tradition was hard, rather like St. **David**'s, but without the harshness or arrogance that was attributed to David. Finnian was said to be full of **learning** and compassion.

FOGOU

A low-ceilinged subterranean passage in Cornwall. *Fogous* are similar to *souterrains* in being associated with settlements, but they are made in a different way. The Breton *souterrains* were burrowed out of sand, while the Cornish *fogous* were built in open trenches with side walls of stone and roofed with capstones; they were then covered with backfill. There is the same discussion about their function as with *souterrains*; on balance it is most likely that their primary use was as grain stores.

The fine *fogou* at Carn Euny in Cornwall was made in the first century BC. The passage is 66 feet (20m) long with, unusually, a circular side chamber.

FOILL

See Religion: **Headhunting**.

FOOD AND FEASTING

Ceremony surrounded the Celtic domestic hearth. Even more ceremony surrounded the provision of large meals. Banquets and feasting were major characteristics of the Celtic way of life.

Posidonius described a feast:

The Celts sit on hay and have their meals served up on wooden tables raised slightly above the earth. Their food consists of small numbers of loaves together with a large amount of meat, either boiled or roasted on charcoal or on spits. This food is eaten cleanly, but they eat like lions, raising up whole limbs in both hands and biting off the meat...

When a large number dine together they sit around in a circle with the most influential man in the centre, like the leader of the chorus, whether he surpasses the others in warlike skill, or lineage, or wealth. Beside him sits the host and next on either side the others in order of distinction...

The Celts sometimes engage in single combat at dinner. For they gather in arms and engage in mock battles, and fight hand-to-hand, but sometimes wounds are inflicted, and the annoyance caused by this may even lead to killing unless the bystanders restrain them. In former times, when the hindquarters were served up the bravest hero took the thigh piece, and if another man claimed it they stood up and fought in single combat to the death.

Feasts such as these were designed to reinforce the pecking order among the warriors, and to strengthen the ties among members of the band.

The main drinks in an Iron Age Celtic feast were beer and mead, though the nobility adopted wine as soon as the trade routes to the Mediterranean allowed. At first it was a very expensive luxury. There was even a tale current in Rome that the Celts had crossed the Alps and invaded Italy just to get closer to the vineyards.

FORTIFICATIONS

On some of the hilltops there were large hillforts, surrounded by complex ramparts and palisades. Although called forts, they had several functions. They were stock enclosures and refuges in times of danger, they housed permanent settlements, and they were the focus of tribal gatherings and feastings (*see* **Food and Feasting**, **Tribes**). They probably also had a ceremonial and religious function, as well as acting as clear territorial markers—literally landmarks—that would help to create a sense of cohesion among **people** who were normally scattered across the landscape in separate homesteads.

The hillfort was usually laid out on the summit of a hill and surrounded by an earthwork that was intended to be clearly visible from below. The massive squared ramparts were faced front and back by rows of upright timbers tied by horizontal crossbeams. The earthen rampart was topped by a stout palisade, to defend the fighting-platform behind it, as at Hollingbury in Sussex. All the timber breastworks have disintegrated now, and the earth and rock they supported has slipped sideways, yet the ramparts can still be imposing. **Maiden Castle** in Dorset is the most impressive of the hillforts, with a complex mazelike entrance; it was the capital of the **Durotriges** tribe.

In Galicia, there were lots of defended homesteads built on hilltops. The presence of these *castros* distinguishes Galicia from the rest of the Iberian peninsula; they are the hallmark of its ancient Celtic past. The *castro* is a hilltop settlement, like a miniature hillfort, defended by multiple walls. Within, there is an ordered settlement, mostly with round stone houses built to a high density. **Castro de Baroña** is a fine example (*see* **Dwellings**).

FUNERAL ODES

One of the duties of a Celtic **bard** was to write a funeral ode on the death of his king. A fine example has survived, entitled *Marwnad Uthyr Pendragon,* which can be translated as *The Funeral Ode to the Wonderful Pendragon.* For a long time this was thought to be the funeral ode for Uther, **Arthur**'s father, but the word "uter" can be an adjective meaning "terrible" or "wonderful," while *pendragon* is a Celtic title for High King or *dux bellorum.* This means that the ode might have been addressed to Arthur himself:

The longing and lamentation of the multitude
Are unceasing throughout the host.
They earnestly yearn for the joyful prize of blue enamel.
There your stone with your name became a riddle.
They also wish for their Prince.
All around appears the rule of order at the head of the feast.
They seek to dress the head of the feast with black.
They unendingly shed blood among the war-bands,
Longing for you to defend them and give them succour.

The sword that was in the van in
taming the brothers of Caw of the
Wall.
They crave with longing for a
portion of your cause
And for refuge in the manliness of
Arthur.
They long for your coming in a
hundred fortresses.
A hundred manors long for your
assurances.
They long for your coming in a
hundred schools.
A hundred chieftains long for your
coming:
The great and mighty sword that
supported them.
They look for your best judgements
of merit,
The restoration of principalities.
Your sayings are remembered,
soothing the aggressive.
The eloquence of the bards is not
great enough:
Toiling for weeks with the eagerness
of beavers,
With the names of men and war-
bands to compare you.
Above the eagles, above the fear of
disorder,
I am the one who is with the great
Warrior.
I am the bard, the bagpiper. I am
with the Creator;
Seventy musicians create the great

rhapsody of the first power...
The Leader of Heaven has left the
nation without a roof.

"Caw of the Wall" seems an odd phrase. *The Life of Cadoc* tells us that Caw (**Cauus**) lived in southern Scotland, not far from Hadrian's Wall; he was the father of **Gildas**.

In another poem, *The Dream of Rhonabwy*, Arthur is described as sitting with Gwarthegydd, another son of Caw.

Other evidence confirms that Arthur and Caw were contemporaries, so the ode was written at the right time to have been for Arthur. If it is his eulogy, it tells us a great deal about the way he was regarded at the time of his death. The final image is the most telling of all: "The Leader of Heaven has left the nation without a roof."

The Element Encyclopedia of the Celts

G

GABRAN

See **Bridei**.

GAMES

Celtic chiefs undoubtedly played board games and maybe their subjects did too.

Gaming pieces made out of wood have not survived, but a set made out of glass was found in a royal grave at Welwyn Garden City, just north of London. It consisted of a set of 12 white marbles and an opposing set of 12 black marbles, both highly decorated. The wooden game board was 2 feet (0.6m) square and badly decayed. This was a game similar to Ludo, and it was designed for two players. Although Ludo itself was patented in the nineteenth century, it was based on a very old board game.

Dice have been found at other sites, but in the Welwyn grave there were six fragments of beads and bracelets, which may have been thrown to determine the number of moves each player made.

GENEALOGY

Kings and princes were entitled to their privileges by birthright, in other words according to who their mothers and fathers were. They therefore had a strong vested interest in establishing and committing to **memory** their family trees. No doubt these were transmitted orally for countless centuries and written down only from about the seventh century AD onward, when the process of Christianization made written records much commoner (*see* **Writing**). The lack of interference from the Romans in Ireland has meant that more in the way of Irish genealogy has survived.

King lists were drawn up and doubtless recited on special occasions by **bards**. These were designed to establish the king's entitlement to his position, and doubtless flattering connections with long-dead heroic figures were added as a matter of course. A considerable amount of invention is involved in some of them. The powerful Irish chiefs of the Middle Ages wanted to be descended from Celtic **gods**, or from Egyptian pharaohs. But sometimes the names of heroes and kings follow one another in a credible sequence that recurs in other genealogies, and this corroboration inspires more confidence.

According to bardic sources, Slaine the Firbolg was the first High King of Ireland. From the time of his accession to the year 1, there were 107 High Kings: nine Firbolgs, nine **Tuatha dé Danann**, and 89 Milesians. After the rebellion in the first century AD, the High Kingship was reinstated, and after that there was an unbroken line of 81 High Kings until Rory O'Connor who, in 1175, surrendered his overlordship to Henry II of England.

The texture of the bardic genealogies often shows a shift from the mythic to the historic. Conaire Mor was the son of the bird god Nemglan; by contrast Ollamh Foola, the eighteenth High King, who came to the throne in 714 BC, is said to have provided Ireland with its first law code, which has a more historic ring to it.

GERAINT

A Dumnonian (Cornish) king who was born in about 480 and a contemporary of King **Arthur**. His pedigree survives. He was Geraint (or Gerontius in Latin), son of Erbin, son of Kynoar, son of Tudwaol, son of Gorwaor, son of Gaden, son of Cynan, son of Eudaf Hen, and known as Geraint Llyngesog, the "Fleet-owner."

He was married first to Gwyar, daughter of Amlawdd Wledig, by whom he had four children: Selyf, Cyngar, Iestyn, and Cado. He then married Enid, daughter of Ynywl, Lord of Caerleon. Geraint himself was the son of Erbin, who held lands in both south-east Wales and **Dumnonia**. Early sources name both Geraint and his son and heir Cado or Cato as "rulers who ruled with Arthur." This supports the idea that there were several Cornish sub-kings, with Arthur as their overking.

The poem Geraint may be a genuine sixth-century poem. It is an elegy for the warriors who fell at the Battle of Llongborth, written in the wake of one of Arthur's battles (see **Funeral Odes**). Llongborth means "Port of the Warships" and is thought to be the westernmost of the Saxon Shore Forts: Portchester, at the head of Portsmouth Harbor, a likely location for the battle with the Saxons:

In Llongborth I saw spurs
and men who did not flinch from
spears,
who drank their wine from glass that
glinted.

In Llongborth I saw Arthur,
heroes who cut with steel,
the emperor, ruler of our labour.

In Llongborth, Geraint was slain,
heroes of the land of Dyfnant,
and before they were slain they slew.

GIFTS

Celtic chiefs competed with each other in the giving of lavish feasts, so feasts should be regarded as a form of gift (*see* **Food and Feasting**). There was also a principle of reciprocation: the guest was expected to respond in kind, inviting his host to another banquet.

This set in train an endless cycle of exchanges of food and drink, the purpose of which was to consolidate social ties. Of course the feasts were very enjoyable, but the temptation to be over-zealous was always there, to try to outdo your host. Ariamdes, a Celtic nobleman from Galatia, threw a feast that was so extravagant that it represented a year's supply of food.

GILDAS

Gildas the Wise was a Celtic monk who lived and wrote in the sixth century. He was born in **Alcluith**, the son of **Cauus**, and possibly the brother of Cuillus, who rebelled against **Arthur**. He migrated, probably in infancy, to Wales. He attended **Illtud**'s famous school, along with with **Samson** and **Paul Aurelian**.

Gildas preached in north Pembrokeshire in the time of King Tribinus and his sons. He preached in northern Britain, received a message from Brigit, and sent her a bell. He arranged a marriage between Trifina, the daughter of Weroc of Vannes, and the evil tyrant Conomorus (who died in 560). Conomorus cut off Trifina's **head**, which Gildas promptly restored.

Gildas wrote strongly condemning the harsh discipline of St. **David**, and equally strongly supported the milder rule of

Illtud and **Cadoc of Lancarfan**. He returned from a visit to Ireland, visited Cadoc, and supervised the school for a year, writing a Gospel that would later be bound in **gold** and silver. He spent a winter on Echni (Flat Holm, an island in the Bristol Channel), where he was disturbed by pirates from the Orkneys. After that, in the days when King **Melwas** ruled Somerset, he went to **Glastonbury**, where he died in 570.

Gildas is of special interest in being the only historian or commentator who was actually writing at the time of **Arthur**. His theme was the condition of Britain, which he thought was in a poor state politically and morally, though it was a beautiful land. His book opens with a surprisingly lyrical description of Britain's watery beauty:

This land of such dear souls, this dear, dear land ... decked with lucid fountains, abundant brooks wandering over snow white sands, transparent rivers that glide with gentle murmur, lakes which pour forth cool torrents of refreshing water.

Written in Latin in about 540, the book has the title *Book of Complaint on the Ruin and Conquest of Britain.*

Gildas describes a great British leader called **Ambrosius Aurelianus** initiating an increasingly successful campaign against the Saxons in the run-up to the Battle of **Badon**, which he identifies as a landmark in history. By 540, the battle, which had been fought 20 or so years earlier, was seen as a watershed engagement: one that marked the end of one phase of history and the start of another, much as Trafalgar or Waterloo would have been perceived by a mid-nineteenth century historian. It is strange that Gildas does not mention Arthur in connection with Badon, as great a puzzle as Aristotle's total silence regarding his pupil Alexander the Great.

What Gildas was complaining about above all was the complacency of the British. Those who had struggled to push back the Saxons in the years leading up to Badon had died. The new generation was "ignorant of the storm"—it had no idea what efforts were needed to defend Celtic Britain against the invaders.

It is an articulate and emotionally highly charged account, with a great deal of invective directed at one British ruler after another: Gildas was dissatisfied with nearly all of them. Probably with conscious understatement, he calls his thunderous accusations *admonitiuncula*, "just a little word of warning."

The text is largely compiled from biblical quotations, making it more sermon than history. Another frustration is the obscure Latin style Gildas uses, making it rich in ambiguity when what we want is clarity.

There may also have been more than one version. Bede's specific references to Gildas imply that he, in 731, was working from a different version than the one we have today, and we have no way of knowing which is the more authentic. Gildas died in 570.

THE GODODDIN

A series of elegies in 103 stanzas about a disastrous expedition of the bodyguard of Mynydd Mwynfawr, King of **Din Eidyn** (Edinburgh). The expedition was ranged against the Anglians at Catraeth (probably Catterick).

The Gododdin has survived in a single manuscript called *The Book of Aneirin*. We are told simply, "This is *The Gododdin*. Aneirin composed it." The subject matter and the detail tell us that this is a genuine sixth-century Celtic poem. The **bard** Aneirin lived in the second half of the sixth century. The Gododdin of the title are the men of the Votadini **tribe**, but the warriors on this expedition include handpicked men from kingdoms all over Britain—**Elmet**, Clyde, **Gwynedd**, and **Dumnonia**—which tells us that communications among the British kingdoms must have been effective and that the Britons were ready to help one another against the Anglo-Saxons (*see* **Alduith**).

The Gododdin chief feasted the men for a year at Din Eidyn before sending them to fight the Lloegrwys (the men of England) or the Dewr a Brynaich (the men of Deira and Byrnaich). Aneirin comments grimly, "They paid for that feast of mead with their lives." The British attack on Catraeth was probably pre-emptive, an attempt to annihilate the embryonic Anglian community while it was still relatively small and powerless; the crushing defeat would have been all the more traumatic because it was unexpected.

One line in *The Gododdin* jumps off the page. A warrior is praised for his fighting prowess, "though he was no Arthur."

GORDEBAR

See **Aircol**, **Vortipor**.

GOSCELIN

See Places: **Cerne Abbas**.

GURGUST
LETHAM

The King of York in the early sixth century.

GURON

A hermit living at Padstow in north Cornwall, who was evicted by St. **Petroc**.

GWALLAWG

A king of the Dark Age Pennine kingdom of **Elmet**.

GWRGI

See **Peredur Steel-Arm**.

h

HELMET

A very fine horned helmet made of bronze was deposited in the Thames River at Waterloo Bridge in the first century BC. It was found in 1868.

Like the Battersea shield, also found in the Thames (*see* **Art**), this was almost certainly not an accidental loss, but a deliberate deposit in **water**. The horns may have been intended to combine ferocity and potency symbolism. The bronze was originally enameled. It is a masterpiece of the armorer's craft, and it is possible that it was made to adorn a wooden statue of a **god** rather than to be worn by a mortal in battle; it would scarcely protect the wearer from a well-aimed **sword** blow. The Romans had an equivalent to this in their decorative parade helmets.

Hengist and Horsa

See **Vortigern**.

Hunting

See Religion: **Headhunting**; **Helis**; Symbols: **Dog**, **Stag**.

Hussa

See **Urien**.

I

Iceni

A British **tribe** living in East Anglia. Its tribal focus or capital was at Caistor St. Edmund, for which the Roman name was Venta Icenorum. In the 1930s, when it was partially excavated, the evidence showed that the Iceni had adopted very little Roman **culture**. They were few opulent houses and few substantial public buildings. The surrounding area had few Roman villas, they were few mosaics, and there were few oil *amphorae*. All this was interpreted as showing that the Iceni were poor and backward. We now see the same evidence as showing that the tribe was consciously retaining its Celtic identity and resisting a takeover by the Roman way of life—not a sign of poverty or backwardness at all.

The Iceni famously engaged in a revolt against Rome in AD 60–61, after their queen, **Boudicca**, suffered maltreatment by Roman soldiers.

Illtud

Illtud was a Breton, a cousin of King **Arthur**, and converted to the monastic life by **Cadoc of Lancarfan**. He may, as claimed, have been baptized by St. Germanus. He was ordained by St. **Dubricius** in the time when **Merchiaun** the Wild was King of Glamorgan.

Not long after his death he was described as "an exceptional teacher of the British, in the tradition of St. Germanus." He is still remembered chiefly for his remarkable school at Llantwit Fawr in Glamorgan, where he taught some remarkable boys: **David**, Leonorus, **Gildas**, **Samson**, **Paul Aurelian**, and **Maelgwn**—all became saints except the last, who became the infamous King Maelgwn of **Gwynedd**.

The boys started at the age of five, learning the alphabet. There were no set fees: Illtud relied on customary "donations."

Illtud's teaching method was gentle and lenient. He did not believe it was sensible for growing boys to go in for excessive fasting. He also tried to dissuade the 15-year-old Paul Aurelian from going off to a desert hermitage, but in the end left the decision to the boy.

The monastery was Illtud's own property, which his nephews expected to inherit. He died some time after 525.

J

JULIUS CAESAR

By no means a Celt himself, Gaius Julius Caesar earns his place here as a destroyer of Celts. He made a greater negative impact on the Celts than anyone else in history.

Caesar came from an old patrician family. In 85 BC, when he was only 16, his father died suddenly. Caesar was young to be head of the family, but he started at once working his way up the *cursus honorum*, the ladder of offices and appointments that would enhance his social status. In pursuing his political career and lobbying for offices, he ran up debts and was accused of corruption.

When he was appointed Governor of Cisalpine Gaul (northern Italy), with Transalpine Gaul (southern France) added later, he was glad to get out of Rome. He was deeply in debt: a great spur to military adventure.

From a variety of motives, including self-glorification and ultimate political triumph, Caesar worked his way through Gaul, attacking the Gallic **tribes** one by one and defeating them. Once he had conquered the tribes along the coast of the English Channel, the way was clear to cross and take Britain.

In 55 BC, Caesar blocked an attempt by two Germanic tribes to invade Gaul. Then, in late summer, he crossed the Channel into Britain. But his geographical and political knowledge of Britain was not good enough. He managed to establish a bridgehead on the coast in Sussex, but could not go further. He withdrew to Gaul for the winter.

In 54 BC he returned to Britain with a larger force and achieved more, setting up some alliances that would prove useful later. But there were poor harvests in Gaul, and a widespread revolt there forced Caesar to withdraw from Britain again.

What Caesar did, unintentionally, was to set down a challenge for future emperors who wanted to make a name for themselves. Could they succeed in conquering Britain, where great Caesar himself had failed?

In 52 BC there was a new and larger revolt in Gaul, led by **Vercingetorix**. This was well-coordinated and Caesar was defeated several times before the revolt was put down at the Battle of **Alesia**.

Plutarch claimed that in Caesar's Gallic Wars one million Gauls had died and another million had been enslaved. Caesar had subjugated 300 tribes and destroyed 800 towns. The figures may have been exaggerated, but it is no exaggeration to see this as little short of a Celtic genocide.

K

KENTIGERN

St. Kentigern was the son of Owain, son of King **Urien** of **Rheged**. His mother was **Thynoy**.

Kentigern traveled to **David** at Menevia. He founded St. Asaph's and was attacked by **Maelgwn** of Degannwy. He visited Europe and went to Rome seven times. It seems that he was Bishop of Senlis, near Paris, from 549–65.

While he was abroad, Riderch became King of Alclud (see **Alcluith**), and Kentigern returned to Glasgow. He taught that Woden was a mortal man, a Saxon king, not a **god**. He preached widely, visiting Pictland, and was visited by **Columba of Iona**, who gave him a staff, which is still preserved at Ripon. Kentigern died in around 603.

KYNGAR OF CONGRESBURY

See **Docco**.

L

LANGUAGE

The old languages still spoken in the Atlantic Celtic lands are related to one another, though they are not all as closely related as once believed. The current view among linguists is that historically there are two families of Celtic languages. The Q-Celtic family, known as Goidelic, has a western Gaelic branch from which Irish is descended and an eastern Gaelic branch from which Scottish Gaelic and Manx Gaelic are descended. Then there is a P-Celtic family, known as Brittonic, with a northern Brittonic branch from which Welsh developed and a southern Brittonic branch from which Cornish and Breton are descended. This division may help to explain why Welsh-speakers cannot understand Gaelic-speakers.

The "Q" and "P" families were first identified in the early eighteenth century by Edward Lhuyd. Q-Celtic is recognized from the presence of the "Q" sound in the word *Mac*, "son of." P-Celtic has the "P" sound in the corresponding position: *Map*. This "P/Q" exchange is found in other words as well.

The relationship between the Cornish and Breton languages is the closest. This is explained by the exodus of Britons, via Cornwall, in the Dark Ages, as they were driven out by the advancing Anglo-Saxons. These British refugees fled westward through southern Britain to Cornwall, then crossed to Brittany in considerable numbers, and they took their language with them.

In the Middle Ages, Scotland was divided culturally between Highlands and Lowlands. The

Highlanders spoke Gaelic (Irish "Celtic" or Erse), while the Lowlanders spoke Scots, which was a Germanic language close to English. This difference was perhaps a legacy of the Anglo-Saxon colonization of the Scottish Lowlands in the Dark Ages.

In the late 1980s Professor Colin Renfrew put forward the view that Celtic speech evolved from its Indo-European ancestor in the British Isles and the adjacent continent at some time after 4000 BC. Professor Renfrew believes that the Celtic language was not taken to Britain at all, but developed *in situ*. This is very much in line with the general view emerging of Celtic **culture** as a whole.

Much of what was passed on to others was learned by listening. Little was written down (*see* **Writing**). There were nevertheless the means to write. The **Ogham** alphabet was made of combinations of short and long marks, often chipped along the edges of stones. It was an ideal method for recording someone's name on a gravestone. Ogham was widely used in southern Ireland, and more than 900 examples have been found in Britain and Ireland as a whole.

It is widely believed that the Celtic language was completely wiped out in England, but there are many surviving Celtic place-names. For a long time after the Anglo-Saxon colonization period (about AD 400–700), Celtic and Anglo-Saxon names existed side by side. Sometimes it is the Celtic name rather than the English name that we know today. The Cotswold Windrush **River** had an English name, Dikler, which died out as late as the sixteenth century; we now call the river by its older Celtic name, even though it has (or had) an Anglo-Saxon name. The Cotswold Hills take their name from a Celtic word and an Anglo-Saxon word. Cuda was a goddess of the Dobunni **tribe**; *wold* was the Anglo-Saxon word for a wooded upland.

In the Roman occupation and the post-Roman period, Celtic kings and princes thought it smart to use Latin. Grave markers from the fifth and sixth centuries are often inscribed in Latin. A gravestone at Penmacho in North Wales reads *CARAVSIVS HIC IACIT IN HOC CONGERIES LAPIDVM,* "Here lies Carausius in this heap of stones."

The Element Encyclopedia of the Celts

LEARNING

Celtic **society** was highly structured and it allowed for the cultivation of learning and literature. There were professional classes who were responsible for their maintenance: the **Druids**, the **bards**, and a third order between them, known in Ireland as "the poets."

In Ireland by the seventh century AD the Druids had disappeared, as they bore the brunt of the Church's opposition, and the intermediate group, known as the *filidh*, were the sole inheritors of the druidic tradition. The *filidh* managed to establish a remarkable *modus vivendi* with the Church that enabled the two authorities to continue running side by side and were therefore able to maintain many of their ancient functions. The Irish bards suffered an eclipse too, as they limped on with a reputation as inferior rhymers.

In Wales, it was again the poets, or *filidh*, who emerged from the clash with Christianity in a position of strength, or at least with an enhanced and dignified reputation. Confusingly, the Welsh equivalents of the *filidh* were called bards.

According to **Julius Caesar**'s de-scription, the Druids in Gaul were teachers and disciples of learning. They distrusted the written word, committing vast amounts of poetry to **memory**. Caesar said the period of study necessary to become a Druid lasted 20 years. Similarly in Ireland, it took at least seven years to qualify for the *filidh*.

We know the Druids had views about the size and nature of the universe, but unfortunately we do not know what those views were.

LEONORUS

Leonorus (510–61) was a pupil at **Illtud**'s school and confirmed by **Dubricius** at the age of 15. He emigrated to Brittany with 72 disciples and many servants, landing near Dinard.

They cleared a wooded site of trees, but the seed corn they had brought from Britain had been lost on the voyage. Fortunately, they were miraculously helped by a robin and Leonorus also dug up a golden ram.

The king of the Breton territory, Rigaldus, died and the land was annexed by Conomorus. To escape persecution by Conomorus, Leonorus and others escaped to

Paris. There, Leonorus presented the golden ram he had found to Childebert, in exchange for confirmation of his rights to land in Brittany.

Conomorus was defeated in 560, and Leonorus died soon afterward.

LEUDONUS

Leudonus, or Llew mac Cynvarch, was a brother of **Urien**, King of **Rheged**. He was ruler of Lodoneis and the father of Gwalchmai (Gawain).

LINDOW MAN

See Places: **Lindow Moss**.

LLEW MAC CYNVARCH

See **Leudonus**.

LLYWARCH HEN

See **Rhun, Son of Maelgwn**.

LOEGAIRE

See **Ciaran of Saigar**, **Fiacc of Sletty**, **Patrick**.

LUERNIOS

See **Arverni**, **Bards**.

LUGID

See **Aillel Molt**.

MACLOVIUS

See **Malo**.

MAELGWN

The great king of **Gwynedd**, who ruled in North Wales from about 517 until his death in 547. His father was Caswallon Lawhir, son of Einion Urdd, son of Cunedda Gwledig, son of Edeyrn. He is mentioned in an inscription made in about 540 at Penmachno; there he appears as *MAGLO MAGIS-TRATUS*—"King Maelgwn." He appears in **Gildas**'s *Ruin of Britain* as Maglocunus and of the five kings Gildas singled out for condemnation, it was Maelgwn he dealt with most harshly:

What of you, dragon of the island [Anglesey, where Maelgwn's home was], you who have removed many of these tyrants from their country and even this life? You are last in my list, but first in evil, mightier than many both in power and malice, more profuse in giving, more extravagant in sin, strong in arms but stronger still in what destroys a soul, Maglocunus. Why wallow like a fool in the ancient ink of your crimes like a man drunk on wine pressed from the vine of the Sodomites? The king of all kings has made you higher than almost all the generals of Britain.

Maelgwn died in the Yellow Plague of Rhos in 547, and was succeeded by his son **Rhun** by his concubine Gwalltwen (*see* **Arthur**; Myths: *The History of Taliesin*).

MAGICIANS

The **Druids**, ovates, and **bards** were in some ways part of the public religious cult, because they formed colleges or fraternities. But there were others who were on the fringes: the magicians or sorcerers. These were secret dealers in rituals and beliefs that had come down from remote times and had little to do with mainstream Celtic religion.

The underground cult of **magic** was scarcely visible to travelers and other outsiders. There were probably many magicians and sorcerers living far from the *oppida* (*see* **Oppidum**), far from the mainstream cult centers, out in the countryside, where they trafficked in cures and magic charms.

MALO

St. Malo or Maclovius was a native of Gwent and a cousin of **Samson**. He was a pupil of **Brendan of Clonfert** at Nantcarvan. He was ordained by Brendan and sailed with him and a crew of 95 in a single ship on a seven-year voyage to the Island of Yma. On the way he encountered an island that looked as if it was made of glass—it was an iceberg. He reached Yma and found a bush that sounds like *acanthus*. He celebrated mass on the back of a whale. Then he returned home to plant his bush at Nantcarvan.

On a second voyage, he failed to find Yma but reached the Orkneys and other northern isles.

On yet another voyage, Malo left Nantcarvan for Brittany, revived a corpse, and celebrated mass in the presence of Conomorus, King of Dumnonie.

After many more travels and adventures, he died in 599 or 604.

MANDUBRACIUS

See **Cassivellaunus**, **Catuvellauni**.

MAUCENNUS

Maucennus of Rosnat was the abbot of Ninian's monastery, which was at **Whithorn** in south-west Scotland. Maucennus and Mugentius are the only two named abbots of Rosnat: one in the late fifth century, and the other in the sixth. Maucennus was referred to as a great teacher (librarius) from the far north, and who lived three days' journey from the home of **Samson's** parents in Demetia. The balance of evidence points to Maucennus being the abbot of Whithorn, which was also known as Rosnat.

MEDB OF CONNAUGHT

See **Chariots**; Myths: **The Ulster Cycle**; Religion: **Coligny Calendar**, **Mother Goddess**; Symbols: **Magic**.

MEDRAUT

See **Arthur**.

MELOR

See Religion: **Headhunting**.

MELWAS

A Dark Age king of Somerset. Later tradition associates him with **Glastonbury** Tor.

MERCHIAUN

King of **Rheged** in the early sixth century.

MERCHIAUN VESANUS

"Merchiaun the Wild" was King of **Glevissig** (Glamorgan) in the early sixth century. He may have been given his nickname to distinguish him from his contemporary namesake: the much more important King Merchiaun of **Rheged**.

Mark Conomorus, the south Dumnonian king, was a son of Merchiaun the Wild; he was exiled to the Breton kingdom of Dumnonie.

MERLIN

The wizard who was King **Arthur**'s legendary mentor.

It is generally and understandably assumed that Merlin never existed, and he was to an extent an invention of Geoffrey of Monmouth, but the character was based on a collection of old poems, riddles, and triads preserved in Wales but relating to a real sixth-century Celtic **bard**, or *carminator*, called **Myrddin**, the Celtic form of Martin, who lived in the north close to Hadrian's Wall. The aristocratic Norman-French readers for whom Geoffrey was writing would have pronounced Myrddin *Merdin*, and probably sniggered at a name so close to merde (= excrement). The Latin form of Myrddin, Merdinus, was no better—merda means "excrement" too, so Geoffrey had little choice but to change it. He chose Merlin.

In the Dark Ages, kings regularly employed bards to compose praise poems, occasional pieces on great victories or disastrous defeats, and **funeral odes**. The bards memorized their compositions for recitation in the feast halls (*see* **Food and Feasting**, **Memory**). A major role of the bard of the warband was to entertain the warriors, often with stirring tales of their own great deeds. The impression given by the surviving fragments of Dark Age Celtic poetry is of ceaseless **warfare**, feasting, drinking, boasting, and showing off. Occasionally, bards confronted warriors with uncomfortable truths, perhaps to shame them into trying harder. In *Rheged arise,* **Taliesin** writes, "Not too well did they fight around their king [**Urien**]: to lie would be wrong."

Taliesin served at least three and possibly four kings in succession—Cynan of **Powys**, Urien of **Rheged**, **Gwallawg** of **Elmet**, and Owain of Rheged—and seems always to have had the greater cause of the British—the Cymry, as they called one another—at heart, even if that meant deserting white-haired Urien for the younger Gwallawg. This element of unpredictability is one distinctive trait of the legendary Merlin.

We have no direct evidence of Arthur's bard, but he too would have had such a figure to sing of his exploits: in part to entertain and in part to condition his companions and warriors to see his as the greatest cause and inspire their unswerving loyalty.

Yet Arthur's Merlin has been portrayed by tradition as more than a bard. He is a magus. It is often assumed that this is an invention of the high Middle Ages, perhaps specifically an invention by Geoffrey of Monmouth, but there is plenty of evidence that sixth-century kings invariably had spiritual advisers or chaplains at their sides so that

supernatural help was always on call. **Muirchetach mac Erca**, High King of Ireland from 503 onward, was a contemporary of Arthur's and very much an Arthur-like figure himself. He leaned heavily on a British monk.

Bridei, King of the pagan **Picts** in the years after Arthur's death, had a chief **magician** called **Broichan**, who also functioned as a foster father and tutor to the king in true Celtic tradition. The relationship between these two real, documented, and truly historical figures is very similar to that described as existing between Arthur and Merlin in the fully developed medieval romances.

Arthur's "Merlin" may have even been based on a **priest**-companion. The Dark Age saints were a law unto themselves—wayward, volatile, intensely committed to their mission, fiercely jealous and competitive, and ever on the alert for the voice of God telling them to pack up and move on. This eccentric and unpredictable behavior is very much what we see in Merlin's character, even to the disappearing and reappearing. One tradition is that St. Piran was Arthur's chaplain. Another possibility is that Merlin might be loosely based on

St. **Dubricius**: the bishop credited with crowning Arthur.

Whether **Arthur** had a saint or a wizard at his side is hard to tell. Perhaps one of the things that made him extraordinary in his day was that he kept a wizard even though he was at least a nominal Christian. He may have had a wizard in his entourage to get the other point of view.

MEURIG AP TEWDRIG

A king of Gwent, the son of Dyfrig (also known by his Latin name, St. **Dubricius**).

Meurig married Onbrawst, daughter of Gwrgant Mawr, son of Cynfyn, son of Pebaw, son of Erb, King of Erging. His son was Arthrwys.

MODRED

See **Arthur**.

MORCANT

See **Urien**.

MORINI

An Iron Age **tribe** in Gaul with its main center at Boulogne.

MUIRCHETACH MAC ERCA

High King of Ireland from 503. Muirchetach mac Erca held the High Kingship very conspicuously for 30 years, dominating political and military affairs in much the same way that **Arthur** is thought to have dominated in southern Britain.

MUSIC

"The sound of song and of the harp filled Tara's halls." Music had a place at every feast (*see* **Food and Feasting**), and probably in the musicians' homes as well. Flutes were made out of bones; pan pipes were made out of bone or wood. There were also horns. The large, curved bronze trumpet found at Lough-na-Shade in County Armagh dates from about 100 BC.

The most remarkable Irish hoard, found at Downs in County

Offaly, was a collection of nearly 200 bronze objects that had been deposited in a lake or bog, probably over a long period. Among the objects were 26 great, curving, bronze horns. They would have made a noise somewhere between a **bull**-horn and a didgeridoo, and they appear to be distinctively Irish in character.

MYNYDD MWYNFAWR

*See **The Gododdin**, **Urien**.*

MYRDDIN

The **bard** of Gwenddolau, and the model for the legendary **Merlin**. Myrddin took no part in the Battle of Arderydd, but he watched it. When he saw his lord killed, he lost his reason and retreated to the Wood of Celidon. By the eleventh century, this had become:

The Battle of Arderydd between the sons of Elifer and Gwenddolau the son of Ceidio; in which battle Gwenddolau fell; Merlin became mad.

According to legend, in the time before Albion (Britain) was peopled, it was known as Clas Myrddin—Merlin's Grove (*see* Symbols: **Treasure**).

N

NAMNETES

An Iron Age Celtic **tribe** living in southern Brittany, along the lower Loire, with its main center at Nantes.

In 56 BC the Namnetes formed an alliance with the **Veneti** to fight against **Julius Caesar**'s fleet. The ensuing sea battle was won by the Roman fleet commanded by Decimus Brutus.

An island close to the mouth of the Loire, perhaps the Ile de Noirmoutier, was known as the Women's Island. No man was allowed to land there. The women living on the island had to sail to the mainland for sex. They had a custom of replacing their temple roof on the same day every year: each woman on the island bringing her own load of materials for the work. If any woman dropped her load, she was torn to pieces by the others, who then carried her limbs around the temple, crying, "Ev-ah!" in a frenzy. If the temple roof was made of reeds, it probably would have needed replacing every year, as described. The Celts were also noted for believing that it was unlucky to drop new materials. Circumambulation, the ritual of walking round a building, was also a common Celtic practice.

NATAN-LEOD

The Celtic king of an inland part of Hampshire at the end of the sixth century. He was killed by Cerdic, the leader and later king of the West Saxons.

NATH-I

A High King of Ireland who died while crossing the Alps in 428. He was struck by lightning. It was believed to be divine retribution for his destruction of a tower built by a hermit called Fermenus.

NECTAN

A Cornish saint, the eldest son of King Brychan of Wales. Nectan was killed by robbers who stole his cows.

NINIAN OF WHITHORN

A fourth-century British saint whose father was King of **Alcluith**. Ninian studied for several years in Rome. On his way home he visited St. Martin of Tours, who lent him the masons who built the stone church at **Whithorn**, a holy place with a high reputation in the fifth and sixth centuries. Martin died in 397.

Ninian cured the blindness of King Tuduvallus, the local king, also known as Tuduael or Tutaguel of Alcluith.

When Ninian died, he was buried at Whithorn.

OGHAM

Some of the ancient Celts used a strange alphabet that was developed specifically for making short inscriptions on **standing stones**. One edge of the standing slab was used as the **writing** line and short horizontal linear marks were made from this, to right or left or both. They were carved singly or in groups of up to five. In this way 20 different characters could be created.

The resulting alphabet was sometimes known as Beth Luis Nuin, after the (original) first three letters, just as with ABC for our modern Western alphabet. The surviving layout of the alphabet means that the system should logically be called Beth Luis *Fearn* (one, two, and three horizontal strokes to the right, respectively).

The fact that the alphabet is known as Beth Luis *Nuin* shows that there was a still older Gaelic system, of which only the nickname has survived.

Because the basis of the alphabet was a vertical line and the characters were lines branching to left and right from it, the system was like a tree, and it is sometimes called the Ogham Tree. This idea led on to giving the characters the names of trees. *Beth* means "birch," *Luis* means "**rowan**," and *Nuin* means "**ash**." The system is a tree; the alphabet itself is a forest. Individual trees held high symbolic significance, so the forest alphabet was deemed to be a repository of wisdom. The word for "knowledge" also means "wood."

Inscriptions are read from the bottom up, the way a tree grows.

The name "Ogham" comes from the name of the Irish god Ogma, the **god** of poetry and **learning** who is said to have devised the alphabet himself.

It is likely the Ogham alphabet was used for writing on perishable materials such as wood, leather, and bark, but these have not survived. The inscriptions that have survived are all on stone and they all date from AD 300 to 700.

The intensification of agriculture in Ireland meant that many Ogham stones were threatened. Some were rescued and put on display at University College Cork; the West Wing Stone Corridor there houses the largest collection of Ogham stones in Ireland. These stones are a national treasure, in that they represent the earliest examples of writing in Ireland, unless we count the remarkable Neolithic symbols carved on the Boyne passage graves. Another collection of Ogham stones is housed at Mount Melleray monastery near Cappoquin in County Waterford.

Some of the standing stones were raised as boundary markers. Some, mainly the later ones, were raised to mark graves. Many of the surviving Ogham inscriptions have been translated to read "name of person + name of father + name of **tribe**."

An Ogham stone from Ballymoreagh in County Kerry carries a Latin inscription on its face, which reads *FECT QUENILOC*, "Made by Qeniloc." Along the edge is Qeniloc's name and ancestry in Ogham.

Ogham was not confined to Ireland; Irish migrants took it to Wales.

OLLAMH FOOLA

See **Genealogy**.

OPPIDUM

Each **tribe** had at least one *oppidum*: a big market center with everything except a defensive rampart. By the first century BC every civitas had at least one, which functioned as its capital. It was a kind of town, with residential areas and areas of workshops, though unlike modern towns, it also included pasturage for livestock. **Julius Caesar** noted that he found a great many livestock in **Cassivellaunus**'s *oppidum*.

Caesar's account of the Gallic War is of particular interest because the date of his account is so precise, 58–51 BC, and this is exactly the time when the Celtic *oppida* were at their fullest development.

ORDOVICES

See **Caratacus**.

OSISMII

A Celtic **tribe** in Gaul, living in the extreme north-west of Brittany. They were first mentioned by the Greek traveler Pytheas in the fourth century BC. He located them on the western tip of Brittany, on a headland then called Kabaion; this was later known by the Latin name Finis Terrae, the End of the World, and is still known by the French version of this, *Finistère*.

The main town of the Osismii was Vorgium: modern Carhaix. The tribe submitted to **Julius Caesar** in 57 BC, though the following year they joined the **Veneti** in a revolt against Caesar, who suppressed them.

OSSIAN

Ossian was an ancient Gaelic **bard** invented by James Macpherson. *The Poems of Ossian*, also concocted by Macpherson, were published in the 1760s. They were an immedi-

ate sensation and Ossian acclaimed as a Celtic Homer.

During the next 30 years, the poems were widely read and translated into many **languages**. Goethe translated parts into German. Napoleon carried a copy with him on his march to Moscow. He also commissioned the artist Ingres to paint *The Dream of Ossian*.

The poems were extremely influential. They gave a huge impetus to the dawning Romantic movement. Poets as different from each other as Blake, Byron, and Elizabeth Barrett Browning were affected by them. The composers Mendelssohn, Schubert, and Brahms wrote **music** inspired by Ossian. The poems also stimulated the study of folklore and ancient Celtic languages.

When Macpherson first published his book, he claimed it was a translation of an ancient manuscript in Gaelic: a copy of an original work by Ossian. Several people challenged this, including Samuel Johnson, who said the poetry was the work of Macpherson himself, but Macpherson neither owned up nor produced the ancient manuscript. The controversy went on for many years.

Macpherson's fake Celtic world

was based on some authentic Celtic material. Fingal is based on Fionn Mac Cumhaill; Temora is **Tara**; Cuthulinn is **Cú Chulainn**; and Dar-Tula is Deirdre of the Sorrows. Parallels such as these create an air of authenticity, but most of the incident is Macpherson's own invention.

One of the poems is *Fingal*. Macpherson presented his "translation" in continuous prose. Here I have broken it up into lines to make it easier to read. This is how Book 1 opens:

Cuthullin sat by Tura's wall;
by the tree of the rustling sound.
His spear leaned against the rock.
His shield lay on the grass by his side.
Amid his thoughts of mighty Cairbar,
a hero slain by the chief in war;
the scout of ocean comes, Moran the son of Fithil!
"Arise," said the youth, "Cuthullin, arise.
I see the ships of the north!
Many, chief of men, are the foe.
Many the heroes of the sea-borne Swaran!"
"Moran!' replied the blue-eyed chief.
"Thou ever tremblest, son of Fithil!
Thy fears have increased the foe.

It is Fingal, king of deserts,
with aid to green Erin of streams."
"I beheld their chief," says Moran,
"tall as a glittering rock. His spear is a blasted pine.
His shield the rising moon! He sat on the shore!
like a cloud of mist on the silent hill!'
"Many, chief of heroes!" I said,
"many are our hands of war.
Well art thou named, the mighty man;
but many mighty men are seen from Tura's windy walls."
He spoke, like a wave on a rock,
"Who in this land appears like me?
Heroes stand not in my presence:
they fall to earth from my hand.
Who can meet Swaran in fight?
Who but Fingal, king of Selma of storms?
Once we wrestled on Malmor;
our heels overturned the woods.
Rocks fell from their place;
rivulets, changing their course,
fled murmuring from our side.
Three days we renewed the strife;
heroes stood at a distance and trembled.
On the fourth, Fingal says, the king of the ocean fell,
but Swaran says he stood!
Let dark Cuthullin yield to him,
that is strong as the storms of his land!'

"No!" the blue-eyed chief replied.
I never yield to mortal man!
Dark Cuthullin shall be great or dead!
Go, son of Fithil, take my spear.
Strike the sounding shield of Semo.
It hangs at Tura's rustling gale.
The sound of peace is not its voice!
My heroes shall hear and obey.'
He went. He struck the bossy shield.
The hills, the rocks reply.
The sound spreads along the wood:
deer start by the lake of roes.
Curach leaps from the sounding rock!
and Connal of the bloody spear!
Crugal's breast of snow beats high.
The son of Favi leaves the dark-brown hind.
"It is the shield of war," said Ronnart;
"the spear of Cuthullin," said Lugar!
Son of the sea, put on thy arms!
Calmar, lift thy sounding steel!
Puno! dreadful hero, arise!
Cairbar, from thy red tree of Cromla!
Bend thy knee, O Eth!
descend from the streams of Lena.
Caolt, stretch thy side as thou movest along
the whistling heath of Mora:
thy side that is white as the foam of the troubled sea,
when the dark winds pour it on rocky Cuthon.

Now I behold the chiefs,
in the pride of their former deeds!
Their souls are kindled at the battles of old;
at the actions of other times.
Their eyes are flames of fire.
They roll in search of the foes of the land.
Their mighty hands are on their swords.
Lightning pours from their sides of steel.
They come like streams from the mountains;
each rushes roaring from the hill.
Bright are the chiefs of battle,
in the armour of their fathers.
Gloomy and dark, their heroes follow
like the gathering of the rainy clouds
behind the red meteors of heaven.
The sounds of crashing arms ascend.
The grey dogs howl between.
Unequal bursts the song of battle.
Rocking Cromla echoes round.
On Lena's dusky heath they stand,
like mist that shades the hills of autumn;
when broken and dark it settles high,
and lifts its head to heaven.

The Element Encyclopedia of the Celts

P

PABO POST PRYDAIN

Pabo Post Prydain, "The Pillar of Britain," was a king of the northern Pennines and brother of Eliffer of York. His territory was south of the Tyne, with borders on the Vale of York and the Pennine frontier of **Rheged**. His son Dunawt was chief of the Northern Alliance that eventually destroyed **Urien**.

PATRICK

St. Patrick, patron saint of Ireland, was probably born in South Wales. His father was a Romano-British deacon named Calpurnius, and his own Celtic name was Succat.

According to legend, Patrick was abducted as a 16-year-old boy by Irish slave traders in about 405 or 410 and carried off to Ireland. He was sold in County Antrim to a chief called Milchu. He managed to escape after six years of captivity and made his way 200 miles overland to board ship. He was at sea for three days, then made his way home to his parents. They urged him never to leave again, but a deep restlessness inspired dreams that made him travel to Rome. He became a monk in Gaul, first at Tours, then at Lerins, before returning to convert his captors. According to Patrick himself, he had decided a long time before that he would have to return to Ireland.

Patrick was consecrated a bishop at the age of 45. In 432 he is believed to have been sent by Pope Celestine I to Ireland as a missionary. He landed at Wicklow and from there sailed north to convert his former master Milchu. In Down he was able to convert another chief, Dichu, to Christianity, and at **Tara** he preached to Loegaire, King of Tara. He also converted the tyrannous Mac Cuil, who became bishop of the Isle of Man.

After 20 years of missionary work, Patrick fixed his see at the royal center of Armagh, close to the ancient capital of **Emain Macha**, in 454. He died at Saul in 459 and was probably buried at Armagh.

As a slave himself, Patrick had the strongest personal motive for preaching against slavery. He preached from experience. In an open letter probably written in 445, he censured King Coroticus (**Ceretic**) of Clyde for stealing Irishwomen and selling them to the **Picts** as slaves. King Coroticus was not only a pagan, he was a committed anti-Christian. According to Patrick's hagiographer, Patrick turned him into a fox.

In the 450s, Patrick came into conflict with the wizards of King Loegaire, son of Niall, at Tara (*see* **Magicians**). Murchu describes the trial of strength:

The fierce heathen emperor of the barbarians reigned in Tara, the Irish capital. His name was Loegaire, son of Niall. He had wise men, wizards, soothsayers, enchanters and inventors of every black art who were also in their heathen, idolatrous way to know and foresee everything that happened. Two of them were above the rest, their names being Lothroch and Lucetmael.

They predicted that a strange new and troublesome faith would come and overthrow kingdoms.

A pagan festival, **Beltane**, coincided with Patrick's celebration of Easter. On the eve of Beltane when a great sacred bonfire was lit, a fire was seen to be burning in the direction of Tara: the religious focus of Ireland. This was surprising, as only the magi were authorized to kindle such a fire. They anxiously approached the blaze and found Patrick and his followers chanting psalms round their campfire.

Patrick was summoned to the Assembly at Tara, where he eloquently defended his mission. The magi challenged him to perform a miracle to prove divine support, but he refused. The magi then cast a **spell** and blanketed the landscape in heavy snow. Patrick made the sign of the cross and the illusion evaporated.

All kinds of **magic** feats were performed during this contest between Patrick's white magic and Lothroch's black arts. At one point Patrick caused one of the magicians to rise up into the air, fall headlong, and brain himself on a rock.

A great deal has been written about Patrick but his only certain literary remains are his spiritual autobiography, called *Confession*, and the letter he wrote to Coroticus. The point of his *Confession* was to explain why he would not return to Britain. The implication is that a British synod claimed authority over him and summoned him in order to exert that authority. Patrick implies that he could override the wishes of the British synod, and he evidently had Pope Leo's (440–61) approval to support him.

In spite of his high profile, Patrick did not have any obvious successor and in the years following his death he was seen in Ireland as just one saint among many.

PAUL AURELIAN

A sixth-century Celtic saint, the son of a nobleman, Perphirius of Penychen. He had two brothers, Notolius and Potolius, and a sister, Sativola. He was educated at **Illtud**'s school at Llantwit (some say he was at Caldey Island, which was an offshoot of Illtud's foundation) and wanted to live the life of a hermit. Illtud tried to dissuade him, but let him go when he insisted.

After spending time in a hermitage on his ancestral estates, Paul was summoned to the court of King Mark Conomorus at Villa Banhedos (later Caer Banhed, and now Castle Dore in Cornwall), where he was engaged in two sea defense projects involving building stone embankments to keep the sea back.

He later emigrated to Brittany, landing at Ushant with 12 disciples and 12 relatives. He won the respect of the local chief, Withur (Victor), whose "city" was at Roscoff. Paul then crossed to the island of Batz, where he got rid of a **dragon**. Withur and his people begged him to become their bishop. In about 550 he went to Paris with **Samson**. After foretelling the destruction of Batz by the Normans and directing that his body should be buried on the nearby mainland for the convenience of future pilgrims, he died on Batz.

PEOPLE

In the 1950s it was estimated that there were about 250,000 people in Britain in 100 BC, increasing to 400,000 by the time of the Roman invasion. More recent estimates have been more cautious, and few prehistorians now will attempt even to guess a population figure, but the numbers do seem to have increased in the late Iron Age. This population growth may have been associated with improvements in food production. **Julius Caesar's** description leaves out numbers:

The population [of Britain] is exceedingly large, and the ground thickly studded with homesteads, closely resembling those of the Gauls, and the cattle very numerous… There is timber of every kind, as in Gaul, except beech and fir. Hares, fowl and geese they think it unlawful to eat, but rear them for pleasure and amusement. The climate is more temperate than in Gaul, the cold being less severe… Most of the tribes of the interior do not grow corn, but live on milk and meat and wear skins.

It was Julius Caesar who also created for posterity the enduring image of blue-painted savages: "All the Britons, indeed, dye themselves with woad, which occasion a bluish colour and thereby have a more terrible appearance." It is still not clear whether this meant that the Britons painted their bodies with woad or tattooed themselves.

Diodorus Siculus gave a description of what the Gauls did to their hair. Men and women wore it long, sometimes plaited: "They continually wash their hair with limewash and draw it back from the forehead to the crown and to the nape of the neck, with the result that their appearance resembles that of Satyrs or of Pans, for the hair is so thickened by this treatment that it differs in no way from a horse's mane." This description is supported by the statue of the *Dying Gaul* (*see* Symbols: **Nudity**) and the **coin** portrait of **Vercingetorix**.

Normally, the Celts were warmly clad. They wore close-fitting trousers that the Romans referred to as *bracae*, "breeches." Over these they wore a long tunic made either of wool or of linen, which was held at the waist by a belt. Over this, they wore a **cloak** that was fastened at the shoulder with a brooch. The textiles were dyed bright colors and threads of different colors were woven so as to produce striking striped or checked patterns (*see* **Tartan**). The Roman observers were startled by the colors and patterns, which they were not used to seeing.

Nor were they used to seeing beards and moustaches. The Celts grew both and grew them long. Diodorus commented fastidiously, "When they are eating, the moustache becomes entangled in the food, and when they are drinking the drink passes, as it were, through a sort of strainer" (*see* **Dress**).

The Element Encyclopedia of the Celts

PEREDUR STEEL-ARM

Peredur and his brother Gwrgi were co-rulers of the kingdom of York (north-east England) in the late sixth century. They were the sons of King Eliffer of the Great Army. Peredur Steel-Arm was King of York from about 560 until 580, when he was killed in the Battle of Caer Greu.

A prince called Arthur was associated with Peredur, doubtless named after the great overking of southern Britain who had died not long before (*see* **Arthur**).

PETROC

A Dark Age Celtic saint, the son of Clemens, a Cornish chief. He studied in Ireland for many years, returning to Cornwall with disciples Dagan, Credanus, and Medanus. They landed near Padstow (Petroc's Stowe). Both **Samson** and Wethenoc had set themselves up in oratories in the area, and they were expected to move out to make way for Petroc, which they did with reluctance.

After a seven-year pilgrimage to Rome and Jerusalem, Petroc returned to Cornwall following the death of King **Theodoric**. Then Wethenoc returned and, to avoid a quarrel, Petroc withdrew to Little Petherick. He baptized the Cornish King Constantine. A powerful local magnate, Kynan, built an oratory in his honor near Bodmin.

After many years at Padstow and Petherick, Petroc moved to Bodmin, where he displaced the hermit **Guron**. He was visiting the monks at Padstow and Petherick when he was taken ill; he died at a farmhouse at Treravel.

St. Petroc spent much of his time teaching and despatching missionary monks from Padstow, which was then the main port for southern Ireland, south Wales, southern **Dumnonia**, and Brittany.

PICTONES

A Celtic **tribe** in Gaul, with its main center at Lemonum (Poitiers). **Julius Caesar** depended on the Pictones to build ships for him on the Loire. At the time of the Roman conquest, Duratios was King of the Pictones and frequently aided Caesar in naval battles. The Pictones supported the Romans because they were afraid of the expansionist strategies of other Gaulish tribes. Even so, they did send 8,000 men to support **Vercingetorix** during the Gaulish rebellion of 52 BC.

PICTS

A general Latin name given to the people who lived in the northern half of Scotland, "Pictland," in the third century AD. "The Painted People" was a nickname given by the Romans to northern Brits who wore woad or sported tattoos. "Pict" does not therefore really define a tribal or ethnic group in the Roman period, and Pictland, Alba, and Caledonia seem to have been thought of as being much the same area—Scotland.

In the past it has been suggested that the Picts were in some way the pre-Celtic inhabitants of Scotland, but that presupposes a belief that the Celts arrived in these islands during the Iron Age. Now that we see that they were well-established there by that stage, in fact they had been settled in Britain for thousands of years, the concept of "pre-Celts" has no meaning.

One theory holds that the Picts came originally, in the first millennium BC, from Ireland, having been displaced by incoming Celts—but there seems to be no particular reason for believing this. Any cultural or "ethnic" differences between the Picts and the people living to the south could be explained by their geographical isolation. They did evolve some extraordinary pictorial symbols, which appear to relate to their language. In other words the Picts' carved memorial stones carry pictograms (no pun intended).

The Irish called the Picts *Cruithin*, which is an early Irish transliteration of *Britanni*, so the Irish were not really identifying them as a distinct people either.

PLAID

A plaid is a **tartan** blanket thrown over one shoulder to make a kind of **cloak**. Plaid is the Gaelic word for "blanket."

POSIDONIUS

A Greek philosopher and poly-math (135–51 BC) who studied at Athens. In 86 BC he settled in Rome, where he became a friend of Cicero and other leading figures. He wrote about history and geography and is a source of information about the Celts in the late Iron Age.

PRASUTAGUS

King of the **Iceni** tribe in the first century AD. He was **Boudicca**'s husband. On his death he left half of his kingdom to Rome and assumed Rome would allow his family to inherit the other half. He underestimated the greed of the Roman administrator, who took everything; this led his successor and widow to lead a revolt against Roman rule in AD 60–61.

Prasutagus was the Latinized form of his Celtic name, Prastotagus. One of his **coins** was inscribed in a mixture of British and Latin, *SVB ESV PRASTO ESICO FECIT*, which means "Esico made [this] under Lord Prasto[tagus]." The coin bears Prastotagus's portrait.

PRINCESS OF VIX

Vix is a village in Burgundy at the site of an important ancient forti-fied settlement with several burial mounds.

One of the mounds contained the body of a 30-year-old aristo-cratic woman who died in about 550 BC. Her body was buried with great ceremony on a bier that was made out of the body of a wagon. The **wheels** were taken off and laid against the wall of her burial chamber. Her grave goods included a range of **treasures**, including Greek cups and other drinking vessels, but most remarkable was the huge bronze vessel, a *krater* for mixing wine. This stands as tall as the princess herself and is one of the most beautiful treasures of archaic Greek **art** that have sur-vived to the present day. It is in the museum at Châtillon-sur-Seine in Burgundy.

The *krater* was made in Greece or a Greek colony in about 500 BC, and transported in kit form, in labeled pieces, across the Mediterranean and up the Rhône **River** into central France. The pieces were assembled for the royal client at Vix. This astonishingly exotic and expensive vase was decorated around its neck with a frieze of Greek warriors in full armor with **chariots**. The Greek *krater* does not tell us that the Greeks colonized central France, but that the Iron Age kings of Gaul were rich and powerful enough to purchase luxury goods from far afield.

It was importing artwork of this distinction that inspired the Celtic craftsmen to aspire to ever-higher artistic standards. It fueled cultural growth. The burial of the Greek *krater* also ensured that at least one example of this type of object survived for people of later centuries to enjoy; nothing quite like it has survived in Greece itself. By burying grave goods, the Celts became, unconsciously perhaps, custodians and curators of a European heritage.

R

REDONES

An Iron Age Celtic **tribe** in eastern Brittany, with its main center at Rennes. The Redones sent a contingent to fight against **Julius Caesar** during the siege of **Alesia**.

The Roman conquest of Gaul was a bloodbath. A million Gauls, 20 percent of the population, were killed; another million were enslaved. Three hundred tribes were subjugated and 800 towns were destroyed. All the native Gauls living in Avaricum (modern Bourges) were slaughtered by the Romans—40,000 people.

RHUN, SON OF MAELGWN

The son of **Maelgwn** and his successor as King of **Gwynedd**.

Maelgwn's son-in-law **Elidyr** tried to take Gwynedd from Rhun, but was killed on the beach at Caernarvon. Rhydderch Hael sailed south to avenge the killing of Elidyr, but his raid on Gwynedd

The Element Encyclopedia of the Celts

was unsuccessful and he had to withdraw. Rhun responded by gathering an army and marching it north, through South **Rheged**, probably by way of York. It was a march of legendary distance and duration. Rhun's army was away from home for a very long time and is said to have met no resistance. Elidyr's son and successor, the boy king Llywarch Hen, was in no position to resist and had not the temperament either; it was probably wiser anyway to allow Rhun's great army pass through unopposed. Llywarch Hen was left alone, and eventually died, an elderly Celtic exile **writing** poetry in **Powys**, long after the English had overrun his kingdom.

Rhun marched on, deep into the Gododdin (south-east Scotland), all the way to the Forth, still unopposed. After this impressive parade of military strength, he marched his great army home to Gwynedd. It was a triumph. Yet it also illustrated, just as **Arthur**'s career had 30 years earlier, how the British could organize brilliant and spectacular military *coups de théâtre* and yet fail to hold together the polity of a large kingdom. To judge from **Gildas**, the British disliked kings. They felt no overriding need to unite behind a powerful monarch or submit to central control. They simply did not see, even as late as 560, how dangerous the growing Anglo-Saxon colonies in the east and south-east were. The soldier's loyalty was always to his lord, but this was a local war-band loyalty. Petty rivalries among the war-band leaders, the kings, and sub-kings, would be likely to erupt quickly, easily, and repeatedly into civil war.

The northern British poems express the spirit of the times well. The highest ethic involved the devoted loyalty of faithful warriors to their lord and his personal destiny. The idea of sacrificing or compromising that loyalty by serving an overlord ran against this sentiment. Long-term loyalty to an overking or commander-in-chief would have been alien to the rank-and-file warrior. The effect was that although British resistance to the advance of the Saxons in the sixth and seventh centuries may have been intermittently highly successful, in the end it was doomed, in the same way that resistance to the Roman invasion had been in the first century, as contemporary Roman commentators had recognized (*see* Myths: **The History of Taliesin**).

The Element Encyclopedia of the Celts

Rhun, Son of Urien

Rhun, son of Urien, became a cleric, settling in **Gwynedd**. He may have been the author of *The Life of Germanus* in about 630. Varying accounts of the baptism of King Edwin of Northumbria exist. One is that Rhun baptized Edwin while the latter was in exile, a boy-refugee in Gwynedd, some 15 years before Paulinus baptized the people of Northumbria. Another account (recorded by Nennius) is that Rhun baptized Edwin in 626, in Northumbria, when he was king. Both may be true, as it may have been deemed necessary to stage a repeat baptism ceremony for the king, in public, for the benefit of his subjects.

Bede's account is different again, giving Paulinus the credit, but Bede had a political motive. **Writing** when he did, he may have wanted to show the first Christian Anglian king as sponsored by the Roman Church, not by the Celtic Church. A power struggle between the two had been going on since Augustine's arrival at the end of the sixth century, and Bede would have had a strong motive for reducing the role of the British priesthood and exaggerating that of the Roman. It seems likely, then, that it was Rhun who actually wrote the account of the baptism ceremony, first hand, in 627.

Rhydderch Hael

See **Elidyr**, **Urien**.

Riderch

See **Dyfnwal**, **Kentigern**.

The Element Encyclopedia of the Celts

ROADS

One of the things the Romans did for us was to build roads. That at least is what we have been led to believe. But what was there in the way of a road system before the Romans arrived in the Celtic **west**—in Gaul, in Hispania, in Britain?

Ancient trackways followed the crests of prominent hill ridges, especially where these persisted for long distances. The chalk and limestone escarpments of lowland England and northern France lent themselves to this form of communication. One advantage was that they were raised and on permeable rock, so they were drier and firmer than tracks on lower ground. Another advantage was that navigation was easier; all you had to do was to follow the crest of the ridge. Being raised up also gave better views across the landscape, so you had better opportunities to identify where you were.

There were the South Downs Way and the Pilgrims Way in Sussex and Kent, the Ridgeway in Wiltshire, the Jurassic Way in Northamptonshire and the Icknield Way in Buckinghamshire, Hertfordshire, Suffolk, and Norfolk.

In wetlands, wooden walkways were constructed. In the Somerset Levels, around 40 wooden tracks dating from 3000 BC onward were built so that **people** and livestock could cross from Wedmore to the islands of Byrtle, Westhay, and Meare, and from there to the Polden Hills. These tracks were up to 2 miles (3km) long.

Some roads that we think of as Roman roads were in fact Roman surfaces added on top of pre-existing Iron Age roads. These were roads that had been built by the indigenous people. A rescue dig next to a quarry 2 miles (3km) south of Shrewsbury gave an opportunity to test a long stretch of known Roman road. The road surface was first built in 200 BC after the land was cleared by burning. The route was used for driving cattle, and their hooves churned it into mud (the Irish Gaelic word for road is *bothar*, which means "cow-path.")

To improve the road, a layer of elder brushwood 15 feet (4.5m) wide was laid down, with earth on top, followed by a layer of gravel and sand, then **river** cobbles, which were compacted into this foundation. The result made an all-weather roadway about 16.5 feet (5m) wide. It was subsequently remade a little wider, and then remade again. The road's surface was grooved by parallel ruts, showing that carts with a 6.5-foot (2m) wide wheelbase were being used. And all this happened before the Roman occupation, when a Roman road surface was added on top of the Iron Age road layers.

So, there were decent, dry, all-weather engineered roads in Britain—and Gaul—before the Romans arrived. **Julius Caesar** does not describe these roads, but he does say that the Gallic charioteers preferred to fight off-road, which means that there must have been roads.

Even in Italy, there were roads before the Romans. The Via Gabina was mentioned as early as 500 BC and the Via Latina in 490 BC, when the Etruscan king had only just been overthrown and the Roman republic was scarcely underway, yet it seems the "Roman" road system already existed.

RUADAN

The son of Birra of the Eoganachta (in **Munster**, Ireland). Ruadan was a huge man, said to be 12 feet (3.6m) tall. He revived the son of a British king who was drowned when one of **Brendan**'s ships sank in the Shannon estuary.

His monks lived an easy life, thanks to the manufacture of a "lime juice" that was evidently a distilled liqor. The easy living and the lime juice attracted many monks from other houses. Under pressure from indignant abbots, Finnian told Ruadan to stop production and practice conventional subsistence farming.

Ruadan is said to have written several books, including *Against King Diarmait*, *The Miraculous Tree*, and *The Wonderful Springs of Ireland*. He died at Lothra; his **head** was preserved in a silver reliquary until the sixteenth century. A bell that was found in a well at Lorrha was venerated as the bell he rang at **Tara** against King Diarmait.

Unfortunately the recipe for lime juice has not survived.

S

SAMSON

St. Samson was a sixth-century contemporary of **Arthur**. His father was a Demetian landowner and also an *altrix*, a companion of the king, who was at that time probably Agricola (*see* **Aircol**).

The idea that Samson should attend **Illtud**'s monastic school at Llantwit Major in Glamorgan, next to a ruined Roman villa, came from "a learned master in the far north," probably **Maucennus**, Abbot of **Whithorn**, who is known to have visited Demetia at the right time. Samson was duly sent to St. Illtud's. Illtud was responsible for educating many boys from aristocratic families, from the age of five until they were 16 or 17. He had great influence, in that he turned out men of the caliber and importance of St. Samson, **Paul Aurelian**, **Gildas**, **Leonorus**, St. **David**, and **Maelgwn**, King of **Gwynedd**.

By the age of 15 Samson was already very learned and at an unusually young age was ordained **priest** and deacon by Bishop **Dubricius**. This aroused the jeal-ousy of Illtud's nephews, who feared that he might succeed as the school's head when Illtud retired and so deprive them of their inheritance. Perhaps because of this ill-feeling, Samson gained a transfer to another of Illtud's monasteries, newly set up by Piro on Caldey Island, where his great scholarship and austerity astonished the Caldey monks.

He did not stay long at Caldey. He "longed for the desert," and was really more suited to the life of a hermit than the monastic life. He lived for a time in an abandoned fort on the Severn **River**, and then in a cave at Stackpole. He was guided by visions and his inner voices directed him to cross to the monastery of Landocco, founded by **Docco** at St. Kew in Trigg in Cornwall. This was the earliest monastery we know of in Cornwall; it was already old when Samson arrived there. Docco, a nickname of Kyngar, had been born in about 410, when the Romans were still in Britain. But the abbot at Landocco, Iuniavus, did not want Samson there. He told him plainly, "Your request to stay with us is not convenient, for you are better than us; you might condemn us, and we might properly feel condemned by your superior merit. You had better go to Europe."

When St. **Petroc** landed in Trigg, he found Samson living, not surprisingly, in a cell beside the Camel estuary. After some dispute, Petroc forced him to leave. Samson was stupefied by his rejection in Cornwall.

Before he left St. Kew he had a revealing encounter with a crowd of non-Christians at Trigg. He came upon the crowd, subjects of a Count Gwedian celebrating pagan rites at a **standing stone**. Samson dispersed the crowd and carved a cross on the stone with his pocket knife, an *ad hoc* example of the Christianization of pagan monoliths that was very common in Brittany.

He made his way across Cornwall to "the Southern Sea," visiting Castle Dore, the power base of one of the Cornish sub-kings, Mark Conomorus. In 547, he sailed to Brittany, where he became bishop of the kingdom of Jonas of Dumnonie, based at Dol. Samson's journey southward was repeated by a steady flow of Irish-inspired missionaries.

In 557, he is recorded as attending a church council in Paris. He seems to have died of old age in 563.

The oldest surviving *Life of Samson* dates from about 600, but it is based on a contemporary original written by Samson's cousin Enoch, who is known to have gone to the trouble of interviewing Samson's mother for details about his **childhood**. So, what is written about St. Samson is rather more reliable than the stories we have about some other saints.

SCAPEGOAT

A Roman commentator, Lactantius Placidus, described how the Gauls singled someone out as an emissary victim or scapegoat:

The Gauls had a custom of sacrificing a human being to purify their city. They selected one of the poorest citizens, loaded him with privileges and thereby persuaded him to sell himself as victim. During the whole year he was fed with choice food at the town's expense, then, when the accustomed day arrived, he was made to wander through the entire city. Finally, he was stoned to death by the people outside the walls.

(*See also* Religion: **Human Sacrifice**.)

SENONES

See **Brennus**.

SHIPS AND BOATS

In remote antiquity the logboat was the commonest vessel in use on **rivers** and in estuaries. Possibly composite **boats** were made for use on unsheltered open **water** by lashing two or three logboats together for stability. These trimarans might well have been fitted with decks for transporting goods.

A simple, small, bowl-shaped, one-person boat was made of wicker and covered in hide to make a coracle. Coracles are still made in Wales today, but instead of hide canvas is used, daubed with pitch. These small boats are really designed for paddling across lakes, or fishing in rivers, but in 1974 a

Welshman called Bernard Thomas crossed the English Channel in one. In antiquity, it was usual to use larger vessels on the open sea, but constructed in exactly the same way; they were called *curraghs*.

There are several documentary references to *curraghs*, which are still built in Ireland. Festus Rufius Avienus wrote a poem, *Ora Maritima*, based on a sixth-century BC source, in which he refers to the Oestrymnides (who perhaps lived in Brittany) plying "the widely troubled sea and swell of monster-filled ocean with skiffs of skin... [They] fit out boats marvellously with joined skins and often run through the vast salt water on leather." Pliny quotes a third-century BC source about Britons traveling to an island "to which the Britons cross in boats of osier covered with stitched skins." Strabo mentions "boats of tanned leather." **Julius Caesar** gives a little more detail: "The keels and ribs were made of light wood, the rest of the hull was made of woven withies covered with hides."

We even know what these boats looked like, thanks to a **gold** boat found on a former shoreline of Lough Foyle in County Derry in 1896. It was discovered along with a hoard of other gold objects, including a large torc, two necklaces, and a bowl. It is the gold ship, however, that particularly captures our imagination, not just because it tells us in detail what an Iron Age *curragh* looked like, but because of its beauty:

The ship is broad in the beam, slightly pot-bellied, with a mast and a yard-arm to carry the sail, seven pairs of oars, originally nine benches for rowers, and a steering-oar at the stern.

Such ships carried iron anchors, of a design that continued in use for many hundreds of years, slung on iron chains (*see* Symbols: **Boat**).

SILURES

See **Caratacus**.

SLAINE THE FIRBOLG

The first High King of Ireland (*see* **Genealogy**).

SOCIETY

By the first century BC, there is clear evidence of the nature of Celtic societies. They are heroic, on the Mycenaean model. They are hierarchical, with kings and queens at the top, heading an aristocracy of warriors. Some of the earliest Irish literature shows swaggering, boastful, aggressive heroes who are constantly quarreling and fighting in order to prove their worth to their peers. The quarrels are often over small matters, but even a small snub cannot be overlooked. It is very reminiscent of the sort of society described in Homer's *Iliad*, which was not written down until about 700 BC, but contains material from 500 years earlier.

Priority at the feast was important to these heroes (*see* **Food and Feasting**). Feasting can be detected in the archeology of places such as **Danebury hillfort** in Hampshire, England, where there were hooks to carry **cauldrons**, spits, and middens containing the remains of joints of meat.

In Ireland cattle-raiding was another way in which warriors showed their prowess. Wealth was measured in cattle—the cow was the unit of currency.

Julius Caesar set out the structure of Celtic society clearly. It was organized into **Druids** (learned men), warrior-nobles, and ordinary **people**. He mentioned at least one king, Divitiacus, who in the early first century BC held lands on both sides of the English Channel. At the lowest level there were slaves, so the plebes (ordinary people) must have comprised at least two categories: slaves and freemen. Slaves certainly existed in Britain; the slave-gang chain complete with neck-shackles found at Llyn Cerrig Bach in 1943 proves this. **Diodorus Siculus** says that in Gaul a slave could be bought for an amphora of wine.

Irish sources show that Celtic society was rather more complex than Caesar noticed, which is what we might expect. The Irish texts mention kings, sub-kings, warrior nobles (*flatha*), lesser nobles, freemen (*bo-airigh*), and serfs. Freemen consisted mainly of farmers who paid food-rent to the king, though the class included **priests**, artists, and craftsmen as well as landholders. The main social unit was the extended family or *derbfine*, which included the four generations of descendants from a common great-

grandfather, and groups of these made up the tuath, or **tribe**. The *derbfine* owned land collectively, in common; there was no individual ownership.

Looked at in terms of straightforward hierarchy, Irish society was feudal, with the High King of All Ireland at its head; below him the five kings of the provinces, Ulster, **Munster**, Connaught, Leinster, and Meath; below them the kings of the counties, and below them again the kings of the hills and the peaks. Then came the four classes of nobles, then the cattle-chiefs, then freemen and craftsmen, and then last of all the bondsmen. All of these except the last held land.

Kings were more than political and judicial leaders: they were battle leaders too, and they had priestly functions to perform when making sacrifices and when undertaking divination. In some Gaulish tribes, such as the Santones, the Remi, and the Treveri, the nobility abolished kingship, devolving the kingly powers upon a magistrate called a *vergobret* after an election. He served for a year only, and to prevent a return to kingship a second magistrate was appointed to take military power. The nobles devised every means possible to avert a return to kingship.

The king (Latin *rex*, Gallic *rix*) and his sub-kings bound themselves to one another by personal oaths of allegiance; similar bonds held lower social classes to higher social classes.

By 100 BC Celtic society had taken on a strongly stratified structure. The emergence of craftsmen and artists into the status of freemen was an interesting development. This may reflect the development of long-distance trade and the consequent availability of exotic raw materials for craftwork. The same long-distance contacts would have exposed kings and nobles on the Atlantic fringe to the refined **art** and craftwork produced in the Mediterranean region. The western kings wanted their own craftsmen to produce similarly refined pieces and so the craftsmen and artists achieved enhanced status.

Relationships between people were more ordered than might be expected. Classical writers normally intent on portraying the Celts as savages occasionally found themselves praising them for the structure and restraint of their society. Tacitus wrote a book called *Germania* about the northern tribes. One of his motives seems to have been to warn the emperor about the danger from the north, from these particular barbarians, but Tacitus found some things about them wholly admirable. Monogamy was strongly upheld, he said. Unmarried women guarded their virginity and valued it as something precious; they lived in a state of impregnable chastity. When an act of adultery came to light, which happened only occasionally, the offenders were punished severely, with flogging and public humiliation. All of this was in stark contrast to the scandalous goings-on in contemporary Rome. In certain ways, Tacitus said, the barbarians were more civilized than the Romans.

Inter-tribal politics were complicated. Quarrels and skirmishing were common. But the placing of major religious sanctuaries on tribal frontiers, and sometimes at the point where the frontiers of three tribes ran together, suggests occasional peaceful meetings. In northern France, for instance, the sanctuary of Morvillers was at the place where the lands of the **Ambiani**, **Caleti**, and **Bellovaci** met; Gournay was where the lands of the Ambiani, Bellovaci, and Viromandui met.

No doubt the sanctuaries were, like Christian churches, regarded as places of protection: places where "sanctuary" in the more general sense might be claimed. There may have been annual festivals at which representatives of neighboring tribes would gather to worship together, settle disputes, and negotiate political problems of common interest. In Caesar's time several Gaulish tribes, such as the Bellovaci, had a council, described by a Roman general as a senate, and it allowed the nobles of the tribe to debate issues. But the tribal senate could be a very large body, of 600 members. It met when there was a crisis that affected the fate of the entire *civitas*.

But the tribes were not bound together with one another and did not easily agree. There was no real mechanism to bring them to agreement. This is clear from the response of the British tribes to the two Roman invasions. Some of the tribes were favorable toward Rome, seeing the advantage of greater access to luxury goods. By the time of the Claudian invasion, several of the tribal territories had become client kingdoms, and therefore in effect Roman allies. The British tribes were divided and this made conquest by Rome easy.

But in Caesar's time, the tribes of one region in south-eastern England did come together to resist Caesar: the **Trinovantes** with their capital at Colchester, the **Catuvellauni** with their capital at St. Albans, and to some extent the **Cantii** across the Thames estuary in Kent. The confederation was fragile, however, and perhaps too much depended on the charisma of individual tribal chiefs.

In Britain, in the post-Roman sixth century, the social hierarchy had at its top the king (*tighern* or *gwledig*), though certainly in time of war there was an overking, commander-in-chief, or leader of battles above him (*amerawder* or *pendragon*). Under the king came the nobles (*uchelwr*) and the king's hearth companions (*teulu* or *altrix*). Then came the ordinary people: the free-born citizens (*boneddig*), bondmen (*taeog*), and slaves (*caeth*).

Although the Celtic lands were divided up into countless kingdoms—some large, some small—there was a recognition that there was a need for a joint effort when a common threat appeared. Confederations of kings were formed, appointing one of their number overking to act as military commander-in-chief. He was known by different titles: sometimes by the Latin title *dux bellorum* (leader of battles), or sometimes by a Celtic title, *amerawder* (emperor) or *gwledig* (overking). Geoffrey of Monmouth has often been criticized for imposing a mindset from his own times on the Dark Ages, but his list of the "Kings of Britain" may actually tell us the succession of overkings. Geoffrey was using an early medieval list:

GORTHEYRN. GWETHUYR VENDIGEIT. EMRYS WLEDIC.

UTHERPENDRIC. ARTHUR. CONSTANTIUS. AURELIUS. IUOR.

MAELGON GOYNED.

Translated and expanded, this becomes:

Vortigern the Elder (of Powys); Vortigern the Younger (of Powys); Ambrosius the Overking (of Dumnonia); Uther Pendragon (of Dumnonia); Arthur (of Dumnonia); Constantine (of Dumnonia); Aurelius

(the Aurelius Caninus mentioned by Gildas = Cynan of Calchvynnydd); Ivor(?); Maelgwn of Gwynedd.

This is interesting in that it is consistent with what can be pieced together from other sources. It also shows the high kingship passing from one kingdom to another, but always within the province of Britannia Prima (Wales and the English West Country).

SOUTERRAIN

An underground chamber associated with Iron Age settlements in Brittany. The *souterrain* is tunneled out of the natural coarse granitic sand and then enlarged by making side chambers. It is still uncertain what these chambers were for, but the likeliest function is for storing seed-grain. Some archeologists believe they were built as refuges or for ritual (*see* **Fogou**).

Succat

See **Patrick**.

Suetonius Paulinus

The Roman general who in AD 60 crossed the Menai Strait and attacked the **Druids'** headquarters on the island of **Anglesey**. When he heard of the **Boudicca** rising, he marched his troops across to meet her and her army on Watling Street, where he defeated her.

Suicide

Posidonius said that Gauls might commit suicide in certain circumstances, for instance in exchange for **gifts** that were distributed to their entourage. The Gauls were also ready to kill themselves after defeat in battle rather than surrender to an enemy.

Swords

Swords had bronze or iron hilts that were well made for gripping, but they were also highly decorative. One fine hilt made in about 100 BC is in the shape of a stylized human being, with the arms and legs acting as functional guards.

Swords were worn in scabbards, and the scabbards themselves had decorated mounts made of sheet metal. Scabbard mounts have been found in England, dating from around 100 BC.

Swords were believed to have magical properties and they were given pet names, usually known only to their owner (*see* Symbols: **Magic**). **Arthur** famously had his sword named Excalibur.

T

Taliesin

A **bard**, probably attached to the court of King **Urien** of **Rheged** (Cumbria). His name means "Radiant Brow." Little is known about him beyond what is in his poems, but these are considered to be genuine and historically based; the historical references show that he was active around 550–60. The legendary account of Taliesin's life written in the sixteenth century is probably not based on fact.

Twelve poems by Taliesin are now reckoned to be authentic productions. Eight are conventional praise poems for **Urien** as a "successful battle prince," "generous patron of bards," "protector of Rheged," and "ruler of Catraeth." Seven end with Taliesin's signature tune—an identical formula expressing the wish to praise Urien until death:

And until I perish in old age
in my death's sore need
I shall not be happy
if I praise not Urien.

In one poem, Urien has "overcome the land of Brynaich, but after having been a hero lies on a hearse." This is interesting in showing that the allegedly conquered land was in the last quarter of the sixth century still being called by its British name, Brynaich, rather than by its Anglian name, Bernicia—at least by the Britons.

Taliesin wrote at least two battle-listing poems. In *Rheged arise*, he lists six of King Urien's battles:

There was a battle at the ford of Alclud,
a battle for supremacy,
the battle of Cellawr Brewyn,
long celebrated,
battle in Prysg Cadleu, battle in Aber,
fighting with harsh war-cry,
the great battle of Cludwein,
the one at Pencoed.

The Battles of Gwallawg lists ten battles: one in the land of Troon, one near Gwydauk and Mabon, and the battles of Cymrwy Canon, Arddunion, Aeron Eiddined, Coed Baidd, Gwenster, and Rhos Eira. Taliesin gives only the smallest amount of detail about each encounter. This was probably a standard formula in widespread use for flattering kings, and probably **Arthur**'s bard wrote a very similar poem to celebrate a selection of Arthur's greatest battles.

In *Rheged arise*, Taliesin says to Urien, "I have watched over you even though I am not one of yours" and the praise poem *To Cynan Garwyn* implies that he may have come originally from **Powys**, serving Cynan, King of Powys, before

The Element Encyclopedia of the Celts

moving north to Rheged.

Taliesin was loyal to the British cause above all else and when he saw Urien's power beginning to wane at the close of the sixth century he shifted his efforts to the support of **Gwallawg**, King of **Elmet**: there are two poems in praise of Gwallawg, *The Battles of Gwallawg* and *Gwallawg is other.* Urien was at that time still alive and it was probably then that Taliesin wrote *The Conciliation of Urien* as a way of apologizing to the old king who was nettled at Taliesin's shift of loyalty.

Several important themes emerge from Taliesin's poems. One is that the kingdoms of the north were allied in a loose confederation against the Anglo-Saxon menace, sometimes under one king—sometimes under another—and Urien is portrayed as one of these commanders-in-chief. Another theme is the in-fighting that went on among the British and the wide geographical range of sixth-century military expeditions against other British kingdoms. Cynan of Powys is described as waging war on Brycheiniog, the Wye Valley, Gwent, Dyfed, **Gwynedd**, and **Dumnonia**, and Urien "ranges himself" against Powys.

There are also insights into the motives for warfare. *The Battle of Wensleydale* mentions that Urien is king of the rustlers, farm leader, suggesting that acquiring livestock was a prime motive for fighting. Acquiring wealth was essential in order to make the show of **gift**-giving that was the hallmark of great kingship. In *You are the best,* Urien is Christendom's most generous man: "a myriad gifts you give to the world. As you hoard, you scatter." In *Gwallawg is Other,* Taliesin tells us, "Hoarding kings are to be pitied ... they cannot take their riches to the grave: they cannot boast about their lives."

A further recurring theme is the importance of **horses** in Celtic warfare. *The Spoils of Taliesin* say, "fine are fast cavalrymen" and "fine is the rush of a champion and his horse." Taliesin was unable to go on an expedition with Urien, but wished that he could have gone "on a frisky horse" to be "with the foragers." The sound of battle was dominated by the horses: "From the stamping of the horses a furious din." Horses ranked among the most highly prized gifts: Taliesin claimed that Cynan gave him "a hundred steeds with silver trappings."

Several so-called Taliesin poems

The Element Encyclopedia of the Celts

have to be rejected because they contain contaminating later material or are written in a metaphysical prophetic style, such as *The Battle of Godeu*. Medieval copyists tended to expand and develop early material that was too terse or cryptic for medieval taste. The nature of the problem is most transparently seen in a poem about Gwallawg ap Lleenawg in *The Black Book of Carmarthen*, where a medieval monk has written an additional stanza—his own—in the margin (*see* Myths: *The History of Taliesin*).

TARTAN

A woven woolen cloth with patterns consisting of criss-cross bands in various pre-dyed colors. The name "tartan" is thought to derive from the Gaelic word *tarsainn*, meaning "across," because the bands of color go across one another. Tartan is particularly associated today with Scotland, but its use in antiquity was certainly more widespread.

Tartan was worn by the Iron Age Celts of the Hallstatt **culture** in central Europe. The earliest known tartan has been found near Salzburg, dating from about 400–100 BC. The earliest example of Scottish tartan dates from the third century AD; a piece found at Falkirk was stuffed into the mouth of a pot containing 2,000 Roman coins. This was a simple check design made out of two natural wool colors: one light and the other dark. This was a native British fabric and it is likely that the pre-Roman Iron Age Britons wore this and other tartan patterns (*see* **Dress**).

Diodorus Siculus wrote that the Gauls wore "a striking kind of clothing—tunics dyed and stained in various colours, and trousers which they called by the name of bracae; and they wear striped cloaks fastened with buckles, thick in winter and light in summer, picked out with a variegated small check pattern" (*see* **Plaid**).

Tartans became associated with clans at the time of the Jacobite rebellions, as the main Jacobite supporters were tartan-wearing Highland clansmen. Before the middle of the nineteenth century, tartans were specific to districts, not to clans. Local weavers produced tartans to suit local preferences and they were restricted by the availability of local dyes. It was noted in 1703 that in the Western

Isles the tartans varied from island to island.

The suppression of the 1745 Jacobite Rebellion meant a clampdown on all aspects of Highland culture, which included tartans. In an attempt to bring the Highlands to heel, the 1746 Dress Act banned the use of tartans. Forty years later the act was repealed and during the nineteenth century there was a revival in the use of tartan.

The great craze for tartan began with George IV's visit to Edinburgh in 1822, when Sir Walter Scott, the novelist and founder of the Celtic Society of Edinburgh, encouraged the king and all his guests to wear tartan costumes. One observer scoffed at "Sir Walter's Celtified Pageantry," but the result was a surge of interest in tartans.

This interest was fed by an 1842 book called *Vestiarium Scoticum* by John and Charles Hay. The content of the book was fake, and the authors were fakes too, having arrived in Scotland 20 years before claiming to be Bonnie Prince Charlie's grandsons, which they were not. They claimed that the clan tartans allocated in their book were based on an ancient manuscript, which they were never able to produce.

This book was the origin of the idea, now widespread, that certain tartans are to be associated exclusively with certain clans; in reality, anyone can wear any tartan.

Prince Albert was caught up in the tartan craze and used it to excess in his redecoration scheme for Balmoral: red Royal Stewart and green Hunting Stewart for carpets, and Dress Stewart for curtains and upholstery.

Today the two most popular tartans are said to be Black Watch and Royal Stewart. Modern chemical dyes produce strong, dark colors, but "ancient" tartan colors are lighter in shade. "Muted" tartan colors, developed in the 1970s, are a shade in between modern and ancient and represent the closest match to the tartans produced in the eighteenth century.

The idea that specific tartans have specific meanings is a modern importation. A common misconception is that red tartans were "battle tartans," worn so as not to show blood.

New tartan designs have been commissioned in recent times in order to give Canadian provinces and American states their own tartans. These contain an element of symbolism, such as blue for lakes,

The Element Encyclopedia of the Celts

green for forest, and yellow for corn. This inventive development of tartan is a symptom of the international Celtic movement, or pan-Celticism.

TASCIOVANUS

Ruler of the **Catuvellauni** tribe from about 25 BC until 10 BC, and the father or grandfather of **Cunobelin**.

Tasciovanus's name means "Killer of Badgers." His Catuvellaunian tribal capital was at Wheathampstead near St. Albans, but there was another center at Braughing and Puckeridge: two neighboring villages north-east of Hertford, where coins were minted. Tasciovanus had one of his coins inscribed *TASCIO RIGON*—"Tasciovanus the Great King" or "Giant King." This boast may mark the annexation of the neighboring territory to the east of the Catuvellauni, the lands of the **Trinovantes**, when Tasciovanus deposed the Trinovantian king **Addedomarus**. This major expansion of power must have made Tasciovanus feel like an emperor.

The portrait of Tasciovanus on his coins shows him young, with Romanized short hair. This may be misleading, though, as the portrait imitates the image on coins of the emperor Augustus, even to the very high bridge to the nose.

The coins minted in the enlarged kingdom in Tasciovanus's time imply that there were several sub-kings ruling under him, each with their own coins: Andocomarus, Diasumaros, and Rues.

TEWDRIG

See **Theodoric**.

THANEY

See **Thynoy**.

THEODORIC

In spite of the Gothic name, Theodoric, or Tewdrig, was a Celtic king with estates in both Wales and Cornwall, in about 500–530. His great namesake was still ruling in Ravenna, and the Cornish

Theodoric was evidently named after him. His dates can be inferred from three independent traditions regarding **Fingar**, Cynan, and **Petroc**. He was a contemporary of King Brychan of Wales.

Theodoric saw military action in South Wales, where he was supporting his daughter Marchel in her marriage to the Irish Anlac, son of King Coronac. The inter-relationships between Cornwall, South Wales, and Ireland were very complex, and the Irish attempts to colonize Wales had to be countered. It seems Theodoric was there dealing with one of these incursions.

Later, Theodoric was in Cornwall, dealing with an Irish incursion there. Fingar sailed with 770 men from Ireland to Hayle Bay (St. Ives) and Theodoric descended on these incomers and massacred them.

The *Life of Cynan* portrays Theodoric as a powerful king living at Goodern, close to Truro. He was also active in Brittany.

THYNOY

The mother of **Kentigern**. Thynoy (or Thaney) was seduced by a soldier, became pregnant, and was thrown off the top of Kepduf (in Irish), or Traprain Law, in a cart, but landed unhurt. She was then set adrift in a **boat** without oars and the waves carried her to Culross in Fife, where she was rescued by St. Servan. Then she gave birth to Kentigern.

TIGHERNMAS

Tighernmas, "The Lord of Death," was an Irish High King who is supposed to have set up the cult of the idol called Crumm Cruach on the Plain of Adoration. At the feast of **Samhain**, he was killed in a frenzied riot.

Togodumnus

Torc

A Catuvellaunian king; one of the sons of **Cunobelin**. Togodumnus and his brother **Caratacus** were the joint kings of the powerful Southern Kingdom at the time of the Roman invasion in AD 43. It looks as if Togodumnus ruled the lands north of the Thames River, while Caratacus ruled the lands to the south.

It seems that they did nothing to oppose the Roman landings, which was a tactical mistake. Instead they fell back to the Medway estuary and gathered their armies there. An onslaught from the Romans pushed the Britons back to the Thames, where Togodumnus was killed. This was the turning-point.

Eleven British kings decided to surrender to Rome, seeing that there was little alternative after the most powerful kingdom in Britain had been overpowered.

The Roman conquest of Britain was formally marked by a 16-day visit to **Camulodunum**, Togodumnus's capital, by the emperor Claudius himself (*see also* **Amminius, Catuvellauni**).

See **Dress**.

Tribes

The large communities of kin-related **people** known as tribes occupied distinct territories that varied in size, but typically might be 1,000 or 2,000 square miles (2,500 or 5,000 square km)—the size of a county in England or America.

There were too many of them across the entire Celtic realm to list, but in England and Wales there were the **Brigantes**, Parisi, Coritani, Deceangli, Ordovices, Demetae, Silures, Cornovii, Dobunni, **Catuvellauni**, **Trinovantes**, **Iceni**, Dumnonii, **Durotriges**, **Atrebates**, and Cantiaci (or **Cantii**).

The tribal territory or *civitas* was clearly defined, and made up of a large number of equally well-defined local territories known as *pagi* in Latin. The *pagus* was an identifiable physical landscape, recognizable on a human scale: perhaps a plain, a valley, or an area surrounding a lake.

TRIBINUS

See **Gildas**.

TRIFINA

See **Gildas**.

TRINOVANTES

A British **tribe** whose territory extended across the modern English counties of Essex and south Suffolk. They may have been responsible for founding London at the lowest fording-place on the Thames **River**.

In the time of **Julius Caesar** the Trinovantes were on hostile terms with their immediate neighbors to the west, the **Catuvellauni**, and probably separated from the lands of the **Iceni** to the north by a belt of wooded country.

Some of their kings are known: Mandubracius (ruled about 54–30 BC), **Addedomarus** (30 and 20–10 BC), **Tasciovanus** (Catuvellaunian, usurped 30–20 BC), Dubnovellaunus (10 BC–AD 10), and **Cunobelin** (10–41).

The Trinovantes were conquered by the Romans in AD 43.

This was a familiar experience for them; they had been repeatedly conquered by the Catuvellauni.

TUCHELL

See Religion: **Headhunting**.

TURONES

A Celtic **tribe** in Gaul. Its main center was at Tours.

U

URIEN

The most famous King of **Rheged** (north-west England), who held court at Cair Ligualid (Carlisle). Unfortunately most of what we know about him was written by his bard: a professional spin-doctor who was paid to praise his king. So we keep reading of his wonderful qualities: "Urien, the most liberal man in Christendom."

He had a son called Owain, who succeeded him in about 590. Urien led a coalition of northern British kings, including Rhydderch of Clyde and **Gwallawg** of **Elmet**, in a campaign against the Angles under their king, Hussa, who were encroaching from Bernicia to the east. Urien thus became an unofficial northern *dux bellorum*, like **Arthur** in Britannia Prima some 70 years earlier.

Urien's neighbor to the north was Mynyddawg Mwynfawr, King of Gododdin, who was based at **Din Eidyn**, while his neighbor to the north-west was Rhydderch Hael, King of Clyde, who fought with Urien against Thedoric of Bernicia, the leader of the Angles in the north.

In 590, Urien's ally Morcant commissioned two men, Dyfnwal ap Mynyddawg and Llovan Llawddino of **Din Eidyn**, to murder King Urien out of jealousy for Urien's all-surpassing generalship, "because in him above all the kings was the greatest skill in the renewing of battle." They assas-sinated him while he was out on campaign. Urien's bard, **Taliesin**, sang nostalgically of the greatness of the dead king:

Sovereign supreme, ruler all highest,
the strangers' refuge,
strong champion in battle.
This the English know when they tell tales.
Death was theirs, rage and grief are theirs,
burnt are their houses, bare are their bodies.

These are fine words, but they conceal the truth of what was happening. They convey that the warriors of Rheged were defeating the English. But death was not theirs, not theirs at all. At **Arderydd**, and in the murder of Urien too, the British were destroying one another, not the English (*see also* **Rhun, Son of Urien**).

URNFIELD

See **Cultures**.

V

VELIOCASSES

A Celtic **tribe** in Gaul, with its main center at Rouen. Before the Roman conquest, the Veliocasses controlled a large area in the lower Seine Valley. They joined the tribal coalition that resisted the Romans in 57 BC, fighting beside the **Bellovaci** in the last stand against the Romans.

VENETI

A seafaring **tribe** living on the south-west coast of Brittany. The Veneti built **ships** powered by leather sails; the hulls were made out of **oak** with large transoms fixed by thick, iron nails. They built sturdily to withstand the harsh sea conditions in the Bay of Biscay.

VENUTIUS

See **Cartimandua**.

VERCASSIVELLAUNUS

A leading member of the **Arverni tribe** in Gaul and a cousin of **Vercingetorix**.

VERCINGETORIX

Chief of the **Arverni tribe** in Gaul. At a crucial general council of the tribes in 52 BC, he was appointed war leader in the Gaulish resistance to the Roman conquest. We know what he looked like from a **coin** minted in 48 BC.

Vercingetorix was the Gaulish commander-in-chief in the major confrontation between Gauls and Romans at **Alesia**. In this large-scale battle, he came close to winning, but finally lost.

After formally surrendering his weapons to **Julius Caesar**, he was taken prisoner along with all of the Gaulish warriors. He languished in prison for five years, awaiting Caesar's Roman triumph at the end of the Gallic War. Like a caged animal, he was to be one of the chief exhibits.

When the triumphal procession ended, no more was ever heard of Vercingetorix, but it is said that he was taken to the Mamertine prison and strangled.

VERICA

King of the **Atrebates** in central southern England. He was expelled by the Catuvellaunian chiefs, **Togodumnus** and **Caratacus**, and fled to Rome.

VORTIGERN

A powerful king of **Powys** from AD 425 onward. Vortigern's main stronghold was at Viroconium (Wroxeter). His palace stood among the ruins of the Roman city.

Vortigern is mentioned in several early sources. The *Life of Germanus*, written in about 470 by Constantius, presbyter of Lyons, gives the following information:

He had three sons, whose names are Vortimer, who fought against the barbarians [non-Christian Saxons] as I have described; the second, Cateyrn; the third, Pascent, *who ruled over the two countries called Builth and Gwerthrynion after his father's death, by permission of Ambrosius, who was the great king among all the kings of the British nation. A fourth son was Faustus, who was born to him by his daughter. St Germanus baptized him, brought him up and educated him. This is his genealogy. Fferfeal, who now rules in the countries of Builth and Gwerthrynion, is son of Tewdwr. Theodore is king of the country of Builth, the son of Pascent, so of Gwyddgant, son of Moriud, son of Eldat, son of Elaeth, son of Paul, son of Meuric, son of Briacat, son of Pascent, son of Vortigern the Thin, son of Vitalis, son of Vitalinus, son of Gliou. Enough has been said of Vortigern and his family.*

Constantius has included too many generations between his own time and Vortigern's; ten generations back in time from 470 would put Vortigern in the second century when he obviously belongs to the fifth. Germanus nevertheless picked up significant information on his visits to Britain in 429 and 445. In particular he saw that Vortigern was a powerful king more or less in overall control in southern Britain.

It is possible that Vortigern was a royal title rather than a personal name; it appears to come from *Vawr-tighern,* meaning "supreme leader" or "overking." This is supported by the mentions in documents of more than one king called Vortigern. An account, by Nennius, of a war fought in the fifth century between **Ambrosius Aurelianus** and a chief called Vitalinus may in fact be about Vortigern. Some scholars think that Vitalinus might be Vortigern, and that Vitalinus might be a personal name and Vortigern a title. **Gildas** calls him a "tyrant" and he may have meant "powerful king." One view of Vortigern is that he was responsible for introducing (or reintroducing) into Britain the Irish practice of High Kingship.

If Vortigern is seen as one king, he ruled as High King of southern Britain from around 425 until 447. What happened to him then is unclear, as there are several different lurid versions of his fate. Vortigern the Elder, Vortigern Vitalinus, may have died or abdicated in 447 and been replaced by Vortigern the Younger, whose personal name may have been Britu.

The closing years of Vortigern the Elder's reign were darkened by a double disaster: an overt attack from the north by the **Picts** and a more sinister and treacherous attack from the east by people of Germanic origin—Angles, Saxons, and Jutes. Vortigern unwisely took on Jutish mercenaries under their leaders Hengist and Horsa in an attempt to keep the Pictish invaders from the north at bay, while at the same time opening the door to more Jutes settling in Kent.

A third attack came from within the British community. A nobleman called Ambrosius the Elder launched a rebellion against Vortigern in 430, apparently in protest against his use of Germanic auxiliaries and the costs that this must have involved in increased taxation. But by 440 Vortigern was enlisting more mercenaries from the same source. In the following year their numbers were large enough to begin demanding higher payment from Vortigern, who gave them the Isle of Thanet (East Kent). Gildas, writing a century afterward, was characteristically outspoken:

To hold back the northern peoples,
they introduced into the island the
unspeakable Saxons, hated of God
and man alike… What raw hopeless
stupidity! Of their own free will, they
invited in under the same roof the
enemy they feared worse than death…

The Saxons later narrated the story from their side in *The Anglo-Saxon Chronicle*:

449: In this year Mauricius and Valentinian obtained the kingdom and reigned seven years. In their days, Hengist and Horsa, invited by Vortigern, King of the Britons, came to Britain at a place which is called Ypwines fleot [Ebbsfleet] at first to help the Britons, but later they fought against them. They then sent to Angeln, ordered [them] to send more aid and to be told of the worthlessness of the Britons and the excellence of the land. They then sent them more aid. These men came from three nations of Germany from the Old Saxons, from the Angles, from the Jutes.

The dangers of employing Hengist's and Horsa's mercenaries were now obvious, and Vortigern's son Vortimer led an army to drive the Jutes back though Kent and confine them to the Isle of Thanet, at that time still separated from the mainland by a broad stretch of open water, the Wantsum Channel. Vortimer himself was killed in the fighting.

Three independent sources support this sequence of events. Vortigern's campaign against the Jutes was successful, but in the process he lost two of his sons and his forces were sapped by plague. The Jutish army remained bottled up in Thanet for five years before breaking out in 465. The British response to this new crisis was to rebel against Vortigern, in about 459. As the situation became increasingly unstable and unsafe, many of the surviving members of the British nobility in eastern England emigrated to Brittany.

Vortigern invited Hengist to attend a conference with 300 members of the British Council. Hengist told his men to conceal daggers and then to slaughter the unarmed elders. It was said that only Vortigern himself was left alive, but now a broken man. At this point he disappeared from history. He was toppled from his position as commander-in-chief or *pendragon*—very likely deposed by his successor, **Ambrosius**.

VORTIPOR

A king of Demetia (Pembrokeshire), son and successor of **Aircol**. He became king in 515. The Vortipor Stone at Castell Dwyran appears to be his grave: certainly this inscribed **standing stone** was raised as a memorial to him. The inscription, *MEMORIA VOTEPORIGIS PROTICTORIS*, means "The memorial of Vortipor the Protector." The sixth-century historian **Gildas** corroborates this with his reference to "Vortipor, the usurper of Demetia."

WARFARE

The warrior-prince burials from both Hallstatt and **La Tène cultures** show an interest in fighting. It looks as if, just as with the Mycenaeans, high status was inextricably tied up with outstanding performance on the battlefield. To be a leader, you had to be a war leader.

The classical writers who described the Celts commented particularly on their aggressive and warlike nature. **Diodorus Siculus** wrote:

The Gauls are terrifying in appearance, with deep-sounding and very harsh voices... Their armour includes man-sized shields, decorated in individual fashion. On their heads they wear bronze helmets.

Warriors, according to **Julius Caesar**, acquired status above that of freeman. Warrior-princes rode to battle in **chariots**, collected the **heads** of enemies as trophies (*see* Religion: **Headhunting**), performed feats of skill and engaged continually in individual duels as well as skirmishes.

There are many bronze figurines to show us what Celtic warriors looked like in action. A third-century BC spearman (found near Rome) is naked apart from a torc, a horned **helmet**, and a belt. The belt, which was commonly worn even by warriors who were otherwise naked (*see* Symbols: **Nudity**), has rarely been commented on. It was worn to hold a knife, sometimes tucked through just behind the hip. The knife was used to finish off a wounded enemy—and sometimes to cut off his head as a trophy.

Warriors went into battle looking as ferocious as they could. This meant getting themselves into a strange state of mind and pulling remarkable faces (*see* Symbols: **Shapeshifting**).

Their style of fighting was described by Roman writers, but in contradictory ways. Livy described them as having neither discipline nor strategy and surging about in uncontrollable hordes. But this is in the context of the Celts' third-century BC invasion of northern Italy, and the Romans were experiencing the sharp end of it. Livy had every incentive to portray this act as a feral attack by a barbarian horde. Caesar gives a very different impression of the Celts in his *Gallic War*. The Gauls calculate and trick, and carry out some complicated and dangerous maneuvers. They must have been commanded by imaginative chiefs with ideas of strategy and fairly effective chains

of command, even if they did not always remain in full control of events.

In the early Iron Age the Celts were individual fighters and skirmishers. They formed recognizable armies only at a late date, though they were able to do this when the crisis was great enough.

Success depended on collaboration. The Celts did form military alliances, and they could present formidable opponents to the Roman legionaries, but those alliances were fragile. In the end, the Romans were able to conquer Gaul and Britain by virtue of the disunity of the Celtic **tribes**. Tacitus commented, "They eventually failed because they are distracted between the jarring factions of rival chiefs. Indeed, nothing has helped us more in war with their strongest nations [the tribal confederacies of the British] than their inability to co-operate."

Some of King Arthur's Wonderful Men was written in the tenth century but based on earlier documents reaching back to the Dark Ages. The warriors described as the members of Arthur's war-band are colorful, larger-than-life saga heroes. Morfran, son of Tegid, was said to be so ugly that at the

Battle of Camlann no man raised a weapon against him, thinking he was a devil. Sandde Angel-Face survived Camlann because he was so beautiful that people thought him an angel. Other men who fought beside Arthur were Gwefl, son of Gwastad, Uchdryd Cross-Beard, Clust, son of Clustfeinad, Gilla Stag-Leg, Gwallgoig, and the three sons of Erim: Henbeddestr, Henwas the Winged, and Scilti the Light-Footed.

Some of the claims made on their behalf were fanciful in the extreme, and perhaps we can hear, dimly, the sort of wild drunken boasting that might have accompanied many a feast. Medr, son of Medredydd, could shoot a wren in Ireland from Kelliwic in Cornwall. Gwaddu of the Bonfire's shoes gave off sparks. Osla of the Big Knife could bridge a **river** with his **magic** knife. Drem, son of Dremidydd, could see Scotland from Kelliwic. Finally, there was Cachamwri, who was Arthur's servant.

Weapons and armor changed during the Iron Age. In fact on the European mainland there were significant changes even within the La Tène period, about 460 BC to 50 BC. La Tène A1 was a transition from the Hallstatt culture to the solidly Celtic La Tène, beginning in 460 BC. Offensive weapons were dominated by **spears**. The warriors' graves were fitted out with several spears: usually a single large fighting spear and several lighter throwing spears or javelins. **Swords** were usually short side-arms, with blades 16–20 inches (40–50cm) long; these were little more than substantial daggers and designed for stabbing in close-quarter fighting. Metal shield fittings were rare, often only a reinforcement for the grip. It was common for belt-hooks to be made of ornate openwork. At this stage the warrior-elite, the nobles, were fighting mainly from chariots.

By 400 BC, the start of La Tène A2, slight changes were under way. Swords became more common in warrior graves, and with a fairly standard sized blade of 24 inches (60cm). Spears were still very much in use, and often in pairs or larger numbers. The Waldalgesheim Style (or Vegetal Style) appeared. This is used on helmets, scabbards, and personal ornaments, often covering every inch of the object with decorative line. An S-form using **dragon** or bird images appeared on scabbards. Shields were still mainly organic (wood or leather), but with metal fittings, and sometimes a metal rim. There was a strong emphasis on chariot warfare.

From 300 BC onward (La Tène B), the Celtic warrior reached the height of his power. The most common type of warrior was the heavy infantryman, who fought not only for his own tribe but fought for others as a mercenary. Warrior aristocrats fought as cavalrymen or as chariot warriors; cavalry was on the increase, with chariot warfare now on the decrease. The standard fighting gear was now a single large fighting spear, a sword, and a shield. Swords were now slightly longer, with blades 26 inches (66cm) long, with a midrib, and were heavier. On shields, metal umbos (bosses) began to appear: initially as twin plates nailed to the wooden boss, and later as the strap-boss. Metal rims were still uncommon.

In La Tène C, from 260 BC onward, the standard warrior gear remained the same: heavy fighting spear, sword, shield, and now always an iron belt chain. The infantry were still the most common type of soldier, but cavalry were becoming more important. The typical sword was longer and thinner, a rapier with a blade that was lens-shaped in cross-section; blade lengths vary, but up to 32 inches (80cm) long. Later blades had almost parallel sides. Spears also changed in shape; some developed a long, tapering quadrangular point. The artistic style of this phase was more restrained, with sparer decoration using **triskeles** and flowing asymmetrical lines.

In La Tène D, which lasted from about 125 BC to AD 100, the Celtic warriors reached their final flowering. Professional warriors included an important class of noblemen who were cavalrymen, and also large numbers of infantrymen who were more lightly armed. The equipment consisted of a long, heavy fighting spear or lance, a long cutting sword, and often a helm. The sword was large and its blade was parallel-sided for most of its length; the point was usually short. This design was less for stabbing, more for cutting, with a blade often 32–6 inches (80–90cm) long.

Shields sometimes had a spindle umbo, but as time passed the spindle disappeared and a domed metal boss appeared. The decorative style became simpler and severer.

Whether the Iron Age Celts were more warlike than other, later peoples is hard to gauge. They had a reputation for being quarrelsome, fierce, and ready fighters. In recent years this warlike image has been downplayed. Even the massively fortified hillforts have been presented as peaceful settlements, with probably a ritual and ceremonial function, with the ramparts put up mainly for show.

But new evidence from Fin Cop, a hillfort in the English Peak District, south-west of Sheffield, shows that forts did have a military function, and that defense against violent attack was very necessary. Fin Cop's defenses were built in haste in about 420 BC, in response to a real and immediate threat. The defensive wall 6.5 feet (4m) high on the fort's eastern perimeter was pushed over into the ditch beside it, leveling the fortification. This wall was attacked and destroyed, and its stones pushed on top of the corpses of scores of people. The most gruesome discovery was that of the skeletons that could be identified, all were women and children—none were warriors. They had no bone damage, which suggests that they all died of soft-tissue injuries, perhaps by having their throats cut. It was a massacre of civilians, and it happened within a few years of the fort being built.

WENEFRED

See **Beuno**.

WETHENOC

See **Petroc**.

WINFRITH

See Symbols: **Oak**.

WINNOC

A British ascetic who died in 588. He traveled to Tours from Britain on his way to Jerusalem in 578; a very conspicuous figure wearing nothing but sheepskins. He ate nothing but uncooked vegetables and drank only sips of wine.

Gregory, the bishop of Tours who wrote a detailed *History of the Franks*, was impressed by his extreme abstinence and ordained him **priest**, hoping to keep him at Tours.

In 586 Winnoc fell ill from malnutrition and took to swigging large quantities of wine. He often became drunk and attacked people with a knife or a stone. He was so violent that he had to be chained up. After two years in chains, he died.

This episode was the result of prolonged undernourishment. It goes a long way toward explaining the bad temper, intolerance, and wild and violent behavior of some of the Celtic "saints." It also explains why the majority of monks were against this intensity of self-denial and why **Gildas** condemned St. **David**.

WITHUR OF ROSCOFF

See **Paul Aurelian**.

WORSLEY MAN

See Places: **Lindow Moss**.

WRITING

Celts were reluctant writers. They rarely wrote records of any kind. The Anglo-Saxon colonists in England famously kept a summary record of their history, *The Anglo-Saxon Chronicle*, but the Celts appear to have felt no need to make such a self-account. They do not speak to us directly and this makes them less accessible to us. What we know about them we know through archeology or through the writings of contemporary literate societies. We know about the Gauls and the Britons thanks to the writings of Roman historians and commentators.

The **Druids** passed on their knowledge by reciting it from **memory**. Because knowledge was of divine origin, it had to be kept secret, reserved only for transmission to novice Druids. Here we can see why the Druids shied away from writing. They were not ignorant of writing; writing was available. The Minoans and Mycenaeans had developed well-established written scripts by 1500 BC, and the Romans were great documenters of everything that happened. The Druids, and the Celts generally, chose not to write their knowledge down, which to us is a great loss, but to them it meant that they could control who had access to it and who did not. They excluded us by refusing to write down what they knew.

The Celts did use writing for commercial transactions, and when they did they used the Greek alphabet. One Greek usage came to be what has been described as a Gallic-Latin spelling habit. A Greek "X" was used to represent the Celtic "ch" sound, as in the Scottish loch, especially when followed by the letter "t." This is seen in inscription from Gaul, such as *TIOCOBREXTIO* on the **Coligny calendar**. In South Shields in Britain there is the inscription *ANEXTIOMARO*. It also crops up on some **coins** of the British King **Tasciovanus** in the form *TAXCIAV [ANOS]* in about

20 BC–AD 10. This custom suggests a deliberate modification of the Roman alphabet, using Greek, by Celtic scholars, to accommodate phonetic values that existed in Celtic speech but not in Latin.

It is also an exciting possibility that writing was rather more common in the Celtic world than we may have thought. There is evidence that papyrus may have been imported into Britain in the period between the invasions of **Julius Caesar** and Claudius. If the British were importing papyrus, it can only have been for the production of documents; both imply a higher level of literacy and more widespread literacy in Britain than we normally allow for.

The situation in Ireland seems to have been quite different, with a **society** that was wholly or almost wholly illiterate, though with elaborate systems of oral transmission. It was only from about the fourth century AD that the Irish adopted **Ogham** as an inscriptional alphabet.

The annals recording the pedigrees of Celtic aristocrats were written down from the fifth century AD, probably under the influence of Rome. It seems probable that the **genealogies** were committed to memory and recited from time to time, and so passed from generation to generation orally.

The Welsh and English chronicles seem to base the structure and subject matter of their earliest entries on the Irish Annals. The Welsh Annals for the fifth and sixth centuries have 18 out of the 22 earliest entries copied straight from the Irish Annals. The Irish pedigrees were more developed, more complete, and more ancient than any other in Europe. This may be a reflection of Ireland's freedom from Roman invasion; the Celtic way of life was allowed to continue uninterrupted. An astonishing 20,000 named Irish people are known from the Irish Annals, from the period before AD 900.

PART 2

Celtic Places

ALAUNA

See **Maryport**.

ALBA

BRITAIN

This very early Celtic name for Britain was first noted about 525 BC, when a traveler's description located Ireland "alongside the island of the Albiones." In the Iron Age the name "Alba" seems to have referred to the whole of the island of Britain—the land of the Albiones.

Later, the phrase "the men of Alba" was used to describe the Dark Age Irish colony of Dal Riada (a small kingdom in southwest Scotland) and this led to a narrowing of the word's meaning; from the ninth century AD "Alba" was local to Scotland. Once what we now call Scotland was recognized as a distinct area, it all became known as Alba, and then Albany. In the tenth century this was Latinized—(for us) rather confusingly—as Albania.

The new Scottish Parliament has its name translated into Gaelic as *Pàrlamaid na h-Alba*, and to that limited, almost heraldic, extent Scotland has once again become "Alba."

ALCLUD

See **Alcluith**.

ALCLUITH

SCOTLAND

The Dark Age kingdom of the Clyde. The name of the kingdom was also used to denote its chief stronghold, which was perched on Dumbarton Rock: Alcluith meant "Clyde Rock." The later name of the adjacent settlement, Dumbarton, is derived from Dun Breatann, "Fort of the Britons," which seems also to have referred to the stronghold up on the crag.

In AD 731 Bede called it "a town of the Britons, strongly defended right down to the present day." The site is mentioned in the seventh-century *Life of Columba*, which refers to "King Roderc [= Rhydderch] son of Tothal who reigned in Alclut." The fortress is spectacularly defended by natural precipices falling on three sides into the Clyde estuary. In the Dark Ages there was a timber rampart defending it on the fourth side.

ALESIA

FRANCE

A major Gaulish *oppidum* (town) and fortress of the Mandubii **tribe**; it was the stage set for the decisive event in the Roman conquest of Gaul.

Developed on a hill surrounded by **river** valleys, Alesia was strongly defended. In 52 BC, it was the scene of a remarkable siege, which marked a turning-point in **Julius Caesar**'s campaign in Gaul.

Caesar had subdued the Eburones tribe under their chief **Ambiorix** in 54–53 BC. Then they rose up again, surprising the Roman army in an ambush in which Caesar lost a great many men; this was his first clear defeat in Gaul.

On the initiative of the **Aedui**, a general council of the tribes of Gaul was called at Bibracte. Only the Remi and Lingones decided to maintain their alliance with Rome: the rest decided that the time had come to rebel. The council appointed **Vercingetorix**, chief of the **Arverni** tribe, as the commander-in-chief (or war leader) of the Gallic armies.

The first indication of this new concerted resistance to the Roman conquest was the massacre of all the Roman settlers in Orléans by the Carnutes tribe. This was followed by massacres of Roman citizens in other major towns in Gaul.

Caesar was encamped in northern Italy at the time, but understood the seriousness of the revolt, rallied his army in haste, and crossed the snow-covered Alps into Gaul to try to retrieve the situation. He was in command of the Roman army and was supported by cavalry commanders Mark Antony, Titus Labienus, and Gaius Trebonius. Four legions were sent under Labienus to deal with the Senones and Parisii in the north, while Caesar, with five legions, pursued Vercingetorix.

The Roman and Gaulish armies met at the hillfort of Gergovia: a strong defensive position to which Vercingetorix had made a tactical withdrawal. It was such a strong position that Caesar decided to retreat in order to avoid defeat.

There were several skirmishes during the summer of 52, and

Vercingetorix withdrew to the fortress town of Alesia, trying to avoid a formal pitched battle against Caesar's troops.

Caesar could see that a direct attack on Alesia would be unwise and decided instead on a siege. There were 80,000 Gaulish warriors garrisoned there, in addition to the civilian population, and Caesar hoped to starve them out fairly quickly. To prevent escape and foraging, Caesar had his own encircling **fortifications** built: a circumvallation consisting of 29 miles (47km) of earthworks 13 feet (4m) high. This was followed inward by two ditches 15 feet (4.6m) wide and 15 feet (4.6m) deep, filled with **water** from nearby rivers. Caesar added man-traps and evenly spaced watch towers. It was a masterpiece of large-scale Roman military planning, and indeed Alesia is seen as one of Caesar's greatest triumphs.

Gallic horsemen came out to raid the fortification works, hoping to keep gaps open through which they might escape. In fact one cavalry detachment did manage to escape, and Caesar guessed that it would seek reinforcements from elsewhere. Anticipating that more Gauls would arrive, he constructed a second line of fortifications, the contravallation, this time facing outward. He was laying plans for a siege, but he was also preparing to be besieged himself.

Inside Alesia, conditions were worsening. The Mandubii decided to send their women and children out, hoping to save some food for the warriors and anticipating that Caesar would take pity on them and open a gap to let them out. But he didn't. He ordered that nothing should be done. The women and children were cruelly left to starve to death in the no-man's-land between the Gauls and Romans. This inhumane act was a devastating blow to the Gauls' morale. Vercingetorix tried to keep their spirits up, but some of his warriors were ready to surrender.

Then a Gaulish relief force arrived and the Gauls inside Alesia decided that they would fight on. The relief force, under Commius, attacked Caesar's contravallation wall, while Vercingetorix directed the Gauls inside Alesia to attack Caesar from within. This tactic was at first unsuccessful, but when repeated Caesar was forced to give up some of his fortifications; only quick action by Antony's and Trebonius's cavalry saved the Romans.

By this stage living conditions had become difficult for the exhausted Roman troops. Rationing was introduced. On October 2 a cousin of Vercingetorix, **Vercassivellaunus**, led 60,000 Gauls in an attack on one of the weak points in Caesar's fortifications. This huge onslaught threatened to overwhelm the Romans, and Caesar rode around the perimeter in person to rally the legionaries and keep them in position. It looked as if the massively outnumbered Roman army would be annihilated. In desperation, Caesar ordered a force of 6,000 Romans to attack the relief force from the rear. This so surprised both the relief force and the Gauls inside Alesia that they fell apart in panic and began to retreat. Once they started to retreat, it was easy for the merciless Romans to hew them down. Caesar had turned imminent defeat for Rome into victory.

When, the next day, Vercingetorix surrendered, he did so to save his warriors from being forced into a fresh battle that would destroy them—and to save his **horses**. Addressing an assembly, he said that he had not undertaken the war for private ends, but in the cause of national liberty. And since he

must now accept his fate, he placed himself at their disposal to make amends to the Romans as they thought best, either by killing him or handing him over alive. He solemnly offered himself to save his army; it was the Roman formula of *devotio*, a rite that Caesar would have recognized and respected.

The garrison force and the relief force were taken prisoner and sold into slavery, apart from the warriors of the Aedui and Arverni tribes, who were pardoned and released; this was done in order to secure the alliance of those two important tribes.

ALKBOROUGH

See Symbols: **Labyrinth**.

ANGLESEY

There was an important religious cult focus on the eastern coast of the island, next to the Menai Strait. Normally the Romans left native temples and sanctuaries alone, but this one was singled out for destruction. It was thought to be an important focus of Druidical power, and **Suetonius Paulinus** took his troops there to put it out of action once and for all. Tacitus described the attack:

He prepared to attack the island of Mona [Anglesey], which had a powerful population and was a refuge for fugitives. He built flat-bottomed boats to cope with the shallows. In this way the infantry crossed [the Menai Straits], while the cavalry followed by fording or swimming by the side of their horses.

On the shore opposite stood the opposing army with its dense array of armed warriors, while between the ranks dashed women, in black attire like the Furies, with hair dishevelled. All around, the Druids, with hands uplifted, invoked the gods and poured forth horrible imprecations. The novelty of the sight struck the Romans with awe and terror, so that as if they were paralyzed they stood motionless, exposed to wounds.

Then, urged by their general's appeals and mutual encouragement not to quail before a troop of frenzied women, they bore the standards onwards and beat down all resistance, and wrapped the Britons of their own torches. A garrison was established to keep the conquered in subjection, and their groves, dedicated to superstition and barbarous rites, were levelled to the ground. They [the Britons] deemed it a duty to cover their altars with the blood of captives and to consult their gods through human entrails.

Whether Suetonius Paulinus was correctly informed or not about the importance of the sanctuary on Anglesey or the **Druids** is impossible to know, but the Druids were widely suspected of being subversive; they were regarded as enemies of Rome. It may not be a coincidence that at exactly that moment the Boudiccan revolt erupted in England (see People: **Boudicca**). Suetonius Paulinus had to get his troops across Britain quickly to put down the rebellion.

The Element Encyclopedia of the Celts

Arderydd

SOLWAY FIRTH

A great battle, the Battle of Arderydd, was fought at Longtown on the shore of the Solway Firth in 573. This was remembered in the Triads as one of the Three Futile Battles of the Island of Britain: "the action of Arderydd, which was brought about by the cause of the lark's nest." This strange, cryptic remark may be fairly easily explained. The Lowland Scots word for "lark" is *laverock*, and there is an ancient castle site on the northern shore of the Solway Firth that is called Caerlaverock, literally "The Fortress of the Lark" or more poetically "The Lark's Nest." It is close to the mouth of the Nith **River**. The battle was remembered as being fought for possession of the Scottish shore of the Solway Firth.

The Longtown river-crossing further to the east, at the head of the Solway Firth, was an important strategic point; it was the crossing-place of the Roman **road** from the kingdom of **Rheged** into the kingdom of Clyde. The site was controlled by the stronghold of King Gwenddolau, son of Ceidio; this may have stood at Carwinley, nearby. The king was one of the leading combatants who died in the battle in and around his own fortress.

Gwenddolau had a **bard**, like all other Dark Age Celtic kings, but his bard was called **Myrddin**, which draws us to look more closely at him. Myrddin took no part in the battle, but watched it. When he saw his lord killed, he went mad and became a hermit in the Wood of Celidon, perhaps between Carlisle and Dumbarton. By the eleventh century, this had become:

The Battle of Arderydd between the sons of Elifer and Gwenddolau the son of Ceidio; in which battle Gwenddolau fell; Merlin became mad.

Elifer is Eleutherius of York, so the battle was of the kingdoms of Rheged and York—a classic conflict among Britons. It may have been Myrddin himself who wrote the verse in *The Black Book of Carmarthen*:

I saw Gwenddolau in the track of kings,
collecting booty from every border,
now indeed he lies under the red earth,

the chief of the kings of the North of greatest generosity.

ASCICBERG

See **Hohenasperg**.

AVALON

SCOTLAND?

One of the names of the Underworld; the Land of the Dead ruled by Arawn. It is the Celtic equivalent to the Norse Valhalla; the magical, Otherworldly island to which King **Arthur** was taken, either to die or to be healed, after his final battle. There are many theories about the location of Camlann, this last battle; it is likeliest to be on the Eden **River** just north of Dolgellau in North Wales, where Arthur was ambushed and betrayed by **Maelgwn** of **Gwynedd**.

If he was rescued from the battlefield, the safest route out of enemy territory would be to the **west**, into the Irish Sea. Some have thought that Bardsey Island off the tip of the Lleyn Peninsula might be Arthur's final resting-place.

There are several, perhaps separate, traditions of magical Otherworldly associations in and around the Irish Sea. The Isle of Man was the abode of the Irish sea god **Manannán**, but he was also associated with the supernatural island of Emhain Abhlach, "Emhain of the Apple Trees," which the old Celtic literature identifies with the Isle of Arran in the Firth of Clyde. The island name *Abhlach* is very close in form to *Avallach*, the name of the Lord of the Dead, and Avalon was the realm of Avallach.

There is also a lonely spot along the north coast of the Irish Sea, the Scottish shore, which has a strong claim to be Avalon. The **Whithorn** peninsula was in earlier times called Ynys Afallach, literally "The Island of the Lord of the Dead." It was never literally an island, though it was fairly remote from the rest of Scotland. Whithorn itself (Ynys Wydryn) was a monastery that had the unique distinction of being regarded as the holiest place in

Britain (or Ireland), "The Shining Place."

In Christian Celtic Britain in the Dark Ages there were Three Perpetual Choirs: religious houses where services were chanted or sung continuously. One was Cor Emrys, which was at Mynydd-y-Gaer. The second was Llantwit Major. The third and holiest was the Cor of Bangor Wydryn at Ynys Afallach, and this was surely the fittest place to take the dying overking, the most successful British leader of battles.

One strange and Otherworldly aspect of Arthur's rest in Avalon is the idea of his being in some sort of suspended animation there, somehow not quite dead but capable of being recalled to life. Even stranger is that this idea actually preceded Arthur's lifetime. Stories of a sleeping Arthur entombed in a cave or on an island were shaped by pre-Arthurian Celtic beliefs. In the first century AD, a Roman official called Demetrius visited Britain and noted one of the few myths of the British ever to be recorded objectively in plain, straight terms. His report was transmitted by the writer Plutarch in his book *On the Cessation of Oracles*. It told of an exiled god, whom he called Saturn, lying asleep in a cave on an island—a warm place in the general direction of the sunset.

Probably both of the cave stories about Arthur's end date back to pre-Arthurian beliefs, or those beliefs added a mythic resonance to the actual events of Arthur's last months. Some of the story of Arthur is history, and some of it is myth (*see* Religion: **Otherworld**).

AVARICUM

See People: **Bituriges**.

B

BADBURY RINGS

See **Maiden Castle**.

BADON

ENGLAND

At Badon, a great battle took place in which the British won a major victory over the Saxons. It was **Arthur**'s first recorded battle in the year 516. Its outcome was so decisive that it held back the Saxons for several decades, and it was largely due to Arthur's exploits during this battle that he owes his reputation as a great warrior.

Several locations for Badon have been proposed, but there are early references to the city of **Bath** in which the name is spelt Badon—for example, in *The Wonders of Britain*, Nennius refers to "the hot lake where the baths of Badon are"—and so the likeliest battle site by far is Little Solsbury Hill, about 2 miles (3km) north-east of Bath. This was on the eastern frontier of **Dumnonia**, at the point where the old Roman **road**, Fosse Way, came down the eastern valley-side from Banner Down toward a crossing-place on the Avon **River** at Bath. In the sixth century this was a key location, right on the frontier between Celt and Saxon, and would have been a natural access point to the Celtic kingdom for an advancing Saxon army. Little Solsbury Hill, which had a small fort on its summit, was an obvious vantage point from which the British warriors could have watched the invaders approaching from the east or north-east and then descended to attack as they passed below. The Saxons would have been caught between the steep valley side and the river.

In the annals there is a strange description of Arthur carrying a cross on his shoulders. This may be explained by the misreading of the word for "shoulder." The Old Welsh for "shoulder," *scuid*, is very similar to the Old Welsh word for "shield," *scuit*. Scribes regularly read whole phrases from the documents they were copying and muttered them to themselves as they wrote. It was easy to make mistakes, especially when words both looked and sounded similar to other words. So the original description may have read, "Arthur carried the cross of our lord Jesus Christ on his *shield*." The image of the cross could easily have been painted onto the shield, or designed into the shield's metalwork, or embroidered into a fabric covering for the shield. It may be significant that high-ranking officers in the late Roman army frequently carried portraits of emperors on their shields. It would be quite logical for a Christian British commander-in-chief educated in the late Roman tradition to carry an emblem of Christ: after all, he recognized no earthly overlord.

The Element Encyclopedia of the Celts

The hammering of the Saxons in the Battle of Badon brought about a major change. For a couple of decades the western frontier of the Saxon world was fixed.

BARDSEY ISLAND

See **Avalon**.

BATH: THE SANCTUARY OF SULIS-MINERVA

ENGLAND

Sulis was a Celtic **goddess** with associations with the **sun**. The temple of Sulis was the highest-profile **spring** sanctuary in Britain, drawing in pilgrims not only from Britain but from overseas as well. The mineral springs here are unusual in being hot springs, and in being very prolific—a quarter of a million gallons a day.

The site began as a cult focus on the floor of the marshy valley in the Iron Age. Then, during the Roman occupation, it was lavishly developed, with Sulis herself being identified with the Roman goddess Minerva, though the name of Su-lis was invariably given priority: *Sulis-Minerva*. The Romans called the place Aquae Sulis, "The Waters of Sulis."

The Roman engineers transformed the natural spring and its associated pool into a large rectangular ornamental pool, enclosed by a Greco-Roman-style temple. There were also subsidiary buildings, including baths. The temple dates from the time of Nero.

Visitors threw large numbers of **coins** and lead **curse tablets** into the pool. The coins were frequently deliberately damaged, to "kill" them so that they could travel across to the **Otherworld**: a practice that was common to other ancient **cultures**. Damaging grave goods would also have the practical value of rendering them worthless to potential thieves.

Sulis is mentioned in many of the dedications at Bath, and she was depicted there in a huge and imposing classical-style statue of gilded bronze; unfortunately only her magnificent **head** has survived.

BEWCASTLE

See Religion: **War God**.

BIBRACTE

See **Alesia**.

BOUGHTON GREEN

See Symbols: **Labyrinth**.

BOURBONNE-LANCY

See Religion: **Damona**.

BOYNE

See Religion: **Boanna**.

BRIGETIO

See Religion: **Grannus**.

BROCH OF MIDHOWE

ROUSAY, ORKNEY

A massive drum-shaped tower standing on the south coast of Rousay and looking out across Eynhallow Sound toward the main island of Orkney. Built about 2,000 years ago, it may have been raised partly to mark territory in an imposing way. It was located on a defensive site: a headland between two narrow geos, and a stone rampart and ditch were added on the landward side—so evidently defense was an important consideration.

Another site consideration may have been the presence of a fine Neolithic tomb, Midhowe; doubtless its large, flat roof-slabs, probably then exposed to view, were an attraction to Iron Age builders. They were dragged off the tomb and used to make the huge room dividers in the interior of the *broch*. The two monuments stand side by side.

The *broch* originally had a range of ancillary buildings. Coastal erosion, a problem for all shore sites such as Midhowe, has greatly damaged the remains of these outhouses. The *broch* itself still stands to a height of 14 feet (4.3m) and the interior is well preserved.

There is also a **spring** in a crack in the rocks, which even during a modern archeological excavation went on filling the Iron Age **water** tank with water that was clear and drinkable.

One surprise is that the Iron Age inhabitants of the Broch of Midhowe had Roman goods: pottery and a ladle. This remote location was well outside the arena of Roman activity, so these objects must have been acquired as **gifts** or by trading with Britons further to the south.

BROCH OF MOUSA

SHETLAND

One of the finest and best-preserved prehistoric buildings in northern Europe, built about 2,000 years ago. It featured in the Norse colonization of Orkney and was even mentioned by name in the *Orkneyinga Saga*:

Then Erland gathered men together and took up his residence in the Broch of Mousa and made great preparations for defence … when Earl Harald came to Hjaltland, he laid siege to the Broch and cut off all communication, but it was difficult to take by assault.

It would have been; it was a massively built defensive tower. This is one of the largest *brochs*, standing 44 feet (13m) high, and it is the only one that stands to its full original height. It also has one of the thickest wall-bases, and consequently one of the smallest interiors. Its excellent state of preservation is due partly to its unusually massive construction and partly to its remote location. Because the building is a drystone construction, it would be easy to damage and disrupt.

Access is by a single door at ground level. Inside, it is possible to climb a staircase built into the thickness of the wall to reach an open walkway at the top.

In its first phase, the *broch* was a complex wooden roundhouse, with an upper floor resting on a ledge 7 feet (2.1m) above the ground. A second upper floor or perhaps the roof was supported on a second ledge 13 feet (4m) above the ground. A **water** tank was cut into the bedrock.

The wooden roundhouse was

later demolished and a small wheel-house was erected in the interior.

The Norse occupations that feature in the *Orkneyinga Saga* are reflected in certain features. The early low lintels of the entrance were pulled out and the outer door-way was doubled in height, which implies that the interior and the doorway were so full of debris that the Norsemen had to take out the door lintel and raise the passage roof simply in order to gain access. Today the door has been restored to its original low height.

BRYNAICH

See People: **Taliesin**.

C

CAISTOR ST. EDMUND

See People: **Iceni**.

CALCHVYNNYDD

ENGLAND

A British Dark Age kingdom in the lower Severn Valley, between **Dumnonia** to the south and **Powys** to the north. There were two towns in it: Cirencester and Gloucester.

CAMELOT

See People: **Arthur**.

CAMLANN

See People: **Arthur**.

CAMULODUNON

See **Camulodunum**.

CAMULODUNUM

ENGLAND

The Roman city of Colchester was developed on the site of an existing British *oppidum*, **Camulodunum** (or Camulodunon), which was the capital of the **Catuvellauni tribe**. Earlier, the settlement had been the main center of the **Trinovantes** tribe.

In the first century BC, the Trinovantes were taken over by the more powerful Catuvellauni tribe, who lived immediately to the **west**, and the Catuvellaunian kings moved their headquarters from Wheathampstead near St. Albans to Camulodunum. The reason may have been strategic. Camolodunum was only 4 miles (6km) from the **head** of the Colne estuary and defended to north and south by marshy **river** floodplains and forests; it was artificially defended on its western side by an elaborate system of defensive dykes built in the first century BC and first century AD. The location near to an estuary also meant that it was possible to escape by sea if it looked as though that would be necessary.

At the climax of the second Roman invasion, in AD 43, the emperor Claudius led his army in triumph into Camulodunum, which was then the stronghold of the late British king **Cunobelin** and the capital of the most powerful British kingdom. This symbolic act marked the Roman conquest of Britain.

It has recently been suggested that in the first century BC **Julius Caesar** also marched on Camulodunum, in hot pursuit of **Cassivellaunus**. Caesar's description has usually been taken to refer to Wheathampstead, but it is now thought more likely to be Camulodunum:

He [Caesar] learnt that the stronghold of Cassivellaunus, defended by woods and marshes, lay not far away, and that he [Cassivellaunus] had gathered there a great number of men and cattle. Now, 'stronghold' is what the Britons call a thickly wooded area fortified by a rampart and ditch, and it is their practice to gather together in such a place to avoid enemy raids. Caesar set out for this place with the legions. He found that it was extremely well fortified by both natural and man-made defences; nevertheless he launched an assault on two sides. For a short time the enemy remained there, but they could not resist the assault of our troops and made

The Element Encyclopedia of the Celts

their escape from another side of the stronghold. A great many cattle were found there, and many of the people who fled were captured and killed.

Given that Caesar had taken five legions with him—more than 20,000 men—the implication is that the stronghold was very big: only Camulodunum seems to fit Caesar's account (*see* **Lexden Tumulus**).

CARDIGAN BAY

See Myths: ***The Legend of Ys, The Salty Sea, The Sigh of Gwyddno Garanhir.***

CARN EUNY

See People: ***Fogou.***

CARNAC

BRITTANY

In the area around the town of Carnac, there is an incredible concentration of ancient **standing stones**, stone circles, stone rows, and chambered tombs, dating from 3500 BC to 2500 BC. A 15

mile (24km) stretch of the Breton coast is known as "The Coast of the Megaliths."

The most spectacular monuments, now and in antiquity, must be the rows of standing stones. There are three sets of them: Menec, Kermario, and Kerlescan. Kermario has 999 standing stones, while Menec has 1,099 standing stones arranged in 12 rows. The Kerlescan group consists of 55 surviving stones arranged in 13 rows. They lead to stone enclosures that were set up in 3500 BC but the rows themselves were built later, in 3000–2500 BC.

Like **Stonehenge** in Britain, Carnac has been an integral part of the Celtic cultural consciousness all the way through: a deeply embedded element of the psychological and spiritual landscape of Celtic Brittany. It has often been remarked that the endless rows of standing stones look like a religious procession or a petrified army, and it must have seemed so to many generations of Bretons too. No doubt, hundreds of years ago **people** imagined the stones to be not just monuments built by their ancestors, but actually their ancestors themselves, turned into stone.

CARRAWBURGH

See Religion: **Coventina**; Symbols: **Horse**.

CASTLE FROME

See Symbols: **Knot**.

CASTRO DE BAROÑA

GALICIA

An Iron Age Celtic fortified settlement on a rocky island connected to the mainland by a *tombolo* (sandy beach) that makes a natural causeway. The site was discovered in 1933. Since then it has been excavated and the impressive ruins are accessible to the public from the C550 coastal highway south of the fishing village of Porto do Son, though there is a difficult and dangerous one-mile walk over rocks to reach them.

The *castro* is surrounded by perfect natural defenses—the rocky cliffs and Atlantic breakers on three sides, and a difficult clamber over rocks on the landward side. The sand *tombolo* is really the only point of access.

The settlement was built and inhabited 2,000 years ago. It has a defensive wall, which turns the site into a miniature hillfort. Inside, the enclosure is filled to a high density with stoutly built roundhouses with thick, stone walls. With a high degree of exposure to strong winds and sea spray, it cannot have been an easy place to live (*see also* People: **Dwellings**, **Fortifications**).

CELIDON

SCOTLAND

A forest in the north of Britain, probably in the Southern Uplands of Scotland. Medieval Scottish tradition puts it north of Stirling, extending into the Grampians. It was the wood where the **bard Myrddin** took refuge when he lost his mind after the Battle of **Arderydd** in about 573.

By the Middle Ages, the Wood of Celidon had acquired a sort of mythic Otherworldly status, like the Mirkwood of Tolkien's *The Lord of the Rings*.

CERNE ABBAS

DORSET, ENGLAND

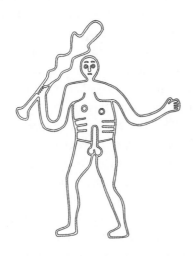

The Cerne Giant is a chalk hill figure: a huge line drawing made by cutting out a turf outline and filling the trench back up to ground level with white chalk rubble. He is 180 feet (55m) high from **head** to toe and in his right hand he waves a knobbly club 120 feet (37m) long. He is famously naked and even more famously displays an erect **phallus** 23 feet (7m) long. He looks vaguely menacing and warlike.

The current fashion is to present the Cerne Giant as a seventeenth-century cartoon. This idea hinges on some rather weak arguments; the main one is the fact that the Giant was not mentioned before 1694. But too much is made of the absence of evidence: we know that documents perish with the passage of time and in any case a lot of things happened in the past that were never written down. There are many arguments in favor of an ancient, Iron Age, origin. One is that it would be an extraordinary coincidence for a seventeenth-century cartoon to imitate so perfectly and in so many details a work of **art** from the Iron Age. There is no other image that looks exactly like the Cerne Giant, but all of his features can be found—in different combinations—in British and European artwork from 500 BC to AD 100.

The Giant is a naked warrior; the way some Celtic tribesmen

took their clothes off before going into battle was an oddity that was commented on by the Romans (*see* Symbols: **Nudity**). Even more telling is the erection. Genital display is common in Iron Age art, where it may have one of two meanings: to ward off evil (and frighten enemies) and to bring good luck.

A virtually unnoticed feature of the Giant is that he is wearing a girdle. **Diodorus Siculus** described the Celts as "descending to do battle unclothed *except for a girdle.*" This belt was for holding a knife, for dispatching enemies and decapitating them.

The club suggests a common man who could not afford a **sword**. The **cloak**-shield also suggests poverty. First-century BC bronze figurines show naked warriors with cloaks wound around their left arms as primitive shields—the routine equipment of non-professional soldiers.

The resistivity surveys that I undertook in the 1990s showed that there was originally a cloak draped over the left arm.

A close contour survey of the low knoll below the left hand (undertaken by the National Trust) revealed the delicately modeled features of a human **head** in low-relief on the hillside. The Giant was swinging a severed human head from his left hand. The cult of the severed head is well documented. **Headhunting** was an integral part of **warfare**. The Giant was returning home from battle with the head of an important enemy— the service an Iron Age **tribe** would expect of its protector **god**.

The fact there may be no early documents that mentioned the Cerne Giant is not a problem. Values change through time, and before the time of John Aubrey antiquities were rarely mentioned in Britain. In 1649 Aubrey visited Avebury by chance while hunting, and described "the vast stones of which I had not heard before," but we know from radiocarbon dates that they were there by 2500 BC.

The Early Modern hypothesis leans heavily on there being no documentation earlier than 1694. But there *are* some earlier documented mentions, in the Middle Ages. Accounts by William of Malmesbury and Walter of Coventry are well known, but an even earlier account by Goscelin in the eleventh century is rarely mentioned. In that, St. Augustine comes into conflict with a pagan community worshiping a low-relief pagan image at

Cerne; he takes control by taking the site over and colonizing it.

Goscelin was a Norman monk who was in Dorset from 1055 to 1078 and later went to Canterbury, where he wrote various saints' lives. His final work was a *Life of St. Augustine*. He was able to incorporate what he had picked up in Dorset about Augustine's humiliating encounter with pagans at Cerne.

The importance of Goscelin's text has been overlooked because a passage describes Augustine as "throwing over the idol to Helia," and this could not refer to the Cerne Giant because it seems to describe toppling a statue, just as in more recent times people have pulled over statues of Lenin, Stalin, and Saddam Hussein. But the passage has been mistranslated for the last 400 years. It should read "Augustine took possession of the *bas-relief* of Hellia" and that certainly could be the Cerne Giant.

Taking possession of the hillfigure might well involve setting up a permanent mission close beside it, conforming to the tradition of an early Christian settlement on the abbey site. The *Life of St. Augustine* reports that he saw offensive images that he felt should be destroyed. We know he sought advice from his superior, the Pope, because Pope Gregory's reply has survived: "Upon mature deliberation the temples of the idols ought not to be destroyed." Gregory explained that he wanted the missionaries to take them over gradually, occupying the pagan sanctuaries and converting them to Christian worship. The Christian missionaries in time did that at Cerne Abbas, eventually building an abbey church between the Giant and a Celtic pagan **sacred spring**.

Taking over and Christianizing existing sanctuaries and temples was an officially approved and recommended practice. In AD 601 Gregory the Great sent an explicit letter of advice to the missionaries in England, specifically to Mellitus:

When (by God's help) you come to our most reverend brother, Bishop Augustine, I want you to tell him how earnestly I have been pondering over the affairs of the English; I have come to the conclusion that the temples of the idols in England should not on any account be destroyed. The temples should be sprinkled with holy water and altars set up in them in which relics are to be enclosed. If these temples in Britain are well-built, then it is better to convert them from the worship of devils to the service of the true God: that the people, seeing that their temples are not destroyed, may remove error from their hearts and adoring the true God may the more freely resort to places to which they have been accustomed.

This is exactly what St. Augustine did at Cerne Abbas, turning a pagan site into a Christian site.

So, a careful look at the medieval texts reveals that there are after all references to the Giant traceable right back to the eleventh century. There was even continuity in his name. Goscelin called him Helia and later writers called him Hele, Helis, and Helith.

When the great pioneering antiquarian William Stukeley visited Cerne Abbas in 1761, the locals told him who the Giant was, but they were uneducated country folk and he was dismissive. "The inhabitants pretend to know nothing more of it than a traditionary account of its being a deity of the ancient Britons," Stukeley laughed up his sleeve, but the thrust of the evidence is that the villagers were right. The Cerne Giant was, and still is, Helis, a tribal guardian god of the ancient Britons.

He was drawn on the hillside perhaps in 100 BC and the Celtic Sanctuary of Helis-Toutatis stood on the site later occupied by Cerne Abbey. The earthworks that were landscaped into formal gardens for the abbey were originally made in the Iron Age: Roman coins have been found in the earthworks, showing that they were there long before the medieval abbey.

Cerne Abbas is a site that has been much misunderstood, like the Celts themselves. The evidence does point to it being a major Celtic rural sanctuary. It was more or less in the geometric center of the territory of the **Durotriges** tribe, which corresponds closely with modern Dorset. Cerne Abbas is more or less exactly midway between the three major hillforts of the Durotriges: Hod Hill, **South Cadbury Castle**, and **Maiden Castle**. The Durotriges were a loose confederation of tribes and may well have met from time to time at their shared sanctuary, close to the spot where their boundaries met.

The **Mars** gods of the English West Country were war leaders, protectors of their tribes, but they also were spirits of well-being and prosperity. Even if the warlike attributes were to the fore, there were peaceful and benign attributes as well, including **healing**. Close to the foot of the hill at Cerne Abbas was a healing spring, St. Augustine's Well, which is likely to have been involved in the Giant's cult (*see* Symbols: **Water**).

In the Cotswolds, the Mars god appears as a benign god of rustic well-being. At King's Stanley in Gloucestershire, he is shown in the full armor of a Roman soldier, for the benefit of Roman legionaries no doubt, but it is very unlikely that the local Celtic tribespeople, the Dobunni, would have seen him like this. For a start, they would have seen him naked; in fact more like the Cerne Giant.

There is a striking similarity between the Cerne Giant image and a depiction of **Ogmios**, the Celtic Hercules, carved in stone at High Rochester in Northumberland. This Romano-Celtic image shows a powerfully muscled naked man with a knobbed club in his right hand and a cloak wrapped round his left arm as an improvised shield.

CHARTRES

See Religion: **Druids**.

CHICHESTER

See People: **Cogidumnus**.

CHYSAUSTER

See People: **Dwellings**.

CIRENCESTER

See **Calchvynnydd**; Religion: **Hooded Dwarves**, **Mother Goddess**; Symbols: **Sky Horseman**.

COLCHESTER

See **Camulodunum**, **Lexden Tumulus**.

COLIJNSPLAAT

THE NETHERLANDS

This remarkable shrine to the **mother goddess**, unusually named here as **Nehalennia**, stood on the East Scheldt estuary. It was discovered in 1970, when fishermen pulled up stone **altars** from a depth of 85 feet (26m). Since that moment of discovery, more than 120 altars and pieces of sculpture have been recovered from under the **water**. It seems that this shrine was in use, standing on the river-bank, in AD 200, and later subsided into the sea.

Nehalennia was a Celtic goddess invoked by Romanized Gauls and Romans. Seafarers and traders were important worshipers at this particular waterfront shrine, dedicating **altars** to her, grateful for safe voyages and profitable trade deals. The images dedicated to her are standardized. She is shown sitting with **baskets of fruit** and horns of plenty (*see* Symbols: **Cornucopia**). She is also usually accompanied by a **dog**.

CULLODEN

See Religion: **Holy Well**.

CURGY

See Religion: **Cernunnos**.

DANEBURY HILLFORT

HAMPSHIRE, ENGLAND

One of the most professionally excavated Celtic sites, this hillfort stands 30 miles (48km) from the sea in the kingdom of the **Atrebates tribe**. It was in use for 500 years until it was destroyed by fire in around 100 BC. Danebury was strongly fortified permanent settlement, with internal streets laid out according to a regular plan, lined by roundhouses (*see* **Fortifications**). About 300–500 **people** lived there. Its modern name, "Fort of the Danes," misleads, as it was really "Fort of the Britons."

The temples were located at the highest part of the *oppidum*. The **road** leading westward from the main east entrance took the visitor directly to the shrines on the hilltop. They consisted of three square structures and an enclosure, all in a straight line. The shrines were built of vertical planks set in slots cut into the chalk.

DEAL

See Religion: **Ritual Shaft**.

DEMETIA

See **Dyfed**.

DIN EIDYN

SCOTLAND

Din Eidyn is now Edinburgh's Castle Rock. It was the principal stronghold of the Gododdin: the Dark Age kingdom that occupied the eastern half of the Scottish Lowlands and much of the Southern Uplands. The people of this kingdom were called the Votadini by Ptolemy in the second century, but the name had been transmuted into Gododdin by the sixth century, when they were immortalized in the heroic poem, written around 600, which refers for the first time to Din Eidyn, ancient Edinburgh (see People: *The Gododdin*).

DINAS EMRYS

WALES

Dinas Emrys, "Fort of Ambrosius," is a place associated with a legend—the confrontation between **Vortigern** and **Ambrosius Aurelianus** is said to have taken place here. But in spite of the name and the legend, it is hard to believe that Ambrosius had any connection with the place. Nennius seems to be referring to this Ambrosius when he uses the title *Gwledg Emrys*—*gwledig* means "prince" in Welsh and *Emrys* is the Welsh form of Ambrosius—but although this might seem to associate Ambrosius with Wales, and therefore conceivably with Dinas Emrys, the Britons living in the West Country, the Severn Valley, the Midlands, and the north of England also spoke a language very close to Old Welsh. The fact that the form Emrys survives now only in Wales does not mean that someone called Emrys in the sixth century was Welsh.

DINAS POWYS

WALES

The principal fortress of the South Wales kingdom of **Glevissig**. An eleventh-century castle was built on the ruins of a sixth and seventh-century fortress. It was a compact but well-defended homestead inhabited by a powerful chief and his immediate family. It contrasts with the much larger Iron Age hillforts of southern Britain, which were designed to house a whole clan or **tribe**.

DOZMARY POOL

ENGLAND

A lake on Bodmin Moor in Cornwall. This is the lake from which **Arthur** is said to have taken the **sword** Excalibur and to which the sword was eventually returned after his death.

DUMNONIA

ENGLISH WEST COUNTRY

A Dark Age kingdom consisting of what is now Cornwall, Devon, Somerset, and Dorset. It was named after the Iron Age **people** who lived there long before the Romans arrived: the Dumnonii.

DUN AONGHASA

GALWAY, IRELAND

An Iron Age castle built on the high cliffs of Innie Mór, the biggest of the Aran islands in Galway Bay. The fortress was first occupied in the late Bronze Age and it was reused repeatedly until the first millennium AD. The first settlement would probably have had a single stone wall perimeter that was rebuilt and repeatedly modified. The present innermost **fortification** is a stone wall 16.5 feet (5m) wide and 16.5 feet (5m) high. It was rebuilt in the Iron Age, but may contain the original Bronze Age wall. The defenses consist of three concentric perimeter walls.

The fort is now semi-circular, because of cliff retreat; presumably when it was new it was circular. Outside the three walls is a *chevaux-de-frise*: a zone of angular stones embedded in the ground close together to make them an obstacle to attackers. They are very difficult to walk across. *Chevaux-de-frises* are found in Scotland, Wales, Ireland, and Galicia.

DUNADD

SCOTLAND

A fortress on a low rocky crag on the Crinan isthmus of the Kintyre peninsula in Argyll. It was fortified in the Iron Age, then reoccupied after the Romans left. When the Kintyre peninsula was colonized by Irish settlers in the fifth century and became part of the British kingdom of Dal Riada, the ruling dynasty made this little drystone-walled citadel its capital. It continued in use like this, as a royal stronghold, for 300 years.

Imported Mediterranean pottery proves Dunadd's high status in the Dark Ages. The survival of the ancient name *Dunatt* from the contemporary Irish Annals almost unchanged right down to the present day makes it absolutely certain that this is the place referred to in the Dark Age documents (*see also* **Tintagel**).

DUNPELDER

See **Traprain Law**.

DURNOVARIA

See **Maiden Castle**.

DYFED

WALES

A Dark Age Celtic kingdom that was also known as Demetia after the Iron Age **tribe** who lived there: the Demetae. It later became the county of Pembrokeshire.

EGGARDON HILL

See **Maiden Castle**.

ELMET

ENGLAND

A Dark Age Celtic kingdom consisting of the Pennines. In the middle of the sixth century, **Pabo Post Prydain**, "Pabo the Pillar of Britain," was king of the Pennines. When he abdicated, the Pennine kingdom was divided between his sons Dunawt (Donatus), who ruled in the north, and Sawyl Benasgell (Samuel), who ruled in the south.

These small units had probably seen an earlier history as tribal territories. What happened during the Iron Age, sub-Roman, and post-Roman periods was a cyclical process of aggregation and disaggregation, and integration and devolution. Elmet was the southernmost of a chain of Brigantian territories that re-emerged after the Romans left. It was probably a return to a much older, perhaps middle, Iron Age territory. But by 550 this splintering process was weakening the Celtic fringe and making it easier for Saxon colonization to resume.

EMAIN MACHA

COUNTY ARMAGH, IRELAND

A round enclosure of 15 acres (6 hectares), on a prominent drumlin ridge just a mile (1.6km) **west** of the city of Armagh. It is known today as Navan Fort. It was, according to historical tradition and Irish mythology, the legendary capital of the Ulaidh: the **tribe** who gave

their name to the province of Ulster.

The large, circular enclosure is 820 feet (250m) in diameter and surrounded by a ditch and a bank. Significantly, the ditch is inside the bank, which shows that the earthworks were not defensive but had a ritual function. This is the same layout that is seen in the Neolithic henges of western Britain, and it may be helpful to regard Emain Macha as a very large (but very late) henge, with correspondingly high status. The reference back to ancient practice is significant; ceremonies often include extremely archaic elements.

Inside the large enclosure, off-center to the north-west, is an earthen mound 130 feet (40m) in diameter and 20 feet (6m) high. To the south-east is a plowed-down ring-shaped monument about 100 feet (30m) in diameter.

The large mound covers the site of a roundhouse that was standing from about 350 BC to the late second century AD and was rebuilt nine times. After the final roundhouse, a new structure was laid out, a huge array of concentric posts 130 feet (40m) in diameter, with an entrance toward the west. The final act in the building of this monument was the raising of an enormous post 43 feet (13m) tall at the center. This happened in 94 BC. Then, in what seem to have been ritual deposition ceremonies, a cairn of stone, clay, and turf was built up around the internal posts, producing a huge mound. The outside timbers were deliberately set on fire and the building as a whole was covered in a turf mound, making something that looked like a Neolithic passage grave. The surrounding bank and ditch were created at the same time.

The whole sequence of events and the architecture of the Emain Macha monument smack of Neolithic rituals from a much earlier time, around 3000 BC, including the deliberate destruction by fire. It is long-held traditions and continuities of this kind that make the idea of a very long-established Atlantic Celtic community seem plausible.

Archeology shows that the hill was in use in the Neolithic, Bronze Age, and Iron Age.

The low ring-shaped monument was a round timber building that was rebuilt twice over. The remains of similar but smaller buildings with hearths were found under the 130-foot (40m) mound;

they were large circular **dwellings** inhabited 600–250 BC, and it is tempting to see them as royal palaces. In the debris from these Iron Age dwellings was the skull of a macaque, perhaps the pet monkey of an ancient Irish king.

The Annals of the Four Masters say that Emain Macha was abandoned after being burned down in AD 331. The ancient place was destroyed by the Three Collas after a battle in which they defeated Fergus Foga, King of Ulster.

In Irish legend, especially in tales of the **Ulster Cycle**, this is one of the most important power centers in pagan Ireland. The ancient capital of Ulster was founded by the **goddess** Macha, perhaps in the seventh century BC, and it became the seat of Conchobar mac Nessa. He had three houses at Emain Macha. One was the Cróeb Ruad (pronounced *creeve-roe*), meaning "The Ruddy Branch," which is where he had his residence; the name "Creeveroe" survives still as a local place-name. Another was the Cróeb Derg, "The Red Branch," where the king's battle trophies were kept. The third was the Téte Brecc, "The Twinkling Hoard," where the war-band's weapons were kept.

Many names celebrated in Irish mythology are connected directly with Emain Macha and the Red Branch warriors: Amergin the poet, **Cú Chulainn** the warrior, Emer his strong-willed bride, Conall Cernach his friend, Cathbad the chief **Druid**, Conchobar mac Nessa, the King of Ulster, and Deirdre of the Sorrows, the most beautiful woman in Ireland.

Today there is little to see beyond a grassy mound; a great contrast to the Emain Macha of myth and legend, which is a grand and mysterious place, the capital of the Ulaidh. The archeology shows a site that was relatively simple and primitive, but with ceremonies rooted in a distant past. The name "fort" is misleading, as the place was laid out for pagan ceremonies.

Navan was threatened by the expansion of a limestone quarry in the 1980s. A Friends of Navan group was formed and a public inquiry led to quarrying being stopped; the site was to be developed for tourism. A visitor center was opened in 1991, closed in 1993 through shortage of funds then re-opened on a seasonal basis in 2005. The Celtic heritage is vulnerable, and not to be taken for granted.

ENTREMONT SANCTUARY

FRANCE

Entremont was the capital of the Saluvii **tribe**. It was sacked by the Romans in 123 BC.

The famous sanctuary at Entremont was placed on the highest point in the area. It was built in the third to second century BC and fitted with limestone pillars 8.5 feet (2.6m) high with incised carvings of human **heads**. There were other sculptures too, mostly connected with severed heads (*see* Religion: **Headhunting**).

FRILFORD

See Religion: **Shrines and Temples**.

G

GERGOVIA

See **Alesia**; People: **Arverni**.

GIANT'S SPRINGS

See Symbols: **Water**.

GLAMORGAN

See **Glevissig**.

GLASTONBURY

SOMERSET, ENGLAND

The Celtic site is not, as might have been expected, the great ruined abbey with all its legendary associations, but an unpromising marshland location nearby where an Iron Age lake village was discovered by Arthur Bulleid in 1892. The lakeside village consisted of more than 90 huts, of which perhaps 30 were occupied at any one time. The round huts were built of closely set upright timbers, with the gaps closed by hurdles.

The floors were clay, with central hearths also made of clay. The village stood on a shelf of peat and was surrounded by a wooden palisade. It was in use from 250 BC to 50 BC.

The waterlogged conditions at the site meant that wooden objects that have been lost elsewhere were well-preserved here: ladles, **wheel** spokes and hubs, tool handles, a ladder, and a loom.

GLAUBERG

HESSE, GERMANY

An important Celtic *oppidum*. It consists of a fortified settlement and several burial mounds. It was the seat of power of tribal chiefs in the late Hallstatt and early **La Tène** periods (*see* People: **Cultures**). In the 1990s it yielded major new evidence about burial, sculpture, and monuments.

The site stands on a spur of the Vogelsberg range, rising 490 feet (150m) above the surrounding fertile landscape. The hilltop, surrounded by **springs**, is very level and about 2,600 feet (800m) across, with a steep drop on all sides.

It had been known for a long time that there were ruins on

the Glauberg plateau, but it was assumed they belonged to the Romans. The chance find of a La Tène torc in 1906 pointed to a more ancient ancestry for the site. Work in the 1930s had a focus on the **fortifications**. In the 1980s and 1990s the burial mound was investigated. Studies in 2004–6 looked at the settlement history and revealed much about the Hallstatt and La Tène periods, though **people** had been living there since the Neolithic (4500–4000 BC), and it is possible the Glauberg may have been fortified even at that early stage. The hill was also occupied in the Bronze Age by the Urnfield people (1,000–800 BC). By the middle Iron Age, the Glauberg was the seat of an early Celtic prince, who ordered the building of extensive fortifications.

In the Roman occupation, the Glauberg was unoccupied. The Romans may have emptied it because of its proximity to their fortified border, Limes Germanicus. The hill was refortified by the Franks in the seventh to ninth centuries. The Celtic fortifications were developed on a large scale in the sixth or fifth century BC and remained in use for 400 years. They define the Glauberg as one of the network of *oppida* existing across most of southern Germany.

The fortified town had at least two gates. There were also additional defenses farther out, to the north-east and south-west. This was a large settlement.

To the south were two royal burial mounds. The larger was originally 160 feet (50m) in diameter and 20 feet (6m) high, surrounded by a ditch 33 feet (10m) wide. At its center was an empty pit, evidently to fool looters, while the real burial chamber was to the north-west. This was a small wooden burial chamber containing a burial; there was a cremation burial as well, which is more characteristic of Hallstatt. Both were the graves of warriors, to judge from their grave goods. The burial chamber was removed to a lab intact in order to excavate it more slowly. Each of the finds in the main chamber had been carefully wrapped in cloth, including a fine **gold** torc and a bronze jug that had once contained mead. A processional way 1,100 feet (335m) long approached the mound from the south-east.

A second mound, 800 feet (250m) to the south, was invisible on the ground, as it had been plowed flat.

The Element Encyclopedia of the Celts

This was a smaller mound than the first, but contained a warrior with a gold ring.

A cluster of 16 postholes was associated with the mound; this structure was a simple astronomical calendar, probably to determine the dates of important seasonal festivals.

The mounds and the processional way were unusual enough, but the find of a life-size pink sandstone statue was very rare. This dated from around 500 BC and was found close to the larger burial mound. Made of local stone, it depicts an armed warrior in great detail: his trousers, armored tunic, wooden shield, and typical La Tène **sword**. On his **head** he wears a strange hoodlike headdress crowned by two extensions, perhaps intended to look like a **mistletoe** leaf. Unfortunately, to a modern visitor they look like the ears of Mickey Mouse. But this was no whimsy on the part of the sculptor: this type of headdress is known from a couple of other statues of the period.

Fragments of three similar statues were found in the area and it is possible that originally all four statues once stood together in the rectangular enclosure.

Remarkable though this site appears to be, the same sort of thing was happening at other Celtic sites in central Europe. There are three other sites of the La Tène period—Holzgerlingen, **Pfalzfeld**, and **Hirschlanden**—where similar large warrior statues were erected.

GLEVISSIG

WALES

A Dark Age kingdom corresponding to today's Glamorgan.

GLOUCESTER

See **Calchvynnydd**.

GLYWYSING

See **Glevissig**.

GOLDBERG

See Religion: **Shrines and Temples**.

GOLORING

See Religion: **Shrines and Temples**.

GOURNAY

NORTHERN FRANCE

A major sanctuary at Gournay-sur-Aronde, close to the northeastern corner of the land of the **Bellovaci** and within easy reach of the **Ambiani**, Viromandui, and Suessiones **tribes**. The sanctuary was probably used as a meeting-place for the four tribes.

The square enclosure bounded by a ditch had its entrance on the south. It was in use from the fourth century BC to the fourth century AD. It was laid out inside but near the edge of an *oppidum*. The sanctuary was perched on a valley slope 175 feet (53m) from a stream, which here widened into a lake about 4 acres (1.6 hectares) in extent. Possibly some of the cult activity at the sanctuary was related to the lake, or the sanctuary was built to commemorate the very early settlement that stood close by in the Bronze Age.

Many animal and **human sacrifices** were carried out, prob-

ably in the *oppidum*, though not in the sanctuary. Selected parts of the slaughtered animals were taken to the rectangular sacred enclosure and deposited in its surrounding ditch. The remains of sheep and pigs were deposited in the middle section of each side, cattle skulls on either side of the entrance, **horse** skeletons at intervals right around, and human remains at the corners. The distribution of the sacrifices was orderly and methodical.

In the middle of the sacred enclosure an array of nine pits surrounded a large central pit. At the end of the sanctuary's life, a small Romano-Celtic temple was built right in the center: a rectangular roofed building surrounded by a roofed verandah. There was exactly the same sequence of events at the sanctuary at Vendeuil-Caply.

GWYNEDD

WALES

A Dark Age kingdom in northwest Wales corresponding approximately to the modern county of Gwynedd.

h

HALLSTATT

See People: **Cultures**.

HAM HILL

See **Maiden Castle**.

HAUSEN-AN-DER-ZABER

See Symbols: **Sky Horseman**.

HAYLING ISLAND TEMPLE

ENGLAND

A Celtic ritual enclosure 260 feet (80m) square. The entrance halfway along its eastern side led the visitor directly to the doorway of a large, circular temple. Offerings deposited here included **chariots**, **horses**, scabbards, and **swords**.

In AD 50 a small stone Romano-Celtic temple was built on the same spot and it looks as though the religious cult activity continued as before (see Religion: **Shrines and Temples**).

HENGISTBURY HEAD

DORSET, ENGLAND

This headland at the mouth of the Wiltshire Avon commanded Christchurch Harbor. In the first century BC this was a major port. The fortified Iron Age settlement stood on the peninsula jutting eastward and forming the southern side of the harbor (*see* **Fortifications**). This peninsula was separated from the mainland by a defensive bank and ditch. A substantial settlement of roundhouses was built on the more sheltered northern slope of the peninsula, overlooking the large harbor (*see* People: **Dwellings**).

The ancient name of this important port is not known, but it has been established that it had strong trading links with ports in Brittany. Breton pottery was imported and a lot of Breton **coins** have been found in the area. Imported wine jars (*amphorae*) that came directly from Italy have been found in a scatter up to 20 miles (32km) from Hengistbury. One of the wine ships sank off the Breton coast; its cargo of wine remains undrunk on the seabed.

Both Strabo and **Julius Caesar** commented that there was a lot of cross-Channel trade, and Hengistbury supplies proof of it. The **Veneti** in Brittany in particular ran a fleet of merchant vessels. Caesar disrupted this trade when he defeated the **tribe** in 56 BC; they had opposed him. The Dorset tribe, the **Durotriges**, were equally opposed to the Roman conquest 100 years later.

THE HEUNEBERG

GERMANY

A fortified settlement on a hill above the Danube (*see* **Fortifications**). It was a very important early Iron Age center in the seventh, sixth, and fifth centuries BC, on the site of an earlier Bronze Age settlement that flourished in the fifteenth to twelfth centuries BC, though it was abandoned in between. This was the key center of power and trade in south Germany in the Iron Age.

A remarkable feature of the settlement was the citadel's circuit wall, built in 600 BC. It was a mudbrick wall 13 feet (4m) high, probably with a roofed walkway on top. Rectangular towers projected from it at intervals. It was destroyed by fire in 530 BC.

Associated with the Heuneberg is the Höhmichele Barrow, an important grave mound built in the sixth century BC. Inside were two wooden chambers. One contained the body of a woman with a wagon. The other contained the body of a man with a wagon and harness, laid on a **bull**'s hide with a woman beside him. The man had with him the grave goods of a warrior-prince: two bows, a quiver, and 50 iron-tipped arrows. What was most surprising about this grave was its opulence. There were bronze vessels and jewelry and rich textiles in the shape of clothing and wall-drapes, which incorporated Chinese silk. It was an exceptionally rich tomb and it challenges classically influenced ideas of a barbaric Iron Age Europe.

The finds at the Heuneberg show that the people here carried on a prosperous trade with the Greeks of Massilia (Marseille).

The Element Encyclopedia of the Celts

Another Celtic tomb dating from about 600 BC has been found not far from the Heuneberg. It is unusually well preserved and contains elaborate jewelry of amber and **gold**. The tomb consists of an underground chamber 16 feet (5m) by 13 feet (4m). Its **oak** floor is intact and well preserved. The finds suggest that a woman was buried there. The entire burial chamber was lifted by cranes onto a flatbed truck and taken to a lab at Ludwigsburg. Other tombs at Heuneberg have been found, but usually they have been looted; this one was not.

HIRSCHLANDEN

GERMANY

A late Hallstatt burial mound north-west of Stuttgart. A remarkable life-sized stone statue was found here, probably originally standing on the summit of the tumulus. Pre-Roman Celtic stone statuary is rare. It seems that in later antiquity the Celts were ready to copy Roman statues, but this one is too early for that to be the explanation: it seems to be the product of a purely native Celtic inspiration. It was carved in sandstone and erected on the mound at the end of the sixth century BC. It depicts a warrior wearing a **helmet**, torc, belt, and dagger, but otherwise naked (*see* **Pfalzfeld**).

HOCHDORF

GERMANY

The country home and resting-place of an Iron Age prince who lived around 525–425 BC (late Hallstatt or early **La Tène** period). His principal seat of power was at **Hohenasperg**, nearby. The three sites—the seat of power, the country residence, and the grave—are all within 10 miles (16km) of Stuttgart on a tributary of the Neckar **River**.

The country home, locally known as Hochdorf Reps, consisted of some very big houses, up to 1,507 square feet (459 square meters), underground huts up to 25 feet (8m) long, and storage pits. All of these were surrounded by a rectangular fence. The main residence was a large, bow-sided house. Local **wheel**-turned pottery dominated the pottery assemblage, but some fragments of Greek *kylices* were found, dating to around 425 BC.

The storage pits were for storing barley, spelt wheat, and millet. Six rectangular trench granaries were identified at the residential site; at least two of them are thought to be associated with the production of barley beer.

The wagon grave at Hochdorf is one of around 100 wagon graves known from 550–500 BC in France, Switzerland, and Germany. It is a huge barrow, 200 feet (60m) in diameter and 20 feet (6m) high when first constructed. The entrance to the mound was to the north. The mound was surrounded by a ring of stones and **oak** posts. Inside the barrow was a central chamber, 15 feet (4.6m) square, made of oak beams. Laid out on a platform inside was a man's skeleton, with a large, bronze **cauldron** filled with honey mead at his feet.

Also in the chamber was a large four-wheeled wagon with harness for two **horses**. Inside the wagon was a dinner service of three serving bowls and nine bronze dishes and plates. Along the walls were nine 9-pint (5-liter) drinking horns, eight made from aurochs' horns and one of iron inlaid with strips of **gold**. The dead king—he must have been a king—was expecting to entertain eight other people

when he reached the **Otherworld**. The chamber was decorated with wall hangings and carpets. There were two further square chambers: one 24 feet (7.3m) across and the other 36 feet (11m) across.

Over the chamber roof was a layer of 50 tons (45 tonnes) of stones, and it may be that it was this layer that prevented the grave-robbers from looting the tomb.

The man in the Hochdorf grave was 40 years old and unusually tall for the period: 6 feet, 1 inch (1.85m). He wore a flat cone-shaped hat (a coolie hat) made of birch bark, decorated with circles and punched decoration. His body was swathed in colored fabric. He wore a golden necklace and golden shoes. Beside him were his toilet requisites: a comb and a razor. There were also items of hunting equipment: a small iron knife, a quiver of arrows, and a bag containing three fish-hooks.

The big, bronze cauldron, probably Greek-made, was decorated with three lions on the rim and three handles with roll attachments. It would have held up to 109 gallons (500 liters) of honey mead; traces of mead were found inside. On top of it was a small, golden cup.

The bronze hearse on which the king was resting is supported by eight female figurines cast in bronze. They are standing on wheels, so that the hearse could be rolled.

Only a highly civilized culture could have produced a kingly burial such as this.

HOD HILL

See **Maiden Castle**.

HOHENASPERG

GERMANY

A steep-sided, flat-topped mountain rising abruptly 300 feet (90m) above the surrounding hill country and above the town of Asperg. The Hohenasperg naturally lends itself to **fortification** and it has been the site of a fortress through many different periods of history. It is clearly visible from a long way off.

In 500 BC, the Hohenasperg was a fortress-refuge and a cult focus for the local Alamanni **tribe**. There are many Iron Age cemeteries in the area, and they have been located in a way that offers a line of sight to the Hohenasperg. The grave site on the Katharinenlinde near Schwieberdingen is one of these; the great chieftain's grave at Hochdorf is another. The Klein-aspergle is a burial mound that lies about half a mile (0.8km) to the south of the Hohenasperg; this offers an exceptionally good close-up view of the Hohenasperg.

The area was overrun by the Franks in about AD 500. After that the Hohenasperg was occupied by the Frankish lord and his legislative assembly. Under the Franks, the mountain was called Ascicberg: the origin of the modern name of the place, Asperg.

HÖHMICHELE BARROW

See **The Heuneberg**.

HOLZHAUSEN

BAVARIA, GERMANY

A **La Tène** ritual enclosure here contained three **ritual shafts**. One of them was 26 feet (8m) deep with a wooden stake placed at the bottom. This post was surrounded by traces of blood and flesh. The implication is that animals or

people were thrown down the shaft as sacrificial offerings. This echoes an almost identical practice at **Swanwick** in England several centuries earlier, in 1000 BC, which implies a very widespread and persistent sacrificial practice (*see* Religion: **Human Sacrifice**).

I

ICHT

The Dark Age Irish name for the English Channel.

ICTIS

ENGLAND

The island of Ictis, mentioned by Diodorus, was St. Michael's Mount in Cornwall.

J

JARLSHOF

SHETLAND

An early stone-built coastal settlement that was inhabited intermittently for a very long time, Jarlshof seems to typify the complex history of the Atlantic Celts. It began in 2000 BC as a late Neolithic village and was reoccupied in the Bronze Age, Iron Age, and later by the Vikings. It was engulfed by sand during a storm, and it was the sand that preserved the remains until modern times.

JULIAN'S BOWER

See Symbols: **Labyrinth**.

k

KEPDUF

See **Traprain Law**.

KERLESCAN

See **Carnac**.

KERLOUAN

See Myths: *The Ballad of Bran*.

KERMARIO

See **Carnac**.

KILDARE

See Religion: **Brighid**.

KLEINASPERGLE

See **Hohenasperg**.

L

LA TÈNE

SWITZERLAND

An important archeological site at the eastern end of Lake Neuchatel. The name *La Tène* means "The Shallows" and it was in the shallow **water** along the lakeshore that evidence of a distinctive middle Iron Age culture came to light. The place has given its name to the La Tène **culture**, which lasted from 450 BC until 50 BC.

The site, near the village of Marin-Epagnier, includes a sanctuary, a walkway, and two bridges: the Pont Desor and the Pont Vouga; these were first discovered when the lake levels were lowered in the 1860s. The site includes features dating from both the Hallstatt and La Tène cultural periods of the Iron Age, from about 650 to 200 BC.

Two hundred feet (60m) out into the lake, scuba-divers have found the most complete remains of a Celtic **ship**, a 60-foot (18m) single-masted cargo ship. Its shadowy shape had been spotted by aerial photography. It is a reminder that

La Tène lies on an important early trade route connecting Rhône and Rhine valleys.

La Tène was first discovered in 1857 and excavated in 1906–17, when it yielded a rich haul of objects that were of new types, including iron **swords** and everyday ironwork—even woodwork. Of the 3,000 or more objects recovered from the site, 60 percent are weapons or artifacts closely connected with weaponry (*see* People: **Warfare**). Other objects include iron tools, sickles, axes, tweezers, fishing gear, basketry, pottery, wooden bowls, and **horse** and cattle skulls—even **chariot wheels**.

The discoveries at the start of the twentieth century and the identification of the new culture sparked a new enthusiasm for archeology. The site does not seem to have been a settlement; it is likely that it was a ritual focus: a place where people came specifically to deposit offerings in the lake.

LAKE BIEL

See Religion: **Sacred Lake**.

LAKE NEUCHATEL

See **La Tène**; Religion: **Sacred Lake**.

LAKE TOLOSA

See Religion: **Sacred Lake**; Symbols: **Water**.

LEXDEN TUMULUS

ENGLAND

A large royal burial mound in Colchester, dating from about 10 BC or a little later. When it was excavated in 1924 it was found to contain the 2,000-year-old burial of a king inside a substantial timber mortuary house. He was laid out on a bed, surrounded by an array of grave goods: shoes, clothes, jars, *amphorae* of wine, **swords**, shields, and **spears**. He may have been one of the Catuvellaunian kings, **Addedomarus**, **Tasciovanus**, or even his son **Cunobelinus**.

The royal burial discovered not

long ago at Prittlewell near South-end was similar—in fact remarkably similar, considering that it dates from about AD 620. There is the same sort of timber mortuary house buried beneath a substantial barrow and accompanied by exotic items from as far afield as the Mediterranean. There is even the same sort of folding stool. At first sight, these two kings belong not merely to the same **culture**, but to the same dynasty—they might be brothers, and yet they are separated from each other by 600 years.

Addedomarus, the likely occupant of the Lexden Tumulus, was King of the **Catuvellauni**, while Saebert (who died in 616), the likely candidate for the Prittlewell Prince, was King of Essex. They are separated by what we have been conditioned to see as two major conquests—by the Romans and the Anglo-Saxons—and by culture changes, yet the evidence shows that there was a strong force for continuity embedded within Britain, and within the lands of the Atlantic Celts generally.

LIBENICE SANCTUARY

THE CZECH REPUBLIC

A third-century BC Celtic or Germanic ritual enclosure. It was laid out with a square plan, which suggests that it may have been a forerunner of the later Celtic rectangular enclosures.

LINDOW MOSS

CHESHIRE, ENGLAND

The well-preserved body of a young, red-haired man with a ginger beard was found here in waterlogged peat. He had been in his early twenties in around 300 BC when he had been poleaxed, garroted, and had his throat cut. He had not just been killed, but killed three times over—the Celtic magic number—and this indicates a ritual killing (*see* Symbols: **Rule of Three**). Apart from a band of fox-fur around his left arm, he was naked, which also implies ritual.

Investigation revealed that his killers first hit him twice over the **head** with ax blows that stunned but did not kill him. Then they carefully tied a cord tightly around his neck, knotted it, and neatly cut off the cord ends from each side of the **knot**. Then they pushed a stick under the cord and twisted it like a tourniquet, garroting him until his neck broke. Then they cut his throat, opening his jugular vein. After the killing, the young man's naked body was put face-down in a crouched position in the bog.

His condition is intriguing. He was well-built, 5 feet, 6 inches (1.68m) tall. He had a full head of hair, grown to medium length, and a short beard. He had well-manicured fingernails, showing that he was not a laborer. His moustache was neatly clipped. Archeologists think he was an aristocrat or a **Druid**. He had eaten a griddle cake shortly before his death. This was a carefully prepared, carefully executed killing, with the character of a sacrifice rather than a normal murder. Lindow Man is one of the most evocative examples of **human sacrifice** to have been found in Britain.

A poorly preserved human head was found in a peat bog in Lancashire in 1958. This has recently been re-examined by computer tomography, and its owner, Worsley Man, was murdered, executed, or sacrificed in the same way as Lindow Man. Worsley Man met his end between AD 70 and AD 400, in other words during the Roman occupation of Britain. It is a reminder that Celtic practices went on "under the Romans," just as they had before.

Irish folk-tales often contain the motif of the Threefold Death, where a human being suffers three different deaths. In one legend, a king is wounded, the house inside which he is trapped burns down around him, and he finally drowns in a vat of liquor as he attempts to escape from the flames. What happened to Lindow Man is that a Threefold Death was planned and carried out deliberately, perhaps to make some prophecy come true.

LINTON

See Symbols: **Dragon**.

LISCANNOR

See Religion: **Brighid**.

LLANGADWALADR STONE

See People: **Cadfan**.

LLANTWIT FAWR

See People: **Illtud**.

LLYN CERRIG BACH

See Religion: **Sacred Lake**.

LLYN FAWR

See Religion: **Sacred Lake**.

LLYN YR AFANC

See Symbols: **Dragon**.

LOCMARIAQUER

BRITTANY, FRANCE

There are several major ancient stone monuments here. The most spectacular is the Grand Menhir Brisé, "The Great Broken Standing Stone." This lies on the ground, broken into five large pieces and apparently felled by a lightning strike in antiquity, though Aubrey Burl thinks it was broken before it could be raised. Dragging it to this spot from the quarry 3 miles (5km) away in about 1700 BC was in itself a huge undertaking. When (and if) standing intact, this 256 ton (232 tonne) monster would have stood at least 80 feet (24m) high.

There is also a fine Neolithic tomb nearby, the Table des Marchands, and another, the Dolmen des Pierres Plats, which is full of decorated stones.

LOUGH NEAGH

See Myths: *The Legend of Ys*.

LYDNEY, SANCTUARY OF NODENS

ENGLAND

Nodens was a British **healing god** who, like Lenus, was equated by the Romans with their god **Mars**. He had an imposing sanctuary at Lydney in Gloucestershire, on high ground overlooking the Severn **River**. It comprised a substantial hostel, baths, and a long building that has been interpreted as an *abaton*: a dormitory for the pilgrims' sacred curative sleep.

Lydney was a wealthy sanctuary, fitted with mosaics, and it was probably built fairly late, toward the end of the third century AD, and renovated a few decades later. The dedications are to Nodens on his own, or Nodens with Mars, or Nodens with **Silvanus**.

Nobody knows what Nodens looked like, because there are no surviving images of him. The cult objects include a number of **dog** figurines, and dogs are often associated with healing; their saliva is thought to heal wounds. Other objects include a votive offering of a model arm.

Some of the imagery at Lydney suggests a marine theme. There is a diadem showing the **sun** god driving a four-horse **chariot** with tritons and anchors; a relief shows a sea god. Maybe the sea connection at Lydney is the Severn bore, which might have been observed from there.

The association of Nodens with Silvanus is hard to explain. Silva-
nus was a hunting god, and dogs were used for hunting; perhaps it is the dogs that connect the two. But Lydney is a strange jumble of images and it may be unwise to look for too many connections.

Among other finds was a seated **mother goddess** carrying horns of plenty—a fertility image (*see* **Cornucopia**).

LYMINSTER

See Symbols: **Dragon**.

LYONESSE

See Symbols: **City Swallowed Up by the Sea**.

LYONS

See Religion: **Lugh, Lughnasad**.

MAGDALENENBURG

GERMANY

A royal Celtic tomb near Villingen-Schwenningen in the Black Forest. A recent re-evaluation in Mainz of old excavation plans of the central royal tomb and the burials around it has led to a new discovery: the layout corresponds with the arrangement of the stars in the northern sky. The approach is similar to the proposition that the layout of the three pyramids at Gizeh represents the stars of Orion's belt.

The burial mound at Magdalenenberg is more than 330 feet (100m) in diameter. The builders positioned long rows of wooden posts on the site of the mound in order to locate the lunar standstill, the northernmost position on the horizon where the moon rises. The standstill is reached every 18.6 years and it marks the completion of a lunar cycle. It is thought that it might have been a key landmark in the Celtic calendar. The northernmost moonrise was certainly of interest to the builders of **Stonehenge**. In about 3000 BC they put up a post each year on the entrance causeway to mark the northernmost position of the moonrise. After observing for more than a century, they had enough data to work out the cyclical pattern, be certain of it, and be confident about predicting it too.

The Magdalenenburg constellation map—if that is what it really is—suggests to Dr. Allard Mees a date of 618 BC. **Julius Caesar** commented about the Celts using a moon-based calendar (the Romans based their calendar on the **sun**). Now there seems to be a little archeological evidence for the Celtic emphasis on the moon.

MAIDEN CASTLE

DORSET

A huge hillfort with soaring earth ramparts enclosing an area of 47 acres (19 hectares). Maiden Castle was the central place of the **Durotriges tribe**. The Durotriges were probably ruled by 10 or 20 petty chiefs, each commanding a *pagus*, or district. They used up a great deal of energy in internal disputes and power struggles, and possibly fending off raids by **Atrebates** or **Catuvellauni** tribesmen. Although they were resolute and bold, they were not organized to defend themselves against Rome. The easy progress of Vespasian's conquering army through Wessex shows that in AD 43 Durotrigian power was decentralized and uncoordinated.

Several centuries before, the Durotrigian heartland had been dominated by six huge hillforts, each with several ramparts: Maiden Castle, Eggardon Hill, Ham Hill, **South Cadbury Castle**, Hod Hill, and Badbury Rings. Tribal territories spread out from these power centers, which were roughly equidistant from each other. By 100 BC, the three biggest hillforts— Hod Hill, Cadbury, and Maiden Castle—had emerged as the most powerful, vying with each other for supremacy; this can be seen in the increasing elaboration of their showy defenses. They evolved into towns, and Maiden Castle was the most important of them. It emerged as the capital, with rows of round, thatched houses ranged along streets (*see* People: **Dwellings**).

The site began as a Neolithic enclosure on the eastern summit in 3700 BC and was turned into an unusual monument, a huge bank barrow, in 3200 BC. In the Bronze Age a small henge was laid out at what would be the center of the Iron Age hillfort. In 350 BC a small hillfort was laid out on the site of the Neolithic enclosure. In 200 BC a much larger hillfort was created by extending the single rampart westward to encompass the western summit. A hundred years later this was elaborated with extra ramparts.

After the Durotriges' resistance to the Romans was crushed, the site was abandoned. In about AD 70 the Romans built an open settlement, Durnovaria, on low ground to the north; this has become Dorset's county town, Dorchester.

Toward the end of the Roman occupation in AD 367, a rectangular temple 20 feet (6m) by 16 feet (5m) was built inside Maiden Castle. It seems to have been a purely Celtic impulse; it in effect replaced a much older round temple that had stood just 40 feet (12m) away 600 years before. An old, native British holy place was being commemorated and revived, just as the Romans were leaving; the old order was being restored. In fact, after the Romans left, another round shrine was built exactly on the site of the original Durotrigian shrine—a clear statement that people were conscientiously going back to the beliefs and customs of the pre-Roman age.

What we see at Maiden Castle is a reminder that who and what the British, French, and Spanish are today is not exclusively or even mainly to be attributed to the Romans. A standard version of school history is that everything started with the Romans, but modern archeology is showing something quite different. First, we can see that there was a relatively flexible Roman incursion into the Celtic world, one that was ready to tolerate, learn from, and incorporate Celtic customs and beliefs. Second, we see that the way people did things after the Romans had gone was in many ways the same as they had been before they arrived. As Francis Pryor comments, "It was said that the Romans gave us roads, language, laws and civilization. All this is false. The Romans invented all this barbarian nonsense."

MARYPORT

CUMBRIA, ENGLAND

A Romano-British port on the north-west coast of Cumbria. The Romans set up a fort there, named Alauna, in AD 122. This was to act as a command and supply base for the coastal defense of the eastern end of Hadrian's Wall. The idea was to stop **people** from going around the western end of Hadrian's Wall by crossing the Solway Firth.

There was a large Roman town around the fort, but after the Romans left the settlement dwindled away.

Several important Romano-Celtic religious cult objects have been found at Maryport. Along Hadrian's Wall, carved stone **altars** were set up with various military dedications. One is from a Spanish auxiliary cohort that was stationed at Maryport. These altars are of special interest because they are evidently of Roman design, yet they incorporate Celtic symbols. One, for example, has the solar **wheel** motif, which is a native Celtic symbol.

Perhaps the most remarkable religious object found at Maryport is the phallic symbol that

The Element Encyclopedia of the Celts

incorporates a human face (*see* Symbols: **Phallus**).

MENEC

See **Carnac**.

THE MIZMAZE

See Symbols: **Labyrinth**.

MONASTERBOICE

See Symbols: **Celtic Cross**.

LE MONT SACON

PYRENEES, FRANCE

A Romano-Celtic sanctuary on a mountain, Mont Sacon, 5,000 feet (1,540m) high in the French Pyrenees. The site was excavated in 1956, when the sanctuary, probably dedicated to the **god** Jupiter, was discovered.

Mont Sacon dominates the area and it is surrounded by legends and fables. It has the reputation of being a strange mountain, with caves and crevices offering access to the Underworld.

The sanctuary was destroyed after the arrival of Christianity in the area.

N

NAVAN FORT

See **Emain Macha**.

NEWGRANGE

IRELAND

One of a cluster of Neolithic passage graves in the Boyne Valley in eastern Ireland. Newgrange is the largest of them. It consists of a huge round mound 36 feet (11m) high and 295 feet (90m) across, its edge marked by a kerb of large, roughly worked boulders laid end to end. A fantastically decorated slab on the south-eastern side is the blocking stone of the entrance passage, made of upright slabs supporting a slab roof. The passage leads to a central chamber with small burial chambers leading off it.

In the Neolithic, the bodies of the dead were allowed to decompose in mortuary enclosures, then, after an interval, the bones were gathered and put into the tomb.

A special feature of Newgrange is the roof box, a specially made "letter box" above the tomb's entrance. Even when the doorway was filled with blocking stones, as it usually would have been, light would have been able to penetrate into the tomb's interior through the roof box. The alignment of the whole monument was carefully designed before it was built so that the first rays of the rising **sun** on the **winter solstice** would pass through the roof box all the way to the heart of the tomb. This was an extraordinary piece of architectural engineering, and it also shows how important the passage of the seasons must have been in the minds of the **people** who carried it out. The middle of winter is the low point of the year, in a sense the death of the year, and the tomb-builders made the life-giving, life-renewing sun shine briefly into the tomb at just that moment, to re-awaken the land and start the new year. Perhaps also the hope was that this **magic** would reawaken the dead and launch them into their new lives.

THE PAPS OF ANU

IRELAND

Two smoothly rounded hills side by side in County Kerry. The ancient Celts thought they looked like a woman's breasts, and so they named them Da Chich Anann, "The Paps of Anu." They are still known in English as "The Paps." The goddess Anu, or Danu, was the mother of the gods (*see* Religion: **Mother Goddess**).

PEMBROKESHIRE

See **Dyfed**.

PFALZFELD

GERMANY

A rare and very elaborate piece of stone carving dating from the fifth century BC, now in the Rheinisches Landesmuseum in Bonn, this peculiar-looking object is described as a pillar. It stands on a hemispherical base and consists of a highly decorated, four-sided, tapering column, the top of which has broken off. The edges of the column are decorated with a rope motif. The central pear-shaped elements on each side have faces crudely carved on them, surrounded by pear-shaped and "s"-shaped motifs that may be symbolic. The pear-shaped elements are likely to be representations of the strange headdress worn by another German figure,

the sandstone statue at **Glauberg**.

The pillar originally had a fifth **head** on the top, but this was broken off in the seventeenth century. The heads probably represent **gods**, but what the image means, and what the pillar as a whole was for, are uncertain. The very high quality of the carving shows that it was a focal feature of some kind—probably an idol.

POWYS

ENGLAND; WALES

A powerful Dark Age kingdom that included central and eastern Wales and the Severn Valley.

PRETANIKÉ

BRITAIN

Pytheas of Massilia (Marseille) sailed north to Britain in the fourth century BC, noting the names of some of the places. Pretaniké, or the Pretanic Islands, was the name of the isles generally. Ierne was Ireland; Nesos Albionon, or Albion, was the island of Britain. Ierne became the Latin Hibernia, and Albionon became the Latin Albionum.

Pretaniké, which became the Latin Britannia, is related to the Welsh word Prydain (Britain), which is linked with a word meaning "painted." Perhaps the original Celtic name for these islands meant something like "Islands of the Painted People," a reference to the widespread practice of tattooing.

PRITTLEWELL

See **Lexden Tumulus**.

R

RAHALLY

IRELAND

A large hillfort near **Tara**. About 90 hillforts are known in Ireland, but only a few of them have been excavated. Rahally is marked out by a series of four concentric circular ditches. **Maiden Castle** has multiple enclosing banks and ditches, but they are bunched at the outer perimeter. Rahally has its bounding ditches spaced out, like the zones of an archery target—in fact very like the arrangement of ditches of the much older Neolithic enclosures.

The small-diameter inner ditches were dug in 900 BC. The outermost boundary, a double ditch, 1,480 feet (450m) in diameter, was laid out 200 years later.

What was initially an exciting discovery that promised to reveal a great deal about Ireland's Iron Age past proved disappointing. The site was almost empty of archeology.

RHEGED

ENGLAND

A Dark Age Celtic kingdom in north-east England, comprising Cumbria and Lancashire. The capital was Carlisle and the most famous king was **Urien**. It was later divided into two kingdoms: North Rheged (Cumbria) and South Rheged (Lancashire).

ROQUEPERTUSE

FRANCE

This cliff sanctuary is located not far from **Entremont**. The shrine has at its entrance three stone pillars that form a portal. The three columns have niches cut into them, containing human skulls dating from the third century BC. They are the skulls of strong young men in their prime, evidently warriors.

A great crossbeam over the portal carried a stone bird. Among the other objects found at this temple were squatting warriors, one bearing a torc, and a Janus **head** held in the beak of an enormous bird. Most of the sculptures at Roquepertuse (and those at Entremont too) were carved in the fourth, third, and second centuries BC.

S

SAINTE-SABINE SANCTUARY

DORDOGNE, FRANCE

A **healing** sanctuary in south-west France dedicated to either the Celtic **god** Atepomarus or the Romano-Celtic god Apollo Atepomarus.

SANDBERG

AUSTRIA

A newly discovered Celtic town in Lower Austria, about 40 miles (64km) north of Vienna, Sandberg may prove to be one of the most important **La Tène** period sites so far excavated. This was not a fortified settlement, yet it was large and powerful (*see* **Fortifications**).

The roughly east–west ridge called the Sandberg is in open, fertile farmland between the villages of Platt and Roseldorf. The Iron Age town lay on its warmer southern and south-facing slope.

The **people** who built and inhabited Sandberg were probably the Boii.

Celtic **coins** were known from the site in the nineteenth century, but the true significance of the area emerged only in the 1990s. Geophysical surveys revealed at least 450 subterranean box structures that are likely to be the remains of timber houses. The settlement extended across at least 258,000 square yards (236,000 square meters) and possibly twice that.

Excavation reveals a barn, a bakery, some houses, and equipment for minting coins. Three rectangular Celtic sanctuaries were opened up, revealing a similar design to the cult center at **Gournay** in northern France. In two of the sanctuary structures, the surrounding ditches contained large amounts of bones, of both animals and people, which looks like evidence of animal and **human sacrifice**.

SHEPHERD'S RACE

See Symbols: **Labyrinth**.

SOMMERÉCOURT

See Religion: **Cernunnos**.

SOURCE DE LA SEINE

DIJON, FRANCE

This, the Sanctuary of Sequana, was one of the most important sanctuaries in Gaul, at the source of the Seine **River**. Its Roman name was Fontes Sequanae, "The Springs of Sequana." Probably this site was visited as a sacred spot for hundreds of years before the Romans arrived, but during the Roman period it was developed on a grand scale. There was an extensive religious complex with a focus on a pool by a **spring**. The cluster of buildings included two temples and a colonnaded precinct.

This major sanctuary was presided over by the **goddess** Sequana, who was portrayed in a bronze figurine as a goddess standing in a duck-prowed boat. Her arms are outstretched in a gesture of welcome.

Among and beneath the Romano-Celtic remains there are the remains of the older Celtic sanctuary. These were discovered in the 1960s when the Roman period buildings were excavated. The Iron Age sanctuary was found in a waterlogged layer, which helped to preserve the almost 200 wooden votive offerings. These offerings included models carved in **oak** or beechwood of various body parts: arms, legs, **heads**, and internal organs. They show that the sanctuary was a **healing** sanctuary and they also show the sorts of ailments people suffered from: arthritis, blindness, goitres, hernias, milk deficiency, and infertility or impotence. In the first century BC, pilgrims journeyed to the healing spring at the source of the Seine to leave models of their physical problems.

Many of the models showing the complete figure are crudely carved, but the head is more carefully depicted. This may be because it was considered important for Sequana to recognize the person she was going to cure, or it may be a by-product of the need to carve the eyes in a way that made it clear that they were closed; many of the

pilgrims were blind or partially sighted.

The late Iron Age votives were distinctly Celtic in character and seem to represent a population that was rather poor.

By the Roman period, the "visitor experience" was more organized, more lavish, and may have catered for people coming from a larger area. In the first century AD, when the buildings were erected, there was an organized healing ceremony, followed by sleep in dormitories to wait for the cure to take effect. It may well be that the colonnaded precinct was designed as a dormitory.

SOURCE DES ROCHES DE CHAMALIÈRES

NEAR CLERMONT FERRAND, FRANCE

This **spring** was the site of a similar **healing** sanctuary to the one at the **source of the Seine**. Here more than 2,000 wooden votive offerings were found in a deposit 3 feet (1m) deep, close to two small natural springs of mineral **water**. **Coins** have been found there, and they suggest that the site was in operation for quite a short time, perhaps 100 years, from the time of **Julius Caesar**'s conquest. So the sanctuary was in use at the same time as the Sanctuary of Sequana (see **Source de la Seine**): first century BC to first century AD.

Here there seem to have been no buildings, just a sacred pool with an enclosing wall on the floor of a marshy valley.

SOUTH CADBURY CASTLE

ENGLAND

A very imposing Iron Age fort on the summit plateau of a free-standing hill. The ancient **fortifications** are mostly tree-covered now, but the four earth ramparts are still impressive. Although often described as an Iron Age fort, Cadbury began earlier, in the Bronze Age. In the Iron Age it became a major focus for the **Durotriges tribe**. During the Roman occupation, the Britons were forcibly removed after a revolt in AD 61, and the site returned to agriculture.

The site was reoccupied in the fifth–sixth centuries, when the advance of Saxon settlers prompted local Britons to use it as a refuge again. **Ambrosius Aurelianus** lived at the right time to organize the refortification of Cadbury in around 470. Buildings were added, including a substantial Dark Age hall. The strategic position of Cadbury near the eastern frontier of **Dumnonia** and its huge area make it a likely muster-point for warriors assembling to do battle with the Saxons in the period 500–70.

The history of this magnificent hillfort is long and complicated, but it was a center of Celtic resistance to invaders at least three times: in the rebellion against Rome in 61, in the **Badon** campaign against the Saxons in 500–20, and in the Dyrham campaign in the years around 570.

In 1532, John Leland visited the site, observing:

At South Cadbyri standith Camallate, sumtyme a famose toun or castelle, apon a very torre or hill, wunderfully enstrengthenid of nature... The people can tell nothing ther but they have heard say that Arture much resorted to Camalat.

STAR CARR

See Religion: **Horned God**.

STONEHENGE

ENGLAND

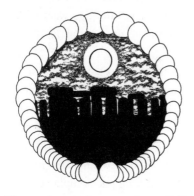

The stone circles stood on Salisbury Plain throughout the long evolution of the Celtic **culture** in Britain. The earth circle was raised in 3000 BC, and the stone circles about 500 years later.

The monument was constantly revisited and reshaped in antiquity, according to shifting beliefs. It was assumed in the eighteenth and nineteenth centuries that it had been a focus of worship by the **Druids**. It looks as if both Stonehenge and the Druids have been somehow amplified, explained, and authenticated by being thrown together by eighteenth and nine-

teenth-century antiquarians. A wonderful fantasy image was published in 1815, showing *The Festival of the Britons at Stonehenge*; hundreds of people form orderly and colorful processions round the monument, while cattle are assembled within for sacrifice. There is no archeological support for any of this, but it is possible that the real Druids of the first centuries BC and AD claimed that they were the legatees of Stonehenge, that their predecessors had built it; this sort of political lie is how power is acquired. A similar story could be told about many of the other megalithic monuments that were built in the lands of the Atlantic Celts.

At the start of the twentieth century, a reformed Druidical order decided to "take back" Stonehenge. By the 1960s, Professor Stuart Piggott was writing about "elements of increasing fantasy, as the Druids, now standing charismatically within the Stonehenge horseshoe, became a compelling magnet for many a psychological misfit and lonely crank."

STRETTWEG

See Symbols: **Wheel**.

T

SWANWICK SHAFT

HAMPSHIRE, ENGLAND

A shaft dug down into the chalk in the Bronze Age and used for ritual offerings. At the bottom was a stake packed round with clay and surrounded by offerings of flesh and blood.

Nothing quite like this sacrificial shaft has been found from the Iron Age in Britain, but the Swanwick shaft is very similar to the Iron Age shaft at **Holzhausen** in Bavaria: even the dimensions of the two shafts are similar. The two sites looked at together suggest a practice of animal (and perhaps human) sacrifice that persisted through many centuries and across a wide area of Europe (*see* Religion: **Human Sacrifice**).

TARA

MEATH, IRELAND

The Hill of Tara, a great ceremonial center in the middle of Ireland, was the seat of the High Kings of Ireland. It is a conspicuous mile-long ridge covered in more than 60 monuments of different periods. The Irish **people**—let us call them Celts—carried out major ceremonies here over a very long period, from the middle of the Neolithic, around 3500 BC, to about AD 450.

The Feast of Tara was a major event of uncertain nature. There are two views about it. One is that it may have been an annual or less frequent event at which rather mundane political issues were settled; the other is that major pagan ceremonies took place. As far as the historical record goes, the Irish Annals only record it in relation to three kings in the sixth century.

The pagan ceremony view holds that on certain ceremonial occasions at Tara, the High King became a **god**. It was common in archaic societies for **priests**, priestesses, kings, or queens to become gods or goddesses, at least for the duration of a religious ceremony. This epiphany (appearance of the god) would have been a major event for the assembled **tribe**. In this case, the High King became **the Daghda**. In that role, he had sex with a maiden who, in her turn, was an epiphany of the goddess of the Boyne **River**, Boann. This public copulation was an enactment of the fertilization of the tribal territory— the High King had become the god of Ireland and the Irish, and he was ensuring the fertility of his island and the prosperity of his people. Specifically, the ceremony was supposed to ensure the survival of viable seed until the following season.

The political conference view points to the surviving documentation, which suggests rather dull events. In 660, an "assembly to regulate the laws and customs of the country" was held. There is nothing in the documents to suggest that the Christian community of the time disliked the Feast of Tara because of any pagan associations. But the political nature of the feast may have involved hostages. Diarmait's fateful execution of the King of Connacht's hostage son

appears to have taken place during the Feast of Tara.

Tara is one of a handful of prestigious royal sites in Ireland. It is central to Ireland's ancient identity, as relatively little has survived from the Irish Iron Age: some metalwork, an oral tradition of epic sagas, and these few royal centers. These remains show how a small elite group lived, but the great mass of Iron Age Irish people remain invisible. They existed, but we cannot see them.

TECH DUINN

See Religion: **Donn**.

THETFORD

NORFOLK, ENGLAND

This was the site of a settlement and major religious center of the **Iceni**. Some think it may have been the site of the residence of **Boudicca**, the Iceni queen. (The tribal capital or *oppidum* of the Iceni was at Caistor St. Edmund, a site renamed Venta Icenorum by the Romans.)

A substantial late Celtic complex was built at Thetford. The site consisted of three large, round structures 100 feet (30m) in diameter, the center of which was approached by a ceremonial avenue. This layout has a marked similarity to that of much earlier Neolithic ceremonial monuments in timber or stone. One of the round structures was two stories high and seems to have been large roundhouse.

There was an elaborate array of timber enclosures around the sacred enclosure, including seven rows of close-set palisades laid out in straight lines. What these were for it is not certain, but it is possible that they were designed to stop people outside from seeing in. All of the site's timbers were stripped out by the Romans following the revolt of Boudicca against Rome in AD 60.

This elaborately laid-out precinct may be a Celtic temple. Alternatively, it may have been the palace of Boudicca. The archeologists are uncertain.

A Roman temple dedicated to Faunus the woodland **god** was built close by. Faunus had no particular British equivalent, but perhaps the Iceni worshiped a woodland spirit before the Roman invasion. Maybe the arrays of posts represented a **sacred grove**, which

might be a relatively small number of trees; the sacred grove at classical Nemea, for example, had only about a dozen trees. The Thetford sacred grove consisted of nine rows of **oak** posts, and it is believed that their branches may have been left on.

THREE PERPETUAL CHOIRS

See **Avalon**.

TINTAGEL

CORNWALL

A fake medieval castle on the island of Tintagel misled archeologists for a long time into thinking that this could not possibly have been the site of King **Arthur**'s castle. But legend is insistent that Tintagel is where Arthur was born.

Geoffrey of Monmouth visited Tintagel between 1120 and 1130, and he viewed it as an Arthurian site—before the medieval castle we now see on the site was built by Richard, Earl of Cornwall. The idea of the site as a castle must therefore have come to Geoffrey from some literary or oral source. He describes "the town of Tintagel, a place of great safety," but when he visited it there were no structures to see at all. The small, rectangular huts that existed there in the sixth century would not have been visible in the twelfth century.

Excavation in the 1930s seemed to show lots of small houses and huts, and they were interpreted as a monastic settlement. Now they have been reinterpreted as a seasonal settlement for a band of warriors. The presence of very high-status pottery shows that it was a royal focus.

Tintagel was the place where a king of **Dumnonia** came for his coronation and on the highest point of Tintagel Island there is a slab of bedrock with a footprint carved into it.

When you stand with your left foot in the footprint, you face the shallow saddle crossing the island, where the war-band's bivouac tents were clustered. Turning through 180 degrees, you find yourself looking just a church-length to the east of Tintagel church. To either side, several miles of the north Cornish coast can be seen. It is easy to imagine an induction ceremony here,

in which a new king planted his foot symbolically into the living rock of his dead father's kingdom, made gestures of command, and uttered an oath of service to the whole of Tricurium—the small local kingdom that was in view from that place. We can imagine the warriors of the war-band standing on the lower ground among the flapping tent-skins of their bivouac, watching awe-struck as the heir silhouetted against the southern sky by the **sun** became their king.

King Arthur's Footprint, as it was already known in the nineteenth century, is not an isolated feature. An even more sharply defined, carved footprint, of almost exactly the same length, was cut in the bedrock on a knoll at **Dunadd**, the royal stronghold of the kings of Dal Riada. It too was probably used for the inauguration of Celtic kings. So, Tintagel may not have been the place where Arthur was born, but it was probably the place where he became king.

The Element Encyclopedia of the Celts

TISSINGTON

See Religion: **Holy Wells**.

TRAPRAIN LAW

SCOTLAND

A hog's back hill between Edinburgh and Dunbar. In the early sixth century, this was the fortress home of **Leudonus** of the Lothians, father of **Thyony**, mother of St. **Kentigern**. Though now called Traprain Law, the place was called Dunpelder in the old British language and Kepduf in Gaelic. The fortifications enclose 32 acres (13 hectares). Inside were many roundhouses, partly built of stone (*see* **Dwellings**).

Many Roman **coins** of the first to fifth century have been found on the site, showing that the British ruler here was in treaty relations with Rome—a client-king. There was a marked intensification of this relationship in the fourth century AD.

Traprain Law is one of two big fortified centers north of Hadrian's Wall, located in northern Votadini territory; it matches **Yeavering Bell**, near Wooler, which was built in the lands of the southern Votadini.

Traprain Law was the residence of Paternus Pesrut, who was appointed by Valentinian I. A rich silver **treasure** hoard was hidden here in the fifth century, right at the end of the Roman occupation.

The fortress remained a Celtic royal center through the Dark Ages; in fact until the English colonized the area.

TRESQUES

See Religion: **Altar**.

TRIER

GERMANY

In the Romano-Celtic period, Trier boasted the most important cult center related to **Mars** the healer, here called Lenus-Mars. This Celtic **god** was worshiped principally by the Treveri **tribe**, who lived in the Moselle Valley, but he did appear at other places, such as Chedworth in Gloucestershire and Caerwent. He was worshiped in the countryside in the territory of the Treveri and also in their tribal capital.

The sanctuary of Lenus-Mars stood in a small, steep-sided, and wooded valley on the bank of the Moselle, opposite the Roman city of Trier. As with other Romanized religious sites, there was a sanctuary here in the Iron Age. Traces of an earlier sacred enclosure have been found that pre-date the second-century temple. This temple was a massive structure, classical in style, with a large **altar** and what may have been a theater for sacred drama. There was a **spring** above the sanctuary, and **water** from this was brought by an artificial channel to fill a small series of baths. This water had an enduring reputation as **healing** water.

Inscriptions show that there were important **priests** at the sanctuary, and pilgrims left many offerings there in the hope of being cured. Sometimes Lenus was worshiped under the name Iovantucarus and was required to give special protection to children, and many of the cult objects at the site show images of children, frequently bringing the god **gifts** of birds. Images of **hooded dwarves** also appear, along with figurines of deities other than Lenus.

Perhaps the sacred water had magical healing qualities; perhaps the power of faith was great enough to heal. Either way, some were cured at the Lenus-Mars sanctuary. An inscription thanks the god for curing a terrible illness (*see* **Ancamna**; Religion: **Ritona, Shrines and Temples**).

TURF MAZE

See Symbols: **Labyrinth**.

TUROE STONE

COUNTY GALWAY, IRELAND

A carved granite block standing 4 feet (1.2m) high that has been shaped into an approximate hemisphere and covered with asymmetrical, decorative, curving shapes. It was evidently a cult stone of some kind. Its half-egg shape, i.e. not quite a true hemisphere, is unusual. It is unlike anything in earlier or later times. But it is, curiously, remarkably similar to the *omphalos*, or navel, stones that were created in Iron Age Greece at about the same time.

The Greek *omphalos* stones were symbols of the physical and spiritual center of the world. The most famous is the one at the cult center of Delphi. The Greeks thought this particular *omphalos* was the channel of communication among three worlds—the worlds of living mortals, the gods, and the dead.

The idea of an Earth navel is similar to the north European idea of the world **ash tree**, which similarly joins the three realms.

U

UFFINGTON WHITE HORSE

ENGLAND

Right across southern Britain there was a preference for depicting the **war god** on horseback, so this image of the steed, at Uffington, may stand in for him. It is the same iconographic shorthand as the images of the cross seen in churches; sometimes it is shown bare, sometimes it is shown with all the paraphernalia associated with the Crucifixion—ladder, nails, **spear**, and sponge—and only Jesus himself is missing. It has even been suggested that originally the Uffington **horse** had a rider, but no archeological evidence for this has been produced.

Stuart Piggott pointed to a strong similarity between the strongly simplified, exploded design of the Uffington Horse and the design on many Iron Age **coins**. This led him to propose that the hill figure was made at the same time as the coins, perhaps a century or two before the Roman conquest. Piggott got this idea from an unlikely source: Anna Fairchild, who was the daughter of the great antiquarian William Stukeley. Anna visited White Horse Hill in 1758 and wrote to her father: "The figure of the horse on the side of the hill is poorly drawn, though of immense bulk but very much in the scheme of the British horses on the reverse of their coins."

The date extracted from the lowest layers of silt on the horse's outline show that the horse was made perhaps as much as 500 years earlier than the coins. Could it be that the coins were based on an already well-established British landmark?

The images are so similar that a connection seems probable.

In 1929 O. G. S. Crawford suggested that the White Horse was the tribal emblem of the Iron Age **people** who created and occupied Uffington Castle, the large prehistoric enclosure on the crest of the chalk hills immediately to the south of the horse. The same connection has been made by David Miles, who excavated parts of the horse in the 1990s and achieved the OSL date of about 700 BC.

The horse may represent the horse goddess **Epona**, or **Rhiannon**.

UISNECH

See Religion: **Druids**.

ULEY

See Religion: **Shrines and Temples**.

VAL CAMONICA

NORTHERN ITALY

One of the largest and most remarkable collections of rock carvings in the world. About 140,000 images and symbols have been officially recognized, but new discoveries take the total of known carvings to around 250,000. The carvings here span a very long period—the Mesolithic, Neolithic, Bronze Age, and Iron Age.

The carvings from the Iron Age were made by the Camunni **tribe**, and they came at the very end of a tradition that had lasted for 8,000 years. Their carvings dominate, accounting for 80 percent of the total. They heavily feature the **stag god**, who was a symbol of strength and potency. The images focus on ideals of heroic masculinity and superiority. There are images of duels, with human figures flaunting their weapons, their muscles, and even their genitals. Some of this is reminiscent of the world of the heroic world of Homer.

There are also figures of cabins, **labyrinths**, and footprints; the

The Element Encyclopedia of the Celts

meaning of which is unclear.

There are death scenes that show four-wheeled wagons carrying funerary urns, accompanied by processions of worshipers or mourners.

The practice of rock carving evidently ceased during the period of the Roman occupation: a vivid illustration of the negative impact the Romans had on some local cultures (*see* Symbols: **Labyrinth**).

VENDEUIL–CAPLY

See **Gournay**.

VIROCONIUM

ENGLAND

The powerful kingdom of **Powys** had its capital at Viroconium (Wroxeter). The visible ruins represent only a small part of the Roman town. When the great British king **Vortigern** made this his capital, much of the Roman town was still standing. There was substantial rebuilding, with stone structures being replaced in timber. These post-Roman timber buildings were large, elaborate, and classical in design.

The abandoned Roman town was revitalized in a way that did not happen at any other British site.

The central building was a massive winged structure raised on the site of the Roman basilica, and this was probably Vortigern's palace. Unfortunately its remains have been cleared to expose the Roman ruins—a reflection of the excavators' cultural values. Nothing of the palace can now be seen on the site.

By 520, Vortigern's dynasty was no longer in power and Viroconium fell out of intensive use. As the Saxons approached from the east, the chief and his family and war-band withdrew to the safety of the ancient hillfort on the Wrekin just to the south-east of the town.

W

WALCHEREN

ZEELAND, THE NETHERLANDS

The Romano-Celtic goddess **Nehalennia** was worshiped intensively in the Dutch province of Zeeland; more than 160 votive **altars** have been found in this province. They all date from the second and early third centuries AD (*see* Religion: **Nehalennia**).

The Dutch altars were found at two particular locations and times. One batch, consisting of 122 altars, was found in the 1970s in the estuary north of **Colijnsplaat**, known in Roman times as Ganuenta. The other batch was found near Domburg on the island of Walcheren in 1647. Unfortunately, all but three of the Domburg altars were destroyed in a fire in 1848. These were dredged from the sea in the seventeenth century, and it is assumed that the site of a temple to Nehalennia has been eroded away by the sea.

The two Nehalennia temples were offered the votive altars, presumably accompanied by a donation, by captains and merchants grateful for a safe sea-crossing. During a storm, or perhaps before a voyage was undertaken, the **goddess** was invoked. The travelers promised her a votive altar provided she saved their lives. After their safe passage, the seafarers bought an expensive piece of imported stone and ordered a mason to sculpt and inscribe it.

It is a little surprising that the inscriptions are in Latin, as the native population spoke a Celtic **language** that had become Germanized. Perhaps these were upwardly mobile, self-improving indigenous **people** who had made an effort to learn Latin; perhaps they were not really Latin speakers, but wanted to impress by using Latin.

The cult of Nehalennia came to an end on Walcheren in the second century AD, when—with perfect irony—the sea destroyed her temple.

WANSDYKE

Two massive earthworks (ditches with banks) built to mark the north-eastern frontier of the Dark Age Celtic kingdom of **Dumnonia** and defend it against marauding Saxons. West Wansdyke runs for more than 7 miles (11km), overlooking the valley of the Bristol Avon, from the Horsecombe Valley south of **Bath** as far as Maes Knoll, where it overlooks Bristol. East Wansdyke runs for 12 miles (19km) from a point north of Devizes to Savernake near Marlborough. Several further short sections of dyke continue eastward. Gaps or breaks in the Wansdyke may have been defended by natural barriers such as dense forests.

The dyke was definitely built in the post-Roman period and it was all built as one single project: not so much as a defensive wall, more as a line of communication along a frontier, enabling a small, mobile force to move quickly and easily along it, marking an enemy in order to tackle him as he attempted to cross into Dumnonia. Saxon colonists could not have crossed into Dumnonia unwittingly, or without being challenged.

If we want to associate this project with a particular Celtic leader, it would most likely be **Ambrosius Aurelianus**.

WHITHORN

SCOTLAND

The Welsh Triads list Three Perpetual Choirs: religious houses where services were chanted or sung continuously. The third and holiest was the Cor of Bangor Wydryn at Ynys Afallach. This corresponds to Whithorn. The word *Wydryn* became Anglicized in the seventh century into the Old English *Hwitern* and later into modern English Whithorn. *Wydryn* or *Hwitern* could be mistaken for *Witrin*, meaning "glass." So the Isle of Whithorn could be "The Glass Island." It was also Ynys Afallach, "The Isle of Avalon" (*see* **Avalon**). The Isle of Whithorn is surrounded by **water** on three sides, not four, but it is remote enough to have been thought of as an island.

Whithorn had a long and complex history, starting with the founding of a small, white-washed stone church by St. Ninian in 397. It became known as the Candida Casa, "The White House." About 100 years later, a religious community called the Magnum Monasterium, the Great Monastery, of Rosnat was set up there. This was the place of special sanctity that stood near the Galloway coast in the sixth century. The circular, walled graveyard was extended in a flurry of activity in about 550, evidently to accommodate a special grave that was dug on the site of one of the monks' cells. Whithorn was the mysterious Rosnat: the holiest of the three holiest places in Britain.

WILSFORD SHAFT

ENGLAND

Dating from the early Bronze Age, this shaft 100 feet (30m) deep and 6 feet (2m) in diameter was dug laboriously down into the chalk. The upper part of the fill had Bronze Age pottery. At the bottom were broken vessels.

Archeologists are still uncertain about the purpose of this shaft. Was it for making offerings to the Underworld? Or was it a well for drawing up **water**? (*See* Religion: **Ritual Shaft**.)

WOMEN'S ISLAND

See People: **Namnetes**.

WOODEATON

See Religion: **War God**.

WROXETER

See **Viroconium**.

Y

YEAVERING BELL

NORTHUMBERLAND,
ENGLAND

A fortress residence of the chief of the southern Votadini in the fifth and sixth centuries AD. It stands close to the head of a tapering valley. It is a safe place, but exposed to strong winds.

Yeavering Bell is half the size of **Traprain Law**, the sister-fortress of the northern Votadini, but it is still larger than most other prehistoric forts north of the Humber. Its perimeter was marked by a thick, stone wall about 10 feet (3m) high, enclosing 13 acres (5 hectares). Inside was a settlement consisting of a large number of round huts 15–30 feet (4.5–9m) in diameter.

Straight after the English took over the area, King Aethelferth (reigned 593–616) built a royal residence for himself at the foot of the hill, presumably to mark the English takeover of this major British site. Even so, some native Britons continued to occupy the old site.

In 627, the Christian missionary Paulinus spent 36 days at Yeavering, baptizing the Bernicians. One of the buildings is probably a pagan temple converted into a church.

The site was abandoned when the English decided on a more convenient location for their center in about 650.

PART 3

Celtic Religion

Abnoba

A huntress goddess of the Black Forest in Germany. She is accompanied by a hunting **dog**.

Altar

Some of the southern Gaulish altars of the Roman-Celtic period are very small. The ones that have survived are made of stone, though it is possible some were wooden. This is reminiscent of the small, portable altars used by the early Christian missionaries, who may well have borrowed this practice from the pagan Celts.

The small altars have religious symbols carved on their fronts, such as a swastika or a **wheel**, to show dedication to the **sun god** or **sky god**. Some have an extra symbol, a palm branch or conifer, that may be a fertility symbol.

Larger altars have carved plinths and cornices, showing classical influence, and they too have a religious symbol or two carved on them.

The altar from Tresques in the Lower Rhône Valley is of particular interest in having a seven-spoked wheel on one side and a rosette with seven petals on the other. The circularity of the two symbols and the repetition of the division into seven suggest that they were connected in some way.

Another altar from the Rhône Valley shows signs that deliberate attempts were made to deface the religious symbols; this may have been the work of Christians.

Some altars were dedicated to two gods at once, such as Jupiter and **Silvanus**. An altar from **Alesia** shows a god seated on a throne that is carved with wheels; he is accompanied by an eagle.

Altars in the Rhineland and Britain were significantly different than the Gaulish altars. They were much more Roman in style, and this is a reflection of their military character; they were set up by the legions, who were bound to be more Romanized than the civilian communities of the Celtic **west**. One outstanding example is the altar found at Cologne. It has a very realistic carving of a wheel below a well-carved inscription to Jupiter.

The altars found along Hadrian's Wall in the north of England are standard Roman military monuments in every way except that they bear a Celtic not a Roman religious symbol: the wheel.

ANCAMNA

The consort of the **god** Lenus at **Trier**.

ANDRASTE

A war **goddess** in Britain, according to Dio Cassius (*see* **Sacred Grove**).

ANGUS MAC OG

The Irish **god** of youth and beauty, and one of the **Tuatha dé Danann**, the gods of the ancient Irish, who later became the heroic **fairies**, the Daoine Sidhe. Their king, **the Daghda**, allocated to them his realms and palaces. He took two palaces for himself, gave one to Lug, son of Ethne, and one to Ogma, but his son Angus Mac Og was away, and so was forgotten. When he returned and complained about being disinherited, the Daghda ceded his own palace on the Boyne (probably the **Newgrange** passage grave) to him for a day and a night. Angus was not satisfied with this, and claimed the Brug na Boinne for himself forever.

ANNWFN

See **Annwn**.

ANNWN

The Celtic Underworld, ruled over by Arawn. Annwn is not a place of punishment or everlasting lamentation, but an Otherworldly place where the power of the ancestors resides (*see* **Otherworld**). Mortal men and women are allowed to visit Annwn and return to the world of the living. From it the **Wild Hunt** rides out.

ARDUINNA

The **boar goddess** of the Ardennes is shown riding a wild boar.

ARIANRHOD

See **Don**.

ARTIO

The **bear goddess**.

ATEPOMARUS

A **healing god** in Celtic Gaul. In the Romano-Celtic period, he was associated with Apollo, and sometimes called Apollo Atepomarus. Small figurines of **horses** were offered to him at some of Apollo's **healing** sanctuaries, such as **Sainte-Sabine** in Burgundy.

The root *epo* refers to the word for "horse," as in **Epona**, and the name "Atepomarus" as a whole has been translated as "Great Horseman" or "possessing a great horse."

B

BADB

An Irish war **goddess**. She is a battle Fury, appearing on the battlefield to confront **Cú Chulainn**. In this mythic confrontation, she drives a **chariot**, wears a red cloak, and has red eyebrows; she is intent on terrifying the young hero.

Badb can **shapeshift** into Badb Catha, "The Battle **Raven**." In this form she flaps round the battlefield, picking over the corpses of fallen warriors, and revels in the bloodshed.

BEAN SI

Pronounced and often spelled "banshee," this refers to the Gaelic fairy woman, the best known of the Celtic **fairies** from Ireland and the Scottish Highlands. She is known as Bean-Nighe, "The Little Washer by the Ford," because she is often seen by the side of the stream, washing the bloodstained clothes of those about to die.

BELATUCADROS

A **god** commonly worshiped 1,800 years ago along the western half of Hadrian's Wall.

BELENUS

A common Celtic healer **god**, often associated in the minds of the Romans with Apollo. Belenus was popular in central and southern Gaul and northern Italy, especially, it seems, in the old Celtic kingdom of Noricum in the eastern Alps. Tertullian says he was the special deity there.

Ausonius, a poet **writing** in Bordeaux in the fourth century AD, mentions that there were sanctuaries dedicated to Belenus in southwestern France. He mentions one of the temple **priests** of the Belenus cult by name: Phoebicius. The link between Phoebicius, Phoebus, and Apollo suggests that this was an adopted name, acquired when he became a temple priest.

The name "Belenus" suggests that there may be a connection with the Celtic name for May Day, **Beltane**. If the word "Beltane" means "shining fire," Belenus could have been a solar god, and this

would explain his "translation" as Apollo, who was also a **sun** god.

BELTANE

A major Celtic annual festival that falls on May 1, May Day, and marks the start of the summer half of the year. The first element, *bel*, probably means "shining" or "brilliant." The second element, *tane* or *tene*, means "fire." This great festival marking the start of summer was celebrated by big gatherings of people and the lighting of May fires. Livestock were driven between twin bonfires to protect them from disease. It is said by some folklorists that the dancing that accompanied this was a ritual enactment of the **sun**'s movement through the sky.

May Day was celebrated as a major festival in various parts of the western Celtic region, especially in southern Britain. The festivities of Tudor England were described in detail:

Against May-day every parish, town and village assemble themselves together, both men, women and children, old and young. They go to the woods and groves, some to the hills and mountains, where they spend all the night in pleasant pastimes; and in the morning they return bringing with them birch boughs and branches of trees with which to deck their *houses.*

But their chief jewel they bring with them is their may-pole, which they bring home with great care; they have twenty or forty yoke of oxen, every ox having a sweet nosegay of flowers placed on the top of his horns, and these oxen draw this may-pole which is covered all over with flowers and herbs, bound round about with strings from the top to the bottom, and sometimes painted with different colours, with two or three hundred men, women and children following it.

And this being reared up with handkerchiefs and flags streaming on the top, they strew the ground about, bind boughs about it, set up the summer halls, bowers and arbours hard by it; and then they fall to leap and dance about it.

Maypole dancing was certainly a major feature of the May Day festivities by the late Middle Ages, but no one really knows how old this custom is. The emphasis on celebrating *outside*, on going off into the woods and groves, is very reminiscent of the old Iron Age Celtic custom of open-air worship, and this suggests that it may be ancient. Maypole dancing is a custom that has survived in the lands of the Atlantic Celts (England, the Basque Country, Galicia, and Portugal), though it is carried on in other places too, such as Sweden and Germany.

As far as the British Isles are concerned, the Maypole seems to have been found mainly in England, which may be taken to suggest a Germanic origin rather than an indigenous western Celtic origin. The places in Wales, Scotland, and Ireland where Maypole dancing became established are said to have been in areas of English colonization, yet the earliest documented reference to a Maypole comes from a part of "Welsh Wales." A Welsh poem written by Gryffedd ap Adda ap Dafydd in about 1350 describes how the people of Llanidloes in central Wales (a "non-English" area) erected a tall birch pole.

The custom of raising posts for ritual purposes has its beginnings back in the Neolithic and even before. It was common in those times to raise avenues and rings of posts, sometimes concentric rings of posts. This happened at Stanton Drew, Mount Pleasant, and most famously at Durrington Walls and Woodhenge. And single posts were raised at the site of **Stonehenge** as long ago as 7000 BC, in the Middle Stone Age.

Whenever the custom had its beginning, there were increasing numbers of references to Maypoles from AD 1350 on. By 1400 the custom was certainly well-established across southern Britain. The Maypole became a community symbol, a focus for communal endeavor. There was a negative aspect of this: they became trophies. In Hertfordshire and Warwickshire in the early seventeenth century, people stole the Maypoles belonging to neighboring villages, which could lead to violent skirmishes.

The anarchic and disorderly behavior surrounding the May Day festivities brought an ever-increasing tide of disapproval from some Protestant groups in the sixteenth and seventeenth centuries. Under the Protestant Edward VI, many Maypoles, such as the famous Cornhill Maypole in London, were destroyed. A Maypole was stored under the eaves of the church of St. Andrew Undershaft in the City of London. Each spring it was taken out and set up for May Day, until 1517, when the riotous behavior of students brought the custom to an end. The Maypole itself survived until 1547 when a Puritan mob destroyed it as "a pagan idol." Mary Tudor, who was intolerant in other ways, rather surprisingly allowed the reinstatement of Maypoles. But the rise of Presbyterianism in Scotland was to lead to their virtual extinction there.

The English Long Parliament's ordinance of 1644 denounced Maypoles as "a Heathenish vanity, generally abused to superstition and wickedness." At Henley-in-Arden in 1655, officials stepped in to prevent them from being erected. The ordinance may have been flouted in many other places, while the authorities turned a blind eye to local custom. Maypole dancing became a symbol of resistance to the Long Parliament and to the Commonwealth that followed.

At the Restoration of the English monarchy in 1660, Londoners put up Maypoles "at every crossway" as a sign that Old England was restored. The tallest of them was in the Strand; it was more than 130 feet (39m) high. It stood beside the church of St Mary-le-

Strand until it was blown down by the wind in 1672.

The Maypole continued to be a symbol of "Merrie England" into the nineteenth century, when the tradition was developed by adding colored ribbons, which produced plaiting woven onto the pole as pairs of boys and girls danced around it. As the plaited ribbons became shorter, the dancers were brought closer to the pole, and closer and closer to one another. This type of quaint conceit was typical of much of the invented custom and folklore of the time.

In some areas, a rather different Maypole tradition developed, called garlanding—small hand-held sticks covered with intricate decorations made of flowers, greenery, and crepe paper. Children were encouraged to design and make these and take them to school on May Morning. A prize was often given for the best garland: it might be tea with the vicar.

The tallest surviving Maypoles in England are at Nun Monkton in North Yorkshire (88 feet/27m tall) and Barwick-in-Elmet (86 feet/26m).

The novel *Fanny Hill* (1750) contains a reference to a Maypole:

...and now, disengag'd from the shirt, I saw, with wonder and surprise, what? Not the play-thing of a boy, not the weapon of a man, but a maypole of so enormous a standard, that had proportions been observ'd, it must have belong'd to a young giant.

The author, John Cleland, may have picked up a long-standing colloquial use of "Maypole" as a euphemism for "penis." This is a long way from proving that Maypoles were *intended* to have a phallic significance. Disentangling folklore from fakelore is often difficult.

BLACK ANNIS

A very tall cannibal hag with blue face and iron claws. She is said to live in a cave in the Dane Hills in Leicestershire, England. There was a great **oak** tree at the entrance to the cave and Black Annis was said to hide in the tree in order to leap down onto stray children and lambs and devour them. It is also said that she gouged the cave out of the rock with her own claws.

Frightening stories about Black Annis were still told in the early twentieth century. Children were told that you could hear her grinding her teeth as she approached, which gave **people** just enough time to bolt their doors and step back well away from the windows. It was possible for Annis to get in through windows, and this was why Leicestershire cottages had small windows (or so it was said). Annis could reach in through a window, with her long arms, and snatch a baby.

By ancient custom, on Easter Monday there was a drag hunt from Annis' Bower to the Mayor of Leicester's house. The dragged bait was a dead cat doused with aniseed. The drag hunt died out at the end of the eighteenth century. The connection is that Black Annis had a monstrous cat.

Annis may be a late version of Anu, a Celtic **mother goddess**.

BOANNA

The Boyne **River**. Angus the Young is the son of **the Daghda** by Boanna: he is the Irish god of love (*see* **Angus Mac Og**). His palace is believed to be at the **Newgrange** passage grave, which stands beside the Boyne.

Boanna is also the **goddess** of the **river**, "She of the White Cows".

There is a legend about Boanna, who is detained by Nechtan when she questions the power of his **sacred spring**, which is the source of knowledge.

BORMANA

See **Borvo**.

BORMANUS

See **Borvo**.

BORMO

See **Borvo**.

BORVO

Borvo, Bormo, or Bormanus was a Gaulish **god** associated with hot **springs**. The name means "bubbling or boiling spring **water**." Although connected with **healing**, Borvo appears by himself, not usually linked with Apollo. This implies that his was an exclusively Celtic cult: one that was not taken up by the Romans.

Worship of Borvo was common in the Rhône and Loire valleys, Provence, the Alps, and Galicia. He had major cult sites at Bourbonne-les-Bains and Aix-les-Bains and sometimes had a female consort called Bormana; she even appears by herself at the healing spring of St. Vulbas.

Borvo's female consort was **Damona**, "The Divine Cow."

BRIGHID

In around AD 900, Brighid was said to be expert in poetry, divination, and prophecy, and was worshiped by the *filidh*, an elite class of poets (*see* People: **Learning**). She was the daughter of the **Daghda** and had two sisters also called Brighid, one associated with **healing** and one with the smith's craft. So there were three **goddesses** called Brighid, which is an interesting example of triplism, or the **rule of three**.

Ironically, Brighid has survived in the shape of her namesake, the Christian St. Brighid. Lady Gregory, in her *Gods and Fighting Men*, proposes that the name "Brighid" meant "Fiery Arrow."

The historical element in St. Brighid is slight, so it is likely that the "Christian saint" is a disguised transformation of the Celtic goddess. Her cult was legitimized by the prefix "Saint"—the Church could scarcely object to the veneration of a saint. St. Brighid's feast day is February 1, which is the major pre-Christian Celtic festival of **Imbolg**, the spring festival.

St. Brighid was born at sunrise neither within nor without a house and she hangs her wet **cloak** on the rays of the **sun** to dry. The house in which she stays appears to be ablaze. She and 19 of her nuns take turns in looking after a sacred flame that burns perpetually;

it is protected by a hedge through which no male may pass. This legend brings the saint close to the Celtic goddess **Sulis**. According to Solinus, **writing** in the third century AD, the sanctuary of Minerva (known by the Celtic name Sulis) also contained a perpetual fire.

No clear boundary can be drawn between the life of the Christian saint and the Celtic goddess. The mortal St. Brighid is supposed to have lived in the fifth century AD.

It is very likely that St. Brighid's great monastery of Kildare was originally a pagan sanctuary. There are stories that in the remote past a community of Druidesses lived there and that they were responsible for maintaining the sacred fire that burned there; by virtue of their duty they were known as the Daughters of Fire. Gerald of Wales mentioned this, stressing the Christian connections of the place, though without disguising its evident paganism. This is the sacred fire surrounded by the hedge that no man was allowed to pass through.

Other Christian monastic sites probably occupied pre-Christian foundations in a similar way. The **holy well** that bears St. Brighid's name at Liscannor in County Clare may have had an earlier existence as another pre-Christian **sacred spring**.

Brigantia, "Exalted One", who was the protectress of the **Brigantes tribe**, is likely to have been another transformation of Sulis-Brighid.

C

CADEIRA DA MOURA

GALICIA

A megalith in the shape of a chair. A **fairy** is believed to sit in the chair at night.

CALAN AWST

See **Lughnasad**.

CASA DA MOURA

The house of the **fairies**. In Galicia, dolmens or megalithic tombs are said to be the homes of fairies, who are associated with the dead. In a similar way in Brittany, megalithic tombs are known as the Maison des Korrigans. Rock-cut tombs are known as fairies' beds (*see* **Cadeira da Moura**; **Mouras Encantada**).

CERNUNNOS

An important **stag**-antlered fertility **god**, Cernunnos is usually shown as a male human figure sitting cross-legged, Buddha-like, on the ground. On the Paris relief known as the Tiberian Sailors' Pillar, he is shown with stag's ears and a torc hanging from each antler; the image bears the name "Cernunnos," which means "Horned One." The image is found in Britain, but it is more common in Gaul, where more than 30 examples are known. One bronze image from Bouray shows the god sitting cross-legged as usual, but instead of human feet he has the hooves of a stag.

Not all of these horned nature gods are named, but the label "Cernunnos" is commonly used to describe them all. Most of these images (as for most of the other gods) are late, but there is a **Val Camonica** carving of Cernunnos that was made as early as the fourth century BC, so his worship prevailed across a long time span.

The finest, most spectacular image of Cernunnos is the one on the **Gundestrup cauldron**, where he is shown as lord of the animals, accompanied by his stag, his ram-horned snake, his **boar**, and his **bull**. Cernunnos and his stag are as one: the artist has very deliberately made the antlers of Cernunnos and the antlers on the stag beside him exactly the same.

He is a god of the forest, of nature, of fertility, of fecundity, and therefore of human prosperity. This is reinforced by an impressive stone relief from Rheims, on which Cernunnos is shown with a sack of money; the coins flow out in a copious stream. Underneath him are a stag and a bull and he is flanked by two naked youths.

At Sommerécourt, a sculpture of Cernunnos was found with sockets in the god's **head** where bronze or perhaps even real antlers were fitted. As usual, he sits cross-legged, but this time he is accompanied by a goddess as well as ram-horned snakes. Another image shows Cernunnos flanked by two youths who are standing on snakes.

A bronze image from Curgy (Seine et Loire) is of special interest. The god is sitting cross-legged, but this time he has three heads, perhaps for emphasis. He is feeding two ram-horned snakes with fruit piled up in his lap; the **serpents** coil round his body. The central head has sockets for the fitting of antlers.

Cernunnos was evidently a mainly Gaulish deity; there are few images of him in Britain. This implies that he was an imported deity, but he was not imported by the Romans. A pre-Roman Celtic silver coin has been found at Petersfield in Hampshire, showing Cernunnos with a **sun wheel** between his antlers. This is a link across to the image of Cernunnos on the Gundestrup cauldron, where he is also associated with a **wheel god**.

It would be possible to describe more individual examples of Cernunnos images, and there were lots of complex variations. One key recurring feature is his association with the stag. Another is the ram-horned snake. The overall impression is one of well-being and prosperity. Cernunnos is a god of nature, perhaps *the* god of nature, as well as the god of fruit, of corn, of beasts, and of plenty. The close co-existence of stag and stag god imply **shapeshifting**; Cernunnos could perhaps appear as a stag and a stag might metamorphose into the god.

With the arrival of Christianity, the old **horned gods**, especially very powerful horned gods such as Cernunnos, became identified with the Devil. Looked at objectively, there is no reason to see Cernunnos as anything other than totally benign, but those conditioned by a Christian upbringing are likely to be uneasy about a god wearing horns.

COCIDIUS

A **god** commonly worshiped along Hadrian's Wall. "Cocidius" means "Red One."

At Otterburn, just below the summit of a ridge, is a square chamber 7 feet (2m) across tucked away among huge slabs of rock. It is a natural chamber that was apparently used in antiquity as a shrine to Cocidius. Originally it had a roof over it. On the right, at the entrance, is a slab with a carefully carved image of Cocidius cut into it. He is shown naked, with a large, pear-shaped **head**, and he is waving a **spear** and a round shield.

Cocidius was worshiped at several places along the western end of Hadrian's Wall and always associated with the Roman legionaries, so it is particularly interestingly that his images are carved in indigenous Celtic style. It seems that, to this extent at least, the Roman soldiers in Britain "went native."

COLIGNY CALENDAR

This unique bronze calendar was found in France, near Bourg-en-Bresse, at the end of the nineteenth century. It was made in the Romano-Celtic period, in the reign of Augustus.

It was evidently made under the auspices of **Druids**, as it shows the Druidical belief in lucky and unlucky days. Each month is divided into a good half, marked *MAT* ("auspicious") and a bad half, marked *ANM* ("inauspicious.") These were appropriate and inappropriate times to act. This idea was shared by the Romans, and it is one that has in a very small way survived to the present, with the idea that the thirteenth day of the month (especially if it is a Friday) is an unlucky day.

The **Ulster Cycle** of tales includes an episode about Queen Medb of Connaught, in which she is prevented from joining battle for a fortnight when the Druids advise her to wait for an auspicious day to fight.

The Gauls counted in nights. This nocturnal custom may have been widespread in the Celtic **west**.

Until relatively recently in Britain it was possible to speak of a "sennight" (seven-nights), meaning a week—Shakespeare used it. "Fortnight" (fourteen-nights) is still in general use for two weeks.

The Gauls' month consisted of 29.5 days. The Druids seem to have wanted to reconcile the lunar calendar with the solar cycle, and did this by having a year of 12 months, alternately 29 and 30 days long, making a year of 354 days (or nights, as preferred). The difference between lunar and solar years was made up every 2.5 years by adding a thirteenth month. The years in turn formed cycles; according to **Diodorus Siculus**, great sacrificial ceremonies were held every five years, and there were "centuries" of 30 years that were used in assembling longer chronologies.

The Coligny calendar, covering a cycle of 62 consecutive months, was inscribed on a sheet of bronze and unfortunately exists only in a fragmentary state. But it is a very important object because it is the oldest extensive document in an ancient Celtic **language**. It uses Roman lettering and numerals, but its content is completely independent of the Roman calendar. It must have been made by Gaulish Druids. It is of outstanding interest in itself, but also because it has points in common with the Greek calendar, which in a similar way used an additional month every so often to catch up with the astronomical year. The month names also have similarities. The Gallic Ellembiu has its Greek equivalent in Elaphebolion, and the Gallic Equos in the Greek Hippios: both meaning "**horse**." The Greek model was evidently an influence on the Druids.

There is no sign of anything like a Celtic timepiece, except in some of the sanctuaries, where there were isolated clusters of posts that could have been used as **sun**-dials.

COVENTINA

Coventina was a northern British **goddess**. She presided over a **spring** inside a sacred enclosure that was bounded by a rough, stone wall. The spring fed a small pool, into which visitors threw offerings of jewelry, figurines, and coins. Pins were thrown in as well, and these are taken as associated with infants and childbirth. The goddess was a **water** nymph, and she may have been associated with water-associated child-bearing. Women may have appealed to her to help them through the ordeal of childbirth.

A beautiful carved plaque found at the shrine of Coventina at Carrawburgh in Northumberland shows three Coventinas, each sheltering under her own elegant archway.

Each goddess holds up a jar, as if toasting her worshiper. Their dresses are shown with parallel curving folds that cleverly suggest the rippling water that is Coventina's element.

When Coventina's Well was excavated in 1876 it was found to be crammed with votive offerings cast into it during the Roman occupation, though it is almost certain that the Romans took over and developed a pre-existing cult spring. There were more than 13,000 coins.

Thirteen stone **altars** depicting the goddess were thrown into the pool, and it is possible that these went in at a time when the sanctuary itself was in danger—they may have been thrown into the water to save them from desecration.

CREIDHNE

See **Gobhniu**.

CROM CRUACH

According to Irish folk-tales, a **god** called Crom Cruach is Lord of the Mound. It was alleged by the anonymous eleventh-century monks who wrote *The Book of Leinster* that bloody rituals were performed in his name:

*…They did evilly
beat on their palms, thumped their bodies,
wailing to the monster who enslaved them.
Their tears falling in showers.
In rank stood twelve idols of stone;
the figure of Crom was in gold.*

Another writer alleged that "the firstlings of every issue and the chief scions of every clan were offered in sacrifice to the god Crom."

These sacrifices, it was said, took place on the Plain of Adoration in County Cavan.

CÚ CHULAINN

An Irish semi-divine hero, the quintessential Celtic warrior, magnified to super-hero scale. Warriors were expected to bring home the **head** of an enemy as a trophy (*see* **Headhunting**). Cú Chulainn could hold *nine* trophy heads in one hand and *ten* in the other—and juggle them.

CUDA

See **Hooded Dwarves**.

CUNOMAGLOS

Cunomaglos is a Celtic epithet meaning "Hound Lord."

At Nettleton Shrub in Wiltshire, the Roman **god** Apollo was known as hound lord. Apollo was a name the Romans gave to the Celtic healer gods. **Dogs** were used for hunting, but they were also associated with **healing**.

THE DAGDA

See **The Daghda**.

THE DAGHDA

The Daghda, or Dagda, is wedded to the land by being married to the territorial **goddess Boanna** of the Boyne **River**. He is the Irish Father of all the Gods. His name may mean "All-Competent" and he is a very strong, club-swinging giant.

The union of Boanna and the Daghda is a classic example of a marriage between a nature goddess who nourishes the Earth and a tribal god, and the Daghda is a fertility figure. He owns a **magic cauldron** that never empties and possesses magical powers of rejuvenation. The **water** the cauldron contains is a fertility symbol. Water is regarded as playing a major role in **healing**.

The Dadhda's other attribute is his magic club. With one end of it he can deal death to the living, and with the other life to the dead. When he drags it behind him it leaves a track as deep as the boundary ditch separating two provinces.

In spite of his great power and his position as father-figure among the gods, he is often treated as a figure of fun. Unlike Zeus or Jupiter, his counterparts in the Mediterranean cultures, he is ugly, rough, crude, pot-bellied, and wears peasant clothing. Short garments are the mark of the peasant and the vagabond entertainer, yet the Daghda's tunic barely covers his backside. His clothes are uncouth, and his behavior is even more so. He is insatiably greedy for porridge and an anecdote in the Irish folk-tales tells how he was lured by the Fomhoire, a mysterious race of evil non-humans who settled in Ireland long ago and were driven out by the **Tuatha de Danann**, into eating a prodigious amount—a king's cauldron full of it.

Yet the Daghda is also an accomplished harpist. The beautiful melodies he plays are, Vivaldi-like, cues to the passage of the seasons (*see* People: **Music**).

DAMONA

A female consort of the **healing god** (Apollo). At Bourbonne-Lancy there is an inscription that connects her with incubation, or healing sleep. At **Alesia**, she was the consort of Apollo Moritasgus, the Celtic god of hot **springs**. "Moritasgus" means "masses of sea-**water**." Damona also appears as the consort of **Borvo**: she had two husbands.

DANA

See **Don**.

DEMETRIUS' SACRED ISLAND

In his book *On the Cessation of Oracles*, Plutarch mentions what Demetrius reported regarding Britain:

Demetrius said that of the islands round Britain, many were deserted and scattered about, and some of them were named after demons and heroes. He said that, for the purpose of inquiry and investigation, by the emperor's order, he sailed to the inhabited island which lay nearest to the deserted islands. It had only a few inhabitants, who were priests, and it was held sacred by the Britons.

Just after Demetrius landed on the island, there was a great disturbance in the air, and many meteors, and blasts of wind burst down, and whirlwinds descended. When it was calm again, the islanders said that the extinction had taken place of one of the superior powers, for, as they explained, a lamp when burning does no harm, but being put out is noxious to many people; in like manner great souls, when first kindled, are benign and harmless, whilst their going out and dissolution, often, as in the present case, stirs up stormy winds, and aerial tumults; it even infects the air with pestilential tendencies. In that region also, they said, Saturn was confined in one of the islands by Briareus, and lay asleep; for that his slumber had been artfully produced in order to chain him, and round about him were many daemons for his guards and servants.

Here, in the sleeping divine king, is one of the mystical ingredients in the Arthurian legend, but dating from long before the time of the historical **Arthur**.

DIVINE COUPLE

Often a Celtic **goddess** is shown together with a god, whether Celtic or Roman. It can be difficult to tell which is the principal deity and which is the consort, though it is clear from Irish mythology that the female may be the dominant figure.

The **Aedui**, a Gaulish **tribe**, venerated a couple whose names have not been recorded. The goddess had a horn of plenty (*see* Symbols: **Cornucopia**) and *patera* (dish) as the badges of her prosperity role. Elsewhere the divine couples have inscriptions to accompany them, and where they do there is sometimes a link to a locality. At Luxeuil, we find Luxovius and Bricta. There are also Ucuetis and Bergusia. **Sucellus** and **Nantosuelta** are another couple.

Perhaps the most interesting divine couple in Britain were **Mercury** and **Rosmerta**. This was a mixed marriage: a Roman god paired with a Celtic goddess. A stone tablet found in Gloucester, at the Shakespeare Inn, shows the pair standing side by side. Mercury is naked, with *caduceus*, **purse**, and cockerel. Rosmerta is fully dressed and carrying a double-ax, *patera*, and wooden bucket. She is thought to be a version of the Celtic fertility goddess. Her name means "The Good Supplier," which makes her a bringer of prosperity. Often she carries a **basket of fruit** or Mercury's purse.

The couple collected some interesting associations in Britain. An image from **Bath** shows them with a ram and three **hooded dwarves**. Rosmerta's bulging purse on a stone from Gloucester shows her importance for prosperity.

DON

Don was the Welsh **goddess** who was the equivalent of the Irish goddess Dana. Dana is the Irish **mother goddess** of the **Tuatha dé Danann**, an ancestral figure associated with the land of Ireland. Possibly Don was an import from Ireland.

The Children of Don also correspond closely to the Children of Dana. Don had three children: **Gwydion** the Wizard, Gofannon the Smith (*see* **Gobhniu**), and Arianrhod, the mother of Llew.

DONN

The god presiding over the Irish Underworld. Donn means "Dark One." **Julius Caesar** said the Gauls claimed they were descended from Dis Pater, who was the Roman Lord of the Underworld. It is unlikely that the Gauls literally claimed descent from a Roman god—Caesar was probably "translating" the Gaulish **god** into what he saw as the Roman equivalent— but the Celtic equivalent of Dis Pater was Donn. It is quite likely that the Gauls would have claimed descent from a common ancestor. Some gods, such as **Lugh**, were claimed as the ancestors of widely separated **tribes**.

Donn is difficult to trace, and it may be that the god **Sucellus** may, in some aspects, have carried out his role. There are representations of Sucellus with a hammer, and Dis Pater is also known to have had a hammer. So the Irish Donn may have been the same as the Gaullish Sucellus.

Donn's Irish abode was a small, rocky island known as Tech Duinn, the House of Donn, off the southwest coast of Ireland. The **people** of Ireland were believed to travel to his island home when they died.

This "going **west**," quite literally into the sunset, was a common way of thinking of death and the journey to the afterlife.

DRUIDS

The Druids were the most famous Celtic **priests**. The name may be derived from *dru-uid*, meaning "very wise."

We have a romanticized view of the Druids thanks to the **art**, literature, and antiquarianism of the eighteenth century—a vision of dignified, long-haired, white-robed priests peacefully embowered in woodland clearings, cutting **mistletoe** from the boughs of sacred **oaks** with **gold** sickles, and presiding over religious ceremonies in the open air. Fanciful though the description sounds, it is partly true. Some of this is supported by contemporary classical writers. But the robes are unlikely to have been white: brown and blue woolen

tartan was a likelier fabric, or unbleached, undyed wool.

We know about the Druids through the **writings** of several Greco-Roman writers, such as Strabo, **Diodorus Siculus**, and **Julius Caesar**. Unfortunately all three of these writers seem to base what they say on just one source, **Posidonius**, and what they say is strongly influenced by personal agenda. What they describe is a very powerful priesthood that was able to control Celtic **society**, but it is difficult to gauge how wide their influence really was. Caesar, for instance, talks about the Druids only in one passage in Book 6 of his *Gallic Wars*. Lucan's comment that the Druids knew the secrets of the universe is thought to have been sarcastic.

Some commentators think that the influence of the Druids was more social than political, but there is evidence that they were the source of the power structure in the hierarchy of Celtic society. Under the impact of Rome, that hierarchy diminished in power, and the power of the Druids ebbed away too. So, as the Roman Empire encroached and impinged on the Celtic lands, the influence of the Druids gradually diminished and could not really have been much of a threat to Rome. Under the emperor Augustus, the Druids were tolerated, so long as they did not seek to interfere with Roman citizens. Under Tiberius, there was a clampdown, and Claudius tried hard to wipe Druidism out.

There was a Celtic rising in Gaul in AD 69–70, led by Civilis, and during this time the Druids made something of a comeback. In the third century they were still active, as they were recorded as making prophesies against Severus Alexander and Maximin, and in the fourth, when the Bordeaux poet Ausonius mentions two famous Druids and the tradition of father-to-son succession. The Irish sources also refer to Druids as prophets and soothsayers. Cathbad of Ulster was one of these.

From the references, it is clear that the Druids were a major religious force in both Gaul and Britain. They were also a political power, holding the balance between civil and military authorities and ensuring that any attempt at tyranny would fail.

Caesar said that the Druids had their main cult center in Britain and that that was where they originated. They were **magicians**

and in their oral tradition was contained the entire liturgy, knowledge of religious ritual, and all the accumulated religious wisdom of the Celts. The Druids officiated at ceremonies in which the **gods** were worshipped; they supervised sacrifices and gave rulings on all religious questions. On a particular day each year they met at a sacred site in the territory of the Carnutes **tribe**, near Chartres in France, summoned by one who held authority over all of them. This gathering-place was regarded as the center of Gaul.

In a similar way, the Irish *filidh* had a leader who was elected from among their number, and they were closely associated with a place called Uisnech, the "navel" of Ireland. This was the location of the primal fire, and it is said that a great assembly was held there. The system in operation seems to have been pan-Celtic.

Pliny describes a feast that was prepared on the sixth day of the lunar cycle. It involved the Druids climbing a sacred oak tree where they cut down a mistletoe bough using a golden sickle and caught it in a white **cloak**. The ceremony also included the sacrifice of two **bulls**.

The Druids were heavily involved in divination and their role as prophets is well documented. They supervised the calendar and they were probably responsible for nominating certain days as lucky and others as unlucky. In both Gaul and Ireland there were traditions of lucky and unlucky days (see **Coligny Calendar**).

The classical writers were fascinated by the Druids' role in carrying out **human sacrifice**. Though the Druids did not actually carry out sacrifices—lesser functionaries did that—their presence was necessary to validate them. Their main purpose in carrying out sacrifice was not propitiation of the gods but divination. Strabo (second century BC) says that the Druid soothsayers of the Cimbri tribe killed their victims with a **sword** stroke in the back and foretold the future from how they fell, the nature of the convulsions, and the flow of blood. The victims' blood was collected and then examined carefully for further clues to the future.

The Druids were also alleged to be interested in harvesting mistletoe. So it is particularly significant that Lindow Man, the man murdered in Cheshire and buried in a bog, was found to have mistletoe as well as the remains of a griddle cake in his stomach. It looks as if he was a Druidic sacrifice (see Places: **Lindow Moss**).

It seems from a number of accounts that the Druids also made great use of bird-watching in divination.

The classical writers mentioned, but did not emphasize, a key role played by the Druids in transmitting knowledge. In a largely pre-literate society, memorizing and reciting knowledge handed down from an earlier generation was of great importance. The Druids worked hard to maintain this oral tradition, committing vast amounts of knowledge, both religious and scientific, to **memory**. Writing was used only for trade, which was regarded by the Druids as a profane activity.

The Druids also wanted to hold back the divine figuration—what the gods actually looked like—in much the same way that they wanted to keep their textual knowledge to themselves. Lucan describes the Druids as living deep in the forest, and claiming to know the secrets of the gods.

Normally very brief and concise, Julius Caesar had much to say about the Druids:

The Element Encyclopedia of the Celts

All the Druids are under one head, whom they hold in the highest regard... The Druidic doctrine is believed to have been originated in Britain and from there imported into Gaul; even today those who want to make a profound study of it generally go to Britain for the purpose. The Druids are exempt from military service and do not pay taxes like other citizens. These important privileges are naturally attractive: many present themselves of their own accord to become students of Druidism and others are sent by their parents and relatives. It is said that these pupils have to memorize a great number of verses—so many that some of them spend twenty years at their studies...

A lesson they take particular pains to inculcate is that the soul does not perish, but after death passes from one body to another; they think this is the best incentive to bravery, because it teaches men to disregard the terrors of death. They also hold long discussion about the heavenly bodies and their movements, the size of the universe and of the earth, the physical constitution of the world, and the power and properties of the gods; and they instruct the young men in all these subjects.

Professor Stuart Piggott had some very wise things to say about the Druids. One of them was that we have to distinguish between Druids-as-known and Druids-as-wished-for. Druids-as-wished-for arrived, as if by stealth, during a slow Celtic revival starting in the sixteenth century.

Several French scholars interested themselves in the ancient Gauls, culminating in Noel Taillepied, who in 1585 wrote his book *Histoire de l'Estat et Républiques des Druides* (History of the State and Republics of the Druids). In 1623, M. I. Guenebault, a medical doctor from Dijon, published a find of a cinerary urn as *Le Reveil de l'Antique Tombeau de Chyndonax, Prince des Vacies, Druides, Celtiques, Diionnois* (The Discovery of the Ancient Tomb of Chyndonax, Prince of Vacies, Druids, Celts, and People of Dijon). Layers of speculative fantasy were added to these accounts during the following century, to a point where in 1649 the English antiquarian John Aubrey could just assume that monuments such as Avebury and **Stonehenge** were connected with the Druids. "Their [the ancient Britons'] religion is at large described by Caesar. Their priests were Druids. Some of their temples I pretend [i.e. claim] to have restored, as Avebury, Stonehenge, &c., as also British sepulchres."

Aubrey's modest inference was taken up by another English antiquarian, William Stukeley, in the 1740s and expanded into a large-scale fantasy. By this time the word "Celt" was coming into general use as an alternative to "Briton." In the end, Stukeley used "British" in his 1740 title, *Stonehenge, a Temple Restor'd to the British Druids*, closely followed in 1743 by *Abury, a Temple of the British Druids*. And Stukeley's Druids were the precursors, somehow, of Christians. Stukeley wrote:

My intent is (besides preserving the memory of these extraordinary monuments, now in great danger of ruin) to promote, as much as I am able, the knowledge and practice of ancient and true Religion, to revive in the minds of the learned the spirit of Christianity.

This was Druids-as-wished-for on a grand scale (*see* Places: **Anglesey**).

EPONA

The **horse goddess** Epona appears in the Roman-Celtic phase as part of a new repertoire of religious imagery. Some features connect her with the fertility and prosperity role of the **mother goddesses**. Many of the worshipers who made dedications to her were soldiers, especially cavalrymen. She is shown nearly always riding sidesaddle on a horse, or in the company of horses, but there are only a few representations of her in Britain.

Like the mother goddesses, Epona is sometimes associated with death, and she appears in cemeteries in Gaul. She seems to have been worshiped mainly in rural and domestic settings. The Celts regularly used mares as work animals on their farms. Epona was probably a patron saint of horse-breeding and regarded as the protectress of horsemen.

In Gaulish sanctuaries, she was associated with **healing waters**; at some of them she was shown naked, like a nymph.

Epona is distinctive among the

Celtic **gods and goddesses** in being mentioned by Roman writers. Juvenal and Minucius Felix describe her as presiding over stables.

ESUS

A Celtic **god** about whom little is known. Two stone reliefs carved in the first century AD show him as a woodcutter. They show an episode from a myth in which Esus played a part, but tell us little about his true mythic role (*see* Symbols: **Crane**). His name appears in only one inscription.

Lucan, **writing** in the first century AD, mentioned three Celtic gods—Esus, **Teutates**, and **Taranis**—as if they were of great importance. He may have been right, but in terms of the inscriptions they seem not to have been very important. This is a reminder that we need to be careful in taking what the classical writers said at face value. Sometimes they latched onto a cult practice because it had some particular interest to them, so they gave it greater importance than perhaps it had to the Celts. **Julius Caesar**, for example, writing about the **Druids**, had his own agenda: the ulterior motive of self-justification. A great deal of Celtic cult practice was in reality no odder than what was going on within the Roman belief system. The Romans seized on things that they could represent as obscene or weird and made much of them, things such as **headhunting**, **human sacrifice**, and divination by ritual murder.

FORTUNA

A carved, stone plaque from Gloucester shows the **divine couple Mercury** and **Rosmerta** together with Fortuna. Mercury has a winged cap and *caduceus*. Rosmerta is also carrying a *caduceus*. Fortuna carries a horn of plenty and a rudder on a globe (*see* Symbols: **Cornucopia**; **Wheel**).

G

Gobhniu

An Irish smith **god**, the Celtic Vulcan. He was known in Wales as Gofannon. Smiths had an aura of supernatural ability about them: an aura that probably dated back to the first Bronze Age metal-workers (*see* Symbols: **Spear**). They were figures who inspired respect, awe, and a certain amount of fear. The words of a hymn written in the eighth century AD ask for God's help "against the spells of women and smiths and druids."

There was an equivalent in Gaul, who was overlooked by **Julius Caesar**. The Gaulish Vulcan was given greater dignity and respect than his Roman counterpart, who was portrayed, like the Greek god Hephaistos, as a figure of fun.

Gobhniu, as Gobban the Wright, was also remembered in Irish folk-tales as a great builder, the master of all masons. He was one of a group of three craftsman gods. The others were Luchta the wright and Creidhne the metal-worker. In the Battle of Magh Tuiredh, these three gods provided the weapons for **Lugh** and the **Tuatha dé Danann**. Gobhniu forged the **heads**; Luchta made the shafts; and Creidhne made the rivets. Together the magic three formed a divine assembly line.

Gobhniu was host and provider at the **Otherworld** feast—the Feast of Gobhniu. Here there may be a link across to the Greek equivalent, Hephaistos, who is made to serve the gods with drink. A dim remembrance of the smith god's role in feasting may be preserved in the Welsh laws, which stipulate that the smith of the court shall have the first drink at a feast (*see* People: **Food and Feasting**).

GODS AND GODDESSES

Julius Caesar commented that the Gauls (the Celts with whom he had most contact) were a profoundly religious **people**. This is true of the Celts in general, and they seem to have seen sanctity everywhere around them. Every mountain, **spring**, and **river** had its own deity. Celtic mythology has been described as "local and anarchical."

One problem we have in identifying the deities worshiped by the Celts is that it is not always clear whether there were many gods or many different manifestations of one god. This is compounded by the processing of the Celtic pantheon by the Romans. Obviously it suited the mobile legions of the Roman army to be able to worship their gods wherever they happened to be, so "translating" local Celtic deities into their Roman equivalents was a useful exercise. The Romans seem to have assumed that the Celtic gods were "really" Roman gods, and it was just a question of identifying which was which.

Often these translated deities were addressed by both their Celtic and their Roman names, such as **Sulis**-Minerva at **Bath** or Lenus-**Mars** at Trier, but Mars was tentatively paired with several Celtic gods with different characteristics, and they may have been separate guardian gods for different **tribes**. At Bath and Mainz, Mars Loucetius, "Brilliant Mars," was given an entirely Celtic consort, in the form of Nemetona. **Mercury** was given a Celtic wife called **Rosmerta**, "The Good Provider," who enhanced his fertility function.

Where **divine couples** existed, the goddess was the one who retained the Celtic name, while the god retained his Roman title. This may be connected with the tendency to associate Celtic goddesses with territory.

The Romans were more interested in an equivalence for the sake of making their soldiers' lives easier, but their translations do not necessarily penetrate into the interior of the Celtic reality. They also used Roman **art**-forms to depict Celtic gods and goddesses who may not have had *any* iconography in the free Celtic world. Examples of Roman imagination being applied to Celtic deities include **Epona**, Sequana of the Seine, **Artio** of Berne, and Arduinna of the Ardennes.

The Element Encyclopedia of the Celts

A common Celtic theme is **shapeshifting**, the ability to change from one form into another. This may explain some of the weird hybrid images we see in the artwork: woodland gods that seem to be half-human, half-tree, or river nymphs that seem to be half-girl, half-**water**.

There was perhaps an element of cultural colonization in this Romanization of Celtic gods and goddesses, but there was no intention on the part of the Romans to belittle—rather the opposite. Quite a number of Celtic sanctuaries were taken up and enormously embellished and enhanced in the Roman occupation. Outstanding examples are the Celtic spring sanctuaries of Sulis at Bath and Nemausus at Nîmes.

The question remains unresolved: did the Celts have a large number of separate gods, or were they worshiping a smaller number with different names for different aspects, or different names in different places? The Celtic world was divided into many separate tribal territories, and it easy to imagine that each had its own local gods. If a tribe quarreled with a neighboring tribe, it would have imagined itself going into battle supported and led by its own unique guardian god, the god of the tribe, rather than a god shared with other tribes. **The Daghda** was a typical Irish tribal god. Distinct and different gods were part of the tribal sociopolitical system. In the **Ulster Cycle**, warriors swear by the gods of their tribe. On the other hand, the **Druids** operated across the whole of the Celtic world and they played a role in creating some uniformity, at least elements of a shared pantheon. This may be why some images are very widespread—the **horned god**, the **mother goddess**, and triplism (*see* Symbols: **Rule of Three**). And there were common recurring themes, such as springs, lakes, bogs, and rivers.

Caesar commented that Mercury was the most commonly worshiped god:

After him they honour Apollo, Mars, Jupiter and Minerva. Of these deities they have almost the same ideas as other peoples; Apollo drives away diseases, Minerva teaches the first principles of the arts and crafts, Jupiter rules the heavens and Mars controls the outcome of war.

He does not mention that the Celts had their own names for

these and other gods, and he was oversimplifying when he said that their ideas were the same as those of "other peoples," meaning of course the Romans; in this he is contradicted by such Celtic documents as survive. He does not allow for the existence of tribal gods such as the *dea Brigantia* and *dea Tricoria*, the goddesses of the **Brigantes** and Tricorii **tribes**.

Caesar gives us the Roman view: the Celtic world as seen through Roman eyes. He also does something more sinister, which is to make a pre-emptive strike at the Celtic pantheon by making it out to be unoriginal: a crude and second-rate copy of the Roman original. The reality is that the Celtic pantheon was far more complex, far richer, and far subtler.

GOFANNON

See **Don, Gobhniu**.

GOLD

In Galicia, the gold of the *mouras* (**fairies**) may be offered as a reward, or it may be found, perhaps in a vase or some other container. This is the Galician version of the fairies' crock of gold.

On St. John's Day, at midsummer, the fairies may appear with their **treasures**. The association of enchantment (or breaking enchantment) at the summer solstice suggests that this may be an ancient belief.

GRANNUS

The Celtic Apollo, **god** of **healing**. Dio Cassius said that in AD 215 the emperor Caracalla was unable to find a cure at the shrines of Serapis, Aesculapius, or Grannus. A temple at Brigetio in Hungary was dedicated to Apollo Grannus and his consort **Sirona**.

GRINE

According to Moroccan myth, every time a human is born in this world, a *djinn* called a Grine is born in another world: a world alongside our own. The actions of the human being influence the actions of the Grine, and the actions of the Grine influence those of the human. The Grine is a kind of spirit double.

GUNDESTRUP CAULDRON

Not very much is known about the detail of Celtic religious ceremonies, except that they involved the use of cult vessels, some of them very big. They were used from the Bronze Age onward and may be associated with **water** cults. The most famous of these cult vessels is the Gundestrup cauldron, which was found in Raevemose Bog in Gundestrup, Jutland, Denmark.

The Gundestrup cauldron is one of the most important pieces of ancient Celtic artwork that has survived. It is spectacular. It is large, over 2 feet (60cm) in diameter, and made of gilt silver. It is covered with decorations in low relief, showing several mythic scenes, and it tells us a great deal about Celtic beliefs in the first century BC. There is a cross-legged Celtic **god** and there is a snake with ram's horns, but the imagery is not easy to interpret. There are certain motifs, such as the shield and war-trumpet, that are of **La Tène** type, and there are also symbols that are not known from any other places in western Europe. One scholar has pointed out that the nearest parallels in artwork are in Romania, and that suggests that the bowl itself may have come from there originally.

The seated **stag-horned god** must be the Celtic god **Cernunnos**, and he belongs to the Celtic **west**, so the imagery seems to be a hybrid, representing religious beliefs from both sides of Europe. That in itself is interesting; why would a wealthy patron, whoever it was, commission a ritual vessel that combined the religious iconography of his own region with that of another? What could the motive have been?

GWYDION

A wizard and **bard** of North Wales who is one of the sons of the Welsh **goddess Don**. In the Mabinogion, he performed many works of **magic** aimed against the men of South Wales.

HEADHUNTING

The male human **head** is an image that recurs again and again in Celtic religious **art**. Everything that made a man what he was resided in his head; it was the seat of the soul. When a warrior killed his enemy in battle, he owned the body of his victim and could dispose of it as he wished. It was his privilege, his right, to take the head if he wanted it as a battle trophy.

This widespread custom appears frequently in accounts by early historians. Here is one, by **Diodorus Siculus, writing** in about 40 BC:

They cut off the heads of enemies killed in battle and attach them to the necks of their horses. The blood-stained spoils they hand over to their attendants and carry off as booty, while striking up a paean and singing a customary song of victory; and they nail up these first fruits upon their houses just as do those who lay low wild animals in certain kinds of hunting. They embalm the heads of their most distinguished enemies in cedar-oil and preserve them carefully in a chest, and display them with pride to strangers, saying that one of their ancestors, or his father, or the man himself, refused the offer of a large sum of money for this head. They say that some of them boast that they refused the weight of the head in gold, thus displaying what is only a barbarous kind of magnanimity.

Strabo repeated this account almost word for word, but adding that **Posidonius**, whose lost work was used by both writers, had actually seen such heads on display in many places when he had traveled through southern Gaul. According to Strabo, Posidonius had initially been disgusted by the sight, but had got used to it.

It was important for a warrior to take home the head of an enemy, not least because he had to prove that he was brave and strong—and victorious. The Celts were great tellers of tales, but tall tales of a distant skirmish were not enough. The bloody head of an enemy warrior said 1,000 times more; it was incontrovertible. Probably the heads of important enemies were valued more highly, and above all the heads of the chiefs, the battle-leaders. The fact that the heads were preserved and kept shows that they might be needed to provide evidence (to the skeptical?) of past bravery in later years.

Before the military engagement at Sentinum in Italy in 295 BC, the Roman historian Livy writes that the consuls received no news of the disaster that had overtaken one of the legions "until some Gallic horsemen came in sight, with heads hanging at their horses' breasts or fixed on their **spears**, and singing their customary of triumph." The heads were not ornamental; they were symbolic. No doubt the best warriors built up substantial collections of preserved heads and

they would have done the boasting without any need for words.

This practice was very widespread across Iron Age Europe, not just in the lands of the Atlantic Celts. The Romans liked to think this was a barbarous practice and Strabo declared that the Romans put a stop to it. We forget, and sometimes the Romans themselves chose to forget, that the Romans were part of that Iron Age world and had absorbed many of its customs; they liked to think of themselves as civilized and the rest of the world as barbarian. But occasionally they too took heads as trophies.

Headhunting by Romans is shown in three scenes on Trajan's Column: on the Great Trajanic Frieze and other carvings celebrating Trajan's victory in his two Dacian Wars (AD 101–102 and 105–106). In two scenes on Trajan's Column, a couple of soldiers offer freshly severed heads to Trajan, who seems to reach out with his right arm to accept them. In a battle scene, a Roman soldier clutches between his teeth the hair of an earlier victim's head, while dealing with a second opponent. In the third image, a soldier climbs a scaling-ladder, holding on his shielded left arm a severed head as he does battle with a defendant on the battlements. As legionaries construct a **road**, behind them stand severed heads impaled on poles. This has been explained in terms of the Roman army using Celtic units to whom this would have been normal practice, but the practice was evidently condoned—not least in the formal commemoration of the warfare on Trajan's Column.

Perhaps surprisingly, **Julius Caesar** does not mention head-hunting by the Gauls, but he does say in a reminiscence about Spain that after a victory outside Munda in 45 BC his own troops built a palisade decorated with the severed heads of their enemies. The soldiers who carried this out were "Roman," but Caesar says they are Gauls of the Larks, the Fifth Legion conscripted by him in Gaul some years before. So the practice of headhunting may on that occasion have been associated with the Celtic recruits, the levied auxiliaries, rather than the regular Roman soldiers. But the Trajanic Frieze shows members of Trajan's own mounted bodyguard with severed heads, so regular Roman soldiers were involved as well, and with the emperor's blessing.

In 54 BC, Labienus launched his troops at Indutiomarus, the chief of the Treveri. The Roman soldiers succeeded in killing the chief and cutting off his head, which they took back to the Roman camp. This brutal gesture had the desired effect: when the Gauls heard that the Romans had the head of Indutiomarus, they gave up the fight. They understood; it was a case of the Romans giving the Treveri a taste of their own medicine.

We know from archeology that severed heads were carried home and carefully stored, some to be set up in niches in **shrines and temples** and offered up to the gods. The imposing stone shrine at **Roquepertuse** in Provence has in its walls skull-shaped niches that were specially made to display severed human heads. The surviving skulls at Roquepertuse belonged to strong young men in their prime, evidently warriors, and they date from the third century BC. At the sanctuary of St. Blaise, again in Provence, there are also niches for displaying heads.

Many shrines carried representations of severed heads carved in low relief in stone or wood. At **Entremont**, also in Provence, a stone slab taller than a man is covered with very stylized severed heads; it apparently represents a niche wall. One of the actual skulls at the Entremont shrine was nailed onto the wall and it still has a javelin-point embedded in it—a clear sign of a battle victim.

The presence of stone heads as well as real human heads shows that the offering of severed heads as battle trophies was absolutely essential. If by any chance the supply of real heads dried up, or the shrine was desecrated and robbed, the stone heads could still stand duty as symbolic offerings to the gods. At Entremont there is a fine life-sized statue showing a warrior god sitting cross-legged: a typical Celtic position. His left hand rests on a severed human head; is this the trophy he wants to be offered, or is he showing his people the trophy head that he himself has harvested to keep the tribe safe? The image could be interpreted either way.

When **Boudicca**, Queen of the **Iceni**, was enraged at the way she and her family had been treated by the Romans, she led a rebellion during which her warriors took their trophies in the form of severed heads. During the rebellion, Colchester was destroyed and London attacked, and the fires that the Britons started left a red, burned layer across the City of London that is still clearly identifiable as "Boudicca's Destruction Layer" and datable to AD 61. The Walbrook Skulls are believed to be some of the severed heads of Londoners massacred by Boudicca at that time.

Folk-tales carry within them vivid memories of headhunting. In the ancient Irish epic, the *Tain*, we hear of the youthful hero, **Cú Chulainn**, taking heads as trophies. He decapitates the three sons of Nechta: the formidable warriors, Fannell, Foill, and Tuchell, who boasted that they had killed more Ulstermen than there were Ulstermen surviving. On his return, wildly triumphant, to the fortress at Emain Macha, a woman there looks out and sees him riding toward the stronghold. She cries, "A single chariot-warrior is here … and terrible is his coming. He has in his chariot the bloody heads of his enemies."

The Romans never conquered or occupied Ireland, or even attempted it, so they would never have seen Irish warriors behaving like this, but they saw it elsewhere, and they always deplored it. They made a point of deploring this universal Celtic custom, even though they occasionally did it themselves. Headhunting, like **human sacrifice**, was one of the badges of barbarism. It was just not the Roman thing to do (officially).

In Welsh storytelling, we find the same emphasis on the severed head, and its special magical quality, but with a twist. In the Mabinogion, the hero Bran is mortally wounded. He asks his companions to cut off his head and carry it with them on their travels as it will bring them good fortune:

"And take you my head, and bear it even unto the White Mount in London, and bury it there with the face towards France. And a long time you will be upon the road. And all that time the head will be to you as pleasant company as it ever was when on my body."

After decapitation, Bran's head goes on talking, which is often a feature of these tales (*see* Myths: *The Ballad of Bran*). In Ireland, the head of Conall Cernach similarly had magical powers. It was prophesied that his people would gain strength from using his head as a drinking vessel.

Turning a skull into a bowl, a magical cult vessel, was evidently something that actually happened in the Celtic world. The Roman historian Livy describes the killing of a Roman general, Postumius, in 216 BC, by a north Italian tribe, the Boii. They beheaded Postumius, defleshed the head, cleaned it, then gilded it, and used it as a cult vessel. Livy also described the Gauls taking the heads of their enemies in battle, and either impaling them on their spears or fastening them to their saddles.

The cult of the head was taken over in the Christian period in stories about the early saints. As soon as a severed head appears in a story, its archaic reference back to an Iron Age pagan world is obvious. St. Melor was one of these Dark Age saints, venerated in Cornwall and Brittany. He met his death by decapitation, but then his severed head spoke to his murderer, telling him to set it on a staff stuck in the ground. When this was done, the head and staff turned into a beautiful tree, and from its roots an unfailing **spring** began to flow. The biblical story of Aaron's Rod was filtered through Celtic pagan lore.

A Scottish folk-tale tells of the murder of three brothers at the

Well of the Heads. Their bodies were beheaded by their father. Three prophecies were uttered by one of the heads as it passed an ancient **standing stone**. The head declared that its owner, when living, had made a girl pregnant and that her child would one day avenge its uncles' deaths. When the boy reached 14, he did indeed behead the murderer, and threw the head down a well. The severed head, the ancient stone, the well, kinship, revenge, and the **rule of three**—all the ingredients of this story from the Western Isles were drawn from long-remembered Celtic archetypes.

The Celts were not by any means the only headhunters in the world, but they carried the custom to obsessive lengths. There was a universal interest in venerating the human head and acquiring trophy heads; it prevailed right across Iron Age Europe. If one single belief can be claimed as pervading Celtic superstition, it must be the cult of the severed head.

HEALING

Healing was a major function of Celtic sanctuaries and Celtic **gods**. The Roman healer god was Apollo, so his name was often added, during the Roman occupation, to the name of the Celtic healer. So, in the Vosges, there was a cult center dedicated to Apollo **Grannus**; one at Aix-la-Chapelle was known by the Latin name Aquae Granni; and an inscription at **Trier** mentions Grannus Phoebus.

HELIS

An Iron Age hunter **god** of the **Durotriges tribe** in Dorset. Hunting was a daily exercise of skill and courage. It was more than a secular activity; as it involved killing animals, which were sacred, it involved transgressing the territory of the gods. Catching an animal meant stealing something from nature, and it was a theft that had to be paid for. It had to be conducted as a form of sacrifice, an offering back to the gods. It also had to involve the consent of the victim or the deity who presided over the victim. According to Arrian, the Celts never hunted "without the gods."

The Cerne Giant in Dorset is a representation of Helis the hunter god who was guardian god of the tribe (*see* Places: **Cerne Abbas**). Returning from the hunt with a battle trophy, with the severed head swinging by its dreadlocks in his left hand, Helis shows that he is ready to hunt human as well as animal victims to help his tribe.

HERNE THE HUNTER

An ancient god of the forest. He is a **horned god**, and so may be a late survival of the god **Cernunnos**. The name survives in England, which means that the name, and the deity, could have either a Germanic (Anglo-Saxon) or an indigenous Celtic origin.

In *Windsor Castle* (1843), the novelist Harrison Ainsworth conjures up a vision of Herne as a forest god presiding over Windsor Great Park: "a wild, spectral object, possessing a slight resemblance to a human being, clad in the skin of a deer and wearing on its head a sort of helmet, formed of a skull of a stag, from which branched a large pair of antlers. It was surrounded by a blue phosphoric light."

John Masefield similarly introduces Herne as a character in his children's novel *The Box of Delights* (1935).

HOLY WELLS

There are large numbers of holy wells in Britain and Ireland, many of which are stone shrinelike structures built around natural **springs** (*see* **Ritual Shaft**, **Sacred Springs**). There are 600 in Scotland, more than 1,000 in England, the same number in Wales and 3,000 in Ireland.

The sanctity of **water** and its sources has always been a key feature of the belief system of the Atlantic Celts.

Sacred wells were honored with dances and religious ceremonies. Some of the wells are now little more than wishing wells, but some have specific rituals attaching to them still. The Clootie Well in Culloden Wood near Inverness in Scotland is one that still has its own ceremony. On Culloden Sunday, in early May, people go to the well and drink from it, making a wish and throwing in a coin as an offering to the spirit of the well. Then a piece of cloth, a clootie, is tied to the branch of a tree near the well. The clootie must be left there to disintegrate—removing it brings bad luck. The custom of hanging rags on thorn bushes was practised at other sacred sites too.

On major feast days, holy wells were decked with flowers. In Derbyshire in England, the pre-Christian custom of well-dressing continues, though it seems to have been intermittent everywhere. Local folklore enthusiasts are often responsible for reviving an old custom and suddenly a village will resume a well-dressing custom that has been allowed to fall into abeyance.

Probably in the early days, well-dressing was no more than someone leaving a posy for a water nymph who was perhaps being thanked for finding a maiden a suitable youth. By the start of the nineteenth century, wells were decorated with simple garlands. Over the years, well-dressing was becoming a more elaborate and intricate art. By 1818, the craft had developed further. Boards were cut to the shape that was to be the design and covered with moist clay to hold the flowers.

A modern well-dressing usually consists of a large picture, usually with a religious subject, and made with a mosaic of overlapping petals, or in some villages whole flower-heads. Other natural organic materials are used as well: bark, moss, lichen, leaves, and berries. Sometimes pebbles, sand, or seashells are used. All of these are held in place by being pressed into soft clay on a background board.

Traditionally, well-dressing was done exclusively by men, but such customary rules are no longer permissible.

Several places in Derbyshire in England maintain the custom of well-dressing. Of these, Tissington is the one with the longest continuous tradition, going back to 1615, when it is said that it was resumed as a thanksgiving after a prolonged and serious drought. Tissington's five wells were the only wells in the area to flow ceaselessly during that drought, supplying not only Tissington but the surrounding communities as well. But there is also a tradition that the practice started in 1350, when Tissington was spared the Black Death while all the other villages around were ravaged by it. Tissington was spared, it was believed, because of the purity of its well water.

However it started (or restarted), Tissington's well-dressing takes place on Ascension Day each year, starting with a service of thanksgiving in the church, followed by a procession of clergy, choir, and congregation to visit each of the five dressed wells in turn.

Buxton's well-dressing takes place on the Thursday closest to the summer solstice. Often it is said that this started in 1840, though this was probably a revival of a much older practice. Well rituals were probably performed beside St. Anne's Well, which in the Middle Ages was a **healing** well. Roman remains have been found nearby, so the practice may have been going on intermittently for 2,000 years or more. In the Middle Ages a statue was found in the well, and people assumed it must be St. Anne. It may have been a Romano-Celtic statue, perhaps of a pagan water sprite, but it was enshrined regardless in a chapel near the well. Many miracles were ascribed to it.

In 1538 it was unfortunately swept away by Sir William Bassett, who was one of Thomas Cromwell's agents. The chapel was forcibly closed and eventually demolished.

Modern well-dressing revives the practice, and includes the blessing of two dressed wells; there is a whole-town festival, presided over by a Wells Festival Queen.

HOODED DWARVES

Hooded dwarves, or *genii cucullati*, are often shown in threes, a common image in the Cotswolds and along Hadrian's Wall (*see* Symbols: **Rule of Three**).

A carved image at Cirencester shows three hooded dwarves with a seated **mother goddess**. The tableau does not make it clear what the relationship is between the dwarves and the seated mother, though we are told that her name is Cuda.

The Element Encyclopedia of the Celts

Also from Cirencester, a single dwarf, or *cucullatus*, accompanies a mother. He holds an egg and she carries fruit. The association of hooded dwarves with mothers is very strong.

There are also groups of three dwarves holding eggs. These images link the dwarves with fertility. On the other hand the hooded and shrouded nature of the dwarves implies a connection with death.

HORNED GOD

The horned **god** has a very ancient ancestry. There are cave paintings dating from the Old Stone Age in France showing a horned god.

Antler masks have been found at a hunter-gatherer settlement called Star Carr in England. As long ago as 8,600 BC, there was a small lakeside camp at Star Carr (the lake has now completely silted up) built on a birch and brushwood hut platform. The hunting camp could have accommodated no more than four families. At that time the area was surrounded by a forest of birch and pine trees, with some **willows** near the lakeside. This was hunting territory, and people camped at Star Carr mainly to hunt the deer who lived in the forest, especially red deer. In the campsite red deer antlers were found that had been carefully splintered to make sharp points for arrows, javelins for hunting, and harpoons for fishing.

The antler masks are thought to have been worn in religious ceremonies in which men became transformed into animals— evidence of an early belief in **shapeshifting**. The existence of a horned man/god across huge spans of time shows how enduring the idea was in western Europe.

The most famous horned god is **Cernunnos**, who wears a fine set of **stag**'s antlers, but there are other gods who are shown with horns but not antlers. Horned gods were worshiped as far back as the Bronze Age. There were even horned birds and horned swans, but horned men were more common. Some carvings show that the horned gods were wearing **helmets**, and that the horns were actually mounted on the helmets rather than growing, supernaturally, out of the gods' **heads**.

Horns were attributed to certain gods at certain times, to emphasize or increase their power as symbols, whatever it was they symbolized. Horns symbolize fertility in particular. Another reason for gods displaying horns was to emphasize their connection with the animal world. There was an intimate connection in the Celtic world between gods and nature—between religion and the natural world. The preference for worship out in the open air, in nature, similarly expressed a deep-seated bond between nature and the spiritual life.

HUMAN SACRIFICE

One manifestation is the Druidical practice of stabbing sacrificial victims, with seers watching their death throes in order to foretell the future.

Diodorus Siculus describes it with an air of disbelief:

They have also certain philosophers and theologians who are treated with special honour, whom they call Druids. They further make use of seers, thinking them worthy of high praise. These latter by their augural observances and by the sacrifice of animals can foretell the future and they hold all the people subject to them. In particular when enquiring into matters of great importance they have a strange and incredible custom; they devote to death a human being and stab him with a dagger in the region above the diaphragm, and when he has fallen they foretell the future from his fall, and from the convulsions of his limbs and, moreover, from the spurting of the blood, placing their trust in some ancient and long-continued observation of these practices.

Tacitus, too, describes human sacrifice in Britain. In particular, he describes what happened on the island of **Anglesey**. There was a **sacred grove** with **altars** drenched in human blood and entrails, which were scrutinized by the **Druids** for the purpose of prophesying the future.

In the first century AD Lucan describes how the Britons "resumed the barbarous rites of their wicked religion". He mentions three **gods**,

Teutates, **Esus,** and **Taranis**, as gods whom the Gauls attempted to appease with human sacrifice. Others, later commenting on Lucan's description, said that there were specific types of sacrifice appropriate to each deity. Taranis was appeased by burning, Teutates by drowning, and Esus by hanging from a tree. It looks as the three elements of fire, **water**, and air were consciously represented. Lucan describes a *nemeton*, a sacred grove, near Marseille where altars were heaped with unspeakable offerings and every tree was spattered with human blood; even the **priests** were afraid to enter the wood at certain times.

Julius Caesar's presentation of the Celtic practice of human sacrifice suggests that he at least thought the power of the Celtic gods could be neutralized only by exchanging one human life for another. When Gauls were threatened by illness or the prospect of battle, the Druids would perform a human sacrifice for them: a life for a life. Sometimes the replacement life offered up would be that of a prisoner-of-war and sometimes it would be that of a criminal. If neither of these was available, it might have to be an innocent life instead.

It appears that those committing serious crimes were incarcerated for five years and then executed by impaling. Those taken prisoner in battle were used as sacrificial victims. Sometimes they were burned alive in a gigantic wicker cage shaped like a man (*see* **Wicker Giant**). Sometimes they were shot with arrows; this is surprising, in that fighting with bows and arrows was unusual at the time. At the same time, a man was executed at **Stonehenge** in the early Bronze Age by being shot and killed with arrows at close range, so there was a long tradition of using the bow and arrow to execute someone.

There is also the possibility that human sacrifice was carried out as a foundation offering. Both at **Maiden Castle** and at **South Cadbury** there were human burials that look like foundation offerings.

The evidence for human sacrifice is much stronger in ancient Gaul. At the Romano-Celtic sanctuary of Ribemont-sur-Ancre in Picardy, the remains of up to 250 young men have been found. At the nearby sanctuary of **Gournay**, there is archeological evidence that sacrificial victims were beheaded with an ax.

The classical writers put special

emphasis on human sacrifice as an indicator of barbarism, because the practice was forbidden in the Roman Empire (*see* Places: **Lindow Moss**).

I

IMBOLC

See **Imbolg**.

IMBOLG

A quarter-day festival in the ancient Celtic year, thought to be connected with the lactation of ewes. February 1 marked the halfway point between the festivals of **Samhain** in November and **Beltane** in May.

A custom associated with Imbolg, of unknown antiquity, is the trial marriage, which survived until fairly recently in County Meath in Ireland. At Imbolg, young men and women might walk toward one another in the street, kiss, and be married; a year later they could come back and walk away from each other, ending the marriage.

IMMORTALITY

Diodorus Siculus remarked that the Celts believed strongly in the immortality of the human soul. One piece of evidence he offered in support of this view was the fact that mourners threw letters to the dead onto the funeral pyre. But this may not have meant that the dead were believed to live for all eternity—it may only imply that there was a short time after death when the spirit of the dead person was still close by and might be communicated with. In fact, many of us have had the experience of visiting the house of someone who has recently died, perhaps to clear their belongings away in readiness to put their house up for sale, and had the powerful impression of the dead person's continuing presence. It is easily explained by the arrangement of all the dead person's possessions, arranged in a characteristic way, conveying the personality, and implying that the dead person has just left the room and may return at any moment. In an archaic **society** such as that of the ancient Celts, that feeling would have been just as strong. But it is because of this type of feeling that, in common with all societies, archaic or advanced, we have funerals. There has to be a leave-taking, a moment of separation when we let the dead person go and when we return to our own lives again. In our advanced and largely secular society, a society in which few people believe in the survival of the human soul, we still write messages to the dead and leave them flowers.

There is nevertheless other evidence that the ancient Celts believed in the immortality of the human soul. Writing about the **Druids**, **Julius Caesar** said, "A lesson they take particular pains to inculcate is that the soul does not perish, but after death passes from one body to another." In other words the Celts believed in reincarnation.

In *Gallic Wars*, **Julius Caesar** comments about Celtic religious beliefs:

The Druids attach particular importance to the belief that the soul does not perish but passes after death from one body to another; they think that this belief is the most effective way to encourage bravery because it removes fear of death.

This belief carried over into the idea of **shapeshifting**, where some beings could adopt a new life-form without even the separating pause of death.

A number of classical writers tell of a warrior elite existing in Gaul and Britain, second in rank to the warrior king. This elite was associated with rich and elaborate graves, and the richness of the grave goods strongly implies that there was a belief in an afterlife in which all the gear necessary for good living would be needed. There was also an elaborate funeral in which these grave goods were assembled. Again, Caesar commented on the practice in Gaul:

Although Gaul is not a rich country, funerals there are splendid and costly. Everything the dead man is thought to have been fond of is put on the pyre, including even animals. Not long ago slaves and dependants known to have been their master's favourites were buried with them at the end of the funeral.

All this points to a belief in an afterlife. Lucan expressed it as a belief in a long life in which death was merely a pause, a bridge between one life and another.

This belief seems to have been real. There were many burials where pairs of hob-nailed boots were provided, perhaps to wear for the journey to the **Otherworld**, or to wear once there. At Cambridge, infants were buried with shoes that were far too big for them; apparently their parents nursed the hope that their children would grow into them as they grew up in the Otherworld.

The Irish had a strong tradition of reincarnation, perhaps several times. The King of the Land of Promise, Manannan, had magical powers, including the power to give new life. Manannan is of interest because he is associated with a real historical figure, the Irish King Mongan, who lived in the seventh century AD.

J

JANUS

The name of the Roman **god** Janus is used now, though probably not in antiquity, to describe gods with two faces or even two **heads** looking in opposite directions.

The sculpted Janus head at the **Roquepertuse** sanctuary in Provence is probably the finest example. This consists of two complete Celtic heads: they are bald with a goose in between them.

JUPITER

See **Sky God**.

L

LLEU

See **Lugh**.

LLUD LLAW EREINT

See **Lud**.

LORD OF THE MOUND

See **Crom Cruach**.

LUCHTA

See **Gobhniu**.

LUD

A British **god** who seems to have no Continental equivalent: a true native god. Some think he may have had the status of a supreme deity.

In a late legend, Lud had a temple on the site of St. Paul's cathedral in London. It is also possible that he gave his name to the city, as Lud's Fort. Ludgate in London seems like another link with the ancient god of the place.

Lud was later known in Wales as Lludd Llaw Ereint. With Mordaf and Rhydderch, he formed a triad.

In Ireland, Lud appears as the Nuade who led the third invasion.

LUGH

A powerful young Celtic **god**, given the name **Mercury** by the Romans. Smertrios is also known as Mercury, but this is not really contradictory, as the Romans often misidentified Celtic gods, for instance calling several different Celtic gods **Mars**.

In un-Romanized Ireland this god was called Lugh, "The Shining One," and he was known as "skilled in many arts together."

In the tale of *The Battle of Magh Tuiredh*, Lugh is credited with commanding all the arts possessed by the craftsmen in the house of Nuadha, King of the **Tuatha dé Danann**. He went to the royal court of **Tara** when a great feast was in progress. The doorkeeper asked him his skill and when Lugh said, "I am a wright," the doorkeeper said he was not needed as they had a wright already. "I am a smith," said Lugh, but the doorkeeper said the Tuatha had a smith already. So it went on, with Lugh listing his skills as harper, champion, hero, poet, historian, sorcerer, and cupbearer, but the Tuatha dé Danann had all of these. Then Lugh asked, "Do you have anyone who combines all these skills?" They did not and Lugh was allowed to enter.

Lugh was worshiped elsewhere too. In Wales he was known as Lleu. His name survived in place-names such as Lugudunum (Lyons) and Luguvallum (Carlisle). The town of Lyons was chosen by Augustus as the capital of the province of Gaul and the location of his own annual festival on August 1. This evidently continued an existing Celtic festival that was dedicated to the town's divine patron, not only the emperor Augustus but also the god Lugh. This is the ancient harvest festival celebrated in the Celtic world as **Lughnasad**, "The Commemoration of Lugh."

Lugh was a more civilized and sophisticated god than **the Daghda**. He had a **spear** and a sling instead of the Daghda's heavy club. He was a lively and colorful figure, youthful, athletic, and handsome, and able to defeat

malevolent beings from the **Otherworld**. His epithet "of the long arm" may refer to the fact that he could kill at a distance with a slingshot or a spear, or it may have the more general meaning that his power had a long reach.

LUGHNASAD

A major festival on August 1, celebrating the first fruits of the harvest. In Gaul during the Roman occupation, the annual fair at Lugdunum (Lyons) was changed so that it could be reconvened under the patronage of the deified emperor Augustus.

Lughnasad was adopted generally into the Christian Church calendar as Lammas. In Ireland in later times the date of the festival was shifted slightly to suit the harvesting of potatoes. The last Sunday in July became Garlic Sunday, which was set aside for the lifting and gathering of the first of the potato crop. **People** kept to this date, even if it meant going without food—July was "Hungry July"—as it was feared that the crop would be spoilt disastrously if it was lifted on the wrong date. This day was marked by a special feast, with the new potatoes being cooked and eaten with cabbage and bacon. It was also a time for assemblies on hilltops, and beside **springs**, wells, and lakes, though these had to be respectably converted into Christian places, often associated with St. **Patrick**. The saint in effect became a Christian replacement for the god **Lugh**.

In Ireland Lughnasad has been continuously celebrated or marked, at least from the early Middle Ages, right down to the present day. One event that still takes place on Garlic Sunday is the mass pilgrimage up Croagh Patrick in County Mayo: a 2-mile (3km) walk up a rocky hill on bare and bleeding feet. The custom of going up this mountain is a very ancient one. In pagan times the faithful ascended to greet wonder-working Lugh, the Shining One who overpowered a primitive Earth god to win the harvest for his people.

In Ireland and parts of Scotland, Lughnasad survives as the Lammas cattle fair. The word "Lammas" is related to the loaf that was made from flour from the first of the grain crop. Lammas also became known as Glove Sunday, when gloves were given as presents. It is difficult to see how *this* element could be an ancient Celtic tradition: 2,000 years ago no one wore gloves.

The same feast was known as Calan Awst in Welsh.

MABON, SON OF MODRON

See **Maponos**.

MAC IND OG

See **Maponos**.

MANANNAN

See **Immortality**.

MANANNÁN MAC LIR

The Irish sea **god**, with his magical powers of creating illusion, carries heroes to the **Otherworld** across the sea or beneath it. His name, meaning "Son of the Sea," connects him with the Isle of Man, and the waters over which he presided are those around the Isle of Man: the Irish Sea.

His **magic horse** is called Aonbarr. One of his magic **swords** is named The Answerer.

He is known in the island of Britain, but by the name of Manawydan.

The legend of the sea journey to the Otherworld has established Manannán's presence in Irish literature. *The Voyage of Bran* was written in the seventh century AD and describes how Manannán travels across the sea in his **chariot** and addresses Bran, a mortal voyager:

It seems to Bran a wondrous beauty
In his curragh on a clear sea;
While to me in my chariot from afar
It is a flowery plain in which I ride.

What is a clear sea
For the proved craft in which Bran
sails,
Is a Plain of Delights with profusion
of flowers,
For me in my two-wheeled chariot.

Bran sees a host of waves,
Breaking across the clear sea;
I myself in Magh Mon [his home in
the Isle of Man]
Red-tipped flowers without blemish.

Speckled salmon leap from the womb
Of the white sea on which you look;
they are calves, they are bright-
coloured lambs,
At peace, without mutual hostility…

It is along the top of a wood
That your tiny craft has sailed across
the ridges,
A beautiful wood with its harvest of
fruit
Under the prow of your little boat.

A wood with blossom and fruit
And on it the true fragrance of the
vine;
A wood without decay or death,
With leaves the colour of gold…

The poem vividly expresses the idea of an Otherworld which is this world turned upside down. The

The Element Encyclopedia of the Celts

sea becomes land, the waves become wooded ridges or the horses of Mannanàn, the foam becomes fruit, and the hostile emptiness becomes a paradisical land of plenty. Gods and mortals see things very differently.

MANAWYDAN

See **Manannán mac Lir**.

MAPONOS

There was a cult of the "Divine Youth" Maponos in northern Britain and also in Gaul, associated with **healing springs**. He was especially popular with the Roman legionaries along Hadrian's Wall.

Maponos is skilled in the art of **music** and in Britain the Romans equated him with Apollo the Harper.

In Wales he appears as Mabon, son of Modron (Matrona, the Divine Mother). Mabon is a hunter. In the tale of *Culhwch and Olwen*, he pursues the magic **boar** Twrch Trwyth and retrieves from between its ears the razor that Culhwch wants.

In Ireland, the nearest equiva-

lent to Mabon/Maponos is Mac ind Og, the Young Lad, also called Oenghus. He is the son of **the Daghda**, the chief **god** of the Irish. Oenghus's mother is **Boanna**, the wife of Nechtan; Boanna was the original **water** deity.

MARS

Julius Caesar commented that the Roman **god** Mars was popular among the Gauls and that booty won in battle was consecrated to him. But Caesar himself cannot have encountered situations where Celts were worshiping Mars. At some time the Romans applied their **war god**'s name to a Celtic god, or more likely to a number of gods with warlike characteristics, and the name Mars may later have been added to the Celtic name. What the Romans met in the Celtic lands was a **tribe**'s protector god, under all sorts of names.

In both Britain and Gaul, the Roman name "Mars" is linked with a large number of Celtic names. Sometimes the link is with Toutatis. Sometimes the pairing is with an epithet that emphasizes a particular personal aspect of the protector god: Caturix (Master of Fighting), Camulos (Powerful), Segomo (Victorious), Rigisamus (Greatest King), Albiorix (King of the World), Belatucandros (Fair Shining One), and Loucetius (Brilliant). Sometimes the epithet is connected with a locality, such as Mars Condatis (Mars of the Watersmeet).

So, we should not see a single powerful god, the Roman Mars, as being worshiped everywhere in the Celtic world. There were many: an infinite number of local protector gods, whom the Romans found it convenient to label "Mars," but the native Celts would probably not have seen any connection among them.

MATRONA

See **Mother Goddess**.

MERCURY

This Roman name is given to an unnamed **god** shown in a bronze figurine found at Heddenheim in Germany. This fine classical statuette shows a young naked god wearing a torc round his neck and a **cloak** wrapped over his shoulder and around his left arm. He holds a bulging **purse** in his outstretched left hand. At his feet are three animals: a goat, a tortoise, and a cock.

Julius Caesar noted that "of the gods they worship Mercury most of all. He has the greatest number of images. They hold that he is the inventor of all the arts and a guide on the roads and on journeys, and they believe him the most influential for money-making and commerce."

The god Caesar called Mercury was known to the native peoples as **Lugh**.

MIRRORS

Some exceptionally well-made metal mirrors were produced by master craftsmen. The Desborough and Birdlip mirrors with their beautifully decorated backs were probably made under royal patronage. Others have been found with simpler patterning, such as the one from Great Chesterford in Essex.

It is often said that these mirrors show how concerned the Celts were about their appearance: a proof of vanity. But even when new and well-polished, they can have given only an unsatisfactory and shadowy reflection. The biblical expression "through a glass darkly" springs to mind.

It is possible that the bronze mirrors were not just used for personal grooming but as aids to foretelling the future. Staring at the dim, dark surface of the mirror may have been an aid to prayerful meditation, and through the darkness might float images of what was to come. The mirrors were more than mirrors: they were windows into the future.

MONSTER OF NOVES

BOUCHES-DU-RHÔNE

The Monster of Noves is a huge stone statue depicting a monster that looks something like a lion. Its great jaws gape slightly, and a half-eaten limb hangs out. It has paws with claws extending to grasp severed human **heads**.

The awful image, designed to disgust and terrify, shows the triumph of death over life. The sculpture may be as old as the fourth century BC.

A very similar stone sculpture was found at Linsdorf in Alsace.

MORITASGUS

A Celtic **god** of hot **springs**. Moritasgus means "Masses of Seawater." At **Alesia** in Gaul, he appears as Apollo Moritasgus with a consort, **Damona**. He had a substantial **healing** sanctuary at Alesia, complete with baths and porticoes, and a polygonal shrine.

THE MÓRRÍGAN

"The Phantom Queen," the Mórrígan is a complex character. She is a spiteful Irish **goddess** of war and destruction, but also a goddess of motherhood and territory. The dual role suggests that she is rather like the Celtic **war gods**, who also have a role in bringing prosperity and well-being. The

Mórrígan nevertheless brings death, destruction, and chaos. She is a battle Fury; she does not fight in battle herself, but uses **magic** to generate terror among contending warriors.

One day **Cú Cuchlainn** is so intent on fighting that he ignores the overtures of a girl who turns out to be the Mórrígan; in revenge, she attacks him, **shapeshifting** into several different animal forms to do so.

Sometimes the Mórrígan is presented as one of a trio of war goddesses: the other two being Badhbh (Crow or **Raven**) and Nemhain (Frenzy). There are occasional references in Irish tales to the Three Mórrígans, the Celtic equivalent of the Valkyries. It may be that these are thought of as a threefold Mórrígan, rather than separate goddesses. Some commentators have tried to equate the trio with maiden, bride, and crone aspects of the same goddess (*see* Symbols: **Rule of Three**).

MOTHER GODDESS

The mother **goddess** is a complex being. Her cult inextricably brings together the living and the dead. She is shown accompanied by images of life and abundance, yet her likeness is buried in tombs with corpses. She also has a destructive aspect. For some reason she is closely associated with **warfare**.

These apparent contradictions may have arisen from the very powerful position women held in ancient Celtic **society**. There are Iron Age tombs in both Germany and Burgundy that were rich burials of princesses or queens. The archeology shows this, and it is supported by literary evidence too.

The classical historians note that there were two British queens who created more fear and chaos among the Roman legions than any king: **Boudicca**, Queen of the **Iceni**, and **Cartimandua**, Queen of the **Brigantes**. Irish literature shows the same story of politically powerful queens. Queen Medb of Connaught is a stronger figure than her husband **Aillel**. The same idea permeates Irish and Welsh myth, where a mortal king may marry a territorial nature **goddess**. In both Irish and Welsh sagas, descent through the female line is mentioned. In the Mabinogion, the Welsh god Mabon, Divine Youth, is the son of Modron (*see* **Maponos**). The Irish divine race, the **Tuatha dé Danann**, are the **people** of the goddess Danu. So the mother as founder of a dynasty and mother as monarch are fundamental Celtic ideas. If the matriarch is the mother of her people and of her territory, she must also be their protectress, and this is where her role in warfare comes in.

The central importance of the matriarchal dynasty-founder is demonstrated by the bronze cult wagon from the grave mound at Strettweg near Graz in Austria. The central figure is by far the largest, and it is a female figure; it is she who holds up the huge disk-shaped bowl.

The physical representation of the mother goddess reached its fullest development in the Romano-Celtic period. As with other deities who had remained largely abstractions in the free Celtic period, the mother goddess was represented in human or humanoid form far more once the Roman occupation came.

The Three Mothers became a common group for portrayal in stone, as in the plaque from Cirencester. Two fully dressed women sit holding what look like apples on their laps, one on each side of a central seated woman who is holding a baby. In inscriptions they are described as *Deae Matres*, Mother Goddesses. There are sometimes extra words denoting the locality, though sometimes that is a whole province—Gaul or Britain. A dedication in southern England mentions the mothers of Germany, Italy, Gaul, and Britain. Another, from York, addresses the mothers of Gaul, Italy, and Africa. But mainly the mothers are tied to a specific location; the Nemausicae were tied to Nîmes, and the Treverae to the Treveri **tribe** around the city of **Trier**.

The mothers sit side by side, fully draped. They have various attributes, and the commonest are **baskets of fruit**, horns of plenty (*see* Symbols: **Cornucopia**), fish, loaves, and children. Occasionally a breast is bared so that an infant may be suckled. An image at Trier shows one mother with a swathing band, indicating that an infant is involved, while the other two have distaffs. This suggests that the

The Element Encyclopedia of the Celts

mothers might be the Fates: the three goddesses who weave the destinies of mortals, from birth onward.

Usually the images are static, but a few are more animated. The elaborate stone relief of Triple Mothers with Children at Cirencester looks rather like a modern coffee morning, with three mature women relaxing while their toddlers play around them. But this is exceptional artwork, and far more Roman than Celtic in character.

Other mother goddesses are shown singly. At a shrine at Trier, the goddess Aveta is shown in several pipe-clay figurines; she is a goddess nursing a baby. Some "single mothers" look very like the figures in the Triple Mother images—seated, draped, and holding a basket of fruit or a horn of plenty. One of these, at Trier, was deliberately decapitated, possibly by Christians in the fourth century.

Matrona, the Divine Mother, is the goddess of the Marne **River** in France.

MOURA ENCANTADA

The *moura encantada* is a **shapeshifting** Galician **fairy**. These charming and beautiful fairies often appear singing and combing their lovely, long red hair with golden combs, promising to give **treasure** in exchange for setting them free by breaking their **spell**.

But they are also dangerously seductive. According to one story, they are the souls of young maidens who were left to guard the treasures that the enchanted *mouros* hid before heading for the **Mourama**. Often they appear as guardians of the pathways into the Earth, and so they can be seen at those special liminal places where mortals might glimpse the **Otherworld**, or even enter it. They might be seen at the entrances to caves, beside wells or **rivers**, or guarding castles or treasures. Folklorists think they may have absorbed memories of local deities, such as **water** nymphs or sprites and other nature spirits.

The fairytales featuring *mouras encantadas* are thought to be of pre-Roman, Celtic origin, with much in common with those of other Celtic water nymphs.

Every Galician town seems to have a tale about a *moura encantada*. Often they have been associated with megalithic monuments, perhaps because in remote antiquity, when these were built, they were intended to be physical links between this world and the next. In the nineteenth century, antiquarians followed the hints embedded in folk-tales about fairies to help them find megaliths.

Some scholars think the name *moura* is connected with death (via Latin *mortuus*), and that the fairies are in fact the deceased or the souls of the deceased. But it is equally possible that the word is related to *mahra*, the Celtic word meaning "spirit."

Mouras encantadas often appear at fountains or springs as **serpents**. It used to be said of a man who married in a foreign country that he had "drunk from the spring." In other words that he fell in love as a result of fairy enchantment. Behind this seems to be a hint of xenophobia: the idea that a man would have to be under a spell to fall in love with a foreigner.

Mouras may be "disenchanted," and if that happens, they may become human. If it is by the intervention of a man, the *moura* may marry him—or simply disappear.

The idea of a fairy becoming mortal and falling in love with a mortal man or falling in love and then becoming mortal in order to live with him is very widespread, and probably has its roots in old Celtic Europe. It forms the storyline of Dvorak's opera *Rusalka*.

MOURA-FIANDEIRA

Galician **fairies**, the *mouras encantadas*, were sometimes seen as spinning maidens. The maiden may carry stones on her head to build the hillforts, while she spins the yarn with a distaff carried at her waist. The *mouras encantadas* were believed to be responsible for building the ancient hillforts, the dolmens, and the megaliths—all the inexplicable works of ancient times. The **coins** found at these sites were called "fairy medals."

MOURA-SERPENTE

In some stories the Galician **fairy** is a **shapeshifter** who can take the form of a snake. Less commonly she turns into a **dog**, goat, or **horse**.

MOURA-VELHA

A Galician fairy who appears in the form of an old woman.

MOURAMA

The Galician fairyland, a **magic** subterranean place where the *mouras encantadas* live. This is the Galician **Otherworld**, the land of the dead.

MOURINHOS

A very small Galician elflike creature living underground.

MUNSTER

The landscape of Munster in the south-west of Ireland was dominated by mountains and a wild sea coast and in legend it became associated with the **Otherworld**. Its lakes and beaches led down to a sunken Land of the Dead.

N

NANTOSUELTA

This Gaulish goddess is given various attributes. In Alsace, in the territory of the Mediomatrici, she is often shown carrying a model of a house on the end of a long pole. This emphasizes her role as a domestic **goddess**.

Nantosuelta is sometimes paired with the hammer-god **Sucellos**. The **divine couple** sometimes have other attributes such as barrels and pots, and this may be a reflection of their association with the protection of wine production in the Alsace region.

Nantosuelta's name, "Winding River," incorporates **water** symbolism, which is common among other goddesses too.

NEHALENNIA

A Romano-Celtic **goddess** who is usually accompanied by a wolf-hound. The Nehalennia cult prevailed at the mouth of the Scheldt **River** in Holland, where there were two sanctuaries dedicated to her. She is mentioned on dedications and her image is shown on more than 100 **altars**. She is associated with prosperity, though the **dog** suggests that she may also be associated with **healing** or with the Underworld.

She is shown as a young woman seated on a throne in a vaulted apse between two columns and holding a basket of apples on her lap. She is always accompanied by the dog, but sometimes the apples are replaced by loaves of bread. In some altar images, she is shown standing beside the prow of a **ship**.

Some of the votive altars bear inscriptions that tell us they were offered in gratitude for a safe voyage across the North Sea. A typical inscription reads:

To the goddess Nehalennia,
on account of goods duly kept safe:
Marcus Secundinius Silvanus,
trader in pottery with Britain,
fulfilled his vow willingly and
deservedly.

NEMETONA

See **Sacred Grove**.

THE NUADE

See **Lud**.

O

OGMIOS

A Gaulish **god**, the equivalent of the Roman Hercules. Lucian says that the Celts saw Ogmios as extremely old and bald, with wrinkled skin, yet in spite of this he was portrayed as Hercules, complete with lionskin and club in one hand. He is sometimes called upon in lead **curse tablets** to bring misfortunes on certain named individuals. He was a god of **eloquence**.

OTHERWORLD

The Otherworld of Irish folk-tale is a true Celtic paradise. There are no diseases there, no worries, no ugliness, and no old age. Instead there are in abundance, **music**, **magic**, and birdsong, and everyone is young.

This pagan paradise naturally became a focus for poets, even for poets who were monks. From the seventh century onward the subject was repeatedly and sensitively reworked.

Before setting off on his voyage to find the Otherworld, Bran mac Febhail first pictured it as an island, later as "three times fifty distant islands," lying far to the **west** of Ireland:

There is a distant isle,
around which sea-horses glisten,
a fair course on which the white
wave surges,
four pedestals uphold it.

A delight to the eye, a glorious range,
is the plain on which the hosts hold
games;
coracle races against chariot
in the plain south of Findargad.

Pillars of white bronze beneath it
shining through aeons of beauty,
lovely land through the ages of the
world,
on which the many blossoms fall.

Unknown is wailing or treachery
in the happy familiar land;
no sound there rough or harsh,
only sweet music striking on the ear.

Another poem from the period dwells in a similar way on the allure, even to medieval Christians, of a pagan paradise:

There, there is neither 'mine' nor
'thine';
white are teeth there, dark the brows;
a delight to the eye the array of our
hosts;
every cheek there is the hue of the
foxglove.

Fine though you think the ale of Ireland,
more exhilarating still is the ale of Tir Mar;
a wondrous land is the land I tell of,
youth does not give way to age there.

Sweet warm streams flow through the land,
the choice of mead and of wine;
splendid people without blemish,
conception without sin, without lust.

Yet, strangely, in this perfect land there is still fighting. Perhaps fighting was seen as necessary for young men to prove their manhood. Perhaps it was seen as a positive pleasure. Late one Friday night on a Northampton street many years ago, I came upon a small crowd of people gathered around a huge Irishman who was lying in a drunken heap on the pavement. His face was covered with blood and he was the worse for drink and fighting. I managed to haul him up onto his feet, while the small crowd looked on impassively. Swaying and beaming with gratitude, the Celtic giant offered to give me a fight. He was offering me a treat.

The story of *Mac Da Tho's Pig* relates how Mac Da Tho, who is really a **god** presiding over the Otherworld feast, acts as host to the men of Connaught and Ulster. These opposing war-bands sit down to a meal of pork and the usual quarrel breaks out over who should have the champion's portion. Pork was always a major feature of these banquets, and archeologists have often found the remains of pork joints in late Iron Age graves, where both wine and a hearth were provided for a dead chief—and a guest, for company.

There is, however, a darker side to the Irish Otherworld. Sometimes it is described as a shadowy place presided over by the god **Donn**. At **Samhain**, when summer turns to winter, it is this more somber aspect that prevails; the spirits of the dead are allowed to move across the boundary into the world of the living and the barrier between nature and supernature temporarily dissolves.

The boundary between this world and the Otherworld is permeable at any time of the year. There are traditional tales of living mortals visiting the Otherworld, often enticed there by immortals, and later being allowed to return.

Yet Otherworldly time is different from everyday time. This

is perhaps rooted in the experience we have all had, of dropping off to sleep for a few minutes and dreaming of events in apparent real time that seem to go on for hours or days. John Masefield develops this idea in his 1935 children's book *The Box of Delights*. The world of dreams is taken to be akin to the Otherworld.

Another example of this is a story told in Pembrokeshire in Wales. A young shepherd joins a **fairy** dance and finds himself in a glittering palace surrounded by wonderful gardens. He spends many years there, very happily, among the fairies. There is one thing he is not allowed to do: drink from the fountain in the garden. As time passes, he increasingly wishes to drink from the fountain. In the end he dips his hands into it. Immediately the garden and the fairy palace vanish and he finds himself back on the cold hillside among his sheep. Only minutes have elapsed since he joined the fairy dance.

This type of experience is often described in mystical trances, in which an enormous amount happens, mentally and spiritually, within the space of a few moments. Some of the (possibly late) fairy tales emphasize the long spans of time it is possible to spend in the Otherworld; after these long visits the traveler returns, like the shepherd boy, to find that only a few minutes have passed. But many of the fairy tales turn this idea around. A fairy dance lasting a few minutes has taken a year or more in the everyday world, as in the tale of *Rhys and Llewellyn*, where a few days of feasting in the Otherworld take 200 years in the everyday world.

It is not always so. In some stories, characters move easily backward and forward between the worlds without any change in time zone. But the mortal traveler to the Otherworld runs the grave risk—among many others—that they may not be able to return to their own time. They could leave to spend a few minutes in the Otherworld and return years, decades, or centuries later to find no one living that they know and all their loved ones dead.

P

PEDRA-MOURA

Galician **fairies** living inside stones. It was once believed that anyone sitting on one of these inhabited stones would become enchanted. If an enchanted stone was removed and taken to a house, all the animals in the house might die. On the other hand, an enchanted stone might have **treasure** inside it.

A fairy might travel to fairyland while sitting on an enchanted stone that could float in air or on **water**.

PILGRIMAGE

An integral part of the Celtic belief system. The seemingly endless journeying described in some of the late romances is often a kind of pilgrimage. The **Grail Quest** in particular shows the medieval approach to pilgrimage: the long, difficult journey toward a climax of spiritual revelation. There were real international pilgrimages of this kind, notably to the shrines of St. James at Santiago de Com-

postela in Galicia and St. Thomas Becket at Canterbury in England.

This was in the Middle Ages. But there is increasing archeological evidence that religious pilgrimages, on a similar scale, went on as much as 3,000 years earlier. Some high-status graves near **Stonehenge** have yielded unexpected forensic results: one man was a visitor from Switzerland. Nor was this an isolated link with mainland Europe. At Stonehenge, a piece of lava was found that can only have come from the Rhineland. In a sense, even the stones were pilgrims. The very big sarsen stones at Stonehenge came from the Marlborough Downs, 20 miles (30km) away, and were probably dragged laboriously on sledges to get them to Stonehenge. More surprisingly, the smaller stones at Stonehenge, the bluestones, were ferried from south-west Wales, 135 miles (220km) away as the crow flies.

Pilgrims brought wealth with them, and left it in the form of **gifts** and offerings, and services purchased. Certainly by the Middle Ages, some saints' relics had become valuable commodities, simply because of their commercial potential. Often, the relics were forgeries. The monks at **Glastonbury** developed an entire mythology surrounding their abbey, concocting elaborate stories about Joseph of Arimathea and the grave of King **Arthur**—all to generate revenue to pay for repairing the abbey.

PRIESTS

There is very little archeological evidence of the priests who officiated at religious ceremonies, beyond the shrines themselves. But there are a few inscriptions referring to priests and there is some priestly regalia.

Crowns and headdresses found in East Anglia, at Hockwold and Cavenham, show the sort of garb that priests wore. Possibly the **gold** chains with **sun** and moon symbols found at Backworth in Durham and Dolaucothi in Pembrokeshire were chains of priestly office. A strange object found at Milton in Cambridgeshire may have been used in ceremonies. It is a flat oval made of bronze and has two perforations that were probably attachments for bells. It was probably carried in procession and shaken to rattle the bells. Another, similar object was found not far away in a Norfolk hoard of religious bronze objects. This was shaped like a spearhead and was evidently mounted on top of a pole. It too had a couple of perforations, this time with surviving rings. This too probably had bells attached.

Metal face masks found at **Bath** and Tarbes may have been used by priests during ceremonies. Conceivably there were moments in rituals when the priest's mortal face had to be hidden: moments when it was forbidden to look at the priest's face. Or perhaps the priest was protecting himself from the presence of the **god**. The Tarbes mask dates from the third century BC. Another mask, a gold mask that is believed to have come from East Anglia, was nailed up on a wall or a post and probably represented the face of the god (*see* **Druids**).

PRINCESA MOURA

A Galician **fairy** appearing as a snake with long, blonde hair.

R

RHIANNON

A **goddess** whose name is derived from the ancient name "Rigantona," meaning "Great Queen." She is closely associated with **horses,** and it has been suggested that she and **Epona**, the horse goddess, may in fact be one and the same.

Rhiannon appears in the Welsh hero-legends, the Mabinogion. There she appears as a beautiful woman in a golden robe, sitting on a white horse. The hero, Pwyll, riding his own horse, tries in vain to catch up with her. At last he calls out to her and she stops. It transpires that she loves him but is betrothed to another; they prepare to marry.

A winding, labyrinthine tale follows, involving **shapeshifting** and **magic** and the birth of a son who disappears. The women who are supposed to care for the lost child collude to put the blame on Rhiannon. When she wakes up, she finds she is daubed with blood (the blood of a puppy) and surrounded by its bones, and is accused of killing and eating her infant child. She protests her innocence in vain. She is condemned to tell her story to every stranger that passes and, if necessary, to carry the stranger on her back. Eventually, she is changed into a horse.

Rhiannon is also associated with birds. The birds of Rhiannon sing so exquisitely that they can send the living to sleep and awaken the dead to life. Both horses and birds are heavily symbolic of the journey to the Underworld: they accompany the spirits of the departed to the afterlife (*see* Myths: **Blackbirds**).

The **Uffington White Horse** may be a visualization of the shapeshifting Rhiannon.

RHYDDERCH

See **Lud.**

RITONA

Goddess of fords at **Trier** in Germany.

RITUAL SHAFT

There was a widespread Celtic custom of digging pits and shafts down into the ground. It is possible that some of these were wells, but some are clearly for some ritual purpose. The custom extended across the Celtic world and into the Greco-Roman world, where special pits called *bothroi* and *mundi* were dug to reach down into the Underworld. The intention seems to have been to create doorways that would connect the two worlds.

There are late Iron Age examples in Britain, but it is likely that they were made throughout the Iron Age because some Bronze Age examples have been found too, at **Swanwick** and Wilsford. It was evidently a tradition of long standing.

In Germany ritual shafts were certainly made in the middle Iron Age, and they were located in rectangular enclosures. At **Holzhausen** there was an enclosure containing three such shafts, one of them containing evidence of animal or **human sacrifice**.

The pits at **Danebury hillfort** in Hampshire may have been dug for grain storage, and the hints at ritual activity around them could be explained as attempts to propitiate the **gods** of the Underworld for disturbing the earth, or perhaps to ensure that the gods looked after the grain properly.

Most of the pits in Britain belong to the first centuries BC and AD, and probably only a quarter of them were dug for ritual purposes.

The shaft at Muntham Court in Sussex was 200 feet (60m) deep and associated with a shrine containing the remains of many **dog** burials. Dogs were associated with the Underworld, so their presence here was apt.

At Newstead in Scotland several shafts were dug, one of them containing the body of a man.

One of the most interesting of the pits is the one at Deal in Kent. This was excavated to make an underground shrine at the bottom of a shaft 8 feet (2m) deep. The oval chamber contained a crude figurine carved out of a block of chalk. The base of the figurine is a shapeless block of chalk. This tapers into a carefully made neck. On top is a well-carved round face, perfectly Celtic in style. It is believed to have stood originally in a niche high up in the wall of the chamber. Foot-holds cut in the wall of the shaft show that it was intended that the chamber should be accessible—it was not just a tomb chamber—and it might have held as many as five people. The pottery found in the chamber suggests that the shrine was made in the first century AD.

There is a problem in distin-guishing some of the ritual shafts from ordinary wells. Sinking wells for drawing **water** had become commonplace in the Roman world by the first century AD. The objects we see as ritual offerings could just as easily be accidental losses dur-ing the normal daily usage of the well. Sometimes there are complete vessels, which had probably been lowered to the bottom of the well to draw water.

When a well was considered to be of no further use, it was usually filled in for safety with ordinary domestic rubbish, and this too is difficult to distinguish from objects dropped in as offerings.

ROSMERTA

A **goddess** often associated with a wooden tub. Images from Gaul showing tubs sometimes have a paddle and a griddle, suggesting an activity such as dyeing. Rosmerta with a tub and a **purse** might be a patroness of commercial textile manufacture. Alternatively, the tub may be a small-scale symbol of endless plenty: a mini-**cauldron**.

Rosmerta is paired with Smer-trios (the closest Celtic equiva-lent of the Roman god **Mercury**). The **divine couple** are sometimes shown as simple Gaulish peasants and carved in a natural way that implies that these are images made by Celts for Celts. Mercury is pre-sented in a fairly standard way, but his female partner adds a homely concern for well-being in all as-pects of life and death.

One possibility is that a Roman god has been deliberately paired with a native Celtic goddess. This produces a wide spectrum of responsibilities for the couple. He supplies good luck, success in agriculture and commerce, fertility, and well-being. Rosmerta brings depth. She protects from harm and from the caprices of fate, she lights the darkness, and she guides us through death to resurrection and regeneration. She represents spiritual comfort.

S

SACRED GROVE

The Iron Age Celts built a few shrines and rather more sacred enclosures, but they also made widespread use of natural features as holy places. This is a very ancient practice that goes right back to Minoan Crete in 2000 BC, when mountaintops were regularly the focus of religious ceremonies. The Minoans also designated certain trees as sacred. The Celts, on the other side of Europe, had a very similar approach.

The Celtic word *nemeton* means "sacred grove" and the word survives in some Roman-Celtic place-names, such as Drunemeton in Turkey, Nemetobriga in Galicia, Medionemeton in Scotland, and Aquae Arnemetiae (Buxton) in England. The Irish equivalent to *nemeton* is *fidnemed*.

Roman commentators on the Celtic world mention sacred groves. Strabo mentions the reunification of three **tribes** in Galatia (Turkey) as being accomplished in a grove of sacred **oak** trees. The sacred location was chosen for the discussion of important administrative matters, perhaps for its neutrality and therefore safety for all parties attending, perhaps because the **gods** were expected to participate.

Tacitus describes the forest clearings on the island of **Anglesey** as the **Druids**' last stronghold against the might of Rome. Dio Cassius describes a sacred wood where **human sacrifices** were offered to the war goddess **Andraste**. Lucan too describes sacred woods in the south of Gaul: woods that were spattered with human blood. Later commentators, explaining Lucan, said that the Druids worshiped their gods in woods without using temples, in other words explicitly saying that worship took place in the open air.

The names of deities were sometimes specifically related to a grove. At Altripp near Spier, the name Nemetona is found, "Goddess of the Grove," and the tribe living in her territory were known as the Nemetes.

Sometimes a tribe identified itself with a particular tree species, probably the species growing in its sacred grove: the Eburones (Yew-tree People) and Lemovices (Elm-tree People). In Gaul, offerings were dedicated specifically to the beech tree. The very large posts raised as focal features in some of the sacred enclosures were probably symbolic of the tribe's sacred tree.

SACRED LAKE

Offerings were frequently deposited in sacred lakes. A small bay at the east end of Lake Neuchatel in Switzerland was a focus for this kind of ritual deposition. In a bed of peat off the shore of the lake a huge deposit of metalwork was found. It was put there in around 100 BC. People stood on a specially built timber platform, like a jetty, and from there they threw their offerings out into the lake: 170 **swords**, 270 **spears**, 400 brooches, and 27 wooden shields.

At Port at the north-eastern end of Lake Biel in Switzerland there was another concentration of offerings, mainly of swords and spears.

In Britain, Llyn Fawr in South Glamorgan is now a spread of peat, but in 600 BC it was a lake. Buried in the peat at Llyn Fawr were some imported Hallstatt material—harness, fittings for wagons, socketed axes, sickles, and two **cauldrons** made of sheet bronze. It is thought that the Llyn Fawr hoard was all deposited on one occasion, but at a time when the cauldrons were already antiques.

Llyn Cerrig Bach on **Anglesey** in Wales yielded a similar cache of metalwork, but seemingly from a longer period. Offerings were deposited there from the second century BC to the first century AD, so they may have been left, item by item, over the whole of that period, or collected elsewhere and then deposited in the lake all at once. Llyn Cerrig is a wild and awe-inspiring place. The metal objects all come from the edge of a bog deposit overlooked by a sheer rock cliff 11 feet (3m) high; this made a fine vantage point from which the worshipers could throw their offerings out into the lake. The metalwork was uncorroded, showing that it was thrown straight into **water**. The offerings are military and upmarket in character: trumpets, **chariot** fittings, harness, weapons, slave-chains, iron-working tools, and cauldrons. Some of the objects are flawless apart from the deliberate damage done to them immediately before being deposited. This was to kill the objects, to enable them to travel across to the **Otherworld**.

Llyn Cerrig was probably in use for sacrificial offerings until the Romans attacked the **sacred groves** of the Druidic center on Anglesey in AD 60 (*see* **Druids**). Tacitus described the scenes on Anglesey that greeted the horrified eyes of the Roman troops: bloodstained groves, howling priests, and black-robed, screaming women brandishing firebrands. But perhaps Tacitus exaggerated; the Romans were keen to justify the suppression of opponents.

The most famous sacred lake was Lake Tolosa at Toulouse in south-west France. The local inhabitants, the Volcae Tectosages, worshiped **Belenus**. They honored him by throwing offerings of **gold** and silver into the lake. When the Roman consul L. Servilius Caepio conquered the territory in 106 BC, he could not resist the temptation; he had 110,000 pounds (50,000kg) of silver hauled out of the lake and almost as much again in gold.

SACRED SPRINGS

Sacred **springs** and **holy wells** are hard to separate. What often happened is that a natural spring that was venerated in the Iron Age was later Christianized—and dedicated to a named saint to make that clear. It was often embellished with masonry and the **water** guided by a duct to fill a small tank or pool. In this new form, it often became known as a well.

There is a fine granite-built baptistry at Dupath Well, Callington, Cornwall. Other examples include St. Nun's Well at Pelynt in Cornwall and St. Hilda's Well at Hinderwell in Yorkshire.

At **Cerne Abbas**, immediately below the graveyard and the site of Cerne Abbey, is St. Augustine's Well. This is a shady hollow beneath some trees, where a natural spring has been surrounded by paving. The water from the well is supposed to have all kinds of magical **healing** properties, though this is hard to square with the fact that it runs out of the graveyard.

Sacred Vessels

The most famous Celtic sacred vessel is undoubtedly the **Gundestrup cauldron**. This bowl of solid and gilded silver is 14 inches (36cm) high and 28 inches (71cm) diameter, with a capacity of 28 gallons (105 liters). But there was an even bigger **cauldron**, the Bra Cauldron, which also came from a bog in Jutland, and that could hold more than 130 gallons (490 liters).

A good many sacred sites where ritual offerings were made to **water** are associated with cauldrons.

Samhain

A major Celtic festival on November 1, connected with rounding up livestock and choosing which of the animals would be killed and which kept for breeding. It marked the pastoral year's end and the year's beginning; it was the Old New Year. It was a moment out of time, when the boundary between this world and the **Otherworld** was down and the spirits of the dead were free to roam. The world was overrun by the forces of **magic**. A dim shadow of this feast, which was adopted into the Christian calendar as All Saints' Day, survives as Hallowe'en: All Hallows Eve.

The name "Saman" is inscribed on the **Coligny calendar**, so we know that the name of the feast is at least 2,000 years old.

Many **cultures** have a special celebration of the dead: a day when they are deemed to live again, on parole. To an extent, by performing certain rituals, the reawakening of the dead may be conjured. One way is to go to an ancient burial mound or **standing stone**, or some other place that has an association with **fairies**, and run around it nine times.

The Celtic year is divided into four by the major solar events: the solstices and equinoxes. These are the longest and shortest days in the year and the days when day and night are of equal length. These are also the days that can be found out in the landscape, by observing where the **sun** rises and sets, and they mark out the year's calendar (see Places: **Newgrange**, **Stonehenge**). There were also four quarter-days, which marked the halfway points between the solstices and equinoxes. In late antiquity, these festivals— **Imbolg**, **Beltane**, **Lughnasad**, and Samhain—seem to have been celebrated more than the solar events. The total of eight calendar festivals may be represented by an eight-spoked **wheel**.

SEQUANA

See Places: **Source de la Seine**.

SEVERED HEAD

See **Headhunting**.

SHRINES AND TEMPLES

Although there are some examples of built temples and shrines, the Celts did not build many permanent, roofed temples. The stone-built temples at **Entremont** and **Roquepertuse** were extremely unusual.

The Celts did, however, build wooden temples in the pre-Roman period. One interesting example is at Frilford in Oxfordshire. In the Roman period two circular structures stood side by side, each about 33 feet (10m) across. One was a building with a porch, and the other was a horseshoe-shaped ditch surrounding a structure made of six substantial posts with votive offerings. These two structures were each preceded by an earlier, pre-Roman, circular shrine. A small Roman town was set up close by. It looks as if Frilford might have been an Iron Age cult site of some kind, and the Romans wanted to perpetuate and develop it.

The Romano-Celtic shrine at Worth in Kent was also probably built on the site of an older, pre-Roman, temple; three Iron Age model shields were found at the site. A similar follow-on from the Iron Age happened at **Hayling Island** in Hampshire, **Maiden Castle** in Dorset, and Haddenham in Cambridgeshire.

At Hayling Island, the Iron Age Celtic temple consisted of a circular shrine placed off-center inside a square enclosure, the entrances of both facing to the east. The Roman period temple that replaced it sat on exactly the same site. Although it was larger and more formal in style, its layout was the same: a circular shrine placed off-center inside a square enclosure, the entrances of both facing east. The older temple was replaced and respected by deliberate imitation: the Roman version was simply bigger and "better."

At Uley too a rectangular Roman-Celtic temple was built directly over the site of a rectangular Iron Age Celtic shrine, and on the same alignment.

Sometimes we see the Romans as sweeping away whatever was there before, but as far as shrines and temples went they conscientiously continued the local traditions.

There are parallels to the British shrines on the European mainland. At St. Margarethen-am-Silberberg in Austria, there is a similar situation to the Frilford sanctuaries. At St. Germain-les Rocheux in Côte d'Or and at Schleidweiler, **Trier**, in Germany, again there are Romano-Celtic temples on the sites of Iron Age shrines. It is a common pattern. The double-square Romano-Celtic temples (square shrines with verandahs) were common right across southern Britain, Belgium, the whole of France, Switzerland, and south-west Germany.

The double-square temples consisted of a square *cella*, a box shape with a door and a pitched roof, and around this was built a low wall to provide a footing for the rows of columns to support a lean-to roof for the ambulatory. The walls of the *cella* rose higher than the ambulatory roof, allowing the possibility of inserting clerestory windows to light the interior. A statue or idol stood inside. The temple usually stood to one side of a rectangular enclosure. The central space in front of the temple door was the place for ceremonies—in the open air. It was here, probably, that sacrifices were made by the official the Romans called the *victimarius*, presided over by the **priest**.

Enclosed and roofed shrines were perhaps not built everywhere, though. Where there are well-preserved remains of shrines, they are often small, 16–33 feet (5–10m) across, and they often stand at one end of a fenced enclosure. Then they look more like a focal point, perhaps the dwelling of a deity represented by a wooden idol, while the main ritual activity went on in the enclosure outside. And *outside* is the key to Celtic

The Element Encyclopedia of the Celts

religious practice. The emphasis was on an open-air relationship with nature. This is very evident at **Val Camonica** in Italy, where there is a whole gallery of religious cult carvings on rock outcrops in a remote forest area.

Ritual enclosures existed at Aulnay-aux-Planches (Marne) and **Libenice** (Czech Republic). These were widely separated geographically and in time too—the Czech shrine was created in the third century BC, and the French in the tenth century BC—yet they were similar in design. Both were roughly rectangular, about 280 feet (85m) long and 82 feet (25m) wide, with cult stones at one or both ends. Both were places where **people** and animals were buried, and it may be that these represent animal and **human sacrifices**. The Czech site contained remnants of burned posts adorned with neck-rings, and these may have been idols representing **gods**.

There were two enclosures in Germany, at Goloring and Goldberg, following a similar pattern. At Goloring there was a massive central post, a cult focus similar to Libenice and Hayling Island, and it is likely that the post was a symbolic sacred tree or sacred column.

The remarkable stone at **Pfalzfeld** was probably a sacred column too; the high quality of its carving suggests that it was a focal point.

There is not much surviving evidence of offerings at Celtic shrines, by contrast with Roman shrines. This sometimes makes it difficult to be sure whether a site such as a rectangular enclosure was really for religious ritual or had some secular function instead. There are hints that human and animal sacrifices took place at some shrines, such as **South Cadbury Castle**, Aulnay, and **Maiden Castle**. Models of objects are found at some shrines, such as Frilford. Celtic **gold coins** were offerings to the gods at Harlow. At Hayling Island, coins were covered with gold to present an appearance of a richer offering; it is interesting to see that in the Iron Age it was thought possible to deceive and swindle the gods in this way.

At some shrines in Britain and mainland Europe, Neolithic axes were given as offerings in Iron Age shrines. In Gaul, these antiquities (already antiquities in the Iron Age) were deliberately smashed. This breaking is in itself a very ancient and widespread practice, and it represented a symbolic killing of the object offered, not to destroy it but to take it across the boundary that separates this world from the **Otherworld**, to send it to the realm of the gods. The collection of Neolithic stone axes for this purpose tells us something else about the Celts, which is their evident awareness of antiquity. They seem to have known that these distinctive objects came from the ancestors, and the no-longer-living ancestors were now in the Otherworld; so breaking and offering the stone axes was in effect a way of *returning* the ancestors' possessions to them. This would please the ancestors and make it likelier that they would intercede with the gods on the mortals' behalf.

The Romans commented on the isolated rural sanctuaries of the Celts, especially in Gaul and Britain, because to them this was a strange idea. But remarkably nearly half of the Roman shrines built in Britain were also built in isolated rural locations. Of those, half were built in completely isolated spots, and the other half next to or on the sites of old native shrines. The Romans were following and copying local customs.

What went on in these shrines and temples?

Prayers and chanted hymns were offered to the presiding god or goddess and offerings were left. The offerings consisted of gold, silver, or bronze coins and weapons, both real, full-sized weapons and miniature, model weapons. Jewelry was another important type of offering, usually in the form of copper alloy brooches with safety-pin-style attachments. Yet another category was **horse** harness. So, a rich variety of **gifts** was left in the shrine for the use of the gods. By the Romano-Celtic period, there was usually a complex of ancillary buildings around the shrine, and one of them would have been a shop, where worshipers might purchase something to leave as an offering.

Animal sacrifices would routinely have taken place, probably outside in the enclosure, and selected parts brought in as offerings. Animal sacrifices were widespread

The Element Encyclopedia of the Celts

and commonplace events at Celtic shrines. There were special decorated sacrificial knives and special utensils and cutlery for presenting and serving the roasted offerings at sacrificial feasts. Some of these have been found in the **sacred spring** at **Bath**.

Though small, the shrines were carefully designed with strategically placed window openings to create dramatic lighting effects on the cult images. Lamps enhanced these effects. The homes of the gods were kept fragrant with incense, burnt in special clay vessels. Herbs were scattered on the sacrificial **altars** and hearths: herbs that would make the meat tastier to the gods and their worshipers.

Mysterious and Otherworldly sound was added with musical instruments. In a Romano-Celtic temple, rattles, tambourines, cymbals, and bells were used. In a purely Celtic shrine, the harp provided gentle melody to hint at the sweetness of the Otherworld.

SILVANUS

Silvanus is the Italian woodland **god**. His cult includes hammers, pots, and billhooks as its icons.

SIRONA

The female consort of **Grannus**, the Celtic Apollo, in the Mainz and Moselle areas. Sirona also has a role as a fertility **goddess**, as she is shown with corn and fruit, or with a snake and a bowl of eggs.

SKY GOD

The **wheel god** is a Celtic version of Jupiter, the sky god. Some Jupiter figures are accompanied by a second, smaller human figure standing or kneeling to the god's left. Sometimes this second figure is made to appear sad. It is thought that it represents the Earth and the pairing of the two represents the dominion of the sky over earthly forces.

At Séguret (Vaucluse) the god is shown in the **dress** of a Roman general, but accompanied by an eagle, a thunderbolt, and a large **wheel**. In the background is an **oak** tree, which is a classical symbol of the god, enwrapped by a snake, which is not Roman but Celtic, symbolizing Earth or the Underworld (*see* Symbols: **Serpent**). It may seem odd to portray Jupiter as a Roman general, but the intention may be to show him in military triumph: the victory of light over darkness.

The association of the sky god image with oaks is a reference to the Roman association of Jupiter with oaks. In the second century AD Maximus of Tyre said that the Celtic image of Zeus was a tall oak tree. Valerius Flaccus commented that the Coralli **tribe** (probably Celts) worshiped images of Jupiter associated with wheels and columns (*see* Symbols: **Sky Horseman**).

SMERTRIOS

See **Lugh**; **Rosmerta**.

SPRINGS

The Celts were drawn to springs as places of mystery. The life-giving **water** came up out of the ground without any reason or cause, so it was supernatural: it must have a divine driving force. **Springs** often became associated with specific deities or sprites, and the water that flowed out was regarded as possessing special **healing** properties.

Some springs became major cult sites, such as the **source of the Seine** and **Bath**. Others were visited by pilgrims and were of no more than local significance, such as the Source des Roches de Chamalières (south of Clermont Ferrand). A typical one was Les Fontaines Salées (Yonne), which offered mineral water with medicinal properties and was in use from the early Iron Age. In the first century AD it was developed with a formally paved pool in a circular enclosure; around it were the remains of an older oval structure. At the healing spring at Mavilly (Côte d'Or) several interesting objects were found, including a figure of **Mars**, a Celtic **ram-horned snake**, and a **La Tène** shield. Vichy was another healing spring sanctuary, which may have replaced the Chamalières site. At Vichy, failing eyesight seems to have been the main health problem, but there was a bronze figure showing a twisted spine, so we have to assume people came with a wide range of problems, in the same way as they come today to a general hospital.

The evidence for cult spring sites in Britain is less obvious than in France, but there were such sites. The most important was the temple of **Sulis** at Bath, which had an international clientele, but there were many lesser sites for more local use as well. The Roman name for Buxton in Derbyshire was Aquae Arnemetiae (the waters of the **goddess** who lives in the **sacred grove**). The healing springs at Buxton are close together on the valley floor and yield two different kinds of water. The Buxton springs are still noted for their mineral water.

SUCELLOS

See **Sucellus**.

SUCELLUS

Sucellus (or Sucellos) was the Gaulish hammer **god**. He is shown wielding a long-handled hammer and nicknamed "The Good Striker." In the south of Gaul he was given some of the attributes of the woodland god **Silvanus** as protector of harvest and cattle. At some locations at least he is paired with the goddess **Nantosuelta**.

He was a very popular god in Gaul, though, from the evidence we have, less popular in Britain. An inscription in the Rhône Valley reads *"Sucellum propitium nobis"* (Sucellus is favorably disposed to us).

It has been pointed out that the "hammer" is really a mallet and that it has an unusually long handle. This suggests that it is not a real, earthly hammer, but has some supernatural use. Perhaps the hammer or mallet was seen as useful for symbolically banging bad luck on the head.

SULIS

The **healing spring goddess** worshiped at **Bath**, known to the Romans as Minerva. One of Minerva's epithets is Sulevia. **Julius Caesar** lists her as one of the principal deities of the Gauls. She was especially popular among ordinary people as the patroness of domestic crafts, and this devotion continued into the Christian period.

In the seventh century AD, St. Eligius rebuked people for invoking the pagan goddess Minerva when they were weaving or dyeing, which shows that it was an ingrained custom.

The nearest equivalent in Ireland is the goddess **Brighid**.

SUN GOD

The sun god is represented in a variety of ways. One is the **wheel god**, with the **wheel** as an obvious symbol of the **sun**. But the sun is also represented by the swastika, with the legs of the swastika apparently representing the rotating movement of the sun. It is not clear, though, how people in antiquity could have arrived at the idea that the sun rotates. We now know

that the sun spins on its axis, but how could people have known that 2,000 years ago? The legs on the swastika may instead represent the sun's ability to travel, to "walk," right across the sky each day.

There are quite a few images where wheels, swastikas, and dedications to a **sky god** occur together. Sometimes the wheel stands as a symbol on its own, decorating the front surface of an **altar**, like the one found at Gilly, near Nimes.

T

TARANIS

Taranis is the **god** of thunder. The poet Lucan, **writing** in the first century AD, referred to three Celtic gods encountered by

Julius Caesar and his army in Gaul, one of which was Taranis. Lucan describes his worship as "crueller than the cult of Scythian Diana"—the Celts offered him **human sacrifices**.

There is a small but widespread amount of archeological evidence for the worship of Taranis. At Scardona on the Adriatic there are inscriptions to a "Thunderer" and **altars** at Tours, Orgon, and Chester were dedicated to "Thunder."

But the scarcity of Taranis's name suggests that Lucan may have been wrong; maybe he was not a major god. There is also the possibility that he was an aspect of the **sky god**: one of the several faces of Jupiter. Some inscriptions support this view. "Taranis" means no more than "Lord of Thunder," and so could be an epithet of Jupiter. Linking the two in an inscription merely puts the Celtic epithet with the name of the Roman god, to emphasize the thundering aspect of Jupiter, who had other aspects as well, such as light-bringer and all-powerful ruler of the sky. The name "Taranis" does not seem to have been used in Ireland or Wales, and it may be that the thunder god was known by different names there.

He could be represented by the wheel or the **spiral**, which is sometimes used to symbolize lightning.

TEMPO DA MOURARIA

The time of the **fairies** in Galicia. Legends and folk-tales take place "once upon a time."

TEUTATES

The **god** Teutates was described by the Roman commentator Lucan (first century AD) as "cruel Teutates propitiated by bloody sacrifice." Another writer took this up and expanded on it, explaining that the victims of Teutates were drowned by being plunged headfirst into a full **cauldron**. Some scholars think this was an invention designed to please a Roman audience. Others point out that a scene on the **Gundestrup cauldron** does in fact show a god plunging human victims into a vat, so something of the kind may have happened. In Irish legend there are recurring stories of ritual murder in vats of alcohol.

are put under a vow of secrecy. If they violate this, then the weight of their mortal years can come upon them.

THREEFOLD DEATH

See **Human Sacrifice**; Places: **Lindow Moss**.

TIR NAN OG

The ancient Irish **Otherworld**, the Celtic heaven, literally "the Land of the Young," Tir nan Og lay far to the **west** across the sea. It was one of the lands to which the **Tuatha dé Danann** retreated after they were defeated by the Milesians (*see* Myths: *The Book of Invasions*).

In Tir nan Og time runs to a different pace compared with earthly time. It is a land of beauty, where the grass is forever green and where **music**, feasting, hunting, love, and fighting (the ancient Celtic pleasures) go on all day. There is no death; if any of those fighting are killed, they are brought back to life again the next day.

It is possible for mortals to visit Tir nan Og, by invitation, but they

TUATHA DÉ DANANN

These were the **gods** of the ancient Irish, who later became the heroic **fairies**, the Daoine Sidhe. When they were defeated by the Milesians, they retreated to an underground realm (*see* Myths: *The Book of Invasions*).

V

VERBEIA

See Symbols: **Water**.

VIERECKSCHANZEN

Four-cornered enclosures without any sacrificial remains are known by the German name *Viereck-schanzen*. They date from the Iron Age. **Holzhausen** in Bavaria is an example.

VINDONNUS

A **god** of eyesight, a curer of eye problems, Vindonnus is shown as a **sun god**, giving off rays of light. His name means "Clear Light" and he is connected with **healing water**. Votive models of various limbs were offered to him, among them bronze models of eyes.

VOW

Taking a vow was a well-established rite. The vow was a solemn promise, conditional upon the deity granting what was requested. The Celts applied this rite exclusively to **warfare**. **Julius Caesar** wrote:

When they have decided to fight a battle they generally promise to Mars the booty they hope to take, and after a victory they sacrifice the captured animals and collect the rest of the spoil in one spot.

The vow shows the Celts' piety. Booty that could have been a source of enrichment for the warriors was entirely devoted to the **gods** and their sanctuaries.

WAR GOD

Every **tribe** had its war god whose responsibility it was to protect the tribe, lead it into battle, and ensure its victory. The Romans applied the label "**Mars**" to every Celtic god with warlike attributes, but it is not clear whether the Celts had a concept of a general war god beyond the tribal guardian gods. The images are often presented unnamed; where there is a name it is prefixed "Mars."

Surviving **shrines** to war gods are very scarce. There was one at Bewcastle, to judge from the finds of dedications to the war god **Cocidius**. Later Roman geographies, such as the *Ravenna Cosmography*, mention a *fanum Cocidi*, a shrine of Cocidius, and it is thought that Bewcastle was probably where this stood.

There was a temple at Woodeaton too, to judge from the finds of cult objects there. These included several miniature **spears**. Miniature weapons were often left as votive offerings by worshipers: a practice common to many ancient cultures. At Woodeaton there were also two images of a war god.

Images of the war god vary across the spectrum, from completely Celtic in style to completely Roman. One of the simplest images is the one from Maryport in Cumbria. Carved in low relief on a square plaque, it shows a crudely drawn male with a large, round face, horns, a spear, and a shield. Often these images show naked warriors—Celtic warriors often fought naked—and often

they are shown with erections (*see* Symbols: **Nudity**). Images such as these are described as ithyphallic. The reasons for showing warriors in this state of arousal have been the subject of a lot of speculation (*see* Symbols: **Phallus**).

Sometimes the war god is shown with a goose. The goose is a good equivalent in the animal world for the tribal guardian god. Geese are very alert, react immediately and fearlessly to the approach of strangers, and are very aggressive; they "see off" strangers. These are exactly the characteristics required of an effective tribal protector god. Mars-Lenus at Caerwent is an example of a war god with a goose for a companion. It may be significant that Julius Caesar mentions the goose as a taboo animal: a sacred creature that may not be eaten.

In southern Britain, the war god was often a horseman, which may indicate the prevailing way of fighting. The horseman god was particularly venerated in the land of the **Catuvellauni** in eastern England. There was a sacred enclosure at Brigstock in Northamptonshire where several bronze horsemen were found, and this precinct may have been dedicated to the horseman god. At

Kelvedon in Essex, a first-century BC pot was stamped with horsemen with stylized spiky hair, hexagonal Celtic shields, and objects that look like shepherds' crooks. Images of horsemen in sacred contexts have been found at many sites across southern England, showing that there was a preference for rendering the war god on horseback. A stone plaque from Nottinghamshire shows a crudely stylized warrior on horseback and carrying or rather displaying a round shield and a spear. At the Romanized end of the scale is the finely made bronze horseman from Westwood Bridge, Peterborough.

In some places the titles given are very grand. Mars Rigisamus (Mars Greatest King or King of Kings) suggests that the war god was preeminent among the deities. Perhaps locally this was the case. At Corbridge, the warrior-god image bears the **wheel** symbolizing the Celtic sky and **sun** god. The horseman-god images reach a climax in the depictions on the Jupiter columns, where the **sky god** is a horseman overriding evil and death. On a smaller scale, the Martlesham statuette of Mars Corotiacus shows a horseman god riding down an enemy, who may merely represent human enemies or, on a grander scale, evil, night, death, and other negative forces (see **Cocidius**, **Helis**; Places: **Cerne Abbas**, **Maryport**; Symbols: **Sky Horseman**).

WHEEL GOD

A bronze figurine found at Le Châtelet (Haute Marne) in France shows how the wheel god was imagined: naked, with a mane of hair on his head and a bushy beard, reminiscent of Greco-Roman depictions of Zeus and Jupiter. In fact this might be the Celtic Jupiter. In his left hand, he is holding a six-spoked **wheel**, which is a **sun** symbol, and in his right hand he brandishes a thunderbolt; below the thunderbolt is the **spiral** symbol of lightning. The wheel god is evidently a powerful **sky god**, and the equivalence with Jupiter and Zeus is clear.

Images of the wheel god were mass-produced in pipe-clay in central France (the Allier District). These cheap images were probably made for poor people to leave as offerings or to carry as talismans. Two main Jupiter types were produced: one with eagle and thunderbolt, and one with wheel and thunderbolt. It looks as if the eagle and wheel are interchangeable, with the eagle for Romanized customers, and the wheel for Celtic customers.

A figure from Landouzy-la-Ville (Aisne) shows a bearded, naked god. He has a grim expression as he holds a wheel over an **altar**. The dedication on the supporting plinth reads "To Jupiter Best and Greatest and the Spirit of the Emperor." This is a Celtic **god** in terms of attributes and attitude, yet Romanized to the extent of having the inscription in Latin and the Roman emperor mentioned;

the long hair and curly beard are typical of Roman images.

Another wheel god image associates the god with fertility. This is not a normal association for Jupiter, but the Celtic world was essentially rural and the Celts were preoccupied with fertility and venerating fertility. So a seated wheel god might be flanked by horns of plenty, *cornucopiae* (*see* Symbols: **Cornucopia**).

Celtic sun-wheel signs were left as votive offerings at some of the hot **spring** sanctuaries in Gaul. Sun wheels were also thrown into Gaulish **rivers**, such as the Seine, Marne, Oise, and Loire. In southwestern France there was a custom of rolling a flaming wheel down into a river; the pieces were then retrieved and reassembled in the **sun god**'s temple. The ritual was a reflection of the solar cycle.

WICKER GIANT

Julius Caesar describes a particular form of **human sacrifice** carried out by the **Druids**: colossal human figures were made out of wickerwork, sacrificial victims were shut inside, and the wicker giants set alight. It is certain that the Celts carried out human sacrifices, though probably not by this method; it is hard to see how any wicker structure could hold people inside it once set on fire. The image is nevertheless compelling and memorable, which is what Caesar needed in his campaign to portray the Celts as barbarians who needed Roman conquest.

The idea was borrowed, with great dramatic success, for the film *The Wicker Man*, written by Anthony Shaffer and released in 1973.

WINTER SOLSTICE

The Celts seem, from the evidence we have, not to have celebrated a midwinter festival. The Romans had Saturnalia, which was in time replaced by Christmas, and the absence of an Iron Age Celtic midwinter feast is strange. The Neolithic communities certainly did honor the winter solstice, as well as the summer solstice, and attached great importance to both (*see* **Newgrange**). It may be that this was one tradition that did not carry through into the Iron Age. Alternatively, it may be that there *was* a pre-Roman midwinter feast, on which Saturnalia was based, but no evidence of it has survived.

PART 4

Myths, Legends, and Stories

Celtic storytelling has a very distinctive character and atmosphere: hard to describe, yet instantly recognizable in the selection that follows. Many of the stories have a sad and mournful quality, showing that the Celts have a keen sense of the tragedy of the human condition. The Breton tale *The Marquis of Guérande* is a characteristic example—sad and dark in the extreme. There is also a wistful hankering for a much better world, which comes across in descriptions of the **Otherworld**.

Some of the tales that have been handed down to us from the Celtic past are mythic, such as the Irish *Táin* (or, to give it its full name, *Táin bo Cuailnge*, "The Cattle Raid of Cuailnge.") Other stories have their origins in history, in the careers of people such as Hannibal, **Vercingetorix**, and **Julius Caesar**, and in distant memories of lands lost to a slowly rising sea (*see* Symbols: **City Swallowed Up by the Sea**). Still others occupy a strange ambiguous world that lies somewhere between myth and history, and fact and fantasy, such as the tales of St. **Brendan**, St. **Patrick**, and King **Arthur**. This spectral shifting backward and forward between the two worlds—this world and the Otherworld—is itself a major characteristic of the Celtic way of thinking.

A

AILELL

See *Midhir and Etain*.

ALOIDA

See *The Marriage Girdle*.

AMHAIRGHIN

See *The Book of Invasions*.

ANNAIK

See *The Marquis de Guérande*.

ARIANRHOD

See *The Four Branches of the Mabinogi*; Symbols: **Magic**, **Treasure**.

B

THE BALLAD OF BRAN

BRITTANY

In the tenth century, Kerlouan on the coast of Leon was raided by the Norsemen. The Bretons, led by their chief, Even the Great, marched out to repel the raiders. They managed to chase them away, but the Norsemen were, even so, able to capture and carry off several prisoners, and among these captives was a Breton warrior called Bran. A village called Kervran, "The Village of Bran," is still there, and this is where, according to tradition, Bran was wounded and taken prisoner by the Norsemen.

Finding himself onboard an enemy ship, Bran began to weep bitterly at his misfortune. When the ship reached the land of the Norsemen, he was imprisoned in a tower. He persuaded his gaolers to allow him to send a letter to his mother. They agreed and a messenger was found. Bran advised the messenger to dress as a beggar, for his own safety. He also gave him his gold ring so that his mother would know that the message had really come from him.

"When you reach my country," he told him, "go at once to my mother. If she is prepared to ransom me, show a white sail when you come back. But if she refuses, you must raise a black sail."

When the messenger reached Bran's home in Leon, the lady was at supper with her family and the bards were playing their harps. The messenger showed her Bran's ring and asked her to read the letter at once. She told the harpers to cease playing. Then she read the letter carefully and became agitated. She ordered a ship to be made ready so that she could set sail for her son in the morning.

In his tower, early one morning, Bran called out, "Sentinel, sentinel, do you see a sail on the sea?"

The guard replied, "No. I see nothing but sea and sky."

A few hours passed in futile waiting, until at midday, Bran asked again, "Sentinel, sentinel, do you see a sail on the sea?"

The guard replied, "No. I see nothing but the billowing sea and the gulls aloft in the sky."

More hours passed and in the evening, Bran asked again, "Sentinel, sentinel, do you see a sail on the sea?"

This time the guard lied. "Yes, there is a ship close by."

"What color is the sail?" Bran asked.

Again the guard lied. "It is black, lord."

Bran was overwhelmed by despair.

When his mother arrived at the town, she asked an old man in the street why the bells were tolling. He told her, "Alas, a noble prisoner kept in that tower died last night."

She walked to the tower and said to the guard, "Open the door, I want to see my son."

Once the door was open, she threw herself down on the body of her son and she too died of despair.

At Kerlouan, on the site of the battle between the Bretons and the Norsemen, an oak tree overhangs the shore and marks the place where the Norsemen fled. At night, the birds gather on this oak, whose leaves shine in the moonlight: birds of black feather and birds of white feather, among them an old gray rook and a young crow. The birds sing such a beautiful song that the sea itself falls silent to listen to it. All the birds sing except the old gray rook and the young crow. The crow says, "Sing, little birds, sing; when you die you will at least end your days in Brittany." The crow is Bran transformed. The rook is perhaps his mother.

In Breton tradition, the dead may return to Earth in the shape of birds.

Several incidents in the story have parallels in the poem *Sir Tristram*, such as the journey to a foreign land, the **gold** ring to prove the authenticity of the messenger, the treacherous gaoler, and the black or white sail. *Sir Tristram* was probably written in the twelfth century and the source is likely to be Breton. If this story is the original, it is interesting that an old woman, the mother, has been replaced in the later tale by a young woman, a lover. The truth may be unreachable, but what seems to have happened is that a fund of stories and legends was passed back and forth among the Atlantic Celts, from Brittany to Ireland to Cornwall to Wales—and back again—so that the ultimate origin of a tale is untraceable (*see* Symbols: **Rule of Three**).

THE BATTLE OF SAINT-CAST

BRITTANY

This is a "late Celtic" eighteenth-century ballad about a remarkable incident that happened in 1758.

A British army landed on the Breton coast, with the object of making sure the English Channel was safe for British merchant shipping. A secondary objective was to create a diversion for the German forces, who were at that time British allies.

A company of soldiers from the towns of Tréguier and Saint-Pol-de-Léon was marching against a detachment of Scottish Highlanders. When the Bretons were about a mile from the Highlanders, they could hear their enemies singing. The Breton soldiers stopped in their tracks, as they recognized the air the Scots were singing. They knew this music. Electrified by it, they joined in singing the patriotic song. All the time the two companies were getting closer and closer together.

When the officers considered them to be close enough, they ordered their men to fire. The orders were given in the same language. At this, the soldiers on both sides stood stock-still. After a moment, emotion swept training and army discipline to one side, and they dropped their weapons as they ran toward one another. The ancient Celts, so the story went, renewed the ties of brotherhood that had once united their fathers.

Although this story may sound too romantic to be true, it seems to be based on a reliable and credible tradition. The air that was sung was apparently "The Garb of Old Gaul," which was composed by General Reid, who was born in 1721 and died in 1807. The song may have been newly written and popular with both Bretons and Scots, so it was probably not an ancient patriotic song.

Perhaps the most interesting aspect of this story is that it shows the effectiveness of Edward Lhuyd's early eighteenth-century promotion of the idea of a common **language** uniting the Celts of the **west**.

BENDITH Y MAMAU

WALES

"The Mother's Blessing." This is a euphemistic Welsh name for **fairies**. The fairies were not by any means a blessing. They visited people's houses and made mischief there: they stole things, elf-rode **horses**, and abducted children. People tried to forestall their malicious pranks, buying their favor by leaving milk for them.

BEN-VARREY

ISLE OF MAN

The Manx name for a **mermaid**. Many tales about mermaids were told around the coast of the island. The Manx mermaids have the characteristics of mermaids everywhere, including treachery: enchanting men and luring them to an untimely death.

BERTILAK

See **The Green Knight**.

BLACKBIRDS

The birds of the goddess **Rhiannon** are blackbirds. They sing on the branch of an everlasting tree that grows in the middle of the Earthly Paradise. Their sweet singing so enchants the listener that it transports them into the **Otherworld**. They sing for Bran and his followers, the Assembly of the Wondrous **Head**, as they feast between the worlds.

The song of the blackbird is so beautiful that it is self-evidently a being from the Otherworld—and capable of spiriting us away there with its singing.

BLODEUWEDD

See **The Four Branches of the Mabinogi**.

THE BLUE MEN OF THE MINCH

SCOTLAND

The Minch is the wide stretch of open water between the islands of the Outer Hebrides and the Inner Hebrides. It is haunted by the Blue Men, who swim out to intercept and wreck passing ships. They can be fended off by seafarers who are skilled at rhyming and able to have the last word in an exchange of banter.

The Blue Men live in underwater caves and are ruled by a chief. They whip up the sudden storms that arise without warning around the Shiant Islands.

THE BOGLE

SCOTLAND

The bogle is a mischievous spirit who likes to perplex, bewilder, and frighten people rather than to hurt them.

The Element Encyclopedia of the Celts

One bogle is Shellycoat, a spirit residing in the **waters**, who has given his name to many a rock along the Scottish coast. He is festooned with weed and sea-shells, and it is the clatter of his shells as he moves that warn of his approach. The coat of shells gives him his name. This is one of the pranks he played:

One very dark night two men approaching the banks of the Ettrick River heard a doleful voice from the water repeatedly cry, "Lost! Lost!" They followed the sound, which seemed to be the voice of a drowning person, but to their astonishment it was traveling up the river. The night was long and stormy, but still they followed the voice of the malicious spirit.

Before dawn, they arrived at the source of the river. The voice could now be heard going down the other side of the mountain.

At this point, the two exhausted travelers gave up their pursuit. As soon as they had done so, they heard Shellycoat applauding his successful prank in loud bursts of laughter.

The spirit was particularly supposed to haunt the old house of Gorinberry, on the Hermitage **River** in Liddesdale.

THE BOOK OF INVASIONS

IRELAND

Leabhar Gabhala Eireann, "The Book of the Conquest of Ireland," is often referred to as *The Book of Invasions*. It represents Ireland's foundation myth. The conquest in the title refers to the arrival of the Gaels in Ireland, but the surviving text is about the last of six waves of immigration.

The first immigration happened before the Flood and was led by Cesair, who was a daughter of Bith, son of Noah. She told her followers, "Take an idol, and worship it."

All of these initial migrants died in a Great Flood. Cesair herself was drowned, but her brother Ladra was carried by the sea-current north along the eastern coast of Ireland, taking 16 maidens with him. He died "of excess of women" and was buried under a great mound on the shore, the first mortal man who went under the soil of Ireland.

Fintan was the only one who survived from that first wave of immigrants, because he had the power to change himself into the shape of a salmon, an eagle, and a hawk. So he could be invoked as a witness to Irish history. He was summoned by the High King at the time when Christianity arrived; he was then the oldest man in Erin (Ireland) and he could recite its history in its entirety:

"I was in Erin
when Erin was a wilderness,
until Agnoman's son came,
Nemedh, pleasant in his ways."

Next came Partholán and his followers. He fought a battle against a race of demonic beings known as the Fomhoire, and this was the first battle fought in Ireland. Partholán cleared four plains; before there had been only one. During his time seven lakes appeared. Many crafts and customs were instituted. The first guesthouse was built and the first beer brewed. But Partholán and his followers were wiped out by a plague.

The third invasion was led by Nemedh. Four lakes were formed in his time and 12 plains were cleared. By creating its physical features and naming them, this and the two earlier invasions were seen as giving Ireland its geographical identity.

After Nemedh's death his people lived under the sway of the Fomhoire. Each year at the festival of Samhain they were required to pay in tribute two-thirds of their corn, their milk, and their children. They rose up against the tyranny of the Fomhoire and attacked their stronghold. Of the few who survived, some went to Greece and some to the north of the world. Those who went to Greece multiplied and eventually returned as the peoples known as the Fir Bholg, the Gailioin, and the Fir Dhombhnann.

By now the geography of Ireland had become as it is today. The main innovations credited to the Fir Bholg are political and social. They divided the island into five provinces: Ulster, Connaught, Leinster, Munster, and Meath. Meath was the area around the center of the island, Uisnech. The

Fir Bholg also introduced the idea of sacred kingship. One of their kings, Eochaidh mac Eirc, was the prototype of a just king: "No rain fell during his reign, only dew; there was no year without harvest; falsehood was banished from Ireland; and he it was who established the rule of justice there."

These people are the first in the story to have a foothold in history. The Gailioin may be the same as the Laighin, who gave their name to Leinster. The Fir Domhnann of Connaught are thought to relate to the Dumnonii tribe in Britain.

The next invasion was by the Tuatha dé Danann, the People of the Goddess Danu. They had become versed in Druidry and the art of magic during their stay in the islands at the north of the world. They brought with them four talismans. One was the stone of Fáil which shrieked under a lawful king. The second was the sword of Lugh—the sword that ensured victory. The third was the spear of Nuadha—the spear from which none could escape. The fourth was the cauldron of the Daghda—the cauldron which none would leave unsatisfied.

When these people arrived in Ireland they demanded the kingdom from the Fir Bholg; if they would not give the land up willingly, they would have to fight for it. This led to the First Battle of Magh Tuiredh, during which the Fir Bholg were defeated. But the supremacy of the Tuatha was not to last long; they soon had to defend their kingdom against the ancient foe: the Fomhoire.

All these events were a prelude to what followed: the coming of the Sons of Mil. They landed in southwest Ireland at Beltane and, as the poet Amhairgin set his right foot upon Irish soil, he sang this song in which he claimed to subsume all being within himself:

"I am an estuary into the sea.
I am a wave of the ocean.
I am the sound of the sea.
I am a powerful ox.
I am a hawk on a cliff.
I am a dewdrop in the sun.
I am a plant of beauty.
I am a boar for valour.
I am a salmon in a pool.
I am a lake in a plain.
I am the strength of art."

After defeating the Tuatha dé Danann, the Sons of Mil set out for Tara. On the way they met the three goddesses of Ireland—

Banbha, Fódla, and Ériu—each of whom made the Sons of Mil promise that the island would bear her name.

At Tara they found the three kings of the Tuatha—Mac Cuill, Mac Cécht, and Mac Gréine—the husbands of the three goddesses. The Sons of Mil called on the three kings to surrender their kingdoms, but the kings claimed a respite, wanting to refer the matter to the judgment of the poet Amhairghin. The poet decided that the Sons of Mil should withdraw out to sea, beyond the ninth wave; to the Celts this was a magic boundary. When the Sons of Mill tried to cross it and land again, the Tuatha dé Danann conjured a druidic wind that blew them still further out to sea. Amhairghin stood up and addressed the people of Ireland. But then the wind dropped and the sea calmed and the Sons of Mil were able to land again, and then they inflicted a final defeat on the Tuatha dé Danann. This happened at Tailtiu, scene of the annual festival inaugurated by Lugh.

In spite of their defeat, the Tuatha dé Danann kept the power of their magic arts. They were able to deprive the Gaels of corn and milk until they came to terms. The agreement was that Ireland should be divided into two: above ground and below. The Gaels were to live above ground, the Tuatha below. And so the Tuatha retreated underground. The Daghda assigned to each of their chiefs a fairy mound or *sidh*.

Throughout Ireland, ancient burial mounds are still regarded as the dwelling-place of **fairies**. In the seventh century, St. **Patrick**'s biographer referred to the **gods** who dwell in the Earth, a statement that shows that the early Christians accepted the mythic tradition about the **Tuatha dé Danann**. People needed to explain the existence of the mounds (*see* Religion: **The Daghda**, **Lugh**; Symbols: **Shapeshifting**).

BRAN

See **The Ballad of Bran.**

Bran the Blessed

See **Branwen**; Symbols: **Giant**.

Bran, Son of Febal

IRELAND

Bran was out walking one day when he was overwhelmed by the sound of music that was so sweet that he could not stay awake. When he woke up, he found a silver branch covered with white apple-blossom in his hand. He carried it back to his fort.

When all his people were gathered round him, a woman in strange costume suddenly appeared in front of him, singing a song about Emhain, the Island of Women: a place without want, winter, or grief, where the golden horses of **Manannàn** cantered on the beach and games went on ceaselessly. She urged Bran to sail to that island and the silver branch leapt from his hand into hers.

The next day, Bran and his company set off in a fleet of *curraghs*, rowing far out across the sea. They met a warrior driving a chariot across the waves as if it had been the land. He told Bran that he was Manannàn, son of Lir, and sang about the Island of Women, inviting Bran to visit.

On the way to Emhain, Bran's *curraghs* passed the Island of Delight, but when they tried to hail the inhabitants, they could get no reply beyond pointing and laughter. Bran landed one of his men on the island, but he too started laughing.

Soon they reached the Island of Women, where they enjoyed all the pleasures of the island.

After they had been there for what seemed like a year, they decided it was time to return home; they pined for Ireland.

Bran approached the Irish coast at a place called Srub Bruin. People on the shore called out to him. When he told them his name, they said that no man of that name was alive, though they did have a very old story that told how a man named Bran, son of Febal, had sailed away to look for the Island of Women.

When one of Bran's companions, Nechtan, heard this, he leapt out of his *curragh* and waded ashore through the surf. But the moment he stepped up onto the beach, all his mortal years came upon him all at once and he crumbled into a handful of dust.

Bran stayed awhile, still in his *curragh*, to tell his countrymen all of his experiences. Then he turned his fleet away from the shore and rowed away. He and his companions were never seen in Ireland again. (*See* Religion: **Otherworld**; Symbols: **Isles of the Blessed**.)

BRANWEN

WALES

When Pryderi was Lord of Dyfed, Bran the Blessed was King of the Island of Britain. He had a full sister, Branwen, who was one of the Three Great Ladies of this Island. He also had a full brother, Manawydan, and two half-brothers. One was Nisien, who brought peace to contending armies and friendship to men, and the other was Efnisien, the most quarrelsome man in Britain.

One day, Bran was sitting with his brothers and nobles on the great rock of Harlech and they saw 13 ships sailing toward them from the south of Ireland. Bran asked his brother Manawydan to go and meet the ships to discover their purpose.

One of the ships drew ahead of the others and Manawydan and Nisien watched as a painted shield was lifted high above the ship's deck, point uppermost, a token of peace. Manawydan lifted his shield in the same way.

The men on the ship came ashore in small boats, greeting Bran. "These, king, are the ships of Matholwch, King of Ireland. He has come in person to ask for Branwen, your sister, in marriage. Will you bid him land?"

Matholwch duly came ashore, greeted Bran, and there was a joyous gathering of the two hosts. The following day, it was agreed that Matholwch should marry Branwen and that the marriage would serve as a peace treaty between Britain and Ireland.

The marriage feast was to be at Aberffraw; Matholwch and his host set sail in their ships, and

Bran and his host set off over land. The feast was held in the open air, as there was no house big enough to hold the godlike Bran, who was enormous.

While billets were being found for the horses and grooms, the quarrelsome brother, Efnisien, arrived. He was annoyed that he recognized neither grooms nor horses and asked what was happening. He was even more annoyed that Branwen had been given in marriage without his consent and swore revenge, maltreating both the horses and the grooms.

Word of this reached Matholwch, who was puzzled and made arrangements to set sail again for home. Bran in turn was perplexed by Matholwch's discourtesy and sent word that Matholwch's grievance was against his brother Efnisien, not against him. "Tell him I shall give him a sound horse for each horse spoiled, and for his injured pride I shall give him a staff of silver as thick as his finger and as tall as himself, and I shall give him a plate made of gold as broad as his face. If he is not content with this, then he should come to see me and my brother Nisien shall make peace between us on terms that he

shall name. I will not have Matholwch return to Ireland in anger; I will not have sorrow brought on Branwen."

Matholwch was persuaded to accept Bran's friendly offer. He ordered his ships' sails to be furled again and returned to Bran's court.

Matholwch and Bran fell into conversation and Bran offered to give something else in reparation: "Tomorrow when the counting of the new horses is done, I will give you the Cauldron of Rebirth. If one of your men is killed, cast him into the cauldron and the next day he will live again. He will be as good as new, except that he will have lost the power of speech."

After that, Matholwch was merry enough and Bran was as good as his word. He gave Matholwch the Cauldron of Rebirth, which all knew was one of the chief treasures ever found in the island of Britain.

Matholwch set sail for Ireland with his 13 ships. On the swiftest of them sat Branwen on a throne of gold and ivory. Horns and trumpets sounded from ship to shore and back again, and Bran watched his sister go with tears in his eyes. Manawydan and Nisien told him he should be happy on this wedding day, but he was filled with foreboding.

For a year, Branwen lived in honor and friendship in Ireland. But then the insult to Matholwch was remembered by some of his men, who taunted him with cowardice. "A king's shame is the shame of his warriors," they said.

The king was persuaded to banish Branwen from his court; she was made to work in the kitchens. Matholwch knew how angry Bran would be at this, and ordered every person visiting from Wales to be imprisoned, so that Bran should never know what had become of his sister. So it continued for three years.

Branwen wrote a letter describing her misfortunes and fixed it to a starling's wing. The starling flew across the sea to the court of Bran and alighted on his shoulder. It ruffled its feathers so that Bran could see the letter. He unfastened it and read it. He was so grateful to the starling that he gave it a bowl for food and a bowl for water and a perch for resting—in every palace in his lands.

Bran assembled his council and read aloud the letter, and they decided to sail for Ireland. Seven knights were left behind to guard the kingdom and Bran's son Cradawg was their leader.

There was no ship large enough for Bran, so he crossed the sea by wading, carrying his minstrels on his back. Matholwch's swineherds saw this strange mountain approaching through the waves and a forest growing out of the sea and tried to describe it to Matholwch. He asked Branwen to explain what the swineherds had seen and she understood: the forest was the many masts of Bran's fleet and the mountain was Bran himself.

Matholwch and his men withdrew to the west, beyond the Shannon River, and broke down the bridge behind them. There were stones on the riverbed that stopped ships sailing along it.

When he reached the Shannon, Bran offered the solution: "He who is chief, let him be the bridge. I myself will be a bridge." He lay across the river and his army passed over him.

Matholwch sent messengers with friendly greetings, offering the kingdom of Ireland to Gwern, Branwen's son, as reparation for the wrong done to Branwen.

Bran replied, "You need not tell your lord that I am other than angry with him."

The Element Encyclopedia of the Celts

Matholwch took advice and set about building a house large enough to accommodate Bran, since that feat had never been achieved. The plan was to offer Bran homage and the kingship and make peace.

But the Irish turned the house into a trap. A bag was hung on either side of every pillar in the house, and in every bag an armed man was concealed.

Efnisien came and inspected the house, hoping to find fault with it. He asked what was in one of the bags. A nervous Irishman answered, "Flour, sir."

"Then this will do no harm," said Efnisien, feeling around the bag until he found a head. He squeezed the head until he felt his fingers break the skull. Then he went on to the next bag and did the same. And so it went on until there was only one bag left. This time Efnisien felt a helmet, but he would not leave it until this last man too was dead.

Then the two hosts arrived and there was peace between them. The only discordant voice was Efnisien's. "Why does my sister's son, the boy Gwern, not come to me? Am I less in his eyes than my brothers? Is he too proud, now that he is King of Ireland?"

Bran urged the boy to go to his uncle. But when he did, Efnisien seized him and hurled him into the flaming fire.

Branwen would have leaped in too, to save her son, but Bran's brothers held her back. Every man in the house stood up and drew his sword and a great battle broke out.

The Irish kindled a fire beneath the Cauldron of Rebirth. As their men fell, they flung their corpses into the cauldron and the next day they stepped out again, renewed.

Efnisien saw that there was no room in the cauldron for his own countrymen and was ashamed that he had brought this disaster on them. He crept in amongst the Irish corpses, lay still, and soon he too was flung into the cauldron. Once inside, he stretched himself out and burst the cauldron into four pieces; in doing this, he burst his own heart too. But for this, no British men would have survived.

Bran was wounded with a poisoned spear. Knowing he would die, he ordered Manawydan to cut off his head, take it to the White Mount in London, and bury it there with the face toward France.

Bran warned that it would take a long time to reach London. The company was to go first to Harlech and then to dwell in happiness at Grassholm in Pembrokeshire for 80 years, until the door toward Aber Henfelen was opened. Once that door was opened, they must stay no longer, but make for London to bury the uncorrupted head.

Manawydan cut off his brother's head and the seven British survivors of the battle returned to Britain, taking Branwen and the head of Bran with them. Branwen was overwhelmed with sadness at the devastation of the two islands—all, she thought, because of her. Her heart broke and she was buried on the bank of a river.

As the seven men journeyed, they heard the news that Caswallawn, son of Beli, had fallen on Cradawg, the son of Bran, and killed him and six other men while wearing a magic cloak that made him invisible. He had conquered the Island of the Mighty and was now King of Britain.

The company of Bran spent seven years at Harlech. While they were there, three birds of Rhiannon visited them and sang a song that was sweeter than any other music they had ever heard.

Then they went to Grassholm, where they found a royal hall.

Two of its doors stood wide open, but the third stood closed. There they stayed for 80 years and the head was pleasant company all this time. The company became known as the Assembly of the Wondrous Head.

One day Heilyn, son of Gwyn, decided the time had come to open the third door. Through it they saw Cornwall and Aber Henfelen. Then they became conscious of every loss they had sustained and felt each as keenly as at the first moment. Then they knew no rest. They had to set off for the White Mount and bury the head there.

That was one of the Three Happy Concealments of the Island. It would be one of the Three Unhappy Disclosures when it was disclosed, but while the head remained concealed, no plague could cross the sea to Britain.

C

BREOGÁN

See **Trezenzon the Monk and the Great Island**.

THE BUGGANE

ISLE OF MAN

A particularly unpleasant and vicious type of goblin, skilled at **shapeshifting**.

A buggane haunts Spooty Wooar, a waterfall, in the shape of a black calf that sometimes crosses the road and jumps into the pool with a sound like chains being shaken.

One day, shapeshifting into near-human form, he went to a house and picked up a girl working there, carried her off, and was intent on taking her down to his home beneath the pool below the waterfall. Luckily, the girl had a knife in her hand, and she used it to cut the string of her apron and get herself free.

CALATIN

See Symbols: **Magic**.

CARIDWEN

See **The History of Taliesin**.

CEASG

SCOTLAND

A **mermaid** in the Scottish Highlands, also known as *maighdean na twinne*, "maiden of the wave." Her body is the body of a beautiful woman, while her tail is the shape of the tail of a young salmon.

If you can catch a mermaid, you can make her grant you three wishes. The *ceasg* can also sometimes be persuaded to marry a man, though these relationships usually end badly.

CESAIR

See **The Book of Invasions**.

CIGFA

See **The Four Branches of the Mabinogi**.

THE CLARK OF GARLON

See **The Marquis de Guérande**.

COMORRE THE CURSED

BRITTANY

Triphyna was the beloved daughter of Guerech, Count of Vannes, the Land of White Corn. One day an embassy arrived from Comorre, Prince of Cournuaille, the Land of Black Corn, demanding Triphyna's hand in marriage.

Triphyna and her father were alarmed. Comorre was a wicked giant, known for his cruelty. When he chased and failed to catch a peasant, he would set his dogs loose to tear him to pieces. But, from Triphyna's point of view, the most distressing aspect of Comorre's reputation was that he had married four wives and killed all of them, or at least it was suspected that he had, whether by fire, water, poison, or the knife.

Guerech would not agree to the ambassadors' demand. He sent them away and went out to meet Comorre, who approached with a band of warriors. It seemed that bloodshed was inevitable.

St. Gildas visited Triphyna, who was sheltering in her oratory, and persuaded her to consent to the marriage. He gave her a magic silver ring, which would turn as black as a raven's wing when she was in imminent danger.

Comorre's army halted, the marriage was agreed, and the wedding took place amid great celebrations.

Comorre's nature seemed to have changed. His prisons were empty; the wind blew through his empty gibbets. Yet Triphyna was uneasy, and every day she went to pray at the tombs of his four earlier wives.

An assembly of Breton princes was called at Rennes. Comorre gave Triphyna his keys before he set off and asked her to entertain herself while he was away. He was gone five months and when he returned, he found her trimming a baby's cap with gold lace. Comorre turned pale when he saw this. Triphyna told him he was soon to be a father and he left her in a rage. She could not understand it, but noticed that her silver ring had turned as black as a raven's wing, so she knew she was in danger. She went down into the vaulted chapel to pray.

When she rose at midnight to return to her chamber, there was a sound of movement in the chapel. Frightened, she hid in a recess. From there, she saw the four tombs of Comorre's wives slowly opening. Out they stepped in their winding sheets.

The spectral wives cried out to Triphyna, "Take care, poor lost soul! Comorre will seek to kill you."

"But what have I done?"

"You have told him you will become a mother. He knows from consulting a spirit that his child will kill him. We died at his hand when we told him what you have told him."

"What can I do? How can I save myself?" Triphyna cried.

"Return to your father," the spectral wives replied.

"But how can I reach him, when Comorre's savage hound stands guard?"

"Give him this poison, which first killed me," said the first wife.

"But how can I climb down the high castle wall?"

"Use this cord, which first strangled me," said the second wife.

"But how can I find my way home through the dark?"

"By the light of the fire, which first burned me," said the third wife.

"But how shall I make such a long journey?"

"Lean on this staff, which first broke my skull," said the fourth wife.

Armed with the staff, the rope, and the poison, Triphyna made her way out of Comorre's castle. She silenced the dog, climbed down the curtain wall, and found her way by a magical glowing light that led the way to Vannes.

The next morning, when Comorre woke, he discovered that his wife had gone and pursued her on horseback.

Triphyna, still on the road, saw her ring turning black, black as a raven's wing. She stepped aside from the road and hid until night-fall in a shepherd's hut, with only a magpie in a cage for company. There, in the hut, the baby was born.

Comorre gave up the chase, turned back, and then heard the magpie imitating the voice of Triphyna, and calling out, "Poor Triphyna!" He guessed that his wife must have passed close by and unleashed his savage hound.

Triphyna was exhausted now and though she had set off again she had to lie down on the ground with her newborn child to rest. She looked up and saw in the sky a falcon wearing a golden collar, which she recognized as her father's. She called to it and it flew down and came to her. She gave it the magic silver ring of St. Gildas and told it to take it to her father.

The falcon flew away like the wind, but just then Comorre arrived. Triphyna only just had time to conceal her baby in a hollow tree before he savagely threw himself upon her. He whirled his sword and with a single stroke severed her head from her body.

The falcon flew into Count Guerech's hall while the count was at dinner with St Gildas. It hovered over the count and dropped the magic ring into his silver cup.

Guerech and St. Gildas recog-nized it at once, and it was black, black as a raven's wing. Guerech cried out, "Saddle the horses and let Gildas here come with us."

They followed the falcon, which took them to the spot where Triphyna lay dead on the ground. Guerich and Gildas knelt in prayer.

Then Gildas said to Triphyna, "Rise up. Take your head and your child, and follow us."

The body obeyed, but gallop as fast as they could, it was always ahead of them, never behind, bear-ing the bloodless head in its right hand and the baby in its left.

Soon they reached the castle of Comorre. As they stood at the gates, St. Gildas shouted to Co-morre, "Count, here is your wife, just as your wickedness has made her, and your child, just as heaven has given it. Will you receive them under your roof?"

Comorre did not answer.

Three times St. Gildas repeated his question and three times Co-morre made no reply.

St. Gildas took the baby from its mother and set it on the ground. The child walked to the edge of the castle moat, picked up a handful of earth, and threw it at the castle wall, piping, "Let the Trinity take judgment."

The Element Encyclopedia of the Celts

The great towers of the castle trembled and fell with a crash, the walls yawned open, and the ruined castle sank into the ground, taking Comorre and all his supporters with it.

St. Gildas then took Triphyna's head, set it on her shoulders and brought her back to life. Guerech was overjoyed.

CONN OF THE HUNDRED BATTLES

See **Lia Fáil**.

CRADAWG

See **Branwen**.

DAHUT

See **The Legend of Ys**.

DAOINE SIDHE

See **Fairies**; Religion: **Angus Mac Og**.

THE DOOMED RIDER

SCOTLAND

The Conan flows darkly, whirling in mossy eddies. It runs past an old burial ground, with the ruins of an old church with the rose-grown mullions of an arched window. Two hundred years ago, or maybe more, the building was complete and where the wood grows thickest there once was a cornfield.

Some Highlanders were busy one day harvesting the corn in that field. At noon, when the sun shone brightest and they were busiest, they heard a voice from the river cry out, "The hour but not the man has come."

When they looked, they saw a kelpie standing on what they call a false ford, just in front of the old church. There was a deep, black pool both above and below, but on the ford there was a ripple that showed, as you might have thought, shallow water. And just in the middle of that stood the kelpie. Again it cried, "The hour but not the man has come." Then, flashing through the water like a drake, it vanished into the lower pool.

The folk were standing wondering what the creature might have meant when they saw a horseman riding down the hill in haste, making straight for the false ford. Then they understood the kelpie's words.

Four of the strongest among them sprang from the corn to warn the rider of his danger. They told him what they had seen and heard and urged him to turn back and take another road—or stay for an hour where he was. But he would not listen to them and would have taken the ford in spite of them, had the Highlanders, determined to save him whether he would or no, not gathered round him and pulled him from his horse. Then, for the sake of his own safety, they locked him in the old church.

When the hour had passed, the fatal hour of the kelpie, they flung the church door open and called out that he could now continue on his journey. But there was no answer.

They called out a second time and still there was no answer.

Then they went in and found the rider lying stiff and cold on the floor, his face resting in the water of the stone trough that still stands among the ruins.

His hour had come, and he had fallen in a fit, head-foremost, into the trough. And there he had drowned.

THE DREAM OF MACSEN WLEDIG

WALES

The Emperor of Rome, Macsen Wledig, dreamed of a beautiful maiden living in a wonderful far-off land. When he woke, he sent his men all over the world to search for her. Eventually they found her in a castle in Britain. She was the daughter of a chieftain living at Segontium (Caernarvon).

The princess was Helen (or Elen) and she accepted Macsen and loved him. He made her father overking of the island of Britain and commanded that three castles should be built for his bride.

While Macsen was away, a new emperor seized power in Rome and warned him not to return. But Macsen now had new allies. With the aid of the Britons, led by Helen's brother Conanus, he marched across Gaul and into Italy and recaptured Rome.

As a reward for their loyalty and help, Macsen rewarded the Britons with the province of Gaul that became Brittany.

ELLYLLON

Tiny, translucent Welsh elves. Their leader is Queen Mab. (*See* **Fairies;** Religion: **Angus Mac Og**.)

ELPHIN

See **The History of Taliesin**.

ENGLYN

A distinctive short Welsh poem with strict rules governing the number of syllables, length of each line, and positions of rhyming words. There are eight recognized types of *englyn*, some of three lines, some of four. The type especially loved by the Canadian novelist Robertson Davies (1913–95) was a quatrain consisting of 30 syllables arranged across four lines. The sixth syllable of the first line announces the rhyme and the last syllable of the next three lines rhymes with it. The final syllable of the first line is rhymeless.

EOCHAID

See **Midhir and Etain**.

Fairies

Fairies are the medieval and post-medieval versions of the old Celtic spirits of place. Among the lesser deities in the Celtic pantheon are the sprites who inhabit **springs** and streams and the dryads who inhabit trees. Among these elementals are the gnomes, the spirits of the Earth who appear out of cracks in the rock to frighten Cornish miners. There are also sea-nymphs or **mermaids**, and sylphs, the spirits of the air.

A feature of the Celtic mindset is a blurring of the boundary between the everyday world and the **Otherworld**, and between human beings and spirits. Just as it is possible for **people** to travel, under special circumstances, to the Otherworld and back again, so it is possible for people to have dealings with fairies, though it is not always wise to do so. European folklore generally is full of tragic tales of relationships between mortals and fairies.

There are different views about the origins of fairies. They are sometimes thought of as the spir-its of the dead, sometimes as fallen angels, sometimes as astral or elemental spirits. In the Highlands in the seventeenth and eighteenth centuries, fairy hosts were regarded as the evil dead. In Ireland, fairies are the spirits of the recent dead as well as the long dead. The **Tuatha dé Danann** became the heroic fairies, the Daoine Sidhe.

In Cornwall, fairies are the ancient pagan dead who died before the age of Christianity; they are not good enough to go to Heaven, nor wicked enough to go to Hell, but linger on, gradually diminishing until they become as small as ants before disappearing altogether. In Cornwall and Devon the souls of unbaptized babies are called piskies, and they appear at dusk as little white moths. In a dark version of the Glastonbury legend about Joseph of Arimathea, the knockers in the tin mines are believed by the miners to be the souls of Jews who were transported to Britain for their part in crucifying Christ.

In Wales, the belief that fairies are the souls of the dead seems to be less common. They are described in more general terms as a race of beings halfway between something material and spiritual and rarely seen, or as a race of spiritual beings living in an invisible world of their own.

Some of the lore is neo-Celtic, dating from the Celtic revival of the eighteenth and nineteenth centuries. Nursery sleep fairies were invented at this time, presumably to make managing small children easier. The best-known of these was the sleep fairy featured in the hugely popular nursery rhyme *Wee Willie Winkie*, which was written and published by William Miller in 1841. The earliest version of the first verse runs:

Wee Willie Winkie runs through the toun,
Up stairs and down stairs in his nicht-goun,
Tirling at the window, crying at the lock,
"Are the weans in their bed, for it's now ten o'clock?"

In the Middle Ages, fairies formed distinct communities or kingdoms. Shakespeare's Renaissance version of a fairy realm ruled by Oberon and Titania is not far removed from the medieval concept of the world of the fairies—though a long way from the Iron Age concept of that world, 2,000 years earlier.

Fairies are usually very small, about 1 foot (30cm) tall, and some are no bigger than insects. The smallest are known as pigwidgeons. They are usually very attractive in appearance, in contrast to goblins, elves, imps, and pixies.

Fairies are gifted with supernatural powers. They have the ability to fly very quickly from place to place and are invisible most of the time. Only people with second sight can see them, though others are able to see them on certain occasions.

They behave rather like children. They are insecure, easily offended, mischievous, and can be quarrelsome. Some think this is because they once owned the landscape and have been displaced by newcomers. They may be responsible for causing fog and dew.

Fairies use toadstools as seats or tables. The flint arrowheads we now know were made by Neolithic people were once believed to be elf-bolts made and used by fairies to fire at cattle (*see* **Fairy Blight**). Sometimes fairies leave objects that are picked up by people.

Fairies like dancing on grass. Sometimes rings of a darker green are seen in the grass, and these "fairy rings" are thought to mark the path danced by the fairies. The dancing takes place at night and the fairies vanish when the cock crows.

Fairies often visit women in childbirth, sometimes casting good or evil **spells** on the babies. The worst thing they do is to steal babies, leaving changelings in their place. Whether the changelings are fairies or mortal children acquired somewhere else is not known.

Occasionally fairies fall in love with mortals, usually with re-sults that are disastrous for both parties (*see* Religion: **Gods and Goddesses**, **Otherworld**).

A knight about to enter a fairy mound:

Fairies are generally held to wear green, which is one reason why some Scottish women dislike wearing that color; another is that green is associated with death. In Ireland the small trooping fairies, the Shefro and the Daoine Sidhe, wear green coats and red caps, but solitary fairies such as **leprechauns** generally wear red. The silkies of northern England wear glistening white silk, the White Ladies on Man wear white satin, and the Tylwyth Teg of Wales also wear white. The self-confessed witch

Isobel Gowdie described the Fairy Queen in her *Traffic with Fairies*: "The Qwein of Fearrie is brawlie clothed in whyt linens, and in whyt and browne cloathes." On the other hand, a fairy queen who visited a cottage in Galloway was described in more vivid terms by J. F. Campbell:

She was very magnificently attired; her dress was of the richest green, embroidered round with spangles of gold, and on her head was a small coronet of pearls. One of the chil-dren put out her hand to get hold of the grand lady's spangles, but told her mother afterwards that she felt nothing.

Manx fairies sometimes wore blue. One description gives us a little, gnomelike man 2 feet (60cm) high, "wearing a red cap and a long blue coat with bright buttons, white hair and bushy whiskers. Face very wrinkled. Very bright, very kind eyes, carrying a small but very bright lantern."

Brownies wear ragged clothes and many hobgoblins run around naked.

The tradition is that the life of a fairy is as long as the life of the world, so it would not be possible

The Element Encyclopedia of the Celts

to witness a fairy funeral. Yet beside this there is a parallel tradition of fairy funerals. The poet William Blake claimed to have seen one. "Did you ever see a fairy's funeral, madam?" he asked a lady who happened to be sitting next to him.

"Never, sir," said the lady.
"I have," said Blake, "but not before last night."

He went on to describe how he had seen in his garden "a procession of creatures of the size and colour of green and grey grasshoppers, bearing a body laid out on a rose-leaf, which they buried with songs, and then disappeared."

FAIRY BLIGHT

The word "stroke" as used for a sudden paralyzing seizure is bor- rowed directly from beliefs about **fairies.** It is a short form of "fairy stroke" or "elf stroke." It was thought to have been caused by an elf-shot or elf-blow, which strikes the victim down.

THE FENIAN CYCLE

IRELAND

This sequence of folk-tales relates the deeds of Irish heroes. The setting is the provinces of Leinster and Munster in the third century AD.

One key characteristic of the Fenian Cycle stories is their strong links with Irish-speaking "colonies" in Scotland, and they differ from the **Ulster Cycle** tales in being mainly in verse and being romances rather than epics. The stories are about Fionn mac Cum- haill and his band of warriors: the Fianna.

One of the greatest of the Irish tales, *The Pursuit of Diarmuid and Grainne*, forms part of the Fenian Cycle. The story of Diarmuid and Grainne is believed to be one of the sources of **Tristan and Iseult**.

FIANNA

See **The Fenian Cycle**.

FINTAN

See **The Book of Invasions**.

FIONN MAC CUMHAILL

See **The Fenian Cycle**.

THE FIR BHOLG

See **The Book of Invasions**.

THE FOMHOIRE

See **The Book of Invasions**.

THE FOSTER BROTHER

BRITTANY

The original of this story is in ballad form and it gives us a brief and tantalizing glimpse of the beauty of the Celtic **Otherworld**, as well as containing several other classic Celtic motifs.

Gwennolaïk was the most beautiful maiden in the town of Tréguier, but her misfortune was that she had lost her mother, her father, and her two sisters when she was very young. Her only remaining relative was her stepmother. She stood weeping at her door, nursing the faint hope that one day her foster brother might return from overseas. Often she gazed out to sea, hoping for the ship that would bring him home. But six years had passed, and when she thought of him it was as the boy she had played games with, not as the young man he had become.

The stepmother broke into her daydreams: "Hurry up and attend to the animals. I don't feed you for idling."

Though noble by birth, Gwennolaïk was forced by her harsh

stepmother to get up very early in the morning to light the fire and sweep the floors.

One winter evening she was at the well, breaking ice in order to draw water, when a passing knight asked if she was spoken for.

She did not answer.

"Don't be afraid," the horseman said. "Just answer my question."

She said she was not betrothed to anyone.

"Good," said the knight. "Take this gold ring and tell your stepmother you are betrothed to a knight from Nantes who has fought a great battle and lost his squire in the fighting. Tell her the knight has a sword-wound in the side. In three weeks and three days, when the wound is healed, I shall return and take you to my manor."

Gwennolaïk went back into the house. When she looked at the ring she realized it was the same as the one her foster brother used to wear.

Three weeks passed and the knight did not return. Then Gwennolaïk's stepmother said, "It's time you married and I have found you the man you should marry."

The maiden found the courage to speak. "Saving your grace, good stepmother, I only wish to marry my foster brother, who has returned from across the sea. He has given me a gold wedding ring and promises to come for me in a few days."

The stepmother would hear nothing of this plan. "A fig for your gold ring! *Bon gré, mal gré,* you'll marry the stable boy, Job the Witless."

Gwennolaïk was distraught, but her stepmother was unmoved by her tears. "Howl out in the courtyard if you must, but you'll be married in three days."

Meanwhile the gravedigger was walking along the road, swinging his bell and taking news of those newly dead from one village to the next. Mournfully he chanted, "Pray for the soul of a worthy knight who was mortally wounded in the side with a stroke of sword in battle. Today he's to be buried in the White Church."

At the marriage feast, the bride was in tears. All the guests wept with her—all but her stepmother.

When the dancing began and it was proposed that the bride should lead the dance, she was nowhere to be found. She had fled the house.

She was slumped in the garden, feverish with despair, when she hard someone close by.

"Who is it?"

"It is I, your foster brother, Nola."

"Can it really be you? Dear brother, you are truly welcome!"

Nola swung her up onto his white horse and they rode off into the night.

"We must have ridden 100 leagues," she said, "but I am happy with you. I will never leave you again."

Owls hooted and the sounds of the night filled her ears.

"Your horse is swift," she said, "and your armor shines so brightly. How happy I am to have found you. But are we near your manor?"

"In good time," Nola answered. "We shall be there in good time, sister."

"But your heart is so cold, your hair is so wet! How cold your hands are!"

"Sister, listen. Do you hear the noise of the musicians who will play at our wedding?"

Gwennolaïk found herself on an island where a great crowd of maidens and youths were dancing beneath green trees laden with apples. The music they danced to was heavenly; she had heard no music like it. The sun rose in the east and this strange new world was flooded with rich light. Then Gwennolaïk saw her mother and her two sisters and her heart was filled with beauty and joy...

The next morning, as the sun climbed the sky, the young women carried the body of Gwennolaïk to the tomb of her foster brother in the White Church. They laid it inside.

THE FOUR BRANCHES OF THE MABINOGI

WALES

The mythic tales included in the Mabinogion collection, written down in the eleventh century AD, are entitled "The Four Branches of the *Mabinogi*." They focus on the activities of various British deities who have been Christianized into heroes and kings. The one character common to each of the four branches is the King of **Dyfed**, Pryderi fab Pwyll. He is born in the first branch and killed in the fourth. It is thought that he may be a humanized version of the **god Maponos**.

Pryderi's mother, **Rhiannon**, is related to the horse goddess **Epona**. The British queen

Rigantona is another character who is a transformed deity. There is also the peaceable British prince Manawydan, who later becomes Rigantona's second husband. Manawydan is a transformation of the Irish sea god **Manannán mac Lir**.

THE FIRST BRANCH:
PWYLL, PRINCE OF DYFED

Pwyll changes places for a year with Arawn, the ruler of the Underworld, Annwn. There he defeats Arawn's enemy Hafgan. On his return he meets Rhiannon, a beautiful young woman whose horse is too fast to catch. He manages to win her hand at the expense of Gwawl, to whom Rhiannon is betrothed. She bears Pwyll a son, but shortly after his birth the baby disappears. Rhiannon is accused of murdering him and is punished by being made to carry guests on her back. In reality the baby has been abducted by a monster and is rescued by Teyrnon and his wife. They bring him up as their own child, giving him the name Gwri of the Golden Hair. But as he grows up, his resemblance to Pwyll becomes apparent, and Teyrnon

and his wife return the child to his real parents. Rhiannon is released from her punishment and the boy is given the name Pryderi.

THE SECOND BRANCH:
BRANWEN FERCH LLĐR

The story of Branwen, Bran the Blessed, and Matholwch (see **Branwen**). At the end of the story just five pregnant women survive in Ireland; it is left to them and their offspring to repopulate the land of Ireland.

THE THIRD BRANCH:
MANAWYDAN FAB LLĐR

Pryderi returns to Dyfed with Manawydan. There Manawydan marries Rhiannon and Pryderi marries Cigfa. Fog descends on the land, leaving it desolate. The four live at first by hunting, but then go to England where they make shields, saddles, and shoes. Their work is of such high quality that local craftsmen cannot match it and the locals drive them away. They move from town to town, eventually returning to Dyfed, where they resume hunting.

While they are hunting, a white boar leads them to a mysterious castle. Manawaydan advises against going in, but Pryderi does so. He does not return. Rhiannon goes to find him and finds him clinging to a bowl: he has lost the power of speech. The same thing happens to her, and the castle vanishes.

Manawydan and Cigfa travel back into England, where they resume their shoemaking, but as before the local craftsmen drive them out. They are forced to return to Dyfed.

They sow three fields with wheat. The first is destroyed before it can be harvested. The following night the second field is destroyed. Manawydan keeps a careful watch the next night over the third field. When he sees it destroyed by mice he catches the leader of the mice and decides to hang it.

Three men appear—a priest, a scholar, and a bishop—and each in turn offers him gifts if he will spare the mouse's life. He refuses.

When they ask what he will accept in return for the mouse's life, he asks for the release of Rhiannon and Pryderi and the lifting of the enchantment that hangs over Dyfed.

The bishop agrees to this: the mouse is in fact his wife. He has been waging a war of magic against Dyfed because he is a friend of Gwawl, whom Pryderi's father, Pwyll, humiliated.

THE FOURTH BRANCH:

MATH FAB MATHONWY

Math, son of Mathonwy, is King of Gwynedd. His feet must be held by a virgin, except when he is fighting. His current foot-holder is a maid called Goewin, and his nephew Gilfaethwy is in love with her. His brother Gwydion tricks Math into going to fight Pryderi so that Gilfaethwy can have access to Goewin. Gwydion kills Pryderi in single combat. Gilfaethwy rapes Goewin. Then Math marries Goewin to rescue her from disgrace and banishes Gwydion and Gilfaethwy from his kingdom, changing them into a pair of deer, then pigs, and then wolves. After three years he restores them to human form and allows them to return.

Math needs a new foot-holder. Gwydion proposes his sister Arianrhod. Math has a way of magically testing her virginity and she gives birth to two sons. One, Dylan, goes to sea. The other is brought up by Gwydion, but he is warned by Arianrhod that he will never have a name or arms unless she gives them to him. She refuses to give him either, but Gwydion tricks her first into giving him a name, Lleu Llaw Gyffes (Bright, of Skillful Hand), and then into giving him arms.

Arianrhod warns Lleu that he will never marry a wife of any race that lives on the Earth, so Gwydion and Math make him a wife out of flowers, called Blodeuwedd (Flower-face). However, the flower-maiden falls in love with a hunter named Gronw Pebr and the two of them plot to kill Lleu. Blodeuwedd tricks Lleu into telling her how he may be killed, but when Gronw attempts to kill him Lleu changes into an eagle and escapes.

When Gwydion finds Lleu he turns him back into human form. He also turns Blodeuwedd into an owl and curses her. Gronw offers compensation to Lleu, but Lleu turns this offer down, insisting on returning the blow that Gronw aimed at him. Gronw tries to hide behind a rock, but Lleu throws his spear so hard that it passes right through the rock and into Gronw.

GAWAIN

See **The Green Knight**.

GERAINT, SON OF ERBIN

WALES

A romance about the love of one of King **Arthur**'s men, Geraint, and the beautiful Enid. The story corresponds to Chrétien's story *Erec and Enide*.

Geraint and Enid marry and settle down together, but rumors circulate that Geraint is neglecting his knightly duties. Enid reproaches herself for keeping her husband from chivalry, but Geraint misunderstands her unhappiness and assumes her comments mean that she believes he has been unfaithful to her.

Geraint forces Enid to accompany him on a long and perilous journey, ordering her not to speak to him. Several times on the journey, Enid is forced to disobey this command in order to warn him of danger. Incidents and adventures along the way prove Geraint's fighting skill and Enid's love. There is a happy reconciliation between them at the end of the story, as Geraint inherits his father's kingdom.

GIANT OF GRABBIST

See Symbols: **Giant**.

GILFAETHWY

See The Four Branches of the Mabinogi.

GLYN

See **The Salty Sea**.

GOEWIN

See The Four Branches of the Mabinogi.

GRADLON MEUR

See **The Legend of Ys**.

THE GREEN KNIGHT

BRITAIN

A mythic story about a strange beheading ritual. In this sinister game, a mysterious stranger, usually a **giant** or Green Knight, enters the hall in the middle of winter and offers his ax to any hero who will cut off his **head**—in return for a similar beheading blow. A hero accepts, cuts off the Green Knight's head, and is horrified to see the challenger rising and immediately taking up the ax ready to deliver his return blow.

In the version of the story in which Gawain is the hero, he is allowed a year's grace before he must receive the return blow. In the version in which **Cú Chulainn** is the hero, he kneels and submits immediately and is accordingly judged the bravest knight in Ulster.

The game is part of the north European midwinter festival, and is an allegory about New Year. The Old Year enters in the form of the Green Knight, the old spirit of the forest, and is decapitated by the vigorous young hero who represents the New Year in all its strength and hardiness. Yet the Old Year is irrepressibly and infinitely self-renewing, like the cycle of the seasons.

The Green Knight's name is Bertilak.

GRONW PEBR

See **The Four Branches of the Mabinogi.**

GUERCH

See **Comorre the Cursed.**

GWENNOLAÏK

See **The Foster Brother.**

GWÉNNOLÉ

See **The Legend of Ys.**

GWION BACH

See **The History of Taliesin.**

GWYDDNO GARANHIR

See **The History of Taliesin, The Sigh of Gwyddno Garanhir.**

GWYDION

See **The Four Branches of the Mabinogi.**

A HARP ON THE WATER

WALES

A long time ago, there was a wicked king who lived in a palace where Lake Bala is today. It was said of him, "He killed whom he would; he spared whom he would." It was also said that there were few who were spared.

Not long after this king came to the throne, he was walking in his garden, contemplating some cruel act, when he heard a voice. The sound was somewhere between a bird's cry and the tinkling of a silver bell. The voice said, "Vengeance will come. Vengeance will come."

Then the king heard a second disembodied voice a little further off, asking, "When will it come? When will it come?"

The first voice answered, "In the third generation. The third generation."

The king laughed. "What do I care about that!"

Years afterward, when he had three sons who showed signs of being crueler even than he was, he heard the same voices in the same garden.

"Vengeance will come. Vengeance will come."

"When will it come? When will it come?"

"In the third generation. The third generation."

The king laughed defiantly. "And where is the king who is mighty enough to wreak vengeance on me?"

More years passed and the pal-ace walls rang with celebrations over the birth of a son to the king's eldest son and heir. A command went out across the countryside, ordering everyone to come to the palace to take part in the rejoicing. A guard was sent after a white-haired harper who lived up in the mountains; he was to provide the music for the feasting and dancing that night. He was reluctant, but he went.

The harper was amazed to see the king's wealth on display: the silver candlesticks, the golden goblets, the ladies' rich robes, and the flowing mead. He was ordered to play and played for hours until, toward midnight, he was allowed an interval for rest. He was given nothing to eat or drink, so he went to a quiet corner of the garden. There he heard a voice saying, "Vengeance will come. Vengeance will come." He saw a small brown bird fluttering near him and it seemed to be encouraging him to follow it. He followed some distance and hesitated, but the brown bird repeated, "Vengeance will come," and he followed it up into the hills.

At last they reached the top of a hill. Now the bird was silent and the moon had slipped behind a cloud. The harpist suddenly remembered his harp. He had left it in the palace. "I must go back. I must, before the dancing starts again." But he was exhausted after playing all evening; sleep and night overtook him.

In the morning he awoke to an unfamiliar landscape. He looked back toward the palace, but it had gone. In its place was a huge lake, absolutely calm. His harp was floating toward him on the water.

HEININ VARDD

See **The History of Taliesin**.

THE HISTORY OF TALIESIN

WALES

This story is not in *The White Book of Rhydderch* or *The Red Book of Hergest* and was written down relatively late, perhaps after 1500.

Even so, it contains elements that are ancient. It is not to be confused with *The Book of Taliesin*, a collection of poems attributed to the enigmatic **Taliesin**. Here it is in full, in all its strangeness and inscrutability:

There lived in Arthur's time in Penllyn a man of noble lineage, named Tegid Voel, and his dwelling was in the midst of Lake Tegid, and his wife was Caridwen. And there was born to him of his wife a son named Morvran ab Tegid, and also a daughter named Creirwy, the fairest maiden in the world; and they had a brother, the most ill-favored man in the world, Avagddu.

Caridwen thought his ugliness would exclude him from the company of men of noble birth, unless he had some special knowledge. So she boiled a cauldron of Inspiration and Science for her son, until she could distil three drops of the grace of Inspiration.

She put her servant boy, Gwion Bach, to stir the cauldron, and a blind man named Morda to kindle the fire beneath it, and she ordered them to boil for a year and a day. She gathered charm-bearing herbs every day.

One day toward the end of the year, while Caridwen was making incantations, three drops of the charmed liquor flew out of the cauldron and fell upon the finger of Gwion Bach. He put his finger to his mouth, and that instant he foresaw everything that was to come, including that his chief care had to be to guard against the wiles of Caridwen, for vast was her skill. He fled toward his own land. And the cauldron burst in two, because all the liquor within it was poisonous—except the three charm-bearing drops.

Caridwen saw the toil of the whole year lost. She seized a billet of wood and struck the blind Morda on the head until one of his eyes fell out upon his cheek. He cried, "Wrongfully have you disfigured me, for I am innocent. Your loss was not because of me."

"You speak true," said Caridwen. "It was Gwion Bach who robbed me." She ran after him.

When Gwion Bach saw her, he changed himself into a hare and fled. But Caridwen changed herself into a greyhound and headed him off. He ran toward a river and became a fish. In the form of an otter she chased him under the water, until he turned

himself into a bird of the air. As a hawk, she followed him and gave him no rest in the sky. Just as she was about to swoop upon him, he saw a heap of winnowed wheat on the floor of a barn, dropped among it, and turned himself into one of the grains. Then Caridwen transformed herself into a black hen, scratched the wheat with her feet, and found him out and swallowed him. And, as the story says, she bore him nine months, and when she was delivered of him, she could not find it in her heart to kill him, by reason of his beauty. She wrapped him in a leather bag and cast him into the sea.

At that time the weir of Gwyddno was on the beach between Dyfi and Aberystwyth, near Gwyddno's castle. Gwyddno had an only son named Elphin, the most hapless of youths and the neediest. Gwyddno granted him the drawing of the weir that year, to see if good luck would befall him and to give him a start in the world.

When Elphin went to look, there was nothing in the weir. Then he perceived the leather bag upon a pole of the weir. One of the weir guardians said to him, "You were never unlucky until tonight, but now you have destroyed the virtues of the weir. It always yielded 100 pounds' worth of fish a year and now there is nothing but this leather skin."

"There may be 100 pounds in it," said Elphin.

The weir-ward opened the leather bag and saw the forehead of the boy inside. He said to Elphin, "There's a radiant brow!"

"Let him be called Taliesin," said Elphin, lifting the boy in his arms.

Elphin made his horse amble gently and he carried the boy as softly as he could. Then the boy praised him:

"Fair Elphin, cease to lament!
Let no one be dissatisfied with his own,
Despair brings no advantage.
No man sees what supports him.
Never in Gwyddno's weir
Was there such good luck as tonight.
Fair Elphin, dry your cheeks!
Being too sad will do no good;
Nor doubt the miracles of the Almighty:
Although I am but little, I am gifted.
From seas and from mountains,
And from the depths of rivers,
God brings wealth to the fortunate man.
Elphin of lively qualities,

Your resolution is unmanly;
You must not be over-sorrowful:
Better to trust in God than to forbode ill.
Weak and small as I am,
On the foaming beach of the ocean,
In the day of trouble I shall be
Of more service to you than 300 salmon.
Elphin, do not be displeased at your misfortune:
With me as your protector
You have little to fear;
None shall be able to harm you."

Gwyddno Garanhir asked the boy what he was, whether he was man or spirit. Then Taliesin sang this tale:

"First, I have been formed a comely person;
In the court of Ceridwen I have done penance;
Though I was seen but little, and received indifferently,
I have been a prized defense, the sweet muse the cause,
And by law without speech, I have been liberated
By a smiling old hag, when irritated,
Dreadful her claim when pursued;
I have fled with vigour, I have fled as a frog,

The Element Encyclopedia of the Celts

I have fled in the semblance of a crow, scarcely finding rest,
I have fled as a thrush of portending language,
I have fled as a fox, used to bounding,
I have fled as a martin, which was of no avail,
I have fled as a squirrel, that vainly hides,
I have fled as a stag's antler, of ruddy course,
I have fled as iron in a glowing fire,
I have fled as a spear-head, which is woe to those who wish for it,
I have fled as a fierce bull fighting bitterly,
I have fled as a bristly boar seen in a ravine,
I have fled as a white grain of pure wheat,
On the skirt of a hempen sheet entangled,
That seemed the size of a mare's foal,
That is filling like a ship on the waters.
Into a dark leather bag I was thrown,
And on a boundless sea I was set adrift;
Which to me was an omen of being tenderly nursed,
And the Lord God then set me at liberty."

Then Elphin came to the house of Gwyddno, his father, and Taliesin with him. Gwyddno asked him if he had had a good haul at the weir and he told him that he had got something better than fish.

"What was that?" asked Gwyddno.

"A bard," said Elphin.

Then said Gwyddno, "What use will he be to you?"

Taliesin himself replied, "More good than the weir ever profited you."

Gwyddno asked, "Are you able to speak, when you are so small?"

Taliesin answered, "I am better able to speak than you to question me."

"Let me hear what you have to say," said Gwyddno.

Then Taliesin sang:

"In water there is a quality endowed with blessings;
On God it is most just to meditate aright;
To God it is proper to supplicate with seriousness,
Since there can be no obstacle to obtaining a reward from him.
Three times have I been born, I know by meditation;
It would be wretched if people could not come and learn

All the sciences of the world, that are
gathered in my heart,
For I know what has been, and what
will come to pass in future.
I will entreat my Lord to give me
refuge,
A regard I may obtain in his grace;
The Son of Mary is my trust, great
is my delight in him,
For in him the world is continually
upheld.
God has been to instruct me and to
raise my expectation,
The true Creator of Heaven, who
affords me protection;
It is rightly intended that the saints
should pray every day,
For God, the redeemer, will bring
them to him."

Elphin's wife nursed Taliesin tenderly and lovingly. From then on, Elphin increased in riches day by day and increased in love and favor with the king. Taliesin lived with him until he was 13 years old, when Elphin accepted a Christmas invitation to stay with his uncle, Maelgwn Gwynedd.

Maelgwn held open court at Christmas-tide in the castle of Degannwy for all his lords and a discussion arose among the vast thronged host of knights and squires. Someone asked, "Is there in the whole world a king so great as Maelgwn, or one on whom Heaven has bestowed so many spiritual gifts? First, form, beauty, meekness, and strength, and all the powers of the soul besides!"

Others said Heaven had given one gift exceeding all the others: the beauty, comeliness, grace, wisdom, and modesty of his queen; her virtues surpassed those of all the ladies and noble maidens in the whole kingdom. And with this they put questions one to another among themselves. Who had braver men? Who had fairer or swifter horses or greyhounds? Who had more skillful or wiser bards than Maelgwn?

At that time the bards were in great favor with the exalted of the kingdom; none performed the office of those who are now called heralds unless they were learned men, not only expert in the service of kings and princes but studious and well versed in the lineage, arms, and exploits of the princes and the kings, and in discussions concerning foreign kingdoms, the ancient things of their own kingdom, and the annals of the first nobles. They were always prepared with their answers in various languages—Latin, French, Welsh, and English. They were great chroniclers and recorders, skillful in framing verses and ready in making *englyns* in every one of those languages. In the palace of Maelgwn there were at that feast as many as four-and-twenty bards, and chief of them all was Heinin Vardd.

When they had all made an end of praising the king and his gifts, it fell to Elphin to speak. "Truly only a king may compete with a king; but if Maelgwn were not a king, I would say that my wife was as virtuous as any lady in the kingdom. I would also say that I had a bard who was more skillful than all the king's bards."

The king's friends quickly reported Elphin's boasts to him. Maelgwn ordered him to be imprisoned until he learned the true virtues of his wife and the wisdom of his bard. Elphin was thrown into a tower of the castle with a heavy chain around his feet.

Then Maelgwn sent Rhun, his son, to inquire into the demeanor of Elphin's wife. Rhun, the most graceless man in the world, went in haste toward Elphin's house, minded to bring disgrace upon Elphin's wife. She was forewarned, however: Taliesin told her that Maelgwn had placed Elphin his master in prison, and that Rhun was coming to bring disgrace upon her. He persuaded his mistress to dress one of the kitchen maids in her apparel, which the noble lady gladly did, loading the best rings she and her husband possessed onto the maid's hands. Then Taliesin sat the disguised maiden down to supper in her mistress's room.

Rhun arrived and was taken by the servants to the room of their mistress. The maid playing the mistress rose and welcomed him then sat down again and Rhun with her. He began jesting with her and slipped a sleeping powder into her drink. She fell asleep and slept so soundly that she never felt it when Rhun cut off her little finger bearing the signet ring of Elphin. He returned to the king with the finger and the ring as a proof that he had cut it from her hand without waking her from her drunken sleep.

Maelgwn rejoiced at this news. Then he had Elphin brought out of his prison and rebuked him for his boast. "Elphin, it is but folly for a man to trust in the virtues of his wife further than he can see her. You may be certain of your wife's vileness. See, her finger, with your signet ring upon it, cut from her hand last night, while she was in a drunken stupor."

Elphin said, "Mighty king, I cannot deny that that is my ring, but that finger is not my wife's. There are three notable things about it. The first of the three is that this ring was hard to draw over the joint of this little finger. The second is that the nail of this little finger has not been pared for a month. The third is the hand from which this finger came was kneading dough three days before the finger was cut therefrom, and my wife has never kneaded dough since she has been my wife."

Maelgwn was angry with Elphin for standing up to him and ordered him to prison a second time, saying that he should not be released until he had proved the truth of his boast concerning the wisdom of his bard and the virtues of his wife.

In the meantime Taliesin told Elphin's wife that he would go to Maelgwn's court to free his master. She asked how he would set Elphin free and Taliesin answered:

"A journey I will undertake,
And to the gate I will come.
The hall I will enter,
And my song I will sing;
My speech I will pronounce
To silence royal bards
In the presence of their chief—
And Elphin I will free.
Should contention arise,
In the presence of the prince,
With summons to the bards
For the sweet flowing song,
And wizards' posing lore,
And the wisdom of the Druids.
In the court are some
who did appear intent on cunning schemes,
By craft and tricking means,
Let the fools be silent,
As once in Badon's fight,
With Arthur the leader of free men,
with long red blades,
Through feats of testy men,
And a chief together with his foes.
Woe be to them, the fools,
When revenge comes upon them.
I, Taliesin, chief of bards,
With a wise Druid's words,
Will set kind Elphin free
From a haughty tyrant's shackles.
To their fell and chilling cry,
By the act of a surprising steed,
From the far distant North,
There soon shall be an end.
Let neither grace nor health
Be to Maelgwn Gwynedd,
For this force and this wrong,
And let there be extremes of woes
And an avenged end
To Rhun and all his race.

The Element Encyclopedia of the Celts

Let the course of his life be short,
Let all his lands be laid waste,
And let exile on far Iona be assigned
To Maelgwn Gwynned."

After this, Taliesin took leave of his mistress and came at last to the court of Maelgwn, who was about to dine in royal state, as was the custom for kings at every feast.

When Taliesin entered the hall, he sat in a quiet corner, close to the place where the bards and the minstrels sat. The bards and the heralds came to cry largesse and proclaim the power of the king and his strength and, as they passed by the corner where he crouched, Taliesin pouted at them, and made a "Blerwm, blerwm" noise with his finger upon his lips.

The bards and heralds took little notice of him as they walked past and went before the king, to whom they bowed in the usual way. But then they said nothing but pouted, making faces at the king, and made a "Blerwm, blerwm" noise upon their lips with their fingers, just as they had seen the boy do.

The king wondered if they were drunk. He commanded one of his lords to go and tell them to collect their wits and to consider whether their behavior was appropriate.

Nevertheless, the bards and heralds carried on making this strange childish noise.

Maelgwn sent to them a second and a third time, telling them to leave the hall. At last he ordered one of his squires to cuff the chief of the bards, Heinin Vardd. The squire took a broom and hit Heinin Vardd on the head, so that he fell back in his seat. Then Heinin went down on his knees, and pleaded with the king that it was not the bards' fault, nor was it through drunkenness, but by the influence of some spirit that was in the hall in the form of a child.

The king immediately commanded the squire to find the boy and bring him forward. The squire went to the nook where Taliesin sat and brought him before the king. Maelgwn asked him what he was and where he came from. Taliesin answered the king in verse, singing:

"Chief bard am I to Elphin,
And I come from the region of the
summer stars;
Idno and Heinin called me Merddin,
In time, every king will call me
Taliesin.
I was with my Lord in the highest
sphere,

On the fall of Lucifer into the depth
of hell:
I have carried a banner before
Alexander;
I know the names of all the stars
from north to south;
I was in Canaan when Absalom was
slain;
I conveyed the Divine Spirit to the
vale of Hebron;
I was in the court of Don before the
birth of Gwydion.
I was instructor to Eli and Enoc;
I have been winged by the genius of
the splendid crozier;
I have been talkative before being
gifted with speech;
I was at the place of the Crucifixion
of the merciful Son of God
I have been three periods in the
prison of Arianrod;
I have been the chief architect of the
work of the tower of Nimrod
I am a wonder whose origin is not
known.
I have been in Asia with Noah in
the ark,
I have seen the destruction of Sodom
and Gomorrah;
I have been in India when Rome
was built,
I am now come here to the remnant
of Troy.
I have been with my Lord in the
manger of the ass;

I strengthened Moses through the
water of Jordan;
I have been in the firmament with
Mary Magdalene;
I have obtained the muse from the
cauldron of Caridwen;
I have been bard of the harp to Lleon
of Lochlin.
I have been on the White Hill, in the
court of Cynvelyn,
For a day and a year in stocks and
fetters,
I have suffered hunger for the Son of
the Virgin.
I have been fostered in the land of the
Deity,
I have been teacher to all
intelligences,
I am able to instruct the whole
universe.
I shall be until the day of doom on
the face of the earth;
And it is not known whether my
body is flesh or fish.
Then I was for nine months
In the womb of the hag Ceridwen;
I was once little Gwion,
And now, at last, I am Taliesin."

When the king and his nobles
heard Taliesin's song, they were
filled with wonder, because they
had never heard anything like it
from a boy as young as he. And
when the king knew that Taliesin

was the bard of Elphin, he bade Heinin, his first and wisest bard, to answer Taliesin and to compete with him.

But when Heinin came forward, he found he could do nothing but make the noise "blerwm." When Maelgwn sent for the other four-and-twenty bards, they all did the same; they could make no other sound.

Maelgwn asked Taliesin what his errand was and Taliesin once more answered him in song:

"You puny bards, I am trying
To win the prize, if I can;
By a gentle prophetic strain
I am trying to win back
Any loss I may have suffered;
Complete the attempt I hope,
Since Elphin is in dire trouble
In the fortress of Degannwy.
On him may there not be laid
Too many chains and fetters.
Strengthened by my muse I am powerful.
On my part, might is what I seek,
For 300 songs and more
Are combined in the spell I sing.
There ought to stand where I am
Neither stone, neither ring;
And there ought not to be about me
Any bard who may not know
That Elphin the son of Gwyddno

Is in the land of Artro,
Secured by 13 locks,
For praising his instructor.
Then I, Taliesin,
Chief of the bards of the west,
Shall free Elphin
From his golden fetters.
If you are primary bards,
To the master of sciences
Declare mysteries
That relate to the inhabitants of the world;
There is a noxious creature,
From the rampart of Satan,
Which has overcome everything
Between the deep and the shallow;
His jaws are as wide
As the mountains of the Alps;
Death will not subdue him,
Nor will human hand nor blades of swords;
There is the load of 900 wagons
In the hair of his two paws
There is in his head an eye
Green as the limpid sheet of icicle.
Three springs arise
In the nape of his neck;
Sea-roughs thereon
Swim through it.
The names of the three springs
From the midst of the ocean;
One generated brine
Which is from the Corina,
To replenish the flood
Over seas disappearing;

The second, without injury
It will fall upon us,
When there is rain abroad,
Through the whelming sky.
The third will appear
Through the mountain veins,
Like a flinty banquet,
The work of the King of kings.
You bards are blunderers,
with too much solicitude;
You are not competent to celebrate
The kingdom of the Britons.
And I am Taliesin,
Chief of the bards of the west,
It is I who will free Elphin
From his golden fetters.
Be silent, now, you luckless rhyming
bards,
For you cannot judge between truth
and falsehood.
If you are primary bards formed by
heaven,
Tell your king what his fate will be.
It is I who am a diviner and a
leading bard,
And know every passage in the
country of your king;
I shall liberate Elphin from the belly
of the stony tower;
And shall tell your king what will
befall him.
A most strange creature will come
from the sea marsh of Rhianedd
As a punishment on Maelgwn
Gwynedd's iniquity,

His hair, his teeth, and his eyes being
as gold.
This will bring destruction upon
Maelgwn Gwynedd.
Discover what it is,
This strong creature from before the
flood,
This creature without flesh, without
bone,
Without vein, without blood,
Without head, without feet.
It will be neither older nor younger
Than it was at the beginning.
Great God! How the sea whitens
When first it comes!
Great are the gusts of wind
When it approaches from the south;
Great is the rainfall
When it strikes on the coasts.
It is in the field, it is in the wood,
Without hand and without foot,
Without signs of old age,
Though it may be co-eval
With the five ages or periods of the
Earth,
And older still,
Though they be years without
number.
It is also as wide
As the surface of the Earth
And it was never born,
Nor was it ever seen.
It will cause consternation
Wherever God wills it.
On sea and on land,

It neither sees, nor is it seen.
Its course is devious
And it will not come when desired
On land and on sea,
It is indispensable.
It is without an equal,
It is four-sided;
It is not confined,
It is incomparable.
It comes from four quarters,
It will not be advised,
It will not be without advice.
It commences its journey
Above the marble rock.
It is sonorous, it is dumb,
It is mild,
It is strong, it is bold,
When it glances over the land.
It is silent, it is vocal,
It is clamorous,
It is the noisiest thing
On the face of the Earth.
It is good, it is bad,
It is extremely injurious.
It is concealed,
Because sight cannot perceive it.
It is noxious, it is beneficial;
It is yonder, it is here,
It will discompose,
But will not repair the injury;
It will not suffer for its doings,
Seeing it is blameless.
It is wet, it is dry,
It frequently comes,
Proceeding from the heat of the sun,
And the coldness of the moon.
The moon is less beneficial,
Inasmuch as her heat is less.
One Being has prepared it,
Out of all creatures,
By a tremendous blast—
All to wreak vengeance
On Maelgwn Gwynedd."

While Taliesin was singing his verse near the door, a mighty storm of wind arose, and the king and all his nobles thought that the castle would fall on their heads. The king ordered them to fetch Elphin in haste from his dungeon and placed him before Taliesin. The moment Taliesin sang a verse, the chains opened from about Elphin's noble feet and fell away from him. Taliesin sang:

"I adore the Supreme Lord of all animation,
Him that supports the heavens, Ruler of every extreme,
Him that made the water good for all,
Him who has bestowed each gift, and blesses it;
May abundance of mead be given Maelgwn of Anglesey, who supplies us,
From his foaming meadhorns, with the choicest pure liquor.

Because the bees collect and do not enjoy,
We have sparkling distilled mead, which is universally praised.
The multitude of creatures which the Earth nourishes
God made for man, with a view to enriching him;
Some are violent, some are mute; he enjoys them all.
Some are wild, some are tame; the Lord makes them.
Part of their produce becomes clothing;
For food and beverage till doom will they continue.
I entreat the Supreme Sovereign of the region of peace,
To liberate Elphin from banishment,
The man who gave me wine and ale and mead,
With large princely steeds of beautiful appearance,
May he one day give me; and in the end,
May God of his good will grant me, in honour,
A succession of numberless ages in the retreat of tranquillity.
Elphin, knight of mead, may your life be long!"

Afterward he sang the ode that is called *The Excellence of the Bards:*

"What was the first man
Made by the God of Heaven?
What was the fairest flattering speech
That was prepared by Ieuav?
What meat, what drink,
What roof was his shelter?
What was the first impression
Of his primary thinking?
Who sported a disguise,
Owing to the wildness of the country,
In the beginning?
Why should a stone be hard?
Why should a thorn's point be sharp?
Who is hard like a flint?
Who is salt like brine?
Who is sweet like honey?
Who rides on the gale?
Why should a wheel be round?
Why should the tongue be gifted with speech
Rather than another member?
Heinin, if your bards are able,
Let them reply to me—Taliesin."

And after that he sang the address that is called *The Reproof of the Bards:*

"If you are a bard completely imbued
With a genius that cannot be controlled,
Do not be intractable
Within the court of your king;
Until your rigmarole shall be known,

The Element Encyclopedia of the Celts

Keep your peace, Heinin,
As to the name of your verse,
And the name of your vaunting;
And as to the name of your grandsire
Prior to his being baptized,
And the name of the sphere,
And the name of the element,
And the name of your language,
And the name of your region.
Avaunt, you bards above,
Avaunt, you bards below!
My beloved is below,
In the fetter of Arianrod.
It is certain you do not know
How to understand the song I utter,
Nor clearly how to discriminate
Between the truth and what is false.
You puny bards, crows of the district,
Why do you not take to flight?
A bard that will not silence me,
may he not obtain silence,
Till he goes to be covered
Under gravel and pebbles;
Such as shall listen to me,
May God listen to him."

Then he sang the piece called *The
Spite of the Bards:*

*"Minstrels persevere in their false
custom,*
Immoral ditties are their delight;
Vain and tasteless praise they recite;
Falsehood at all times do they utter;
They ridicule poor innocent people
And married women they destroy.
*Innocent virgins of Mary they
corrupt*
*As they pass their lives away in
vanity;*
*At night they get drunk, and they
sleep all day long*
In idleness, without work.
*They hate the Church, and they
frequent the tavern;*
*They associate with thieves and
perjured fellows;*
At courts they inquire after feasts.
*They bring forward every senseless
word;*
They praise every deadly sin;
They lead every vile course of life;
*They stroll through every village,
town, and country*
*Thinking nothing concerning the
pain of death.*
*They give neither lodging nor
charity,*
They do not use psalms or prayers,
*They do not pay tithes or offerings
to God,*
*Nor worship on feast-days or
Sundays;*
They do not heed vigils or festivals.
The birds fly, and the fish swim,
Bees collect honey, and worms crawl;
*Every living thing works to get
food,*
*Except minstrels and lazy useless
thieves.*

I do not scorn songs, I do not scorn minstrels,
For they are given by God to lighten thought;
Only those who abuse them,
For blaspheming Jesus and his service."

Taliesin had set his master free from prison and protected the innocence of his wife. He had silenced the bards—not one of them now dared say a word. Now he brought Elphin's wife before them and showed that she had not one little finger missing. Elphin rejoiced, and so did Taliesin.

Then Taliesin asked Elphin to wager the king that he had a better and swifter horse than any of the king's horses. This Elphin did. The day, the time, and the place were fixed, and the place was that which today is called Morfa Rhiannedd. The king went there with all his people, and four-and-twenty of the fastest horses he possessed. The course was marked out and the horses placed for running.

Then Taliesin came with four-and-twenty twigs of holly, which he had burned black, and he told the youth who was to ride his master's horse to place them in his belt and gave him orders to let all the king's

horses go before him and then to overtake one horse after the other, and as he did so to take a twig and strike the horse with it over the crupper, and then let the twig fall; and after that to take another twig, and do the same thing to every one of the horses as he overtook them. He also told the horseman to watch out for when his own horse stumbled and to throw down his cap on the spot.

All these things the youth did and his horse won the race.

Afterward Taliesin brought Elphin to the spot where his horse had stumbled. He asked him to get workmen to dig there, and when they had dug a deep hole, they found a large cauldron full of gold.

Then Taliesin said, "Elphin, here is the payment and reward for you for rescuing me from the weir and for bringing me up from that time until now."

On that spot today stands a pool of water, which is called Pwllbair.

After all this King Maelgwn ordered Taliesin to be brought before him and he asked him to recite the creation of man from the beginning. In response, Taliesin composed the poem which is now called *One of the Four Pillars of Song:*

"The Almighty made,
Down the Hebron vale,
With his sculpting hands,
The fair form of Adam:
And 500 years,
Devoid of any help,
He remained there and lay there
Without a soul.
Again he created,
In the tranquillity of Paradise,
From a left-side rib,
Bliss-throbbing Eve.
For seven hours they were
Content in that orchard,
Till Satan brought strife,
With cunning from hell.
From there they were they driven,
Cold and shivering,
To gain their living,
Into this world.
To bring forth with pain
Their sons and daughters,
To have possession
Of the land of Asia.
Twice five, ten and eight,
She was self-bearing,
The mixed burden
Of man-woman.
And once, not hidden,
She brought forth Abel,
And Cain the forlorn,
The homicide.
To him and his mate
Was given a spade,
To break up the soil,

Thus to get bread.
The wheat pure and white,
Summer tilth to sow,
To feed everyone,
Till the great yuletide feast.
An angelic hand
From the high Father,
Brought seed for growing
That Eve might sow;
But she then hid a tenth of the gift,
And did not sow all
Of what was dug.
For this thievish act,
It is necessary now
For every man to pay
A tithe unto God.
Of the ruddy wine,
Planted on sunny days,
And on new-moon nights;
And of the white wine too.
The wheat rich in grain
And red flowing wine
Christ's pure body make,
Son of Alpha.
The wafer is flesh,
The wine is spilt blood,
The Trinity's words
Sanctify them."

The Element Encyclopedia of the Celts

K

KER-IS

See **The Legend of Ys**.

ROBERT KIRK

The seventeenth-century author of *The Secret Commonwealth*. It is believed that he was carried off into a **fairy** hill: the Fairy Knowe at Aberfoyle. He went against his will and it is thought that he was abducted by the fairies because he betrayed fairy secrets.

L

LADRA

See **The Book of Invasions**.

LAIRD OF LORNTIE

See Symbols: **Mermaid**.

THE LEGEND OF YS

BRITTANY

This old Breton folk-tale was first published in 1637 and it finds strong echoes in folk-tales from both Ireland and Wales:

Many hundreds of years ago, the city of Ys, sometimes called Keris, was ruled by a prince named Gradlon (sometimes spelled Grallon) Meur, which means Gradlon the Great. His palace was built of marble, cedar, and gold. Gradlon himself was a good, even a saintly, man. He was the patron of Gwénnolé, the founder and first abbot of the first monastery ever built in Brittany.

Gradlon was a pious man, but he was also prudent and practical. He defended his capital, the city of Ys, from invasion by the sea by creating an enormous basin that took the overflow at high tide. This basin had a secret sluice gate and the king alone had a key to it; he alone was able to open and close the gate with the changing tide.

Gradlon's daughter, Princess Dahut, was wayward. On one occasion, while her father slept, she arranged a secret banquet for her lover. They drank and drank and behaved more and more foolishly. In a final act of recklessness, it occurred to the princess that she might open the sluice gate. She crept silently into her father's bedchamber and took the key from his girdle. Then she went and opened the gate. In rushed the water, pouring unstoppably into the city of Ys, until it was entirely submerged.

One version of the story adds the cautionary note that Ys was a city that was given over to the arts and the making of money. It was so devoted to the pursuit of luxury that it attracted criticism from St. Gwénnolé. He saw the city as a latter-day Sodom and Gomorrah and predicted that it would come to a similarly catastrophic end. An ancient ballad elaborated on this theme. The pursuit of luxury would be the city's ruin:

St. Gwénnolé woke King Gradlon up and told him to run for his life. He mounted his horse, swept up his worthless daughter, and rode at a gallop toward higher ground, the rising sea seething and boiling at his horse's hooves.

The sea was on the point of overwhelming Gradlon when a disembodied voice said, "Throw the demon you are carrying into the sea, if you want to save yourself!"

Princess Dahut fell back off the horse's rump into the water and the sea immediately stopped rising. Gradlon safely reached Quimper...

...and there the story ends.

The ballad version of the tale ends with Dahut turning into a **mermaid**, haunting the **waters** that cover the site of her father's city:

"Fisherman, have you seen the daughter of the sea, combing her hair in the midday sun on the margins of the beach?"

"Yes," says the fisherman, "I have seen the white daughter of the sea, and I have heard her sing, and her songs are as plaintive as the sound of the waves."

The Element Encyclopedia of the Celts

Another version has Princess Dahut using the key to unlock a gate that she thought was the city gate, only she opened the sluice gate by mistake.

One tradition puts the location of the lost city of Ys in the Etang de Laval on the shore of the Bay of Trépassés. Another tradition places it on what is now the floor of the Bay of Douarnenez. Similar stories were told in other Celtic lands too, about a sunken city in Cardigan Bay or Lough Neagh:

On Lough Neagh's bank as the
fisherman strays,

When the clear, cold eve's declining,
He sees the round towers of other days
In the wave beneath him shining.

The story was retold by Gerald of Wales in his *Topography of Ireland*; a certain Irish **tribe** was punished for its sins by the inundation of its territory:

There was a saying among this tribe that whenever the well-spring of that country was left uncovered (for, out of reverence, from a barbarous superstition, the spring was kept covered and sealed), it would immediately overflow and inundate the whole province, drowning and destroying the whole population.

It happened that a young woman came to the spring to draw water; after filling her pitcher but before she had closed the well, she ran in great haste to her little boy, whom she had heard crying at a spot not far from the spring where she had left him. But the voice of the people is the voice of God, and on her way back she met a huge flood of water from the spring. It swept her away with her boy, and the inundation was so violent that they both were drowned in an hour in this local deluge, and the whole tribe with its cattle. The waters covered the whole surface of that fertile district, and became a permanent lake.

A not improbable confirmation of this occurrence is found in the fact that the fishermen in that lake are said to see distinctly under the water, in calm weather, church towers, which, according to the custom of the country, are slender and lofty, and moreover round; and they frequently point them out to strangers traveling through those parts, who wonder what could have caused such a catastrophe.

There is also a Welsh poem about the submerging of Cantre'r Gwaelod in Cardigan Bay and another folk-tale about the disappearance of Llys Helig beneath the waters of Lake Bala. Possibly the Cornish legend of the lost land of Lyonesse (thought to lie between Cornwall and Scilly), flooded by the sea, belongs to the same tradition: an ancient legend common to the Atlantic coastlands (*see* Symbols: **City Swallowed Up by the Sea**).

The idea of losing land to the sea is easily explained. It was a natural process due to erosion and the gradual 7,000-year-long rising sea level. Both of these continue into the present. A conversation with a 97-year-old man living on the Sussex coast was recorded in the middle of the nineteenth century:

Seeing him looking sadly at the sea, I asked him, "What are you looking at?" and he said to me, "I am looking at where I was born."

"What! Were you born in the sea?"

"Yes, there, where the sea is now, in a house which the sea has swept away. The well was hereabouts, somewhere, but I cannot see it now."

LEPRECHAUN

An Irish **fairy**. Leprechauns are hoarders, but a man who is bold enough to seize one may be able to bully the little fellow into giving up his pot of **gold**. There is no record of anyone succeeding in catching a leprechaun, however. They are very quick, and even if you succeed in catching them they can slip through your fingers and away.

LIA FÁIL

IRELAND

Lia Fáil, or *Lia Fál*, the Stone of Destiny, situated at **Tara**, was the stone on which the High Kings of Ireland were crowned. According to legend, it was brought to Ireland by the **Tuatha dé Danann**. Again according to legend, it recognized the true High King of Ireland by giving a loud shriek when he stood on it.

An early tale told about the stone concerns King Conn of the Hundred Battles, who went one day at sunrise to the battlements of the royal fortress at Tara, the Ri Raith. He took with him his three **Druids**—Mael, Bloc, and Bluicné, and his three **bards**—Ethain, Corb, and Cesare—so that they could watch the skies without any hostile being from the air descending on Ireland without his knowing. As he walked the battlements, Conn happened to tread on a stone, which shrieked so loudly that it could be heard all though East Meath. He asked his Druids what this meant. So profound was the meaning that they took 53 days to reach a decision.

The Druids told him that the name of the stone was Fál and that it came from the island of Fál. The number of shrieks the stone gave forth was the number of kings that would succeed him. Later the **god Lugh** led Conn to his house to tell him the length of his reign and the names of his successors.

This remarkable stone was one of the four precious things brought to Ireland by the Tuatha dé Danann.

LLEFELYS

See Symbols: **Dragon**.

LLEU LLAW GYFFES

See *The Four Branches of the* Mabinogi; Symbols: **Magic**.

LLUDD

See Symbols: **Dragon**.

LOCHLANN

See Symbols: **The Grail Quest**.

LORGNEZ

See **Morven, the Prop of Brittany**.

LYN

See **The Salty Sea**.

MAC CON GLINNE

*See **The Vision of Mac Con Glinne.***

MACSEN WLEDIG

*See **The Dream of Macsen Wledig.***

THE MAGIC ROSE

BRITTANY

An old Breton couple had two sons. The elder son went off to Paris to make his fortune. The younger son, La Rose, was timid and stayed at home. His aging mother urged him to marry. At first he resisted, but his mother pressed him and eventually he gave in and took a wife. But he had been married no more than few weeks when the new bride fell sick and died. La Rose was distraught with grief. He went every evening to his wife's grave and wept.

One evening when he was about to go into the graveyard he saw a terrifying phantom, which asked him what he was doing there.

"I have come here to pray at the grave of my wife," La Rose replied.

"And do you wish she was still alive?" the spirit asked.

"Oh yes!" La Rose replied. "I would do anything to have her restored to me again."

"Listen, then," the phantom said. "Come back to this place tomorrow evening at the same time. Bring a pick and you shall see what will come to pass."

The following evening came and La Rose walked to the graveyard as instructed. The phantom appeared and said, "Go to your wife's grave and strike at it with your pick. The earth will fall away and you will see her lying in her shroud. See this little silver box, which contains a rose. Take it, open it, and pass the box under her nose three times. Then she will wake as if from a deep sleep."

La Rose hurried to his wife's grave, where everything happened just as the phantom had foretold. He struck the ground with his pick and the earth fell away. He placed the box under his wife's nose and she woke up with a sigh, as if from a deep sleep. La Rose had brought clothes with him for her to put on, and together they returned to the parents' house. There was much rejoicing.

Some time afterward, La Rose's father died of old age and his mother was not long following him. La Rose wrote a letter to his brother in Paris, telling him that he should return to receive his share of their inheritance, but he could not leave Paris just then, so La Rose was forced to travel to Paris instead. Before setting off, he promised his wife he would write to her every day.

When he reached Paris, he found his brother very ill. Preoccupied with nursing him back to health, he forgot to write to his wife. So the weeks passed.

The wife became increasingly fearful that something terrible had happened to her husband. She sat every day at the window, watching for a courier bringing her a letter or message, but nothing came.

A regiment of dragoons was billeted on the town. The captain was lodged at the inn immediately opposite La Rose's house and he was strongly attracted to La Rose's wife. He made inquiries about who she was and why she was so sad. He wrote her a letter, pretending to be her brother-in-law in Paris and telling her that her husband had died. Then, after a tactful interval, he started paying court

to the young widow. He proposed marriage and she accepted. They married and when the regiment left the town, they both went with it.

Meanwhile, La Rose's brother recovered and La Rose remembered his wife and rushed back to Brittany. When he got home, he was startled to find the doors of his house closed and bolted. The neighbors told him what had happened.

For a time he was too numb to act. Then he decided to enlist in the same regiment of dragoons as his wife's new husband. He had fine handwriting and was taken on as secretary to one of the lieutenants. He tried to catch sight of his wife, but repeatedly failed to do so.

One day the wicked captain came into the lieutenants' office, saw La Rose's fine handwriting, and asked the lieutenant if he could borrow him for a few days to help him with his correspondence. This was agreed.

While La Rose was helping the captain, he saw his wife, but she didn't recognize him. The captain was very pleased with La Rose's letter-writing and asked him to dinner. During the meal, a servant who had stolen a silver dish and feared discovery slipped it into La

Rose's pocket. When the loss of the silver dish was discovered, the real thief accused La Rose of stealing it. The evidence spoke loudly against La Rose and his judges sentenced him to be shot.

In prison, while he was awaiting execution, La Rose struck up conversation with Père La Chique, the friendly old guard who brought him his food. "Père La Chique," said La Rose, "I have 2,000 francs. If you do as I ask, the money is yours."

The old man agreed at once. The young man requested that after the execution La Chique go to the graveyard where he was buried and bring him back to life with the magic rose, which he always carried carefully with him.

When the fateful day came, La Rose was shot, but Père La Chique went off to inn after inn with his money. As he was drinking more and more wine, occasionally the thought of La Rose crossed his mind, but he dismissed it: "Well, the poor fellow, he really is better off dead. The world is a wearisome place and he is better out of it. Whyever should I bring him back?"

After several days of drinking with his friends, Père La Chique had used up most of the money and began to regret that he had not done as the young man had asked. He took a pick to the graveyard and struck the ground with it. The earth fell away, exposing the corpse of La Rose. The old man was terrified and ran away. He needed a gulp or two of wine to give him the courage he needed to complete the task. But back he went and passed the rose in the silver box three times under the corpse's nose.

La Rose sat up at once. "That was a good sleep, but where are my clothes?"

The old man gave him his clothes and when he was properly dressed they quickly left the graveyard.

Now La Rose needed to make a living. He followed the sound of a drum beating in the street and listened to a crier announcing a large reward for any who would act as a sentry to guard the chapel where the king's daughter had been incarcerated; she had been magically turned into a monster.

La Rose volunteered, then discovered that every sentinel who watched the chapel between the hours of 11 and 12 had disappeared, never to be seen again. By chance, on his very first night he was given that perilous midnight watch. He was on the point of running away when he heard a voice: "La Rose, where are you? Listen, and no harm will come to you. A fearsome great beast will appear. When it does, leave your musket by the sentry box and climb onto its roof and the beast will not touch you."

The hour of 11 struck. La Rose hurried to get up on top of the sentry box. A hideous monster emerged from the chapel, belching flames and bellowing, "Sentinel of my father, where are you, that I may devour you?" It blundered into the musket, which it seized in its teeth and took back into the chapel to eat.

La Rose cautiously got down from his perch to find the musket crunched into a thousand pieces.

The king was pleased when he heard about La Rose's success; he knew that if the same sentry kept guard on the midnight watch for three consecutive nights his daughter would be freed from her enchantment.

On the second night, the mysterious voice told La Rose to place his musket against the chapel door before climbing to safety and the same thing happened as on the first night.

On the third night, the voice told him to open the door of the chapel and when the monster came charging out he should run inside the building himself. There he would find a leaden shrine that he should hide behind; he would also find a small bottle containing a liquid that he had to sprinkle on the monster's head.

La Rose did as he was told, escaping from the monster just in time and reaching the leaden shrine. When he sprinkled the contents of the bottle on the monster's head, it changed instantly into a beautiful princess.

The king was delighted to have his daughter restored to him and gave her to La Rose as his bride. Shortly afterward, the king gave up his throne in his son-in-law's favor.

One day, the new king inspected the regiment of dragoons to which he had once belonged and pointed out that a man was missing. The colonel was startled, but said, "It is true, sire. A useless old man called Père La Chique. We left him back at the barracks playing the fiddle!"

"Well, I want to see him," said the king.

La Chique was very frightened as he was dragged before the king, but the king tore the epaulettes off the captain who had deceitfully stolen his wife and placed them instead on the trembling shoulders of Père La Chique. Then he gave the order for a great bonfire to be lit, and onto it were thrown the deceitful captain and the faithless wife who had so quickly forgotten her husband.

Then the king and his queen lived happily ever after.

MALDWYN

See **The Salty Sea**.

MANAWYDAN

See **Branwen**, *The Four Branches of the* Mabinogi.

MARK

See **Tristan and Iseult**.

THE MARQUIS DE GUÉRANDE

BRITTANY

A wild young nobleman, Louis-François de Guérande, Seigneur of Locmaria, lived a reckless life in the early seventeenth century. He terrorized the neighborhood, so whenever he went out on the rampage his virtuous mother rang the bell of the château to warn her neighbors.

One day, the Clerk of Garlon was visiting the family of his wife-to-be, Annaik. He asked the girl's mother where she was, as he wanted to take her dancing on the green. The mother answered that the girl was upstairs asleep and that he should take care not to wake her.

The Clerk of Garlon ran upstairs and knocked at Annaik's door. He could not understand why she was asleep in bed when everyone else was out, intent on dancing on the green.

"I don't want to go to the dance because I fear the Marquis," she said.

"The Marquis can do you no harm so long as I am with you," said the Clerk. "Come, Annaik, I will look after you."

The girl rose and dressed in velvet embroidered with silver. The Clerk too was finely dressed, with a peacock's feather in his hat.

The Marquis de Guérande leaped onto his horse and rode out from his château. As he galloped along the road, he overtook the Clerk of Garlon and Annaik. "Ah, you go to the dance. It is customary to wrestle there, is it not?"

"It is, sir," the Clerk said, politely.

The Marquis smiled roguishly at the girl and tried to persuade the Clerk to take off his doublet and wrestle with him. But the Clerk declined; he did not think it appropriate because of the difference in their social status.

"You are the son of a peasant, you say," said the Marquis, "yet you take your choice of the village girls!"

"I did not choose this maiden, sir," said the Clerk. "God gave her to me."

Annaik was now very frightened. She could see that she was threatened by the Marquis. The Clerk tried to reassure her by holding her hand, while the Marquis was reveling in the fear he inspired. He tried to lure the Clerk into a sword fight.

"I wear no sword, sir. The club is my only weapon," said the Clerk.

Then, without any sense of honor whatever, the Marquis drew his sword and ran the Clerk through with it.

Annaik was overcome by grief and rage. She leaped at the Marquis and pulled his sword out of his hand. Then she dragged him to the green, where the dance had begun, and pulled him around until he was exhausted. She dropped his senseless body on the grass and hurried home.

"Good mother, if you love me, make my bed, for I am sick unto death."

The mother thought she had danced too much; that was what had made her ill.

"I have not danced at all,' said Annaik. "The wicked Marquis has killed the poor Clerk. Tell the sexton who buries him not to throw in too much earth. In a little while he will have to put me beside him. We may not share the same marriage bed, but we shall sleep in the same grave. We shall be joined at least in heaven."

The Element Encyclopedia of the Celts

THE MARRIAGE GIRDLE

BRITTANY

This ballad is about the Breton expedition to Wales in 1405 to help the Welsh to free themselves from English rule; this was the time of the Owen Glendower revolt. The Bretons gave significant support to the Welsh and had the satisfaction of knowing that they had succeeded in invading English territory, which no French king had ever managed to do. The expeditionary force of 10,000 men was led by Marshal Jean de Rieux.

The morning after his betrothal, a young man received orders to join the standard of de Rieux to help the Bretons overseas. He went with heavy heart to say goodbye to his betrothed, Aloida. He told her that duty demanded that he sail to England. She begged him not to go, reminding him how changeable the wind and sea were. She asked him what she would do if he died; every day she would be impatient for news of him. "I shall wander by the seashore, from cottage to cottage, asking the sailors if they have heard anything of you."

The young man asked her to stop weeping. He would send her a girdle from over the sea: a purple girdle set with rubies. They parted.

The man went to board his ship, and as he did so, he heard some magpies cackling, "If you think the sea is changeable, young women are much more so."

When autumn came, the girl said, "I have looked far out to sea from the mountain heights. Out on the water I saw a ship in danger. I sense that the man I love was on it. He had a sword in his hand and he was fighting fiercely. He was wounded to the point of death. I am sure he must be dead."

Not many weeks passed before she was betrothed to someone else.

Then the news came that the war was over. The cavalier went back home. As soon as he could, he went to find his beloved. As he got nearer to her house, he heard the sound of music and saw that every window of the house was lit as if for a celebration. He met some revelers outside and they told him it was a wedding.

It was the custom in Brittany to ask beggars in to weddings and because of this, the soldier was invited in, but he sat apart, silent and sad. The bride noticed this and went up to him to ask him why he wasn't joining in the feasting. He said he was tired from traveling and his heart was heavy with sorrow. The bride asked him to dance and he agreed.

As they danced, he murmured in her ear, "What have you done with the golden ring that I gave you in this very room?"

The bride stared at him in dismay. She had thought she was a widow and now she realized she had two husbands.

"Then you think wrongly," the "beggar" hissed, "for you have no husband at all this side of the grave." He drew a dagger and struck the faithless young woman through the heart.

The magpies had been right.

In the abbey of Daoulas is a statue of the Virgin. She has a splendid girdle of purple with sparkling rubies and they came from across the sea. If anyone wants to know who gave it to her, they may ask the penitent monk who lies prostrate on the ground in front of the figure of the Mother of God.

It is curious that the faithless bride should have "seen" her lover perish in a naval skirmish off the Breton coast, as there was a real skirmish at just the right time. In 1405, the very year the ballad refers to, a Breton fleet encountered an English flotilla off Brest and there was a terrible battle. Perhaps this was the sea fight the lady saw.

MATH

See The Four Branches of the *Mabinogi*; Symbols: **Magic**.

MIDHIR AND ETAIN

IRELAND

Etain was the second wife of Midhir, King of the Fairy Hill of Bri Leith. His first wife, Fuamach, was jealous of her and with the aid of the Druid Bresal Etarlaim she turned her into a fly and blew her away into the land of the mortals. There she was blown about for seven years in misery.

Fuamach's wicked actions eventually became known and Angus Mac Og beheaded her.

After seven years, Etain was blown into the hall where Etar of Inver Cechmaine was feasting. She fell from the roof into the gold cup of Etar's wife, who swallowed her when she drank some wine. Nine months later, Etain was born as Etar's daughter and was again named Etain. She became the most beautiful woman in Ireland. When she grew to womanhood, Eochaid, the High King of all Ireland, saw her, paid court, and took her back with him to Tara.

All this time, Midhir knew where she was.

At the wedding feast, Eochaid's younger brother, Ailell, fell in love with Etain. He tried to suppress his longing and fell ill. The doctor said it was love-longing, but he denied it.

Eochaid had to journey around Ireland to receive homage from the kings; while he was away, he committed Ailell to Etain's care. She tried to persuade Ailell to tell her what it was that was bringing him to the gates of death, but he would not. At last she guessed, and realized that the only way to save his life was to yield to his longing.

She arranged to meet him early the next morning outside the town.

Ailell was happy and lay awake all night. At dawn he fell into a deep sleep and so didn't go to meet Etain.

At the time that she had arranged to meet Ailell, Etain saw another man approaching. They looked at each other, Etain realized he was not Ailell, and he went on his way. When she went back, she found Ailell awake and angry with himself for missing their meeting.

The next morning the same thing happened again.

On the third morning the same thing happened again. But this time Etain spoke to the strange man. She explained to him that she had not come to meet a man out of wantonness but to heal him.

The stranger said to her, "You would do better to come with me. I was your first husband, in days long gone."

"What is your name?"

"It is easy to tell you that. I am Midhir of Bri Leith."

He went on to tell Etain how she had been spellbound by Fuamach, turned into a fly, and blown out of the Land of Tir nan Og. Then he asked if she would go back with him.

The Element Encyclopedia of the Celts

But she said, "I will not leave Eochaid to go away with a stranger."

Midhir told her that it was he who had put the spell of yearning on Ailell and it was he too who had prevented Ailell from going to meet her in order to save her honor.

Then Etain went back to Ailell and found that he had recovered. The yearning had left him. They were both relieved that they had been saved from betraying Eochaid. When Eochaid returned, they told him everything that had happened. Eochaid praised Etain for her kindness to his brother.

Later, Midhir appeared again to Etain in the likeness of a stranger. No one else saw him. No one else heard him sing his song in praise of the wonders of the Land of Tir nan Og. He begged Etain to return with him, but still she refused to leave Eochaid. Then he asked her if she would go if Eochaid willingly gave her up to him, and she agreed.

Midhir then appeared to Eochaid and challenged him to three games of chess. According to the custom in those days in Ireland, the stakes were not named by the winner until after the game was won. Eochaid won two of the games, asking first for a great tribute of horses,

then for three tasks that took all Midhir's fairies to accomplish. But Midhir won the third game and he asked for Eochaid's wife. Eochaid refused to agree to this, so Midhir softened his demand. Could he instead kiss Etain? Eochaid agreed. The stakes were to be exchanged in one month.

When Midhir reappeared at the end of the month, Eochaid had gathered all his warriors around him and as soon as Midhir entered, he barred the doors behind him so that he couldn't take Etain away. Midhir drew his sword with his left hand and embraced Etain with his right hand and kissed her. Then they rose together through the roof. The warriors rushed outside, where they saw two swans flying over the palace of Tara, linked together by a golden chain.

But the story did not end there. Eochaid could not forget Etain. After years of searching he discovered where she was. He made war on the realm of fairy and Etain was given back to him. But the wrath of the Tuatha dé Danann fell upon Eochaid and all of his descendants for the harm they had wrought on the Land of Tir nan Og.

MORDA

See *The History of Taliesin*.

MORVAN, THE PROP OF BRITTANY

BRITTANY

Morvan, Prince of Leon, was a historical figure. In the ninth century he achieved fame as an upholder of Breton independence, hence his nickname, "The Prop of Brittany." He became the hero of a series of ballad tales that, assembled together, almost amount to an epic. They describe Morvan's life, travels, adventures, and death, and the wonderful feats he performed along the way. He occupies a similar place in Breton legend to **Arthur** in British legend.

The ballad ultimately composed by Villemarqué was drawn from ancient Celtic sources. There are resemblances to Arthurian romances. The description of the flight of young Morvan is very similar to the episode in the Arthurian saga *Percival le Gallois* in which the boy Percival leaves his mother's care in exactly the same way. The Frankish king and his court are depicted in a style similar to that of the *Chanson de Gestes* celebrating the deeds of Charlemagne. The severed **head** represents much more ancient material (*see* Religion: **Headhunting**).

MORVAN'S FIRST ADVENTURE

The boy Morvan was sitting at the forest edge on day when a knight rode out from among the trees on a great charger. The boy was alarmed by the dramatic appearance of the knight, thought he was St. Michael, and ran away. But the knight overtook him. The boy cried, "Seigneur St. Michael, please do me no harm."

The knight laughed. "I'm not St. Michael, just a belted knight: there are scores of us about!"

"I've never seen a knight before," said the boy. "What is it you are carrying?"

"That is a lance, my boy."

"And what are you wearing on your head and chest?"

"A *casque* and breastplate. They are meant to protect me from the blows of swords and spears. Tell

The Element Encyclopedia of the Celts

me, boy, have you seen anyone pass this way?"

"Yes, *seigneur*. A man went by on this very road not half an hour ago."

"Thank you, boy. If anyone asks who spoke to you, say the Count of Quimper."

He spurred his horse and set off down the road in the direction Morvan had indicated.

Morvan went back to his mother to tell her of his meeting. He was full of the knight's military bearing, his gallantry, and his grace. "Mother, you never saw such a splendid man, nobler than the Archangel Michael whose image is painted on the wall of our church."

Morvan's mother patted him fondly. "No man looks as noble as the Archangel Michael!"

But Morvan was convinced that he was right. "I wish I could grow up to be like that and become a knight too."

His mother was so dismayed that she fell down in a faint. She had lost her husband in battle and dreaded that the same fate might overtake her son. The boy was so preoccupied with his vision that he scarcely noticed. He went to the stable and led out a horse. He jumped up onto its back, turned its head, and cantered off after the knight.

THE RETURN OF MORVAN

Young Morvan passed the next ten years in martial adventures. Then he was suddenly seized with a desire to revisit his ancestral mansion and made his way home.

He was dismayed to find brambles and nettles growing over the threshold of the house and the walls disintegrating and overgrown with ivy, that exploiter of neglect.

As he was about to go inside, he noticed an old blind woman standing near the entrance. He asked if he might have hospitality for the night.

"We have little to offer, sir," she said. "The house has gone to ruin since its son and heir left."

A young maiden came out, looked at Morvan, and burst into tears.

"How now, why do you weep?"

"Alas, my lord, my brother left us ten years ago to lead the life of a soldier. Every time I see a youth of about his age it reminds me of him."

"And your mother? What of her?" asked Morvan.

"Alas, my lord, she too is gone. There's no one here now but me and my old nurse. My mother died of grief when my brother rode away to become a knight."

Morvan was deeply stirred. "Wretch that I am, I have been the cause of my mother's death!"

The maiden turned pale. "In heaven's name, who are you?"

"I am Morvan, son of Conan, and Lez-Breiz is my surname. And you are my sister."

The maiden stared at him, then fell into his arms, praising God that her long-lost brother had come back.

THE KING'S KNIGHT

Morvan could not remain long at his home. His fireside was the tented field, his recreation was the clash of battle. One day he said to his squire, "Rouse yourself, young squire. Furnish my sword, shield, and *casque* and let me smear them with the blood of the Franks. Today, with this right arm, I hope to carry slaughter into their ranks."

The squire wanted to join him in the battle. "Shall I not fight at your side today, my lord?"

Morvan smiled, remembering his own over-eagerness to join the fray when he met the Count of Quimper. "Think of your mother, boy. You might never return to her. Just think of her grief if you should die today."

The boy would not be put off. "Oh, lord, if you love me, please grant my wish. Please let me fight beside you!"

So it was that when Morvan rode off to battle one hour later his squire rode beside him. As they passed the church of St. Anne of Armor, they went in.

Morvan prayed to St. Anne. "Most holy lady, I have been in 20 battles, yet I am but 20 years old. All gained by your aid. And if I come back again alive, I shall make you a rich gift. I shall give you enough candles to go three times round your church and three times round your churchyard. As well as this I shall give you a white satin banner with an ivory staff. And I shall give you seven silver bells to ring gaily day and night above your head. And I will draw water for your use three times—on my knees."

The enemy watched Morvan approaching them from a long way off. He was mounted on a small, white donkey with a halter of hemp, as a gesture of contempt. Morvan's chief enemy, Lorgnez, launched himself at Morvan with a band of warriors, while Morvan had only his little squire behind him. On the enemy came. At first

The Element Encyclopedia of the Celts

the little squire was alarmed, but he rallied when his master spoke to him and drew his sword and spurred his horse forward.

Morvan came face to face with Lorgnez and hailed him politely. "Seigneur Lorgnez! Good day to you, sir!"

Lorgnez replied with equal courtesy. "Good day to you, Seigneur Morvan! Will you join with me in single combat?"

But then the courtesies were done. "I will not," said Morven. "Go back to your king and tell him I despise him. I scoff at you and those you have about you. Go back to Paris, take off your mail, and put on the silken armor of fops. That would suit you far better!"

The face of Lorgnez flushed with rage. "The lowest scoundrel in my company will knock the helm from off your head for this."

Then Morvan drew his great sword…

The ancient hermit of the wood heard knocking at his door. He opened it quickly and saw the little squire standing there. He was startled at the sight of the boy's bloodstained armor and pallid face. "My son, you are badly hurt. Let me wash your wounds at the fountain. Then rest here awhile."

The boy shook his head. "I may not rest, good father. I have come for water for my master, who has fallen in the fight. He has slain 30 warriors, and Lorgnez was the first."

The hermit showed concern. "Alas that he has fallen."

The boy said, "Do not grieve. It is true that he has fallen, but only from exhaustion. He is not wounded and shortly will recover."

Once recovered, Morvan went back to the chapel of St. Anne. True to his word, he bestowed on her all the gifts he promised.

"Praise be to St. Anne," he cried, "for it is she who has won this victory."

THE KING'S BLACKAMOOR

The King of the Franks sat among his courtiers, listening to news of a fresh exploit of Morvan. "I wish someone would rid me of this troublesome Morvan," he said. "He constantly afflicts the Frankish lands and kills my bravest warriors."

The King's Blackamoor stood up, a giant among men, towering head and shoulders above them all. "Let me fulfill your wishes. Sir Morvan has sent me his glove. If tomorrow I do not bring you his head, I will let you have my own."

The following morning, Morvan's squire went to his master in a state of alarm. "Lord, the King's Blackamoor has come. He says he defies you."

Morvan took up his sword.

The boy was even more alarmed. "Dear master, take care what you do. This moor is a demon who practises enchantments."

Morvan laughed. "Can the demon resist cold steel? Go, saddle my black charger."

"Saving your grace," said the boy, "you will not choose the black charger. He has been bewitched. You will notice that when you enter the lists to fight the Moor will throw his cloak to the ground. You must not do the same; if you do and your cloak falls underneath his then the power of the giant will be doubled. When the Moor attacks, use your lance to make the sign of the cross. When he rushes at you, attack him with the steel."

Then the heroes met in the lists. The King of France and his noblemen followed the giant to witness the combat. The trumpets sounded and the two champions rushed furiously at each other. They circled each other, watching for an oppor-

tunity for a strike. Then one man struck, the other retaliated, and blood flowed over the bright armor.

The King of the Franks shouted for action from his Blackamoor. "Ho! Black crow of the sea, pierce me now!"

At this, the giant Blackamoor fell upon Morvan. Their lances crossed, but the Moor's broke like matchwood. They leaped to the ground and exchanged many powerful strokes. Sparks flew up from their armor as they clashed. The Moor gripped his sword with both hands and prepared to strike a mighty killing blow. Morvan, swift as thought, plunged his own blade deep into the Moor's armpit, through to the heart, and the giant fell to the ground like a toppled tree.

Morvan put his foot on the dead giant's chest, pulled out his sword, and used it to cut off the Moor's head. He tied this bleeding battle trophy to the pommel of his saddle, rode proudly home with it, and mounted it on his castle gate.

All men hailed Morvan's heroic deed, but he was modest and gave the grace of victory to St. Anne alone. He would build a chapel in her honor up on the heights between Léguer and the Guindy.

The Element Encyclopedia of the Celts

MORVAN DOES BATTLE
WITH THE KING

One day Morvan rode out to do battle with no less a foe than the King of the Franks himself. The king rode out with 5,000 mounted men-at-arms, a huge army, and as he set off a mighty clap of thunder boomed across the vault of heaven.

The king's nobles, riding with him, knew it was an omen. One of them said, "My lord, turn back. The day has started with such an evil sign."

The king replied briskly, "I have given the order. We must march."

That same morning, Morvan's sister said to him, "If you love me, dear brother, do not seek this battle with the king, for if you do you must surely meet your death. Then what will become of me? On the shore I see the white seahorse, the symbol of Brittany, entwined about by a monstrous serpent, grip-ping him by the hind legs. The sea stallion rears round to bite the ser-pent, but the fight is too unequal. You alone, and the Franks without number!"

But Morvan was on his way, cantering out of earshot...

The hermit who lived in the greenwood of Helléan lay sleeping. He was woken by three knocks at his door. Outside someone said, "Good hermit, please open your door. I need sanctuary and help from you."

A cold wind blew from the land of the Franks. It was that time of night when wild beasts wander the woods, looking for prey. The hermit was reluctant to open his door. "Who are you, knocking at my door in the night, demanding to be let in? How can I tell if you are true? How can I tell if I can trust you?"

"Good priest, I am well known in this land. I am Morvan Lez-Breiz, the Ax of Brittany."

"I'll not open my door to you," the hermit answered quickly. "I know you for a rebel and a mortal foe of the King of the Franks."

Morvan grew angry. "No! I am a Breton true: neither traitor nor rebel. It is the King of the Franks who has betrayed this land."

The Element Encyclopedia of the Celts

The hermit unlocked the door and pulled it open. He recoiled in terror when he saw what was waiting outside. A terrible headless phantom advanced toward him, holding its severed head in front of it as it approached. Its eyes seemed to boil with blood and fire, rolling around and around. The hermit was revolted and frightened by what he saw.

The head laughed at him, and spoke: "Old Christian, fear not. God permits this. God allowed the Franks to cut off my head, but only for a time. What you see now is only a phantom. But God will allow you, old hermit, to put my head back on my shoulders—if you will."

The hermit was reluctant. He drew back. He had seen things from the Otherworld before—things he had reason to dread. But he had also fallen under Morvan's spell, Morvan the hero of the Bretons, even though he believed himself the subject of the King of the Franks. He overcame his natural fear and said, "If God is willing for this to happen, then I too am willing to place your head back on your shoulders."

"Silence!" the hermit replied. "The King of the Franks is a man of God. You may not slander him so."

"No man of God, but rather of the devil. He has ravaged the lands of the Bretons and the gold that he wrests from the people of Brittany is spent on the work of the devil. Open the door, hermit!"

"I will not, my son. If I did, the Franks would find fault with me."

Morvan was furious. "You refuse? Then I shall break down your door." He threw himself against the door, which creaked but held shut.

"Stop, my son!" cried the old hermit, fearing for his door. "Stop and I will open the door."

He took up a torch, lit it from the embers of his hearth-fire, and went to open the door.

"Take it," said Morvan's bloody head, "take it, then."

The Element Encyclopedia of the Celts

The quaking priest took the repulsive trophy from Morvan's hands and placed it on the chief's broad shoulders. "In the name of the Father, the Son, and the Holy Sprit, I replace your head, my son."

With that benediction, the phantom once more became a man.

"You must do a great penance, Morvan," the hermit told him. "You must carry with you for seven years a cloak of lead, chained to your neck. Each day at noon you must fetch water from the well at the top of that mountain over there."

Morvan was happy to do as the hermit asked. "I will abide by your wish, old man."

The seven long years of penance passed. By the end of the seventh year, the leaden cloak had chafed and cut Morvan's skin, his beard had become gray, and his hair fell almost to his waist. No one recognized him now, except a lady dressed in white who passed one day through the greenwood and gazed earnestly at him with tear-filled eyes.

"It is you, Morvan, my son. Come here, so that I may free you of your burden."

With a pair of golden scissors, she cut the chain that fastened the leaden cloak to the penitent's shoulders.

"I am your patron, Saint Anne of Armor."

For seven years, the squire of Morvan had been searching for his master. One day he was riding through the greenwood of Helléan. "Alas," he said to himself, "I have killed the man who murdered him, but I have lost my dear lord."

Then he heard the whinnying of a horse at the far end of the wood. His own horse sniffed the air and answered the distant whinny. Then, between the branches, the squire saw a great black charger. It was Morvan's fine steed. It whinnied plaintively, as if it stood upon its master's grave.

But Morvan will return one day to fight the Franks and drive them out of the land of the Bretons.

The Element Encyclopedia of the Celts

N

JOHN AND MARY NELSON

See **Redeemed from Fairyland**.

NEMEDH

See **The Book of Invasions**.

NOROUAS, THE NORTH-WEST WIND

BRITTANY

A cycle of Breton folk-tales deals with the winds, which play a major part in Breton folklore. Fishermen on the north coast are said to speak to the winds as if they are living beings, shaking their fists and swearing at them if they blow in the "wrong" direction.

There was once a goodman and his wife who had a little field where they could grow flax. One year their field produced a particularly fine crop. After cutting it, they laid it out to dry. Then Norouas, the North-West Wind, with one sweep of his great wings tossed it up into the air as high as the tree-tops. It fell into the sea and was lost.

The goodman saw what had happened and began to swear at the North-West Wind. He took a stick and set out to find and kill Norouas for spoiling his crop.

He was impatient to set off and took no food or money with him. When night fell, hungry and penniless, he came upon an inn. He explained his situation to the hostess. She gave him some bread and allowed him to sleep in a corner of the stable. When morning came, he asked her the way to the abode of Norouas and she took him to the foot of a mountain, where she said the wind lived.

The goodman climbed the mountain and on the summit he met Surouas, the South-West Wind. The goodman asked if he was Norouas, but the wind denied it.

"Where is that rogue Norouas?" the goodman cried.

Surouas hushed him. "Not quite so loud, goodman. If he hears you he will throw you up into the air like a straw."

Then Norouas appeared, whistling wildly.

"Ah, you thief!" cried the goodman. "It was you who stole my lovely crop of flax!"

But the North-West Wind took no notice of him.

"Give me back my flax!" the goodman shouted furiously.

"Hush!" said Norouas. "Here's a napkin that may keep you quiet."

The goodman howled in frustration, "But with my crop of flax I could have made a hundred napkins like this. Give me back my flax!"

"Hush, you fool," said the North-West Wind, "this is no ordinary napkin I am giving you. You have only to say 'Napkin, unfold' and you will have the best-laid table in the world."

The goodman grumbled as he took the napkin and went down the mountain. Disinclined to believe what Norouas had said, he placed the napkin down in front of him and said the words "Napkin,

unfold" as he had been told.

Instantly a table appeared spread with a banquet. The smell of finely cooked dishes filled the goodman's nostrils and rare wines sparkled and glowed in glittering vessels.

When he had finished eating, the goodman folded up his napkin and returned to the inn where he had slept the previous night.

The hostess asked, "Well, did you get any satisfaction out of Norouas?"

"I did indeed," the goodman said, eager to demonstrate his success. He produced the napkin and said, "Napkin, unfold." Instantly the magic table appeared, laden with food and drink.

The hostess was speechless with astonishment. She wanted that napkin for herself. That night she placed the goodman in a handsome bedchamber with a beautiful bed and a soft feather mattress. He slept more soundly than he had ever slept in his life. While he was asleep, the cunning hostess tiptoed into the room and stole the napkin, leaving one that looked similar in its place.

In the morning the goodman set off for home and eventually arrived at his little farm. His wife eagerly asked him if Norouas had made reparation for the damage done to the flax and he said that he had. He proudly produced the napkin from his pocket, anticipating how pleased his wife would be when he demonstrated what it could do.

"Well," said the wife, unimpressed, "we could have made two hundred napkins like this from the flax that he destroyed."

"Ah, but this napkin is not the same as the others," said the goodman. "I only have to say 'Napkin, unfold' and a table loaded with food appears."

He said the words but nothing happened.

"You are an old fool," said his wife.

The husband's jaw dropped and he grabbed his stick. "I have been tricked by that scoundrel Norouas!" he shouted. "I shall not spare him this time."

He rushed off toward the home of the winds.

As before he slept at the inn and the following morning climbed the mountain. He called loudly on Norouas, demanding for his crop of flax to be returned.

"Be quiet!" Norouas shouted back.

"I shall not be quiet!" The goodman shook his stick. "You cheated

me with that napkin of yours."

"Very well," Norouas answered. "Here is an ass. You have only to say 'Ass, make me some gold' and it will fall from his tail."

The goodman was eager to test the value of his new acquisition and led it to the foot of the mountain. He said, "Ass, make me some gold." The ass shook its tail and a shower of gold pieces fell to the ground.

The goodman hurried back to the inn, where he showed the magic donkey to the hostess. That night, she went to the stable and exchanged the magic ass for an ordinary one and the goodman took the wrong ass home to show to his wife.

Once again the goodman launched into a demonstration of his prize. The ass failed to respond to the magic words and the goodman's wife ridiculed him a second time.

He set off in a towering rage, arriving on the mountain of the winds for a third time, and called on Norouas, heaping insults on him.

Norouas replied, "Gently, gently. Ease off, my friend. I am not to blame for your misfortune. You must know that it is the hostess at the inn where you slept who is the guilty party. She is the one who stole your napkin. She is the one who stole your ass. Take this cudgel. When you say 'Strike, cudgel' it will attack your enemies for you. All you have to do is to say '*Ora pro nobis.*' When you want it to stop.'

The goodman was eager to try it out, so he said at once, "Strike, cudgel." The cudgel set about beating him soundly, which he deserved. He shouted, "*Ora pro nobis!*" and made it stop.

He went back to the inn in a black mood, loudly demanding that the hostess return his napkin and ass. She threatened to call the constables. He cried, "Strike, cudgel," and the cudgel straightaway set about giving her a beating. She begged the goodman to call it off and said she would give him back his napkin and his ass.

Once he had his property back, the goodman hurried home, where his wife was overjoyed by the treasures he conjured up. He rapidly became rich.

But his neighbors were suspicious at the sight of so much wealth acquired invisibly. They reported him to the constable and he was accused of wholesale murder and robbery and taken before a judge,

who sentenced him to death.

On the day of his execution, he made a final request: that his cudgel might be brought to him. This favor was granted.

He cried, "Strike, cudgel," and the cudgel beat the judge, the constables, and the neighbors so hard that they all fled. It beat the scaffold too, breaking it up, and cracked the hangman's head. There was a general cry for mercy and the goodman was instantly pardoned.

After that, he and his wife were left alone to enjoy the treasures the North-West Wind had given him as compensation for his ruined crop of flax.

THE NUBERU

GALICIA, SPAIN

The Nuberu is a character in Galician mythology. He is the Cloud Master, the god of clouds and storms. He is sometimes represented as a man with a bushy beard, wearing goat leathers and a big hat. He wields control over the weather and entertains himself by setting off storms and launching gales, striking down livestock with bolts of lightning, and wrecking the harvests of men with storms of rain and hail. He can be cruel to people, but he can also be kind to those who have helped him:

Long ago, the Nuberu arrived on a cloud, but was unlucky enough to fall off and land on the ground. He asked for shelter, but no one wanted to help him. Eventually, late at night, a peasant took pity on him and took him into his house. In gratitude, the Nuberu watered his dry fields and gave him good harvests.

Some years later, this peasant had to travel to Egypt and when he arrived there he heard that his wife was about to marry someone else; she evidently thought, because her husband had been gone a long time, that he was dead. The peasant then asked for Nuberu's help. Together they traveled back to Galicia riding on clouds, and they arrived in time to halt the wedding.

According to myth, the Nuberu lives in the city of Orito, in Egypt. Some folklorists believe he is a late memory of the Celtic **god Taranis**, who similarly ruled over the skies. If he is attacked, he does not hesitate to hurl lightning in retaliation.

The Nuberu is greatly feared for the damage he causes. There are superstitious folk who think they can scare him away by lighting candles and ringing bells. Fishermen fear him because of his ability to whip up strong winds at sea, forcing them to hurry back to the safety of their harbors.

OWAIN, OR THE LADY OF THE FOUNTAIN

WALES

The hero of this folk-tale, Owain, is based on the historical figure Owain mab Urien. In the later continental tradition he appears as Ywain. The story is a romance.

A hero marries the maiden he loves, the Lady of the Fountain, but he loses her when he neglects her in order to engage in knightly exploits. One of these exploits is to

The Element Encyclopedia of the Celts

save a lion from a serpent. Later, with the lion's help, he finds a balance between his marital and social duties—and is reunited with his wife.

The story is related to the French romance *Yvain, the Knight of the Lion* by Chrétien de Troyes.

P

PARTHOLÁN

See **The Book of Invasions**.

PÈRE LA CHIQUE

See **The Magic Rose**.

PEREDUR, SON OF EFRAWG

WALES

Another Welsh poem with an uncertain relationship with the work of Chrétien de Troyes, this time *Pereceval, the Story of the Grail*. Peredur may preserve some of the ancient material that found its way into Chrétien's source. The sequence of events is different in *Peredur* and there are many orginal episodes, such as the hero's 14-year stay in Constantinople, where he co-rules with the Empress (a remnant of a sovereignty tale). In *Peredur* the Holy Grail is replaced by a severed **head** on a platter, which is an older archetype. But in spite of these differences, it is possible that the poem was influenced by the French romance.

Peredur's father dies when he is young and his mother takes him into the woods to raise him in isolation. He later meets a group of knights and resolves to become like them. He travels to King Arthur's court, where he is ridiculed by Cei. He sets off on further adventures, promising to take revenge on Cei for his insults, and on those who supported Cei.

While he is traveling he meets two of his uncles. The first (taking the role of Percival's Gornemant) educates him in the use of arms and warns him not to ask the meaning of what he sees. The second (taking the role of Chretien's Fisher King) shows Peredur a salver bearing a man's severed head. The young man refrains from asking any questions about this and goes on to further adventures. These include a stay with the Nine Witches of Gloucester and an encounter with the woman who wants to be his true love: Angharad Golden-Hand.

Peredur returns to the court of Arthur, only to embark on a new series of adventures that (this time) do not correspond to incidents in *Perceval*. Eventually he discovers that the severed head at his uncle's court belonged to his cousin, who had been killed by the Nine Witches of Gloucester. Peredur avenges the wrongs done to his family and is acknowledged and applauded as a hero. (*See* Religion: **Headhunting**; Symbols: **Grail Quest**.)

PIXIES

DARTMOOR, ENGLAND

An old woman who lives on Dartmoor is returning home from market with an empty basket. As she approaches the bridge over the Blackabrook at the Ockerry, a small figure leaps onto the road and starts capering in front of her. He is a pixy about 18 inches (45cm) high. She wonders what to do, as she fears being pixy-led (ab-ducted). She remembers her family are waiting for her and walks on.

When she gets to the bridge, the pixy hops right up to her. She suddenly bends down, scoops him up, and drops him into her basket, latching the lid.

The pixy starts scolding and chattering in some unknown language while the woman hurries home, pleased that she has something so interesting to show her family. The scolding and chattering stop, so she lifts the lid a little to peep inside. There is no sign of the pixy. He has gone.

PRYDERI FAB PWYLL

See The Four Branches of the Mabinogi.

JIM PULK

See Symbols: **Dragon**.

JIM PUTTOCK

See Symbols: **Dragon**.

R

REDEEMED FROM FAIRYLAND

SCOTLAND

James Campbell lived near Aberdeen. He had a daughter called Mary, who was married to young John Nelson. Shortly after they married the young couple went to live in Aberdeen, where John carried on his trade as a goldsmith. They lived happily together, until the time approached for Mary to produce her first baby.

The midwives who were with Mary had had too much to drink. Near the hour of 12 at night, they were frightened by a dreadful noise. All of a sudden the candles went out, causing great confusion. The midwives called in the neighbors to bring lights. When they looked at Mary, they saw that she was dead.

The next day, while preparations were made for Mary's funeral, the Reverend Mr. Dodd looked at her corpse and said, "This is not the body of a Christian. Mrs. Nelson was carried away by the fairies and what you take to be her body is not her, only some substance left in her place."

The others could make no sense of what he said and did not believe him, so Mr. Dodd stayed away from the funeral. The following day Mary was buried.

After sunset, John, the grief-stricken husband, was riding across his own field when he heard pleasant music. He saw coming toward him a woman dressed in white. She wore a veil, so he could not see her face. He rode up to her and asked her in a friendly way who she was to walk alone so late.

At this she lifted her veil and burst into tears. She said, "I am not permitted to tell you who I am."

John knew she was his wife and asked what disturbed her and why she had appeared at that hour.

She said, "Appearing at any hour is of no consequence. Though you believe me dead and buried, I am not, but was taken away by the fairies. You only buried a piece of wood in my place. I can be recovered if you take the proper means. The child has three nurses to attend it, but I fear it cannot be brought home. I depend more than anyone on my brother Robert, who is captain of a merchant ship and will be home in ten days' time."

John asked what he had to do to win her back. She told him he would find a letter the following Sunday on the desk in his room, addressed to her brother. In it there would be instructions for winning her back.

"Since I was taken from you, I have been treated like a queen," she added, "and if you look behind me you will see my companions."

He did, and a short distance away he saw a king and queen sitting beside a moat on thrones in splendor. To each side he saw other kings.

He said, "I fear it will not be possible to win you back from such a place."

She said, "Were my brother Robert here in your place, he would be able to bring me home, but you must not attempt it, as that would mean that I would be lost to you forever. I am threatened with severe punishment for speaking to you. To prevent that, you must ride up the moat and threaten to burn all the brambles around it, unless you get a firm promise that I shall not be punished."

John promised and instantly lost sight of all he had seen. He rode resolutely up to the moat and vowed he would burn everything around it if he did not get a promise that his wife would come to no harm.

A voice asked him to throw away a book that was in his pocket and then make his request. John answered that he would not part with his book and insisted that his request be granted. The voice said that upon its honor Mary would be forgiven but he should suffer no prejudice to approach the moat. He agreed to this and heard most pleasant music.

John then returned home. He sent for the Reverend Mr. Dodd and told him what had happened. Mr. Dodd stayed with him until the following Sunday morning. Then, as his wife had said, John saw a letter on his desk. It was addressed to Mary's brother, who came home a few days later and read it:

Dear Brother,
My husband can relate to you my present circumstances. I request that you will, the first night after you see this,

come to the moat where I parted from my husband. Let nothing daunt you, but stand in the center of the moat at the hour of 12 at night, and call me. I, with several others, will then surround you. I shall have on the whitest dress of any in the company.

Take hold of me, and do not forsake me; you must not be surprised at all the frightful methods they shall use, but keep your hold, even if they continue till cock crow, when they shall vanish all of a sudden, and I shall be safe and return home and live with my husband. If you succeed in your attempt, you will gain applause from all your friends, and have the blessing of your ever-loving and affectionate sister,
Mary Nelson

Robert vowed to win back his sister and her child or die in the attempt. He went back to his ship and told his sailors the contents of the letter. He stayed with them till ten at night, when he left. His loyal sailors offered to go with him, but he refused to take them: he had to go alone.

As soon as he left his ship a terrifying lion came roaring at him. He drew his sword and struck at it. The sword passed straight through—the lion was of no sub-

stance, only the appearance of a lion to terrify him. This encouraged him.

He went to the moat where he saw a white handkerchief. Suddenly he was surrounded by screaming women uttering frightful cries. He saw his sister in the whitest dress of any around him. He seized her right hand and said, "With God's help, I will save you from all infernal imps."

At this the moat seemed to fill with flames and the sky rang with dreadful thunderclaps. Terrifying birds and beasts seemed to lunge at Robert from out of the fire, which he knew wasn't real, so nothing daunted his courage. Steadfastly, he kept hold of his sister for an hour and three-quarters.

Then the cocks began to crow, the fire disappeared, and the frightful imps vanished. Robert took his sister in his arms and thanked God for his help that night. Mary's dress was thin and he wrapped her in his overcoat for warmth. She embraced him, saying she was safe now. He took her home to her husband and there was great rejoicing.

John said he would destroy the moat in revenge for the child the fairies had taken from them, but instantly they heard a voice saying, "You shall have your son safe and well, on condition that you will not plow the ground within three perches of the moat, nor damage bushes or brambles around that place."

They agreed at once and a few moments later the child appeared on his mother's knee.

THE RETURN FROM ENGLAND

BRITTANY

When Duke William of Normandy conquered England, a large number of Breton warriors accompanied him. Many of these men were rewarded with lands in England.

One young Breton who followed the Conqueror was called Silvestik. This story tells how his mother mourns his absence:

"One night I lay on my bed, and could not sleep. I heard the girls at Kerlaz singing the song of my son. Dear God, my son, where are you now? Perhaps you are 300 leagues away, drowned in the great ocean and the fishes feed upon your fair body. Perhaps you are married to some Saxon girl. You were to

have married a lovely Breton girl, Mannaik de Pouldergat, and by now you and she might have surrounded us with beautiful children.

"I have taken to my door a white dove. It sits in a small hollow in the stone. I have tied to its neck a letter, using the ribbon from my wedding dress, and I have sent it to my son. Go, my dove, rise on your wings, up into the sky, fly far across the sea, and find out for me if my son is alive and well."

Silvestik was resting in the shade of an English wood. A familiar note fell upon his ear.

"That sound," he said, "is like the voice of my mother's dove."

The sound grew louder and seemed to say, "Good luck to you, Silvestik. Under my wing I have a letter for you."

Silvestik read the letter and was very happy. He decided to return to his grieving mother.

Three years passed and the dove had not returned to Brittany. Day after day the grieving mother walked along the seashore, waiting and hoping for the ship that never came.

One stormy day she was walking along the beach when she saw a ship being driven ashore upon the rocks. Shortly after that, the bodies of its drowned crew were washed up on the beach.

When the gale died down, the mother searched among the corpses on the beach. Among them she found her son, Silvestik.

This ballad was probably written in the eleventh century, contemporary with the Norman Conquest of England. Many Bretons who sailed with the Conqueror did not return for several years and, inevitably, some did not return at all. The ballad is a cautionary tale of sorts, warning against meddling with destiny.

LA ROSE

See **The Magic Rose**.

S

THE SALTY SEA

WALES

A very long time ago, when the sea was still fresh water, there were three Welsh brothers. They had been born in a yellow house on the Welsh Tramping Road and were now grown up into three young men: Glyn, a farmer plowing the land, Lyn, a mariner plowing the sea, and Maldwyn, the youngest of all, who did nothing, plowing only his own furrow. Glyn prospered and had honey on his bread. Lyn prospered too and had apples with his cheese. But Maldwyn and his wife did nothing but wander the highways, sharing between them whatever they could beg. Whenever they passed the yellow house, they would stop and cadge something from Maldwyn's older brothers.

Glyn tired of Maldwyn's cadging and decided to be rid of him forever. He asked him, "What would you promise me, if I gave you a pig?"

Maldwyn said, "Anything you ask, brother."

Glyn said, "Then I'll take you at your word. Here's your pig. Now go to blazes."

Maldwyn said, "My word's my word. I'll trouble you no more."

For the rest of the day, Maldwyn and his wife wandered about, with their pig on a string, looking for Blazes.

Toward evening, they came upon a cottage with a lighted doorway. In the garden was a white-haired old man who looked like a shepherd. They asked him if he, by any chance, was Blazes.

The old man said, "Mr. Blazes is an old friend of mine. You'll find him in Fernal, the house at the bottom of the valley. He loves nothing better than a roast, and my guess is he'll see your little pig and want to buy it from you. But if you want some advice, and I'll gladly give it to you, don't let the pig go in exchange for anything less than the handmill that stands behind the kitchen door. It is a fine handmill, one that grinds out exactly what you want. If you pass this way again, I'll be glad to show you how to work it."

Maldwyn thanked the shepherd and walked with his wife and his pig down to the bottom of the valley. There was a big house there called Fernal and they knocked at its door. It opened at once, and they were ushered in by Mr Blazes' many servants. Some were tending a huge roaring fire. Others were already prodding the little pig to see how plump it was.

Mr. Blazes offered Maldwyn a thousand years for the pig.

"A thousand thanks," Maldwyn answered politely. "My wife and I have saved up for more than a year so that we could have this little pig for our Christmas dinner. But because I am the kindest-hearted man alive and hate to see anyone disappointed I will let you have it simply in exchange for the handmill behind your kitchen door."

Mr. Blazes resisted Maldwyn's proposal for a long while, offering him all sorts of things instead of the handmill, things that seemed far more valuable and desirable. It was Maldwyn's wife who said, "It must be the handmill or nothing."

By now the servants were howling for the pig. "Give us pig! Give us pig or we'll die!"

In the end Mr. Blazes gave in and let Maldwyn and his wife have the handmill.

The pig had been keeping as close as possible to Maldwyn while all this discussion had been going on. Now it squealed as it found it-self clamped in the crook of Mr. Blazes' arm.

Maldwyn took the handmill back up to the shepherd, who showed him how to start it and, more important, how to stop it. Maldwyn and his wife couldn't wait to get started. First it ground out a house for them, then candles to light it and furniture and food and drink. This going to Blazes was a good thing to do.

Maldwyn drove up to the yellow house in the carriage the handmill had ground out and invited his brother Glyn to come and dine with him.

Glyn, and the neighbors who went with him, were amazed at the gold plates and the fine selection of wines Maldwyn had to offer.

"Little brother," Glyn exclaimed, "where in blazes did you get all this?"

"From behind the kitchen door," Maldwyn said mysteriously, but after a while Glyn got the whole story out of him.

Maldwyn fell asleep after drinking and eating too much, and Glyn seized the opportunity to grab the handmill and walk off with it to the yellow house.

Glyn sent his wife out to work in the field so that he could see what the handmill could do on his own. His first thought was to get the mill to provide servants—if they were pretty, so much the better—and ale. He spoke to the handmill:

"Little mill, little mill,
Grind me maids and ale;
Little mill, little mill,
Grind them dark and pale."

As the words left his lips, a dark-skinned girl appeared, surfing toward him on a wave of beer. Then came a pale girl, then a tawny one, then a white one. The house was suddenly full of maids with different-colored skins and the ale was a foot deep on the floor and getting deeper.

Glyn shouted, "Enough! Stop, mill, stop!" But the handmill went on grinding. Soon the maids of different colors were swimming for their lives in a rising tide of ale. It burst out through the doors and windows, and a torrent of ale went foaming down to the sea.

Out in the fields Glyn's wife was swept away by the torrent and soon she and Glyn were drowning. The maids, though, were in their element, swimming and frolicking in the lake of ale.

The Element Encyclopedia of the Celts

Maldwyn heard the commotion. He had been wondering where his handmill had gone. Now he realized that his brother Glyn had taken it. He ordered the mill to stop grinding out maids then ale. Gradually the flood subsided and Maldwyn retrieved his handmill.

The following week, Maldwyn's brother Lyn sailed into the bay with a cargo of salt. He was surprised to find the water there smelling of ale and full of mermaids splashing about in it. He soon heard what had happened, and went along to Maldwyn's gold-plated house, amazed to find his younger brother so wealthy.

"Where in blazes did you get so rich?" he asked.

"Behind the kitchen door," Maldwyn said cryptically, but Lyn, too, quickly got the full story out of him—everything except the crucial instruction that would stop the mill grinding.

"Will it grind salt?" Lyn asked.

"Yes, enough to make all the sea salt," said Maldwyn.

Lyn said nothing, but thought how useful it would be if he could grind salt. He wouldn't need to go to sea any more. When Maldwyn fell asleep through having eaten and drunk too much, Lyn picked up the handmill and took it to his ship. He set sail at once.

Once he was out in open water in Cardigan Bay, Lyn patted the handmill and chanted to it:

"Little mill, little mill,
Grind me salty salt.
Little mill, little mill,
Grind it without halt."

The handmill ground out salt till it lay like snow, drifting all over the deck of Lyn's ship. Lyn and his crew climbed the mast to get out of the way of the rising heaps of salt, but there was no escape. The ship eventually sank under the weight of salt and Lynn and all his crew were pickled in the brine.

Later the white-haired shepherd walked along the long Welsh Tramping Road. He saw the mermaids frolicking in the sea and tasted the salty water. "Truly," he said, "I move in mysterious ways my wonders to perform."

It seemed good to him to have mermaids in the bay, so he left them there, and smiled at all his works. And the salt of the sea was good, so he left the handmill too, grinding away and making the sea round Wales a little saltier than any other.

The Element Encyclopedia of the Celts

SEITHENIN

See **The Sigh of Gwyddno Garanhir.**

SHELLYCOAT

See **The Bogle.**

THE SIGH OF GWYDDNO GARANHIR

WALES

In the days long ago, before the sea overwhelmed the lost kingdom, Gwyddno Garanhir was king over Cantre'r Gwaelod. This was the low country in the west. This was the best, the richest, of all the kingdoms of Britain; its land was worth four times as much as any other. It was land you would covet, but for one thing: it was land that was lower than the waters of the sea.

A great wall had been built to protect Gwyddno's kingdom from the sea, with sluices and water-gates. As the tide fell, the water might run out, but as it rose again the sluices stopped it flowing back in. Watching over this wall and making sure the sluices were opened and shut at the right times was Gwyddno's main task, and he had entrusted it to Seithenin, a prince of Dyfed. Seithenin was handsome and high-spirited, but he had a weakness for drink. He was in fact one of the Three Arrant Drunkards of the Island of Britain.

The month of the high tides came. One night there was a feast in Gwyddno's court. Meat and drink without limit were served from his larder of plenty.

As night fell a fierce gale whipped up in the south-west, piling up the waters in the sea between Wales and Ireland. This was a night when a watchman was needed, yet never was Seithenin drunker. The sluices were left open and the water-gates too stood open. In rolled the sea as the tide rose, and by dawn the whole kingdom and its 16 towns were under the water.

Still the sea holds sway in Cardigan Bay, but sometimes when the tide is low you may see a tree-stump or a stub of wall, or you may hear the chime of a water-swung bell. This is all that is left of Gwyddno's great kingdom.

The king himself escaped to higher ground with his court and a few of his subjects. They made for the mountains of the north, where they lived by hunting, but it was a hard living.

Gwyddno felt the loss of his kingdom keenly. He had been a proud king, and now he was no more than a squire with a salmon-weir on the Dyfi River. He never could look out at the waters of Cardigan Bay without thinking of his lost kingdom, and reliving the sorrow that he felt on the first morning after the terrible flood. It was a sorrow so great that he could not speak. Instead he let out a sigh over the waters so deep that even now when people want to describe the sigh of deepest sadness they call it:

The sigh of Gwyddno Garanhir,
When the waves rolled over the land.

(*See* **The History of Taliesin.**)

SILVESTIK

See **The Return from England.**

THE SONS OF MIL

See **The Book of Invasions, Trezenzon the Monk and the Great Island.**

SORCHA

See Symbols: **City Swallowed Up by the Sea.**

THE SPOILS OF ANNWFN

WALES

An early medieval poem, 60 lines long, and found in *The Book of Taliesin*, *The Spoils of Annwfn* describes an expedition to the **Otherworld** to retrieve a magic cauldron; it is led by King **Arthur**.

The teller of the tale relates how he traveled to the land of Annwfn (*see* **Annwn**) with Arthur and three boatloads of men, of whom only seven returned. Annwfn is given several names—Mound Fortress,

Four-Peaked Fortress, and Glass Fortress. The Welsh Triads list the Three Exalted Prisoners of Britain; one of these is Gweir, and he is languishing in chains within the walls of the Mound Fortress.

The cauldron of the Lord of Annwfn is described. It is finished with pearl and will not boil food for a coward.

All but seven of the adventurers are eventually killed, but exactly how is not explained. The poem goes on, rather oddly, with a small-minded condemnation of monks and "little men" who do not possess the poet's knowledge.

SUROUAS

See **Norouas, the North-West Wind**.

T

TAIN BO CUAILNGE

See **The Ulster Cycle**.

TOM AND THE GIANT

CORNWALL, ENGLAND

Tom was coming back from St. Ives with his empty wagon, his courage screwed up by virtue of the the three or four gallons of strong beer that he had drunk. It seemed to him that the king's highway ought not to be twisting and turning like an angle twitch [worm], but he went boldly on as well as he could. He came to the gate of the giant's farm and opened it. Then he drove his oxen through.

On went Tom, without seeing anything of the giant, or anyone else, only the fat cattle of every kind grazing in the fields.

After driving his oxen for about a mile, Tom came to a high wall with a pair of gates in it. This was close to the giant's castle. There was no passing around these gates, because there were deep ditches full of water on either side of them, so Tom charged at them. The huge gates creaked on their hinges, and the wheels of Tom's wagon creaked and rattled over the causeway. An ugly little dog began to bark, and at this the giant tore out: a great ugly unshapely fellow, all head and stomach.

Tom fought the giant and killed him. And so Tom acquired the store of silver, copper, and tin the giant had been guarding deep in the cellars of his castle.

TREZENZON THE MONK AND THE GREAT ISLAND

GALICIA, SPAIN

Breogán, son of Brath, was a mythical king in Galicia. In Gallaic, the Galician language, his name was Briganos Maccos Brattae. He was the mythic father of the Galician nation. His sons were Ith and Bile (**Belenus**). Galicia is sometimes poetically described as "the home of Breogán," as in the Galician anthem *Os Pinos.*

The Book of the Taking of Ireland, which is also known as *The Book of Conquests* and **The Book of Invasions**, is a compilation of Gaelic legends made in the eleventh century. According to this book, King Breogán built a colossal tower in the city of Brigantium, so high that from the top his sons could see a distant green shore. The sight of that distant green shore lured them to sail off to the north toward it. In this way they reached Ireland, where they were met by the ancient **tribe** who lived there, the **Tuatha dé Danann**. The Tuatha were hostile. They ambushed the Galicians and succeeded in killing Ith. It was some decades later that one of Breogan's grandsons, the nephew of Ith, Mil Espaine, took revenge on the Tuatha dé Danann. He invaded Ireland, with the intention of defeating them and taking their island for himself; he would settle there.

This story is mostly told in the final chapter of the book, where we hear of the Sons of Mil who, according to Irish myth, were the last wave of invaders.

A very similar story was written in the ninth or tenth century in Galicia. The manuscript is entitled *Trezenzonii de Solistitionis Insula*

Magna, "Trezenzon the Monk and the Great Island." This has a monk seeing a distant green island from the top of the high tower of Brigantia.

TRIPHYNA

See **Comorre the Cursed**.

TRISTAN AND ISEULT

This is just one of several variant forms of the ancient story. The couple are called Tristan and Iseult in some versions, and Trystan and Esyllt in others; in Richard Wagner's famous operatic transformation they are Tristan and Isolde. In this Welsh version, which has a happy ending, they are Trystan and Esyllt.

Esyllt of the White Throat was the wife of Mark, son of Meirchion. The news came to Arthur that Trystan, son of Trallwch, had gone off with Esyllt and they were wandering together as outlaws in the Oakwood of Celidon in the North. They were alone except for Esyllt's handmaid, who was called Golwg Hafddyd (Face Like a Summer's Day), and Trystan's page. The page carried pasties in a satchel and wine in a jar. They slept beneath the trees, with only leaves for bedclothes, but they were sustained by their love for each other, and by the wine and the pasties.

Mark went to Arthur to complain about Trystan's behavior and ask Arthur to avenge the insult. Arthur hesitated, because Trystan was one of the Three Unyielding Chieftains of the Island of Britain, but Mark argued that Arthur too was insulted because Trystan was his subject and openly defied him.

Arthur called up his war-band and rode to the Wood of Celidon; he surrounded the oakwoods. Trystan lay asleep, but Esyllt could hear the sound of warriors and woke him.

Trystan was unafraid. "Many of these men are my friends: blunt Cei, angry Bedwyr, and courteous Gwalchmei."

Even so, for safety, he set Esyllt in a hollow oak, where holly and ivy and a nearby yew hid her from view. Then he set off toward the sound of the warriors, with his sword in his hand.

He saw Mark and spoke directly to him. "Lord, we have a quarrel, you and I. Draw your sword and let us settle it."

But Mark knew Trystan's destiny. He understood that if he killed Trystan it would bring about his own death. He refused to fight and called on his men to tie Trystan up and bring him before Arthur. Mark's men did not understand the destiny that hung over Trystan and thought Mark had refused to fight out of cowardice; they refused to act for a man who would not fight for himself. So Trystan was able to walk away unhindered.

Mark went again to Arthur, who said, "I thought this was how it would be. There is only one way left. We must send the best harpers in the Island of Britain to play to Trystan from afar. As his mood softens, we shall send in poets and praise-makers to praise him. Then we shall be able to talk to him."

This they did. The forest was filled with the sound of the harps; even the birds stopped singing to listen. Trystan summoned the harpers to him and rewarded them handsomely for their music with gold and silver. Then the poets and praise-makers came and exalted Trystan. Trystan summoned them too, and gave them gifts. To the chief song-maker he gave the circlet of gold that adorned his own neck and to the others he gave gold and silver.

Now his heart was softened, and Gwalchmei appeared before him with a message from Arthur. Trystan consented to Gwalchmei's courteous request to visit Arthur, who bound both Trystan and Mark to keep peace with one another until the matter was resolved.

Arthur spoke to the two men separately, but neither would agree to give up Esyllt. Arthur's judgment was that Esyllt should go with one man for as long as the leaves stayed on the trees, and to the other for as long as the leaves were not on the trees. It was for Mark, son of Meirchion, to choose first.

"Lord, this is an easy choice to make," Mark cried happily. "I shall have Esyllt when the leaves are not on the trees. The short, dark days of winter often seem longer than the days of summer, and the nights are longer, and the time passes more slowly then."

Arthur went into the middle of the forest to find Esyllt and report his judgment to her.

"Bless you for this judgment, my lord," she cried.

Cei was puzzled by her reaction. He asked, "Why so, lady?"

As her answer, Esyllt sang this verse:

"Three trees there are, both good and true:
Holly and ivy and yew are they.
They keep their leaves the whole year through,
And Trystan shall have me for ever and ay."

U

THE ULSTER CYCLE

IRELAND

This is a group of Celtic folktales, told in prose and probably not written down until AD 750, though they may have been told and retold for a long period before then. They describe in epic form a sequence of events relating to an heroic society that has a strong resemblance to the one described in Homer. Some scholars have even wondered whether the tales were perhaps written in the Christian era in deliberate imitation of Homer. Against this explanation are several features of the tales. One is that by the fifth century the political framework of Ireland had changed; by then Ulster was smaller and far less powerful politically. It had been reduced by the family of Niall, who died in AD 404. So the events described in the Ulster Cycle must belong to the fourth century or earlier. Another feature is the fact that the characters swear by the **gods** of their **tribes**, not by a universal God.

Another view of the Ulster Cycle is that the stories go back to the second century BC, very much the pre-Christian Celtic Ireland. Yet another view is that they are centuries older still.

These heroic tales are set mainly in the provinces of Ulster and Connaught. They revolve around the lives of Conchobar mac Nessa, King of Ulster, and the great hero **Cú Chulainn**, who was the son of the god **Lugh**. They and the people around them are the Ulaid people. The action takes place mainly at the royal court of **Emain Macha** (Navan Fort), near the present-day town of Armagh. The Ulaid had contact with an Irish colony in Scotland and part of Cú Chulainn's training takes place there. The capital of Ulster was at Emain Macha and its overking or high king was Conchobar. Ulster was opposed by a confederacy of the rest of Ireland led by Ailill of Connaught and his warrior-queen, Medb. The stories are dominated by cattle-raiding, fighting, and feasting.

The main tale in the cycle is the *Tain bo Cuailnge.*

Some of the characters, such as Medb, were probably originally deities, and the hero Cú Chulainn displays superhuman prowess, suggesting that he too may have originated as a minor god. But the characters are presented in the tales as mortals, acting in a particular time and place.

THE VISION OF MAC CON GLINNE

IRELAND

A clever twelfth-century parody of all the earlier adventure tales about voyages to the **Isles of the Blessed**. The phantom from the **Otherworld** tells the hero, Mac Con Glinne, that he is:

"Wheatlet, son of Milklet,
Son of Juicy Bacon
Is mine own name
Honeyed Butter-roll
Is the man's name that bears my bag."

The bag is a reference to the bag of the sea god, **Manannàn**, which holds the **treasures** of all the world. The hero of *The Vision* goes on a marvelous voyage in a boat of fat sailing on a lake of milk. He makes landfall on an island that has earthworks of thick custard; its bridge is made of butter, its walls of wheat, and its palisade of bacon. Inside, there are "smooth pillars of old cheese, fine rafters of thick cream with laths of curds." A sage gives Mac a cure-all that will work for all complaints except the disease of wandering gentlemen, commonly known as loose bowels.

After reciting his vision, Mac Con Glinne cures the King of Cork of gluttony and traps a demon in a cooking pot. The tale ends with details of the reward due to the reciter.

THE VOYAGE OF BRENDAN

The Latin *Navigatio Brendani* describes **Brendan**'s voyage **west**, out into the Atlantic, where he sees the **Isles of the Blessed**. Some once took the story at face value and some still do, believing that St. Brendan actually discovered America. The story was very popular in the Middle Ages and it may even have inspired later attempts to sail west to discover whatever was there.

Many different versions of the story exist. Some say Brendan set off with 60 pilgrims, 14 others, and three unbelievers who joined at the last minute. One of his followers was St. **Malo**.

On his voyage, Brendan is said to have seen St. Brendan's Island, which was covered with vegetation. He also encountered a sea monster. The adventure that is most commonly illustrated is his landing on an island that turns out to be a gigantic sea monster called Jascon or Jasconius.

The Element Encyclopedia of the Celts

The story is essentially a Christian narrative, but it includes stories about natural phenomena and fantasy adventures. This blend naturally gave it a broad appeal.

The adventure begins with St. Barrid (St. Barinthus) describing his travels to the Island of Paradise, which prompts Brendan to go and find it. He assembles a company of 14 monks to go with him. They fast in preparation, then three latecomers join the party.

Brendan discovers an island with a dog and mysterious hospitality: food is left out for the visitors but there is no sign of the hosts. He exorcises an Ethiopian devil from one of the unbelieving latecomers, who dies. He discovers an island with a boy who gives them bread and water; an island of sheep, where they remain for Holy Week; and the island of the monks of Ailbe, where there is no aging and complete silence. Then he comes upon a "coagulated" sea, which is perhaps the Sargasso Sea or more likely the frozen Arctic Ocean. Then Brendan and his followers find an island with three choirs of monks who give them fruit; then they find an island of grapes.

After revisiting the monastery at Ailbe at Christmas, they sail through a clear sea. They pass a "silver pillar wrapped in a net" in the sea. They find Judas perching unhappily on a cold, wet rock in the middle of the sea; this is his respite from Hell: he is let out for Sundays and feast days. Finally, Brendan and his company find the Promised Land of the Saints before returning home.

The story belongs to a particular kind of popular Irish literature called an *immram*, which describes a hero's adventures in a boat. Some of these *immrams* specifically include a search for and a visit to, **Tir nan Nog**, an Otherworldly island far distant in the west (*see* People: **Barinthus**, **Brendan**; Religion: **Otherworld**; Symbols: **Isles of the Blessed**).

The Element Encyclopedia of the Celts

W

THE WILD HUNT

The Wild Hunt is an ancient folk myth, widespread across north, **west**, and central Europe. It consists of a ghostly band of huntsmen with horses and hounds, who tear in a mad chase across the sky, or along the ground, or just above the ground. The hunters may be **fairies** or the spirits of the dead. Seeing the Wild Hunt has often been thought to be unlucky: an omen of some catastrophe, such as plague or war.

PART 5

Symbols, Ideas, and Archetypes

APPLE

The mythic tree of the Under-world, the tree of **immortality**, is a common idea in many **cultures**. In late Celtic mythology, the Isle of **Avalon**, where King **Arthur** was taken to die, was either an is-land of the dead or a portal to the Underworld. The word "Avalon" means "orchard"; compare the Old Welsh word *afal*, meaning "apple." Avalon was the resting-place of heroes and kings: a particular kind of **sacred grove**—of apple trees.

The apple itself is a **magic** fruit, again as it is in many ancient cultures. Although the Bible does not say so, tradition has it that the forbidden fruit in the Hebrew Gar-den of Eden was an apple. In the Greek Epic Cycle, the entire drama of the Trojan War is set in motion by the **goddess** Strife rolling her Golden Apple inscribed "To the Loveliest" among the other god-desses—for them to quarrel over.

In Somerset the oldest apple tree in the orchard is known as the Apple Tree Man, and the fertility of the orchard as a whole is supposed to reside in that one tree. The Apple Tree Man is also believed to be able to speak—with a Somerset accent.

A grafted apple, an "ymp-tree," is very dangerous because it is under **fairy** influence. If a man falls asleep underneath an ymp-tree, he is liable to be carried away by fairy ladies.

The apple recurs again and again in European myths, and it is there too in Celtic myth as the fruit of the World Tree, the axis of the universe. To the Celts, the apple is the fruit of immortality and proph-ecy. In the old European fairy-tale about Snow White, the heroine is poisoned by a shiny red apple given to her by the witch. It makes her fall into a sleep of oblivion. This makes the connection with the Otherworldly orchard at the end of the world, where apple trees form the landscape of rest and oblivion.

The apple orchard as the home of the dead is reminiscent of the ancient Greek idea of the fields of asphodel, a typically Mediterra-nean picture of an idyllic moun-tainside landscape, away from the everyday world, yet carpeted with beautiful flowers. The asphodel often grows today in the dappled shade of olive groves. The newly restored epic *The Apple of Discord* describes the spirit of the hero

Palamedes walking off after his murder by Odysseus to the fields of asphodel. In the same poem, the long-dead spirits who visit Menelaus in the **Labyrinth** at Knossos are sent back to where they belong by a ritual of libation performed by King Idomeneus:

Then back they fell as if sucked away by the wind,
a vortex, both ghosts and gods summoned away
by Hermes of Kyllene, bearing the golden wand
with which he charms the eyes of men or wakens
whom he wills. He waved them on, all squeaking
like the bats in a cavern's underworld, all flitting,
criss-cross in the dark. With ever fainter cries
the shades trailed after Hermes, the pure deliverer.
He led them down dark corridors of time
past shores of dreams and the narrows of the sunset
in swift flight to the place where the Dead have their home,
the wilderness of asphodel at the world's end.

The Apple of Discord, Book 4, lines 194–205

ASH TREE

The ash is said to be the first tree that was ever created. In Teutonic (Germanic) myth, the World Ash Tree is called Yggdrasil. Its roots penetrate to the heart of the Earth, where the three Norns, the Fates, weave the destiny of the human race.

In the Celtic world-view the ash is the queen of the forest; the **oak** is king. The ash is a huge tree with a root system that penetrates deep into the ground, while its branches soar high into the sky. It is a symbol of massive spiritual growth, of expansion, and of integration. The great tree holds together the three worlds—Heaven, Earth, and Underworld—and as such it symbolizes the grandest and most ambitious of visions.

One ash tree in County Cork, in the parish of Clenor, was treated with special veneration. The local people never cut its branches, even when they were running very short of firewood. Another ash tree, in Borrisokane, was called the Old Bell Tree. This one was sacred to May Day rites, and the local **people** believed that if anyone burned in their hearth so much as a single chip from it his whole house would burn down.

In England, the ash has been seen as a magical protection against mischievous spirits.

AWEN

Awen is a Welsh word meaning inspiration, in the specific sense of poetic inspiration. It was used historically to describe the divine inspiration of the Welsh **bards**. A poet or a soothsayer who is inspired is described as an *awenydd*. Today, *awen* is sometimes used to describe poets and musicians.

The word has also become a girls' name. It is related to *awel*, which means "breeze."

The first time the word is known to have been used was in Nennius' book *Historia Brittonum*, written in the late eighth century.

In neo-Druidry, *awen* is symbolized by three straight lines, diverging slightly as they descend, each with a dot at the top. This symbol is not ancient, but was invented by Iolo Morgannwg. Different neo-Druid groups have different interpretations of the *awen* symbol. To some the three lines represent the three elements of earth, sea, and air. To others the three lines are love, wisdom, and truth. They could also symbolize body, mind, and spirit. Some see *awen* as symbolizing the inspiration of truth, and the three lines indicate the understanding of truth, the love of truth, and the maintaining of truth.

The Order of Bards, Ovates, and Druids, a revived druidic order, has described the three lines as rays emanating from three points of light, which represent the triple aspect of deity. The three points also symbolize the points on the horizon where the **sun** rises at the equinoxes and solstices. The emblem of the order of Bards, Ovates, and Druids is ringed by three concentric circles to represent the three circles of creation.

B

BASKET OF FRUIT

The **gods** were expected to be providers. They were in charge of the production of food in all its forms: domestic livestock, wild animals that might be hunted, birds, fruit, grain, and vegetables. A simple way of summarizing this produce in religious **art** was to depict a basket of fruit. The concept was similar to the way a church might be dressed for a traditional harvest festival, with fruit and loaves to symbolize the harvest safely gathered in.

The goddess **Nehalennia** was a fertility goddess, and was invariably shown with vegetation and crops. A Romano-Celtic stone **altar** dedicated to her found in Holland shows her sitting beside a basket overfilled with fruit. She was a provider, and the basket shows her produce (*see* **Cornucopia**).

BEAR

An apt symbol for the strength, wildness, and ferocity of the great warrior. King **Arthur**'s name seems to be derived from the Celtic *artos*, meaning "bear" or "bearlike." The association is not confined to warlike men either: warrior-queens might also be called bears. In Gaul there was a bear called **Artio**.

BOAR

The boar was a wild beast of the forest, like the **stag**, and both were treated as highly symbolic of the forces of wild nature. The boar hunt culminated in a pork banquet, and at this banquet the pecking order among the warriors would be established, usually accompanied by disputes and quarrels (*see* People: **Food and Feasting**). Sometimes pork joints were buried with warriors, presumably as a way of awarding the dead man his "champion's joint of pork." Pork was also a hospitality symbol.

Wild boar, and even nominally domesticated pigs, can be very destructive and unmanageable. In Irish folk-tales, pigs are strong and destructive, and they can lure men into the Underworld. **Magic** pigs are involved in ritual hunts where the point of the story is the invincibility of the pig.

The magical nature of the pig is also found in Welsh tradition; in the *Tale of Cwlhwch and Olwen* supernatural pigs are people transformed.

Certain Celtic divinities, often female, are responsible for beasts that are hunted in the forests. The Romans naturally identified these **goddesses** with their own huntress goddess, Diana. **Arduinna** is one of these Celtic goddesses. She frequents the woods of the Ardennes, riding on the back of a wild boar.

BOAT

A pre-Roman manifestation of a **god**. In the Bronze Age and early Iron Age, objects or attributes were often made to stand in for deities, rather like the double-ax standing in for the Minoan goddess of ancient Crete. In the very early days of Rome, the Rome of the Kings, **Mars** was represented by **spears**, and those spears were deemed to be capable of moving of their own accord in time of danger: they *were* Mars. The pre-Roman conquest world of the Celts was very like this, with few humanoid representations of deities.

Initially, there were few figurative representations of deities because the **Druids** did not want them to be seen unveiled. This changed through time, as the great sanctuaries were developed and large-scale public ceremonies were enacted in them. The gods were required to attend and take part; they therefore had to be visible. The massive posts that stood at the centers of the sanctuary enclosures were almost certainly conceived as "gods." **Julius Caesar** describes *simulacra*, which implies something rather different from the classical statues of gods that he was used to seeing in Rome. Probably these posts were carved in a very stylized way, like Native American totem poles. Maximus of Tyre wrote, "The Celts devote a cult to Zeus, but the Celtic image of Zeus is a great oak."

Through time, and with increasing exposure to Roman **culture**, these Celtic *simulacra* became more realistic. Most, though not all, of the more realistic figurative representations of the gods and goddesses belong to the Romano-Celtic period.

BRIGHID'S CROSS

An Irish pagan symbol that has become a Christian symbol by adoption. It is usually made from rushes and consists of a central woven square and four radial arms that are tied at the ends. It is a specific design of **corn dolly**.

The design is probably related to the swastika, an ancient **sun** symbol, with its four arms pointing to the four points of the compass. The four arms also represent the elements: earth, air, fire, and **water**. Like so many other Celtic symbols, this one has a complex ancestry and expresses more than one idea. This symbolic compression is typical of the ancient Celtic mindset.

The crosses are associated with several traditions and rituals. At one time it was believed that a Brighid's cross had the power to protect a house from fire and evil. It is still to be seen hanging in many Irish and Irish-American kitchens to ward off evil.

The cross is associated with **Brighid** of Kildare, who is one of the patron saints of Ireland. The crosses are traditionally made on February 1, which in the Irish calendar is St. Brighid's feast day, a borrowing from the ancient past: this is the old pagan Celtic feast of **Imbolg**.

St. Brighid and her cross are linked together in a Christian folktale. A pagan chieftain in the neighborhood of Kildare lay dying and some Christians in his house sent for Brighid to talk to him about the Christian faith. When she got there, the man was delirious and conversion was impossible. She tried to comfort him and stooped down to pick up some rushes from the floor, weaving them into the form of a cross, fastening the points together. The man asked her what she was doing and she explained. He listened with growing interest. In the end he was baptized just as he died.

The cross is likely to be far older than this, though. "Saint" Brighid was one of the **Tuatha dé Dannan,** the **goddess** Brighid.

The Christian Brighid's cross is likely to be descended from a pagan cross. Its original meaning may even be preserved in modern superstitions about the cross protecting a house from fire. There is nothing in the Christian story about St. Brighid and burning houses, so this is likely to have been borrowed from some earlier, pre-Christian, belief.

BULL

The bull was in use as a symbol and decorative motif from the Bronze Age onward. This shows an enduring admiration for the bull's characteristics: strength, virility, and ferocity.

The ox, from which the virility and ferocity have been removed, was a symbol of agriculture and prosperity. At Mont Bego in the south of France, a sacred mountain was decorated with rock carvings that feature the ox in plow-teams.

Bronze vessels made in the Bronze Age were often decorated with bull's horns. Clay bull's horns mounted on stands were made in Hungary in the seventh century BC. This veneration of the bull and its horns was shared by the Mediterranean **cultures** too; the bull was important in Minoan and Mycenaean cultures and it

is possible that the bull cult was ultimately inherited from the Minoans.

It is difficult to be sure what the bull may have meant in the Celtic world, when many aspects were borrowed from still more ancient belief systems. It has to be remembered that in the Roman world the bull was an emblem of Jupiter, and in the earlier Mycenaean-Minoan world the bull was a transformation of Poseidon. So the Celts too may have seen the bull as a **god**, or at least as godlike.

A peculiarity of Iron Age bull's horns is that they are shown with knobs on the end. It is not known why, though it could reflect some ritual or ceremonial situation in which it was deemed safer to have the dangerous points of the (real) bull's horns covered.

The (pre-Roman) **Gundestrup cauldron** shows the bull several times, and it carries a large scene on the baseplate showing a bull sacrifice. Bull imagery can be seen in Gaul and Britain, but rarely in conjunction with any human or humanoid images. One significant exception was found at Rheims, where a bull is seen associated with **Cernunnos** and a **stag**—just as at Gundestrup.

Some elaborate ritual deposits have been found that show how important bulls and cattle in general were as religious symbols. At **South Cadbury** there is plenty of evidence of this in the Iron Age. On the approach to a **shrine** the remains of newborn calves were deposited. Cattle skulls were set upright in pits, and deliberately buried in that way. A full-grown cow was buried outside the door of a porched shrine. And this kind of ritual burial of cattle was going on at a great many places in Britain. In about AD 300 there was an underground shrine at Cambridge where more elaborate animal rituals went on; there were burials of a complete **horse** and a complete bull, as well as hunting **dogs**—and all carefully arranged.

The **writings** of classical commentators confirm the sacrificial nature of some of these events. Pliny describes white bulls being sacrificed in the **mistletoe**-cutting ceremony of the **Druids**.

Cattle were an important part of the warrior-hero culture; cattle-raids were a major focus. *The Cattle Raid of Cooley* is an Irish tale in which the supernatural plays a part. The climax of the tale is a conflict between two great supernatural bulls who had in earlier incarnations been divine swineherds; because of their previous existences, the two bulls had the power of human thought.

In Ireland, bulls were connected with the choosing of kings. There was a bull-feast at which a bull was killed and the meat was eaten by a man who then fell asleep. Four Druids chanted their incantations over him and the sleeper saw in a dream the person who was to become king. Possibly this is what lies behind the image on the base of the Gundestrup cauldron, where a large bull awaits sacrifice. Its horns have become detached, and may have been deliberately made so that they were detachable.

C

CAULDRON

The cauldron was a central object in every home—the huge cooking pot sitting on the fire or hanging over it. It was used for most domestic cooking. It was also used for carrying **water** and for bathing. It was probably the finest object owned by most households.

Its central place in the home makes it a profoundly female symbol. The hemispherical shape also looks like the belly of a pregnant woman, which makes it a natural symbol for motherhood, childbirth, and fertility. When used for cooking, ingredients are put into the cauldron and transformed into a stew, so it is also symbol of transformation and regeneration, and of passage from one world to another.

The cauldron holds a central place in the Celtic belief system. It was used for divination and also for sacrificial rites. It was a symbol of the realm of water, and some finely made and beautifully ornamented cauldrons were sacrificed to the **gods** of **rivers** and lakes.

Sometimes the ocean itself was regarded as a huge cauldron.

A big cauldron in the **Otherworld** was the source of inspiration for poets and musicians. The goddess Caridwen owned a great cauldron, and it was from this that the **bard Taliesin** drew his legendary bardic talent (*see* Myths: *The History of Taliesin*).

The Gauls associated the cauldron with the god **Taranis**. Sacrifices to this god by Druidic **priests** are supposed to have been drowned in a cauldron, possibly in a belief that they would be reborn. Celtic myths tell of a cauldron into which dead warriors could be thrown and brought back to life again.

The **Dagda**'s huge cauldron is one of the four legendary **treasures** of Ireland. It is a **magic** object that supplies endless quantities of food and drink. This cauldron of the Otherworld gained a new lease of life in the Arthurian tales, where it remained an object of great mystery and veneration, but this time associated closely with Christ. The Arthurian myth was endlessly told and retold through the Christian era, and the Celtic cauldron, turned into the chalice, became a major focus of Christian liturgy. The two combined in the legend of the Holy Grail, where the two vessels became fused to make a new symbolic object (*see* **Grail Quest**; Places: **Hochdorf**; Religion: **Cernunnos**, **The Daghda**, **Druids**).

CELTIC CROSS

The Celtic cross, sometimes called a ring cross, is a hybrid type of monument that incorporates three very distinct elements: the cross of Christ, a circle that is a **sun** symbol, and a megalith. The megalith, a great **standing stone**, is an ancestral monument that is deeply embedded in the Atlantic Celtic tradition. It is perfectly natural that it should somehow survive the Christian conversion of the communities of the first millennium, at least in this modified form.

There were already some carved embellishments being added to megalithic monuments back in the late Neolithic, such as the "**mother goddess**" carving on one of the uprights at **Stonehenge** and the **spiral** carvings on Breton passage graves. That developed further in the Iron Age with some "all-over" carved designs such as the one covering the **Turoe Stone**. The development of the megalith into a massive cross with all-over figurative decoration was a simple next step.

The ring cross was a very widespread symbol in the ancient world, though with the cross contained inside the circle. It was a sun cross, a **wheel** cross, or Odin's cross. The sign naturally first appeared in the Bronze Age, where it represents very literally a four-spoked **chariot** wheel, the sort of chariot wheel made by the Minoans and Mycenaeans in the period 1700– 1200 BC. It was also an astrological sign, symbolizing not the sun but the Earth—both the planet and the substance. It was a common sun symbol in the pagan Celtic world, and one that was easy for early Christians to adopt and convert. Extending the arms of the cross outward, outside the circle, emphasized the cross at the expense of the circle and some people argue that this too is a symbolic development, showing that Christ worship has overcome sun worship.

The Irish promoted a legend that St. **Patrick** or perhaps St. Declan introduced the Celtic cross during the time of the conversion of the Irish pagans to Christianity. This is hard to support, in that there are no examples from that early period for us to look at. The idea that the joint symbol is to show Christ's supremacy over the pagan sun-worshipers does not work so well psychologically—it is more provocative that persuasive. There may nevertheless be something in the suggestion that the sun symbol was added to the cross in order to make the imagery more familiar and more congenial to converts. Another possibility is that the characteristic perforation of the cross to give the sun symbol four spokes was a deliberate attempt to make the combined symbol into a sun wheel, which was a powerful religious image in the Iron Age. A more important idea, spiritually and psychologically, is that the ring cross brings together, combines, and welds two religious systems; it is the old and the new together.

Given that Christ was sometimes depicted at the center of the cross, and therefore also at the center of the circle, the circle could double as a halo, and it may even be the origin of the halo. The Celtic cross is a quintessentially Celtic symbol, rich in multilayered meaning.

The distinctive British tradition of building monumental high stone crosses was under way by about 750, and it is likely that there were even earlier versions in painted wood, though these have not survived. The Irish crosses were usually shorter. Some of the damaged monuments imply that the sculptors must have become aware early on that the horizontal "arms" of a stone cross were vulnerable and easily snapped off. It may be this that led to the addition of the circle—not so much a symbolic statement, more a structural necessity.

The cross at Monasterboice in Ireland is a particularly fine example of a Celtic cross. Its four branches are all richly decorated, and the circle is also embellished with a beaded pattern. Then the tall pillar or shaft of the cross has six tiers of decoration, with each register carrying, typically, three figures on each face.

Other fine Celtic crosses survive at Clonmacnoise in Ireland and Iona. St. Piran's cross is another, at Perranporth in Cornwall. In Scotland, there are fine examples in the Dupplin Cross, Iona Abbey Crosses, Kidalton Cross, and St. Martin's Cross.

It is interesting to see the overlap between Celtic cross-making and

Anglo-Saxon cross-making. The Ruthwell Cross, in Dumfriesshire, Scotland, represents what Anglo-Saxon craftsmen made of this new fashion.

There are similar Celtic crosses in France, mainly in the **west** (Normandy, Brittany, and Limousin), but many of these were made late, in the fifteenth century. These "crosses with halo," *croix nimbées*, have the same general design (cross superimposed on circle) but are more intricately carved.

Celtic crosses are found in Galicia too, where they are often mounted on top of granaries as a protection against evil. They are also found on churches. A very characteristic Galician take on the Celtic cross design is the Celtic cross with a Celtic **knot**. The St. Maur cross at Glanfeuil Abbey is thought to date from the tenth century. One of the most intricate cross-and-knot carvings is the one on the roof gable of the church of St. Susanna at Santiago de Compostela.

The nineteenth-century Celtic revival in Ireland led to a revival in Celtic cross carving. In 1853, casts of several fine historic high crosses were displayed at the Dublin Industrial Exhibition. In 1857, an illustrated book showing the designs was published. These events stimulated a new wave of interest in the old Celtic heritage. The main manifestation of this was the adaptation of the high cross to make smaller monuments for cemeteries, for individual and family graves, first in Dublin, then elsewhere, then later still for war memorials. The use of the Celtic cross for individual grave markers was a departure from medieval usage; in the Middle Ages the large crosses were communal markers.

Suddenly the Celtic cultural revival had a logo. Celtic spirituality also had its identity realized in an image. The jewelry designed and made by Alexander and Euphemia Ritchie, working on Iona from 1899 to 1940, popularized the use of the Celtic cross. Now the Celtic cross is seen everywhere, in T-shirts, tattoos, and logos for the Gaelic Athletic Association and Northern Ireland's national football team. Somehow, in Ireland and Germany too, it has acquired a white nationalist undertone, rather in the way that the flag of St. George has in England (*see* Religion: **Wheel God**; Celtic Twilight and Revival).

City Swallowed Up by the Sea

The idea of a lost, uncharted, untraceable land somewhere in the ocean away to the **west** is a very Celtic dream. Both Cornish and Breton myths have the story of the lost land of Lyonesse.

The name "Lyonesse" is derived from the French Léoneis. Some think that in turn may be derived from the Latin name for Lothian, Lodonesia, but it is not clear how an area in Scotland could have become associated with submerged lands in the English Channel. The writer of the French Prose Tristan placed Léoneis, a land area, adjacent to Cornwall, and in both French and English versions of French tales, it is associated with Cornwall. Its exact whereabouts were always left vague.

The tale of Lyonesse seems to be a folk memory of a widespread event: the encroachment of the sea due to a rising sea level in prehistoric times. The Cornish name for St. Michael's Mount, now an island in a bay, is Karrek Loos y'n Koos, "The Grey Rock in the Wood." This sounds like a memory of a wooded landscape on the site of the bay, with the rock of the mount sticking up out of it. At low **water** it is still possible to see remnants of a submerged forest. But these trees have not been growing for 4,000 or 5,000 years, so it is stretching the idea of a folk memory of submergence over rather too long a span of time.

When sea-level was lower, several thousand years ago, the Scilly Isles would have been one large island, and some of the seabed between Scilly and Land's End would have been exposed as dry land. Interestingly, the legendary lost land in that area has a specific Cornish name, Lethesow. The Seven Stones reef, where the oil tanker *Torrey Canyon* was wrecked in 1967, was part of Lethesow, which means "the milky ones," a reference to the white water across the reef.

The name Lyonesse was not given to this area until the

sixteenth century. Even so, the mystery of its location has added to its power. By the nineteenth century, in *Idylls of the King*, Lord Tennyson was making Lyonesse the place where the final battle between **Arthur** and Modred took place, and Lyonesse became part of the Arthurian legend.

Then rose the King and moved his
host by night
And ever pushed Sir Mordred,
league by league,
Back to the sunset bound of
Lyonesse –
A land of old upheaven from the
abyss
By fire, to sink into the abyss
again…

Here Lyonesse becomes another transformation of the Celtic **Otherworld**, a mystical Isle of the Dead. Tennyson himself felt this, instinctively. Lyonesse was a place…

Where fragments of forgotten peoples
dwelt,
And the long mountains ended in a
coast
Of ever-shifting sand, and far away
The phantom circle of a moaning
sea.

Naturally, in the Christian era the story of the peopled land over-whelmed by the sea was turned into a British Sodom and Gomorrah. The **people** who had lived there were *wicked*; they had brought down upon themselves the wrath of God. But the place of Lyonesse in myth was also more mysterious than that, and similar to the place of **Tir nan Og** in Irish myth.

In Brittany the parallel is with the Ker Ys, the city of Ys, drowned as a consequence of its sinful life-style, with a single survivor who manages to escape on a horse: King Grallon (*see* Myths: **The Legend of Ys**).

In Wales there is an equivalent to Lyonesse and Ker Ys: a mythical drowned kingdom in Cardigan Bay called Cantre'r Gwaelod.

There were other mysterious lands that lay beneath the seas, known to Gaelic-speaking Celts as Sorcha and Lochlann, places where **magic** ruled. Lochlann was inhab-ited by spirit-folk who brought fer-tility to the land and ensured good harvests.

There is a Welsh tradition that **Merlin** was not only Welsh but foretold that the town of Carmarthen would one day be swallowed up by the sea.

CLADDAGH

An Irish symbol devised in the sixteenth century as a symbol of eternal love and fidelity. It is named after and it seems originally made at a Galway village.

It consists of a cross with a crown at each terminal. At the crossing is a heart, held by a hand on each side. The crowned heart and hands is a motif added to wedding rings. It may be a borrowing from an ancient Roman fidelity ring design, the *Fede*, which featured clasped hands.

CLOAK

The **god Lugh** had a cloak that made him invisible and enabled him to pass unseen among a host of warriors to rescue his son. The idea is an obvious one, as a cloak, especially one with a hood, in effect made the wearer invisible. Wearing a hooded cloak is equivalent to wearing a mask of anonymity. From anonymity it is a short storytelling step to invisibility.

The Cerne Giant had a cloak, no longer visible, but detected by a geophysical survey in the 1990s, draped over his left arm (*see* **Cerne Abbas**). In the Iron Age this was the standard type of shield for a warrior who could not afford proper weaponry. Interestingly, Iron Age people often liked to think of their gods in this way—as People Like Themselves.

Manannán, the Irish sea god, possesses a **magic** cloak; if this cloak is shaken between two people it is impossible for them ever to meet again. This may be a metaphor for the fogs of the Irish Sea. The Lady of the Lake, Vivien, has a similar cloak, again probably symbolizing the mist that often hangs over lakes. The British hero **Cassivellaunus** is said to have worn a magic **tartan plaid** that made him invisible.

CORN DOLLY

Corn dollies are still made today, but more or less as a picturesque wall decoration with little or no symbolic value. In past centuries, the corn dolly was a powerful fertility symbol associated with the agricultural year.

It was once believed that the spirit of the grain harvest resided in the corn itself. When the harvest was gathered, the corn was cut down and the corn **goddess** became homeless. Farmers made a crude image of her out of the last stalks of the harvested crop, as a **dwelling**-place for her. She over-wintered in the farmer's house, waiting to be returned to the plow-land in the spring. When the fields were plowed, the dolly was taken out and plowed back into the soil: the goddess was returning to the earth.

The custom of making corn dollies was widespread and each area had its own design. They are always stylized, and many of them are quite abstract, looking nothing at all like goddesses.

CORNUCOPIA

Iron Age **goddesses** are often shown bearing a long, straight, cone-shaped container brimming with fruit. This is the horn of plenty, often referred to by its Latin name, *cornucopia*, and representing the boundless riches of the Earth. It is the most common symbol of abundance, particularly in relation to food.

A Gallic image shows the god-dess **Rosmerta** offering a cornu-copia and a small offering–dish, a *patera*. On other sculptures, where a goddess is accompanied by a god, she may hold both or just the cor-nucopia, while her male partner holds the *patera*. Another image from Gaul shows a triad of god-desses, all holding a cornucopia, but only the middle one holding a *patera*: maybe this is to show that the middle goddess is a little more important than the other two.

A relief from Aquitaine shows a goddess with a crown holding a cornucopia of fruit and vine leaves, to show the fertility and productivity of the region. The stone image is dedicated to Tutela, a "**Fortuna**" goddess who was the patroness of a town, possibly Massilia. When the deities appear in couples, male and female, it is usually the female who holds the cornucopia, held upright like a sceptre (at Dijon, Pagny-la-Ville, **Alesia**, and Glanum). The frequency of the association of the horn of plenty with a **divine couple** suggests that the "plenty" is thought of as a product of a divine marriage.

There are carvings showing the **horse**-goddess **Epona** carrying a cornucopia while riding her horse. It is a symbol of productivity; some images abbreviate the cornucopia to a single **apple**, as on the fine

Epona sculpture from Kastel, but the symbolic thrust of the image is exactly the same.

Sometimes, as with other religious symbols, the cornucopia stands on its own. A stone **altar** dedicated to the goddess **Nehalennia** has a cornucopia carved onto its front (*see* **Basket of Fruit**; Religion: **Altar**).

CRANE

A well-carved relief from **Trier** shows the **god Esus** chopping at a **willow** tree that contains a **bull's head** and three egrets. A completely separate image of Esus shows him hacking down a willow, while on an adjacent scene another willow is shown associated with three egrets and a bull. The bull here is mysteriously named Tarvostrigaranos. Some of this symbolism is straightforward: egrets favor willows, and they also eat the ticks off the backs of cattle. But it is less obvious why egrets, bulls, and willows should be important in association with a particular god. One idea is that Esus is chopping down the willow as a form of sacrifice and the willow is a Tree of Life; perhaps what we are seeing is the laying-low of life in winter in preparation for the coming spring.

The birds may represent human souls, as in other **cultures**. Chopping down the willow causes the birds to fly away, so the image may be a metaphor for death and the flight of the soul to the **Otherworld**.

Cranes, like willows, are associated with **water** and wetland. Both lake and marsh were foci for ritual offerings, so cranes were birds that frequented sacred places. Cranes and other waterbirds were often shown on **coins**. The crane and the crow were both symbols of the Otherworld, and heralds of death.

It may be significant that in Irish folk-tales, which contain a good deal of ancient material, cranes can represent women. In that context, the **Maiden Castle** bull, with its three female riders, suddenly finds its meaning; the three women can **shapeshift**, in true Celtic style, into three birds (*see* **Rule of**

Three). This is therefore a similar image to the one associated in Gaul with Esus. In both Irish and Welsh literature there are **magic** birds, sometimes appearing in threes. Cliodnu, an Irish goddess, has three birds nourished by everlasting **apples**; the birds are able to sing sick people to sleep. The sweetly singing birds of **Rhiannon** are able to bring joy and forgetfulness for seven years (*see* Myths: **Blackbirds**).

CUP

See **The Grail Quest**.

DAISY

The daisy is a **sun** symbol. It is said that the custom of dressing children in daisy chains arose from a desire to protect them from being carried off by **fairies**.

DEATH BY SORCERY

Killing by an act of sorcery was practised in the remote past. Surprisingly, it has been practised in more recent times as well. The method is to use an image or effigy of the enemy who is to be destroyed and inflict harm on them by way of the image.

A conspiracy is said to have been aimed at Duff, King of Scotland from 962 to 966. The king was suffering from some ailment without any obvious physical cause. He had painful sweats, could not sleep, and was wasting away. A group of sorceresses or witches in the town of Forres was suspected of planning to assassinate him. They were caught in the act of basting an effigy of the king over a fire and reciting **spells** as they did so. The image was destroyed, and the witches were themselves brought to trial, condemned, and burned. King Duff recovered sufficiently to lead his army against the rebels who had conspired against him and deliver retribution.

In the Middle Ages, effigies used for death by sorcery were usually made of wax, which melted easily in a flame. Presumably the idea was that by **magic** this would cause a wasting of the victim's flesh. The witches described these effigies as "pictures." In later times, the effigies were more commonly made of clay. Thorns, pins, and needles were pushed into the soft clay, as if sticking knives into flesh. "Elf-arrows" (crude flint-flake darts) were thrown at the clay image to the accompaniment of spells. Finally the clay image was broken up. At this point it was expected that the victim would give up the ghost.

A few decades ago one of these clay effigies was found in a Highland stream. It had been placed there so the **water** would gradually wear it away, implying that the sorcerer wanted his enemy to suffer a long and slow decline.

Another clay effigy, in the Pitt-Rivers Museum in Oxford, came from Inverness and was donated by a "Major G" of that county. It was "intended for the Major," and had been stuck full of pins and nails and left at his house.

A minister in the Scottish Highlands had a similar experience. He appeared to be suffering from some sort of wasting disease and when his friends investigated they found a clay effigy in the stream beside his house.

Within the last century or so, sheeps' hearts full of pins have been discovered stuck up the chimneys of cottages in both Scotland and Wales.

These things happened in modern communities that professed to be Christian, yet ancient pagan Celtic practices still went on. And perhaps they still do.

DOG

The dog was an important domestic animal—a companion, a guardian, a help in hunting—so it was likely to find some cult-role in Celtic religion. Dogs appear repeatedly in Celtic cult images and their bones are commonly found in ritual deposits.

The dog was not just associated with one deity, but with several. In the Mediterranean world (which might be considered a cousin of the Celtic world), the Greco-Roman healer **god** Aesculapius was accompanied by a dog. The huntress goddess, Diana, was also accompanied by a dog. The mythic monster Cerberus was a giant dog. These different roles for dogs were reflected in the Celtic religious world. The Gaulish **healing-**goddess Sequana was left offerings at the **source of the Seine** in the form of images of **people** with dogs. The magical value of the dog lay in its ability to heal itself with its own saliva, and this gave it a natural position as the companion of a healing god or goddess.

Sucellus, the hammer god, was sometimes accompanied by a dog; in Dacia, he was accompanied by a three-headed dog. In Celtic religion triplism of this kind can be highly significant—and classical mythology also had its three-headed dog. At **Lydney**, the British healer-god Nodens was represented nine times not by a human image, but by his canine helper: a deerhound (*see* **Rule of Three**).

Just as **Epona** was inseparable from her **horse** (or horses), so the Gaulish goddess **Nehalennia** was inseparable from her dog, which is often shown looking intently up at her in the way that dogs often gaze at their owners. As far as posterity is concerned, Nehalennia's identity is defined entirely by the companionship of her dog.

There seems to have been an association of the dog with the Underworld. There were many ritual deposits of dogs in Britain, mainly in pits or wells. In its role as hunting companion, the dog was associated with speed, power, and killing instinct, and perhaps this killing aspect was how it gained an association with the Underworld.

DRAGON

The belief in dragons seems to have been worldwide. Every ancient **culture** had its dragons.

Dragons are multiple symbols. They represent the whole of creation; they are guardians of **treasure**; and they obstruct the road to spiritual gain. Overcoming them is a major rite of passage—a rite of release.

In modern times, dragons are usually represented as gigantic lizards, with two pairs of lizard-like legs and wings, though they rarely fly. A dragon without front legs is known as a wyvern. The nineteenth-century discovery of dinosaurs altered the way dragons were represented; today it is common in artwork and film to depict dragons as fantastic dinosaurs.

Perhaps the most familiar dragon is St. George's dragon: a small heraldic beast with bat's wings, a sting in its tail, and wide-opening jaws that breathe fire. This quaint little creature, familiar to us from any number of works of **art**, is a long way from the dragons of Celtic legend, which tend to be gigantic, wingless, wormlike **serpents**. They are very long and their breath is poisonous rather than flaming. The Celtic dragon is a scaly **water**-snake and haunts wells, pools, and lakes; it also lives in caves.

Dragons have a penchant for maidens and they often diligently watch over hoards of treasure. They are usually depicted as malevolent. Their ferocity symbolizes the wild and destructive forces of nature, yet they are believed to be very wise. They are also long-lived.

Not all dragons are malevolent, however. Y Ddraig Goch, the Red Dragon, is the benign symbol of Wales itself.

Stories of dragons from England are not necessarily of Anglo-Saxon origin. Folk-tales told in the Middle Ages in England are likely to belong to the pre-Anglo-Saxon culture.

The Dragon of Kingston was choked by a great boulder rolled down a hill into his mouth as he opened it to belch out flames.

The Dragon of St. Leonard's Forest, near Horsham in Sussex, was a land-based dragon. There were repeated sightings of it in 1614, which were vividly described in a pamphlet. The details it describes are very difficult to explain:

A True and Wonderful Discourse relating a strange and monstrous Serpent (or Dragon) lately discovered, and yet living, to the great Annoyance and divers Slaughters of both Men and Cattell, by his strong and violent Poison: in Sussex, two Miles from Horsham, in a Woode called St Leonard's Forrest, and thirtie Miles from London, this present Month of August, 1614. With the true Generation of Serpents.

In Sussex, there is a pretty market-towne, called Horsham, and neare unto to it a forrest, called St Leonard's Forrest, and there is an unfrequented place, heathie, vaultie, full of unwholesome shades, and overgrowne hollowes, where this serpent is thought to be bred; but wheresoever bred, certaine and too true it is, that there it lives. Within three or four miles compasse are its usual haunts, oftentimes at a place called Faygate, and it hath been seene within half a mile of Horsham; a wonder, no doubte, most terrible and noisome to the inhabitants therebouts. There is always in his track or path left a glutinous and slimie matter (as by a small similitude we may perceive in a snail's) which is very corrupt and offensive to the scent…

This serpent (or dragon, some call it) is reputed to be nine feete, or rather more, in length, and shaped almost in the forme of an axletree of a cart; a quantity of thickness in the middest, and somewhat smaller at both endes. The former part, which he shootes forth as a neck, is supposed to be an elle long; with a white ring, as it were, of scales about it. The scales along his back seem to be blackish, and so much as is discovered under his bellie, appeareth to be red; for I speak of no nearer description than of a reasonable ocular distance. For coming too nearer it, hath already beene too dearly paid for, as you shall heare hereafter.

It is likewise discovered to have large feete, but the eye may be there deceived; for some suppose that serpents have no feete… He rids away (as we call it) as fast as any man can run. He is of countenance very proud, and at the sight or hearing of men or cattell, will raise his neck upright, and seem to listen and looke about, with great arrogancy. There are likewise upon either side of him discovered, two great bunches so big as a large foote-ball, and (as some thinke) will in time grow to wings; but God, I hope, will (to defend the poor people in the neighbourhood) that he be destroyed before he grow so fledge.

He will cast his venome about four rodde [about 64 feet/19m] from him, as by woefull experience it was proved on the bodies of a man and woman coming that way, who afterwards were found dead, being poysoned and very much swelled, but not prayed upon. Likewise a man going to chase it and, as he imagined, to destroy it with two mastive dogs, as yet not knowing the great danger of it, his dogs were both killed, and he himself glad to return with haste to preserve his own life. Yet this is to be noted, that the dogs were not prayed upon, but slaine and left whole; for his food is thought to be, for the most part,

The Element Encyclopedia of the Celts

in a conie-warren, which he much frequents.

The persons, whose names are hereunder printed, have seene this serpent, besides divers others, as the carrier of Horsam, who lieth at the White Horse in Southwark, and who can certifie the truth of all that has been here related.

John Steele
Christopher Holder
and a Widow Woman dwelling near Faygate.

The belief that St. Leonard's Forest was a dragon lair persisted until the nineteenth century, when it was still believed that the area was the haunt of monstrous snakes. It is possible that the old belief was kept alive by gamekeepers, who had their own reasons for wanting **people** to keep away from the woods.

Many other places in Sussex were deemed to be dragon lairs. There was one on Bignor Hill, another at Fittleworth (reported in 1867), and it was said that there were serpents guarding treasure in a tunnel under the Iron Age camp at Cissbury.

There was also a water-monster at Lyminster, living in one of the knucker-holes on the coastal plain in front of the South Downs. These holes are artesian **springs**, fed by cold and crystal-clear water rising under pressure from the underlying chalk. There were knucker-holes at Worthing, Shoreham, Angmering, Lancing, and Lyminster. "Knucker" is derived from the Anglo-Saxon *nicor*, which means "dragon" or "water-serpent."

The Lyminster Knucker-Hole, out on the bleak water-marshes of the Arun floodplain, was the lair of a notorious dragon. It rampaged around the countryside, carrying off cattle, sheep, and people and devouring them in its hideouts in the marshes. It was said he went swimming in the Arun **River**, "sticking his ugly face up against the windows in the shipyard when people were sitting having their tea." The Knucker was an all-round pest. In the end the King of Sussex offered the hand of his daughter to anyone who could kill it. According to some, a passing knight killed the Knucker in heroic combat, married the princess, and settled in Lyminster. When he died, a gravestone was made for him. It is still there, with a cross superimposed on a herringbone pattern, which is believed to represent the ribs of the dragon, but there is no inscription.

But there is another version of what happened. According to this version, the victor was not a passing knight, but a local farm boy called Jim Pulk. Jim decided to bake the dragon a huge Sussex pie, poison it, and take it on a farm cart to the edge of the Knucker-Hole. He hid behind a hedge to see what happened. The Knucker came up out of the water, sniffed the pie and ate it, along with the cart and **horses**. Then the poison took effect and the dragon curled up and died. Jim came out and cut off the dragon's **head** with a scythe. To celebrate his triumph, he went to the Six Bells Inn for a drink and fell down dead. The mysterious gravestone was Jim Pulk's.

The story was retold with many variations. In some Jim Pulk was Jim Puttock. In some the story is brought up-to-date. This is the nature of a long-enduring oral tradition.

…off Jim goos, as bold as a lion. All the people followed him as far as the bridge [at Arundel], but they dursn't goo no further, for there was old Knucker, lying just below Bill Dawse's. Least, his head was, but his neck and body-parts lay all along up the hill, past the [railway] station, and he was tearing up the trees in Batworth Park with his tail.

And he sees this 'ere tug [cart] a-coming, and he sings out, affable-like, "How do, Man?"

"How do, Dragon," says Jim.

"What you got there?" says Dragon, sniffing.

"Pudden," says Jim.

"What be that?" says Dragon.

"Just you try," says Jim.

He didn't want no more telling. Pudden, horses, cart, tug – they was gone in a blink. Jim'd have gone too, only he hung on to one of they trees what blew down last year.

"Weren't bad," says Knucker, licking his lips.

"Like another?" says Jim…

I used to visit the Knucker-Hole as a boy. It was a lonely, wild place. Recently, after a long time away, I returned to find it completely inaccessible, ringed by a high chain-link fence. There was a door in the fence—a door with a letterbox…

Another monster is said to have once lived in a pool called Llyn yr Afanc on the Conwy River in North Wales. There are uncertainties about its form. Some say it was an enormous beaver, because the word *afanc* is sometimes used in Welsh dialects for "beaver." Some say it was a sort of crocodile.

Llyn yr Afanc is a kind of whirlpool. Anything thrown in will go around and around and then be sucked down, but local people said it was the *afanc* that pulled down people or animals who fell into the Llyn. In the seventeenth century it was said that the *afanc* was drawn to a maiden, who persuaded it to put its head in her lap and go to sleep. As it slept, it was chained up and the chains attached to a team of oxen. But as they began to drag it away, the *afanc* woke up and tore away the maiden's breast, which it was clutching with its claw. Some men joined in pulling with the oxen. They were disputing with each other about who pulled the hardest, when the *afanc* unexpectedly spoke:

"Had it not been for the oxen pulling,
The afanc would never have left the pool."

The parish of Linton in Roxburghshire in Scotland is said to have been plagued by the Linton Worm. It was apparently a legless worm with poisonous breath that killed cattle and people. It was killed by Somerville of Lariston, who thrust a burning peat on the tip of a long lance down its throat. This neutralized its poisonous breath and burned out its entrails. The **spiral** ridges on Wormington Hill bear witness to the Linton Worm's death throes.

Whether the worms of the Atlantic Celts were original Celtic creations or borrowings from Scandinavian lore is not known, but the worm-dragon is certainly a common type in Britain. A typical one is the Lambton Worm from Yorkshire. This grew to monstrous proportions after being pulled from the Wear River by the heir of Lambton, who was fishing on a Sunday, and thrown down a well. When the worm emerged from the well it had taken the form of an enormous lizard that ravaged the countryside. Sometimes it curled its huge, long body around a hill, or sometimes around a great rock in the river. If cut in half, it could rejoin itself.

Another worm-dragon is the Mester Stoorworm in Orkney, a sea-serpent of enormous size. When in its death throes, it screwed up its body to become the island of Iceland.

The Dragon of Loschy Hill was another self-joining dragon, like the Lambton Worm, and it was finally overcome with the help of the hero's **dog**, who carried away the various pieces of the worm as they were chopped off so that they could not reunite. But the poisonous fumes of the dragon's breath eventually proved fatal to both the hero and his dog.

Dragons and worms are curiously absent from surviving Irish traditions. In Irish tales, the foe is more often a **giant** (of which there are large numbers) or a supernatural hag. But there are some Irish dragons. More than one large pool derives its name from a worm or serpent that lived in it in the age of the heroes. Fion M'Cumhaill killed several of them. A hero from Munster killed a fearsome serpent in the Duffrey in County Wexford, and the pool where it lived is still called Loch-na-Piastha.

The Red Dragon of Wales appears on the Welsh national flag. The earliest recorded use of the dragon as a symbol for Wales comes from the *History of the Britons* written in the late eighth century by the monk Nennius. Tradition has it that it was the battle standard of King **Arthur** and other Celtic

war leaders, so the Red Dragon would have been seen leading the Celts into battle. Henry Tudor flew the Red Dragon of Cadwaladr on a green and white field as his personal banner when he marched through Wales on his way to fight Richard III for the English throne at Bosworth in 1485. After the battle, in which Richard III was killed, the flag was ceremoniously carried to St. Paul's cathedral to be blessed. The banner was to represent the House of Tudor. The Tudor monarchs were Welsh in origin, so it was natural for them to incorporate the Red Dragon of Wales into the royal coat of arms, where it still stands as one of the two supporters, the other being the Lion of England.

In the Mabinogion story *Lludd and Llefelys*, the Red Dragon does battle with an invading White Dragon. Its shrieks of pain cause women to miscarry, plants to wither, and animals to die. Lludd, the King of Britain, consults his wise brother, Llefelys, who advises him to dig a pit at the very center of Britain. He is to fill it with mead and cover it with a cloth. Lludd does as his brother tells him. The dragons drink the mead and fall asleep. Lludd is then able to bind them up in the cloth and keep them captive; he keeps them imprisoned inside **Dinas Emrys**, in Snowdonia.

Then Nennius takes up the story. The two dragons remain captive at Dinas Emrys for hundreds of years, until **Vortigern** attempts to build a castle there. By day King Vortigern builds. By night the castle walls and foundations are demolished again by unseen forces. Vortigern consults his wizards, who tell him to seek out a boy without a natural father and offer him as a sacrifice. The king finds such a boy—it is rumored that he is the young **Merlin**—who is said to be the wisest wizard who ever lived. When the boy discovers that he is to be put to death to solve the problem of the self-demolishing castle, he contradicts the advice that Vortigern has been given and tells him about the two dragons entombed deep inside the mountain.

Vortigern has the mountain excavated, freeing the two dragons. On their release into the air, they continue their unceasing fight. Finally the Red Dragon defeats the White Dragon. Then the boy explains what has happened. The White Dragon symbolizes the Saxons. The Red Dragon symbolizes the people of Vortigern: the Britons.

This vivid legend is nothing less than a Welsh foundation-myth. Vortigern's Britons are the Welsh, and they remain undefeated by the Saxons: Wales remains a separate entity, while the Celtic kingdoms to the east are colonized and taken over by the Anglo-Saxons.

Geoffrey of Monmouth repeats the story in his *History of the Kings of Britain*. There, the Red Dragon is a different kind of symbol. It represents a prophecy of the coming of **Arthur**, who will save Britain from the Saxon onslaught.

The symbolic use of the Red Dragon still has the power to inspire, and the equal power to antagonize. In 1953 the Red Dragon badge of Henry VII was given an augmentation of honor, which consisted of a circular riband surrounding the Red Dragon and bearing the inscription (in Welsh) "The Red Dragon inspires action." The British Prime Minister at the time, Winston Churchill, scoffed at it in a Cabinet Minute: "Odious design expressing nothing but spite, malice, ill-will and monstrosity. Words (Red Dragon takes the lead) are untrue and unduly flattering to [Aneurin] Bevan." In spite of

Churchill's contempt, the badge was added to the arms of Cardiff, the Welsh capital, in 1956.

The Highland water-horse, or Each Uisce, is a dragon in all but name. This is a fierce and dangerous monster that haunts both open sea and Scottish lochs. It takes the form of a sleek and handsome horse that invites mortals to ride it; then it careers at headlong speed into the lake and devours its rider as it **shapeshifts** into a monster.

A widely told story involves seven little girls and one little boy out on a Sunday afternoon walk when they see a fine pony grazing beside a loch. One little girl mounts the pony, then another, until all seven of them are on the pony's back. The little boy is more wary, as he notices that the pony gets longer to accommodate each additional child and senses that all is not well. He runs off and hides among some rocks away from the loch. The horse turns and sees him. "Come on, little scabby-head! Get on my back!" The boy will not go near the pony, so the pony rushes toward him, still carrying the little girls, who are now stuck fast to his back. The boy dodges among the rocks and the pony is unable to catch him. In the end,

the water-horse gives up trying to catch the boy and plunges into the loch. The next day the livers of the seven little girls are washed up on the lakeshore.

ETERNITY KNOT

A knotwork design confined within a circle, or a circular interlace. Many designs, ancient and modern, conform to this specification, though not necessarily with any specific symbolism. To an extent, in modern times the symbolic value of designs has been driven forward by commercial considerations. Eternity symbols in particular can be used to promote the sale of jewelry and tattoos.

Exaggeration

(ENLARGEMENT)

One way of taking objects from the everyday world and transporting them to the **Otherworld** was to make them unrealistically large. This might apply to a whole object or just a part of it. Making an image of an animal, otherwise in true proportions, and giving it abnormally large horns was a way of transforming it into something Otherworldly.

The Cerne Giant in Dorset is well-known for his very large **phallus**, and the exaggeration has often been seen as proof that the figure was made as a fertility figure, but in this we have been misled. It was only during a scouring as recently as 1909 that the phallus was lengthened—before that it was in perfect proportion with the rest of the figure. This may have been done as a joke by the laborers who were given the job of cleaning the figure, but it is more likely to have been a mistake. In the eighteenth and nineteenth centuries there was a ring representing the Giant's navel immediately above the phallus. Overgrown with grass, these two features could easily have been joined by mistake. Either way,

the present head of the phallus is exactly where the navel was until 1909. But there are genuine examples of Celtic phallic exaggeration, such as the bronze relief of a naked man found at Woodeaton in Oxfordshire.

Another common form of exaggeration was repeating an image, especially in triplicate (*see* **Miniaturization**, **Rule of Three**; Places: **Cerne Abbas**).

Giant

Giants and ogres are an integral part of later Celtic legend (*see* Myths: ***Comorre the Cursed***, **Morven, the Prop of Brittany,** ***Tom and the Giant***). Some of the giants, such as the colossal Bran the Blessed, clearly were once **gods**. Bran was so big that no house could contain him, and so big that he was able to wade across the Irish Sea from Wales to Ireland. He was enormously strong, but he was benign. His decapitated **head** chatted amiably and brought a blessing wherever it was carried; it protected Britain from invaders so long as it was safely lodged in London (*see* Myths: **Branwen**).

The huge hill figure depicting the Cerne Giant was originally intended as an icon of the Iron Age protector god of Dorset, though he has been interpreted subsequently in all sorts of different ways (see **Cerne Abbas**).

Aggressive, short-tempered giants are stock characters in medieval storytelling. The Giant of Grabbist was a stone-throwing giant, but he was also actively benevolent. He once lifted a **boat** that was in difficulties at sea and set it down safely in harbor. The Giant of Grabbist is slightly comical, and as the storytelling tradition developed, giants became steadily more grotesque and foolish. Increasingly, they became figures of fun.

The Giant of Carn Galva in Cornwall was a kindly giant. He was more playful than warlike. Giants were responsible for placing rocking-stones ("logan-stones") on top of the granite tors of the English West Country. The Carn Galva Giant put in place the rocking-stone on the westernmost hilltop, so that he could rock himself to sleep as he watched the **sun** sink into the sea in the **west**. Nearby is a pile of roughly cube-shaped boulders that the giant used to build up and then kick down again as a pastime, like a bored child playing with building blocks. His main occupation was to protect the **people** of Morvah and Zennor from attack by the Titans who lived on Lelant Hills. The Giant of Carn Galva never killed any of the Morvah people except one, and that was by accident, in play.

The giant was fond of a young man from Choon, who used to walk up to the hilltop occasionally, just to see how the giant was getting on, to cheer him up and play a game of bob to pass the time. One afternoon, the giant was so pleased with the game they had played that when the young man from Choon threw down his quoit ready to go home, the giant tapped him good-naturedly on the shoulder with the tips of his fingers. "Be sure to come again tomorrow, son, and then we'll have another good game!"

But the young man dropped dead at his feet—the giant had broken his skull with his gentle tap. When the giant realized his young friend was dead, he cradled his body in his arms and sat down on the big, square rock at the foot of the hill, rocking himself to and fro. He wailed and cried louder than the noise of the breakers on the cliffs. "Oh, why didn't they make the shell of your noddle stronger? It's as soft as a piecrust and made too thin by half! And how shall I pass the time without you here to play bob with me, and hide-and-seek?" The giant pined away for seven years before he died of a broken heart.

The landscape detail included in stories such as this one help to explain how the stories evolved and why they persisted. They gave people an explanation of strangely shaped landforms that otherwise were a total mystery to them.

At Peel Castle on the Isle of Man is the legendary grave of the first king of Eubonia, the ancient name of the island. It is 30 feet (9m) long.

THE GRAIL QUEST

The **magic** cup is a common element in Celtic folk-tales. In *Finn MacCoul and the Bent Grey Lad*, the hero is sent off to look for the "quadrangular cup of the Feni-

ans," which the King of Lochlann has stolen. The cup has supernatural qualities. Any drink you could wish for may be drunk from it. This is similar to the magic cup given to Huon of Bordeaux by King Oberon.

In another Irish tale, there is a cup that can cure the dumb. The enamel-decorated glass tumbler known as the Luck of Edenhall brings good luck, but if the cup is broken, the luck runs out. In a similar way, the family that possesses and looks after the cup of Ballafletcher on the Isle of Man may expect good luck, prosperity, and peace; but if the cup is damaged there are serious consequences.

The Holy Grail legend is the daughter of two parents and four grandparents. The mother is a Christian legend, and the father is a Celtic myth. There are two Christian origins for the cup. It may be the sacred cup from which Jesus drank at the Last Supper, or it may be the one used to catch the blood that ran from his wounds at the Crucifixion; either way, it is a sacred cup intimately associated with the last hours in the life of Jesus. There are, symmetrically, two Celtic origins. One is the magic **cauldron** of Celtic **gods**: a cauldron that is never empty and keeps everyone replete. The other is the magic chalice that gives spiritual power and kingly authority.

Invariably, when people talk about the Holy Grail as a physical object, they mean the cup associated with Jesus. But in medieval storytelling, somehow all four of these ideas come indeterminately stirred together to produce a misty apparition, an Otherworldly chalice that can only be seen under certain favorable conditions, and then only by the pure and the deserving.

It is said that an incomplete wooden cup, called the Nanteos Cup, and preserved in private ownership in Wales, represents the actual cup described in Christian legend.

This cup, said to be made of olivewood, has its own provenance story, which some may believe and some may not. Robert de Boron's *Joseph of Arimathea* describes Joseph as bringing the cup to Britain. It arrived at **Glastonbury**, where it went into the care of the monks of Glastonbury Abbey. But then much depends on whether you believe the other stories that are told about Glastonbury. After the Dissolution, some of the monks from Glastonbury took refuge in Strata Florida Abbey near Trega-

ron in Ceredigion. When that abbey closed, it is said that the cup was left in the care of the Stedman family, the local landowners, and subsequently passed through marriage to the Powells of Nanteos Mansion near Aberystwyth.

The Nanteos Cup is thought by experts to be a medieval mazer bowl. It resided for many years at Nanteos Mansion, but went with the last member of the Powell family when they moved out in the 1950s. Two independent examinations of the cup have shown that it is made of wych elm, not olivewood, and that it probably dates from about 1400.

The story of the Nanteos Cup is attractive, but unsupported by any evidence. The Grail seems to remain elusive, just out of reach. That was the nature of the legendary Grail too.

The Grail legends of the Arthurian romances represent something very deep-seated in Celtic thought: the dangerous and eventful journey, the adventure, and the quest. The knights of King **Arthur** are striving to find the Holy Grail in exactly the same way that Everyman in medieval Christian Europe was supposed to be striving to find his own personal salvation.

So the Grail becomes a symbol not just of pure spirit, but the purest spirit, and the quest for it becomes the quest for spiritual wholeness, the quest for a personal salvation.

THE GREEN MAN

A sculpture or drawing of a face surrounded by leaves or even made from leaves. Some Green Man faces have leaves for hair and leaves for a beard. The face is almost always male. Sometimes branches or vines sprout from the mouth or nostrils, and the shoots may bear flowers or fruit. The Green Man is mainly found as an architectural ornament on churches.

The earliest known example of a Green Man image with foliage coming from its mouth dates from France in about AD 400. There are earlier Green Man images than this, though. One has been found on an Irish stone carving dating from 300 BC. **Gods** wearing leafy crowns are shown in Iron Age carvings. One of the local Romano-Celtic gods in Gaul, Erriapus, is shown as a **head** emerging out of a mass of foliage.

Leaves were themselves religious cult objects. Leaves made of bronze or precious metal were left as offerings to the gods.

The Green Man is not an exclusively Celtic image. It occurs in other **cultures**, but it was enthusiastically adopted by the Celts for its rich symbolic value.

Some of the cleverest carvings seem at first sight to be only foliage; it is only after a moment or two that the foliage resolves into a human face. The image is that of a pagan nature-spirit: the woodwose, or the wild man of the woods.

There are many variations and the Green Man is found in many different cultures. The image is clearly a vegetation deity and a symbol of rebirth and renewal every spring.

Whether the Green Man can be seen as a specific part of the Celtic belief system is hard to say. Certainly the mythological beliefs regarding him continued alongside medieval Christianity, and it is striking how often this unmistakably pagan image appears in churches, abbeys, and cathedrals. It may be that the creation of Green Man images went on alongside the pre-Christian pagan belief system too. The Green Man almost seems to represent a belief system in itself, a belief in the self-renewal of vegetation that transcends religion.

At the same time, there were several Celtic nature gods who had much in common with the Green Man. It is also significant that one Celtic god has a name that means "The Green Man" in both Latin and Celtic: *Viridios*.

The Green Man was transformed into a folk-dancing character in Jack in the Green. Ancient tree worship entailed venerating the tree itself. From there it was a short step to nominating a young man or young woman to stand in for the tree. Usually, some sort of light wicker frame was carried, slung from the shoulders, and the frame covered with leaves and small branches—the wicker cage ritual again, though this time without a death at its climax (*see* Religion: **Wicker Giant**). In this way the tree, now *The Tree*, was mobilized and could take part in dances

and processions—be directly engaged in the festivities to celebrate the arrival of summer. These were the typical activities of May Morning. The Maypole dancing was a similar transformation of the act of dancing a ring dance around a tree; in Maypole dancing, the pole stands in for the tree. And these customs still continue in England (*see* Religion: **Beltane**).

On May Morning, one dancer from a Morris team dresses entirely in branches and leaves and, as Jack in the Green or The Tree, he whirls about, leading the Morris Men through the streets, deciding the route and conducting the dance. On May Morning 1967, I was Jack in the Green for the Oxford University Morris Men—an animated Green Man. The nature symbolism is obvious. Jack represents the new foliage of early summer: the ritual is a greeting to summer itself and the promise it brings.

After the Middle Ages, the Green Man was given a new lease of life as a decorative image, in stone, stained glass, and manuscripts, and on bookplates. A dramatic, modern 40-foot (12m) tall full-figure version of the Green Man by sculptor Toin Adams can be seen at the Custard Factory in Birmingham, England.

The self-renewing woodland spirit nature of the Green Man was an idea that was repeatedly transformed. We can see it in figures as different from one another as Peter Pan, Robin Hood, Father Christmas, and the **Green Knight**.

h

HARE

All over Wales hares were regarded as heralds of death. There was a case in North Wales where a woman knew, before anyone had told her, that a certain person had died. The local clergyman asked her how she knew and she replied, "I know because I saw a hare come from towards his house and cross over the road before me." She evidently believed the hare was the dead man.

In Wales there was a tradition that witches could turn themselves into hares (*see* **Shapeshifting, Witchcraft**). If a hare made an unexpected escape from the hounds, a huntsman might send his servants to see if some old woman, suspected of being a witch, had been out that morning.

It was also believed that witches could change other people into animals. An instance was quoted by Elias Owen, in his book *Welsh Folklore*, of such a transformation in Cardiganshire, where a man was turned into a hare by a witch.

There is speculation that the **Druids** used hares for prophecy, perhaps deliberately catching and then releasing them in order to watch exactly how and where they ran and then prophesying accordingly.

HAZEL

Hazel is the tree of knowledge. Hazelnuts are believed to carry great wisdom within them. In Druidic lore, the hazel is connected to the Salmon of Wisdom, which was thought to have acquired its knowledge by eating **magic** hazelnuts.

Hazel trees favor damp places. The tree's association with **water** (it is thought to "choose" to live near water) is the reason why hazel twigs are used for dowsing water. The hazel itself is thought to know where underground water lies.

HEAD

The head features very prominently in Celtic religious **art**. It is a powerful symbol, representing the self, the center of being, and the most important part of the human body.

One peculiarity of the Celtic obsession with heads is the association of heads with **water**, and with **spring**-cults and well-cults (see Religion: **Holy Wells**, **Sacred Springs**). Several votive offerings at the **Source de la Seine** sanctuary depicted heads. In first-century London, heads were deposited in a well. The same connection between severed heads and water crops up in folk-tales. The water connection may be linked to the fundamental idea of regeneration: the belief that, somehow, immersion in water might bring a dead head back to life in the same way that it might restore a sick limb to health. The

severed head may be a short-hand statement for death itself, in which case the association with water is a simple dualistic statement: head = death, and water = life, and birth, rebirth.

The **Pfalzfeld** pillar, carved in about 500 BC, has images of human heads on each of its four sides near the base. Sometimes what is shown is very specifically a display of severed human heads, in imitation of an actual practice of **headhunting** and the real-life display of heads as battle trophies. This was separate from the practice of representing **gods** by depicting their heads alone.

HOLY GRAIL

See **The Grail Quest**.

HORSE

The horse was a cult animal in Europe as far back as the Bronze Age. Rock art in Scandinavia shows horses with **sun wheels** and **boats**. The horse and the sun-disk were major symbols in the Urnfield **culture**, and this Bronze Age association continued into the Iron Age; the two symbols often occur together on Iron Age **coins**.

By the middle of the Iron Age, horses were ridden as well as being used for pulling carts and **chariots.** The horse acquired great prestige value by association with its use as a steed by the warrior aristocracy—a special status that went beyond their practical usefulness. This was evident at the terrible siege of **Alesia** by the Roman army. The Gaulish chief **Vercingetorix** finally sent away his horses and surrendered to insure their safety; he was to lose his life, but his horses were to be saved. This gesture may have entailed something beyond a sentimental feeling for favorite animals; the horses may have symbolized his kingship. Vercingetorix might be about to surrender to **Julius Caesar** and be taken off to Rome in chains, but the kingship of his tribe, the **Arverni**, would go on.

The horse's central place in Celtic warrior **society** ensured its central place as a religious symbol. Horse figurines were commonly left as offerings in Britain and Gaul; to give one example, a small bronze horse was left as a votive offering at **Coventina**'s Well, near Carrawburgh, on Hadrian's Wall.

The image of a horseman, a mounted **god**, appears in Romano-Celtic religious **art**, especially in Britain, in the lands of the **Catuvellauni** and Coritani, and related to a local **war-god** cult.

The horse was closely associated with the goddess **Epona**, who was the most conspicuous horse deity (*see* Places: **Uffington White Horse**; Religion: **Coventina**, **Epona**).

I

ICHTHYS WHEEL

See **Wheel**.

ISLES OF THE BLESSED

These islands were the mythic location of the **Otherworld**. In the adventures of Bran, Mael Duin, and **Brendan**, they featured as mysterious islands far out in the Atlantic: a vast sea subject to constant change.

The islands were fantastic in every possible way. One island was a gigantic foot sticking up out of the ocean, with an island on top and a door at its base. Another was a vast, four-sided, silver pillar with a **gold** mesh hanging from the top down into the sea below. Another was an island with a strange beast whirling around its outer wall and turning itself inside its own skin.

J

JUPITER COLUMN

See **Sky Horseman**.

K

KNOT

A characteristic design, one that became conspicuous in Celtic **art** from about AD 700 onward.

Knotwork is made of a single continuous labyrinthine line that winds and weaves all around and through the design, without a beginning, and without an end. It symbolizes eternity. Knotwork is often used in illuminated manuscripts to fill corners or to make decorative borders around the edge of a page of text.

The never-ending interlacing line was also carved in stone. It forms an elaborate decoration on the face of the **Celtic cross** at Carew in Pembrokeshire.

The elaborate interlace pattern was still in use as late as the twelfth century, which is when the remarkable stone font of St. Michael's church, Castle Frome, Herefordshire, was carved. This has, around its rim, three triple never-ending lines that interweave regularly, plaiting just like basketwork—and making the **magic** Celtic three times three (*see* **Rule of Three**). Lower down, on the waist of the font, is another interlace pattern, this time a single never-ending path that weaves about far more randomly. It seems almost to look back to the random wanderings of the **labyrinth** lines on Neolithic tombs. In a Christian church, the community is carrying on with its old ideas just as before. Here, as in so many aspects of Celtic **culture,** there is long continuity of practice and thought through deep time.

L

LABYRINTH

Labyrinths are not unique to the Celts. They occur early on in south-eastern Europe, in the Aegean region, with the building of the Knossos labyrinth in about 1900 BC. This famously mazelike building was commemorated, long after it had fallen into ruins, by a maze symbol stamped on the coins of the classical city of Knossos, which was built right next to the remains of the Bronze Age labyrinth.

In the Bronze Age, the labyrinth was literally mazelike, with many different possible routes. In later times, the design was stricter, allowing only one route in, and one route out. A typical labyrinth design is compact, while allowing the longest possible linear path in from the outside to the center.

Labyrinths constantly reappear in different forms at different stages in the evolution of Celtic **culture**, and some of them are earlier than the Minoan labyrinths. The labyrinth as an idea is closely related to the **knot**: the line that winds all around a design. The difference is that in a knotwork design the line has no beginning and no end, while in a labyrinth there is, usually, a starting-point and a goal.

Both symbolize journeys. This might be a particular journey or adventure, or the overall journey of life itself. Labyrinths therefore form a visual counterpart to the epic folk-tale, which often consists of a long and convoluted journey with episodes that repeat and double back on themselves. They may symbolize a journey of self-discovery too, a journey in to the center of the self and out again, and in this way the ancient symbol emerges as a Jungian archetype: a tool for self-exploration and self-**healing**.

The path representing a long and winding journey makes its first appearance in the Celtic **west** in the Neolithic passage grave **art** seen at Gavrinis in Brittany, **Newgrange** in Ireland, and Bryn Celli Ddu in Wales. These rock-cut mazes dating from 3,500–3,000 BC are asymmetrical.

Later, in the Bronze Age, from around 2000 BC onward, nearly symmetrical labyrinths appear. The classic design, similar to the Knossos maze but circular instead of square, was chipped onto the living rock near Tintagel.

These ancient formal designs themselves have ancestors. It is possible to see early forerunners of the labyrinth idea in the cup-and-ring marks seen on many naturally outcropping slabs of rock, especially in northern Britain. The marks at Old Bewick in Northumberland consist of concentric circles that are entered by winding paths with a cup at each end.

Labyrinths are also found among the **Val Camonica** rock carvings in northern Italy.

In the post-Roman, early medieval Celtic world, some knotwork designs were developed to turn them into labyrinths. Squared off, these could become decorative patterns for floor-tiles.

In the highest developments of Celtic art, reached in the early Middle Ages, and in purely decorative art again in the nineteenth century, knotwork and labyrinth converged. By this stage, Celtic, Anglo-Saxon, and Norse interlace elements became impossible to distinguish; the arts and crafts of the different cultures spilled over into each other.

Labyrinths were adopted by the Christian Church, and occasionally large labyrinth pavements were laid out in tiles on church floors.

The most spectacular one is in Chartres cathedral. It is based on a design made of 11 concentric circles and its path is exactly 666 feet (203m) long. This may be a joke on the part of the designer, as the number 666 is usually regarded as being associated with the Devil, the Great Beast, though apologists argue that it is a sacred number. The Chartres labyrinth has a six-petaled flower, hiding the Seal of Solomon. Curiously, the cathedral-builders in Britain did not include labyrinths in their designs, though there were plenty of mazes available in Britain that could have served as models.

The turf maze is a British invention. Sometimes they are called Troy Towns (Draytons) or the Walls of Troy or, in Wales, Caerdroia, the City of Troy. Sometimes they are called Julian's Bower, apparently after the Julius who was the son of Trojan Aeneas and *burgh* meaning town. The insistent connection with Troy is hard to explain. There was no legend of a labyrinth at Troy, as there was at Knossos. Another name given to the turf maze is Shepherd's Race, which is self-explanatory.

One of the biggest turf mazes is the one on the common at Saffron Walden in Essex. It is circular, 140 feet (43m) across and probably made in the fairly recent past. The maze at Wing in Rutland is apparently older; it stands close to an ancient burial mound. The very irregular turf maze at Pimperne in Dorset, Troy Town, was also fairly old. In 1686 John Aubrey described it as "much used by the young people on Holydaies and by ye School-boies." Unfortunately it was plowed up and destroyed in 1730.

Julian's Bower at Alkborough in Lincolnshire and Shepherd's Race at Boughton Green in Northamptonshire were classic, symmetrical, circular mazes, and both 40 feet (12m) in diameter.

In the early nineteenth century, the people of Alkborough played games at Julian's Bower on May Eve. One villager who was a youth at the time said that he had "an indefinite persuasion of something unseen and unknown co-operating with them" as they ran backward and forward along the paths to reach the center and then retraced their steps to get out again.

The Mizmaze is a nearly lost turf maze in Dorset; perhaps significantly, perhaps not, it lies exactly halfway between two great

Iron Age hill towns of **Maiden Castle** and **South Cadbury**. It could be ancient, but it seems more likely to be medieval. Over the last 200 years, which was ironically a period of awakening antiquarian and archeological interest, the local people have stood by and watched the Mizmaze grow over and gradually disappear from view. John Hutchins, writing about the history of Dorset in the eighteenth century, described it as "a maze of circular form, about 30 paces in diameter, surrounded by a bank and ditch. The banks of which it is composed are set almost close together, and are somewhat more than one foot in width and about half a foot in height."

A later edition of Hutchins's *History of Dorset*, produced in the early nineteenth century, added:

Heretofore it was the custom for the young men of the village to scour out the trenches and pare the banks once in six or seven years, and the day appropriated for the purpose was passed in rustic merriment and festivity. But of late years, either through want of encouragement from the principal inhabitants, or from a less reverence for a curious piece of antiquity, this salutary work has been neglected, and *there is at present great danger that, in the lapse of a few years, the traces of the several trenches or divisions will no longer be discernible, particularly in the centre, where the circle being shorter, and consequently more susceptible of injury, the banks have been trodden down by the numerous cattle that resort to the spot to enjoy the cool breeze in summer. In the year 1800 this common was inclosed, and the part on which the maze was formed, consisting of a small field, being in the possession of an individual who had taken no care to preserve this work of antiquity, it was almost obliterated.*

Hutchins's fears were fully justified. Only the hexagonal and feebly developed enclosing earthwork survives today. The Mizmaze itself has gone.

LEAVES

See **The Green Man**.

Magic

Folk-tales and legends are wreathed in magic, as if it is an integral part of the Celtic mindset. It is, even so, difficult to explore and examine ancient magic because those who practised it invariably did so in secret. The **Druids** made a point of not **writing** things down precisely in order to prevent their knowledge from falling into the wrong hands, or the wrong minds. Lewis Spence tired of searching for a book about Celtic magic, and so in frustration wrote one himself. His impression was that "to no race was it given to cultivate a higher or keener sense of spiritual vision or of the fantastically remote than to the Celtic." For evidence, he looked to medieval Celtic literature, but also to comments made by classical authors. Pliny said that the Britons performed "such ceremonies that it might seem possible that she [Britain] taught magic to the Persians." **Diodorus Siculus** believed that Pythagoras received his mystical philosophy from the Celtic **priests** of Gaul.

From the folk-tales, we can tell that Celtic wizards were believed to be able to **shapeshift**. An Irish magus, Fer Fidail, was able to abduct a girl by transforming himself into a woman. Another was able to deceive **Cú Chulainn**, the Irish Achilles, by adopting the form of the Lady Niamh. In the tale *The Children of Lir*, the three children of the god Lir are changed into swans by their stepmother Aeife.

In the Scottish Highlands there are several tales associated with enchantresses who take the form of deer. Some tales entail sex-shifting as well as **shapeshifting**, so that maidens are transformed into **stags.** One transformation is particularly common: a hideous hag can be released from her enchantment only by having sex with a self-denying hero. In one Scottish tale, the hero, Diarmid, meets a hag who begs him for shelter and "a share of his couch." When he agrees to this (initially) distasteful task, she is transformed into a young woman of surpassing beauty.

As well as shapeshifting, **magicians** are alleged to be able to see things a long way off, raise wind, night, snow, or fire, and induce forgetfulness with a mysterious elixir. They could cause streams to dry up and annihilate time. They could cause confusion by throwing a mantle of fog over a landscape. The spoken word of magic, the **spell**, was known among Gaelic-speakers as *Bricht*.

The **Tuatha dé Danann** are surrounded by many magical incidents. They lived for a time in the north of Europe, in four enchanted cities—Falias, Glorias, Finias, and Murias—where four celebrated magicians—Moirfhais, Erus, Arias, and Semias—presided. From the four cities they took ship for northern Britain and Ireland, taking with them four of the most powerful magic talismans. One was the *Lia Fáil*, a crowning-stone that at a coronation roared its approval beneath the feet of a king. The second and third were the **sword** and **spear** of **Lugh**. The fourth was the **Daghda's cauldron**. All of these elements reappear in the (later) stories about the quest for the Holy Grail, which draws on ancient archetypes (*see* **The Grail Quest**). It is interesting that in this episode the rule of four prevails, instead of the more usual **rule of three**.

Celtic magicians were not above exacting revenge by the use of magic. It is said that King Cormac, who lived in Ireland in the second century AD, attempted to suppress magicians. In retaliation, a magician called Maelcen conjured up an evil spirit who placed a fishbone crossways in the king's throat and choked him to death.

Ireland seems to have had a class of sorcerer that was unconnected with the Druids. The wizard Calatin was conspicuous in Irish magical legend. He had 27 monstrous sons. The number is significant: 3 x 3 x 3. There were several fearsome females in the family too. The Clan Calatin went armed with poisoned spears that never failed to reach their mark. In the end Calatin was killed by Cú Chulainn, but Queen Medb sent Calatin's three daughters first to Scotland, then to Babylon, to be educated in magic. When they returned they were expert in every kind of sorcery and Medbh kept them at her side until she could let them loose upon Cú Chulainn, their father's murderer.

The fourteenth-century Welsh poet Dafydd ap Gwilym states that the three most famous sorcerers in Britain were Menw, Eiddeilic the Dwarf, and Math the monarch. Math appears in the Mabinogion tale of *Math, Son of Mathonwy*. The

Welsh Triads mention **Gwydion** and Uther Pendragon as magicians, as well as Rhuddlwm the Dwarf.

The magician's magic wand is a recurring feature in Celtic tales. Druids, we are told, regularly carried staffs made from **yew**, hawthorn, or **rowan** wood. In the story of *Diarmid and Grainne*, a sorcerer called Reachtaire strikes his son with a magic wand, turning him into a "cropped pig, with neither ears nor tail." Wands could also bear witness to the truth. In a tale in the Mabinogion, there is a question as to whether the Lady Arianrhod is a virgin or not. Math insists that she step over his wand. When she does, she promptly gives birth to a child: the infant Lleu Llaw Gyffes. Covered in confusion, Arianrhod tries to leave the room, but before she can she produces another child: Dylan, later to become a sea **god**. In Yorkshire there is a saying that "if a girl strides over a broomhandle she will be a mother before she is a wife." It is possible that this peculiar saying has its roots in a pre-Anglo-Saxon folk-tale: a version of the Arianrhod story.

Not quite a magic wand, and not quite a natural branch, but something in between: the magic silver branch.

This is used by the gods to lure certain favored mortals toward the **Otherworld**. The silver branch might almost be a symbol for the Celtic belief system, which depends on the connection between the everyday world and the Otherworld. It is cut from a magic **apple** tree and produces magic **music** that is impossible to resist. The apples the branch produces supply the pilgrim with both food and drink while he or she stays in the Land of the Gods. The tree from which the branch is cut grows at the door of the Court in the Plain of Honey.

Cormac MacAirt, High King of Ireland, was walking near his palace one day when he saw a youth holding a branch with nine golden apples hanging on it. The youth shook the branch and the apples made sweet mystical music. Anyone who heard it forgot their sorrows— it had the property of lulling people into a magic forgetfulness. Cormac asked to buy it, and was dismayed when the youth told him the price: his wife and children. Nevertheless, he agreed. Cormac's wife and children were horrified to hear that they had been sold, but when Cormac shook the silver branch they forgot what had happened and went off happily with the youth.

A year went by and Cormac wanted to see his wife and children again. He set off to find them. He was enveloped in a magic cloud, where he encountered a **divine couple**; he knew them to be **Manannán**, the sea god, and his wife. Cormac saw his wife and children come into the hall and then Manannán admitted that he was the youth who had taken them away. Cormac and his family slept that night in Manannán's house. When they woke up next morning, they found themselves back in their own hall at **Tara**, with the silver branch beside them.

The silver branch is as important an idea in Gaelic legend as the golden bough is in classical myth: a passport to the Land of the Gods.

Manannán is himself portrayed as a magician. He travels in a magic **boat** made of copper: *Wave-sweeper*.

The medieval tale of *Math, Son of Mathonwy* tells the magical story of the faithless flower-maiden Blodeuwedd (*see* Myth: **The Four Branches of the** *Mabinogi*). Some scholars believe the original mythic tale came from Irish sources and was brought to Wales by Irish migrants.

In the Mabinogion, Math is presented as a magician, a master of omens, who passes his arcane gifts to his nephew Gwydion, and who in turn becomes a master of illusion. Cú Chulainn was schooled by the Druid Cathbad, who made him "skilled in all that was excellent in visions."

Celtic tales are incredibly rich in magical detail, to a point where it is clear that the ancient Celtic way of life must have been saturated in it. Some of it survives in minor beliefs that were perhaps only half-believed: the little quirks of human behavior that we call superstitions.

Some of these superstitions are very long-lived. Like **Julius Caesar**, Strabo described the sacrifice of men to the gods by burning them to death. In a little-noticed aside, he added, "When there is a large yield [of victims for burning] there is forthcoming a large yield from the land as well, as they [the Celts] think." So the burning of human victims was believed to induce a good harvest. One-and-a-half millennia later, in October 1555, Bishop Hugh Latimer was burned to death in an equally terrible kind of **human sacrifice** in front of Balliol College, Oxford. Onlookers in the crowd were heard to say it was a pity it had not happened earlier in the year, as then *it might have saved the crops*. It was the same idea, the same superstition.

My grandparents were country people who lived in a timber-framed cottage in Kent. My grandfather was a farm laborer and my grandmother used to take in laundry for one of the big houses nearby. They were down-to-earth people, but their lives ran according to a host of small customs. One day I watched my grandmother unaccountably opening an umbrella indoors. My grandfather snapped, "Bad luck to put up an umbrella in the house." My grandmother snapped back, "Pah! Superstitious twaddle! It's only bad luck if you stick it over your head."

MEMORY

Long memories are characteristic of Celtic communities. The **Druids** leaned totally on memory. They had to devote themselves to great efforts of **learning**. **Julius Caesar** noted that the Druids "are said to learn by heart a great number of verses." They went so far as to spurn **writing** in order to intensify their dependence

on memory. In Druidry there is a deep and abiding connection between memory and nature. The Earth itself is regarded as remembering everything; it is a witness to history, in a way that we cannot fully appreciate.

On the outskirts of the village of Trellech in Gwent (South Wales) there is a row of three **standing stones**, erected in the Bronze Age. They stand in a line 40 feet (12m) long, two leaning slightly and one leaning rather more. They are also graded, with the shortest stone in the north-east and the tallest in the south-west, which is the direction of the midwinter sunset.

The three stones are remembered in the name of the village, which comes from *tri-llech*, meaning "three stones"—these particular three stones. They are also memorialized in the sundial made in 1689, which is by the church door; the three stones are carved in low relief, with their heights in feet correctly inscribed on them: 8, 10, 14. Above them is written *MAJOR SAXIS*, "the great stones." The mysterious old stones were regarded as an important part of the village identity.

As the stones were still there in the landscape, no great feat of memory was involved, but on the base of the memorial something else was inscribed: *HIC FUIT VICTOR HARALDAS*, "Here Harold was conqueror." This was a distant memory of Harold Godwinsson's little-known campaigns there in 1055 and 1056 and final victory in 1063. It is surprising to find a 600-year-old military victory remembered in a village.

MERMAID

The characteristics of the mermaid were defined in antiquity and have remained unchanged to the present day. She is a beautiful maiden from the waist upward, but with the tail of a fish. She carries a comb and a **mirror** and is to be seen languidly and vainly combing her long hair and singing with irresistible sweetness on a rock on the seashore, where she lures men to their death.

The appearance of mermaids is an omen of misfortune. In spite of their beauty, they are avid for men's lives; they either drown or devour them.

In some of the early Celtic descriptions they are monsters, enormous in size. One sighting de-scribed a mermaid 160 feet (49m) long with hair 18 feet (5m) long and fingers 7 feet (2m) long. Her nose was 7 feet long (2m) too. These precise measurements were possible because her corpse was washed up by the sea. This is said to have happened in AD 887.

Mermaids are typically sea creatures, but they are not averse to freshwater and may swim up **rivers** and haunt freshwater lakes.

The young Laird of Lorntie in Forfarshire was returning home from hunting one evening, with a servant and two greyhounds. As he passed a lake about three miles south of Lorntie, closely hemmed in by woods, he heard a woman screaming. It sounded as if she was drowning. He spurred his horse to the lakeside, and saw a beautiful woman struggling in the water and shouting, "Help, help, Lorntie!"

He dismounted, rushed into the lake, and made to grasp her long, golden hair as she went under. Suddenly he was seized from behind by his servant and pulled out; the servant understood that this was a trick by a water-sprite.

The master was about to beat the servant, but the servant said,

"Wait, Lorntie. Look! The howling woman was, God save us, no other than a mermaid."

The laird instantly understood that his servant was right, and the mermaid herself rose half out of the water. "Lorntie, Lorntie, were it not for your man, I'd have had your heart's blood fry in my pan."

The Irish equivalent of mermaids are called merrow or the Murdhuacha. They are particularly feared because they make their appearance just before storms. But they are gentler than most mermaids, often falling in love with mortal fishermen. There are male merrows too, which are very ugly but amiable and good-natured, ready for a chat with anyone passing.

MERROW

See **Mermaid**.

MINIATURIZATION

(SHRINKAGE)

Miniaturization is a very ancient practice, going right back to the Neolithic period, and probably we should not see it as distinctly Celtic. It is even seen in ancient Egyptian tombs, where miniature agricultural tools were left so that food production could go on in the afterlife.

However, an important aspect of Celtic religion was taking objects, animals, or **people** from the everyday world and transporting them to the **Otherworld**, and one way of doing this was to change the scale. Things could be made unrealistically large or unrealistically small and each type of **exaggeration** took things into the Otherworld. So, miniaturizing objects made them sacred and sublime. The Celts made models of tools and weapons, and this made them appropriate as votive offerings. Miniature axes and **spears** were quite common.

MISTLETOE

A strong life symbol, because it is evergreen and bears fruit in the winter. Other evergreens with winter berries such as holly and ivy are also symbolic, and all three have remained highly symbolic as Christmas decorations. All three have their symbolic origins in pre-Christian solstice customs and beliefs, and are therefore all three "pagan plants," but mistletoe in particular is singled out as being too pagan to hang inside a church.

Mistletoe still retains its strong pagan association, because of the classical description of the **Druids** and their interest in the plant. Why the Druids attached such great significance to it is not known, though it is possible to guess from some of the plant's peculiarities. Apart from being evergreen and bearing fruit in winter, mistletoe does not grow on the ground but in the sky: it is a heaven-sent plant. It also perches on the oak tree, the most sacred and heavily symbolic tree as far as the Druids were concerned. They took their name from the Celtic name of the **oak** tree, *duir*. The oak is a symbolic door to the **Otherworld**.

The custom of kissing under the mistletoe is of unknown antiquity. It suggests that somehow mistletoe is associated with sex and fertility. The association of mistletoe with kissing is so well-established that the little "x" mark on the under side of the berry has become the written shorthand for *kiss*.

In some places in England it is considered unlucky to cut mistletoe at any time other than Christmas. Among its names was All-Heal, because it was thought to cure many different ailments. It was also thought to avert misfortune and even counteract poison.

MONUMENTAL COASTAL SCENERY

The Atlantic Celts inhabited—and still inhabit—a very distinctive landscape: a wild, rocky coastline with high and rugged cliffs. The coastline of Galicia is fretted by deep, wide sea inlets (*rias*) with steep, rocky slopes rising to uplands on each side. It is an intricate coast, with the *rias* creating numerous sheltered natural harbors. The Brittany coast is similar, with many branching inlets that are the remains of ancient **river** valleys drowned by a rising sea; the biggest of the Breton inlets is the Rade de Brest. In the English West Country, it is the same again, with more large branching inlets at Falmouth and Plymouth, and in Wales at Milford Haven. Further north, the inlets are drowned glacial valleys and the land rises very steeply on each side to mountains.

This is dramatic, sometimes melodramatic coastal scenery. In fine weather it is a coastline that encourages exploration, on foot or by sea. In stormy weather it looks like a setting for myth and adventure; it inspires, but in a different way. The interaction of the coast with the sea—the tides, the wind, and the changeable weather—is a continuous drama: one that demands our attention.

THE MURDHUACHA

See **Mermaid**.

N

NANTEOS CUP

See **The Grail Quest**.

NEVER-ENDING PATH

See **Knot**.

NUDITY

Iron Age Celts often went into battle naked. The famous *Dying Gaul* statue is a marble copy of the original bronze statue raised by Attalos I of Pergamon in the third century BC, after he successfully defeated the Celtic Galatians in Asia Minor. The warrior is stripped naked except for a torc round his neck. This powerful image is the most vivid testimony imaginable that Celtic warriors really did go into battle naked.

Various reasons have been suggested. The Roman historians who first saw this were evidently puzzled, and suggested practical reasons: clothing might hamper the warriors' movement, or it might get caught by shrubs or brambles. The warriors were safer taking their clothes off. But nudity exposed the body to all kinds of injury, as well as to the rigors of variable weather conditions. It seems likely that the overriding reason was ritual, part of the fighting frenzy, to show that the warrior was offering his body to death.

Part of the undressing can be explained by a need to make an effective shield. There are many figurines showing naked warriors who have wound their **cloaks** around their left arms to make a cloak-shield. This has been found experimentally to be effective in absorbing the energy of a blow, and can even give protection against a **sword** blow (*see* Places: **Cerne Abbas**).

O

OAK

A sacred tree, the king of the forest, the oak was held in special regard.

This was shared by the Germanic people of northern Europe: it was not exclusively a Celtic belief.

The oak formed a kind of magical trinity with the **ash** and the thorn. The **Druids** were held to regard the oak as a particularly sacred tree. Subsequently, it has been regarded as the **dwelling-place** of **fairies**:

Fairy folks
Are in old oaks.

Some oaks are haunted by sinister oakmen.

Winfrith (St. Boniface) was born in AD 680 in Devon, the son of Anglo-Saxon immigrants from mainland Europe. He entered the Church and seemed to be set on a life of scholarship and teaching, but decided to give this up in order to become a missionary. His idea was to return to his homeland, Saxony, and convert the pagans there to Christianity. His ambition was to create a continuous corridor of Christianity from Rome all the way to the North Sea. Near Geismar, in the heart of what is now Germany, he came across an oak tree that was venerated as Thor's Oak. To the consternation of the oak's pagan devotees, Winfrith took an ax to it, challenging Thor to stop him.

By chance—or was it a miracle?—a thunderstorm broke at that very moment and a bolt of lightning struck the tree, breaking it up and destroying it.

Because Thor had failed to protect his own tree, many of the pagans abandoned Thor and turned to Christ. Winfrith and his followers gathered up the boughs of the sacred tree and made an oratory out of them. It was a classic example of the conversion of a pagan religious center, as well as being a turning-point in the Christian conversion of Germany.

This happened in AD 723.

We can be sure that many **tribes** in central and western Europe similarly venerated oak trees.

OGHAM

The Ogham signs are alphabet characters. In neo-Celtic spirituality, these characters are said to symbolize different species of tree. The first letter of the Ogham alphabet, a horizontal stroke leading to the right from a vertical edge, is B, or Irish-Gaelic *Beithe*, Birch. The birch in turn represents beginning, renewal, and youth.

This is the complete system:

Ogham: Trees and their Symbolic Meaning

B *Beithe* = Birch: beginning, renewal, youth

L *Luis* = Rowan: protection, expression, connection

F *Fern* = Alder: endurance, strength, passion

S *Sail* = Willow: imagination, intuition, vision

H *Huath* = Hawthorn: contradiction, consequence, relationships

D *Duir* = Oak: strength, stability, nobility

T *Tinne* = Holly: action, assertion, objectivity

C *Coll* = Hazel: creativity, purity, honesty

Q *Quert* = Apple: beauty, love, generosity

M *Muin* = Vine: introspection, relaxation, depth

G *Gort* = Ivy: determination, change, patience

NG *Ngetal* = Reed: harmony, health, growth

STR *Straif* = Blackthorn: discipline, control, perspective

R *Ruis* = Elder: transition, evolution, continuation

A	*Ailm* = Fir: clarity, achievement, energy
O	*Onn* = Gorse: transmutation, resourcefulness, exposure
U	*Ur* = Heather: dreams, romance, feelings
E	*Edad* = Poplar or Aspen: victory, transformation, vision
I	*Idad* = Yew: transference, passage, illusion

PHALLUS

A peculiar feature of Celtic religious imagery is the linking of the **head** and the phallus. The Celts venerated the human head, practised **headhunting**, and in their religious **art** often showed the human head on its own. The image was sometimes combined with the phallus as if to emphasize the connection of the human head with potency.

At Bremevaque, in south-western France, a Gaulish image was found roughly carved in stone. It shows a **god** with erect phallus, **spear**, snake, and swastika.

The phallic heads from Eype in Dorset and Broadway in Worcestershire were probably intended to represent local gods, as well as incorporating other ideas.

War gods were depicted naked, because warriors often fought naked (*see* **Nudity**). But they were also often depicted with erect phalluses. One suggested reason is that this was to demonstrate their virility, and by implication strength. There may have been a secondary intention to associate the war god with fertility and prosperity. A god who could ensure victory in battle would bring general prosperity to a **tribe**; a god who enabled cattle-rustlers to win skirmishes also enabled the tribe to acquire more cattle.

The phallus was an image that recurred, sometimes in forms that are less than obvious. The Pillar of **Eliseg** in Wales bears an inscription saying that it was raised by King Concenn of **Powys** to commemorate his great-grandfather. Concenn died in 854, yet the style of the pillar is Mercian-English and tenth or eleventh century rather than ninth, so there is something of an enigma even about its date. The columnar shape of the pillar, however, with a rimmed capital at the top and a flaring base, is phallic.

The Celts were fascinated by visual puzzles and riddles, and by **shapeshifting**, by things turning into other things. A remarkable stone phallic symbol found at Maryport shows a simple disk-shaped face carved into the ventral face of the erect phallus in such a way that the part of the glans remaining visible round the edge looks like two locks of hair. The Maryport Pillar or **Serpent** Stone, as it is known, is a clever piece of ambiguity.

This kind of visual pun is still to be seen in popular religious art; in tourist shops in the Mediterranean it is possible today to buy statuettes of the Virgin Mary which, when turned round, change into erect phalluses. It is a curious, instant switching between the sacred and the profane, and between the sublime and what today looks like a crude sexual joke. But perhaps putting these two faces of humanity side by side in this way is itself a statement of some weight about the nature of the human condition.

Perhaps the most blatant and explicit depiction is a pottery image made in the Nene Valley and probably intended for use by the Roman troops in Britain. A woman is bending forward and massaging a gigantic phallus while looking behind her and pointing at her own genitalia. A man is running toward her with a huge erection and having a premature ejaculation. But phallus images are rarely as explicitly sexual as this. The phallus is normally depicted as if it was religious icon its own right.

Other ambiguous phallic symbols include some of the **Celtic crosses**. A pillar at St. Buryan near Penzance in Cornwall is thought to be an ancient **standing stone** that has been Christianized by having its top shaped into a **sun-wheel**. Without the "limbs" of the cross extending outside the sun circle, the outline looks phallic—and of course the sun-wheel on its own could be a symbol of the Celtic god **Taranis**, and not a Christian symbol at all. The same applies to another Cornish cross: St. Piran's Cross on Penhale Sands (*see* **Exaggeration**; Places: **Cerne Abbas**).

Purse

Gods are sometimes shown holding a purse or moneybag, representing the worldly prosperity they can bring. The purse is a particular attribute of the Celtic **god Mercury**, who often has a purse in one hand and a caduceus or wand in the other. If Mercury is shown with a goat, the purse is frequently shown close to it, perhaps to emphasize that money comes from livestock. Sometimes goddesses carry purses, and the meaning is the same. In some images of couples, one partner carries the purse (implicitly for both), but sometimes they both carry purses, probably for emphasis.

The purse is often held, resting on one knee, if the god or goddess is seated. One statue of **Rosmerta** shows her holding the purse clasped to her breast, while a snake rests its head on the purse as if feeding from it (*see* **Serpent**).

The purse is often large, and always bulging with coins. A relief of **Cernunnos** shows him sitting cross-legged with a big bag of coins in his lap. Another image of Cernunnos shows the (possibly same) moneybag spilling a cascade of coins toward the greedy worshiper.

In some images the symbols seem to elide with one another. A snake feeds from a purse in one image, and from a dish in another. Some images clearly show the moneybag brimming with coins, and others show coins in a dish.

R

Ram-horned Snake

Snakes are a symbol of the Earth. The snake-limbed monsters on the Jupiter columns show that they belong to and represent the Earth (*see* **Sky Horseman**). Snakes are also believed to be guardians. In Irish tradition, Conall Cernach has to deal with a snake that guards his enemy's fort. But seen from the enemy's point of view, the snake is acting as a protector, and this protecting role is a major aspect of the snake. Snakes are protectors against sickness, against war, and against the terrors of death.

Adding the ram's horn to the image of a snake takes the image out of the realm of the everyday. The image is mainly a Gaulish one, but there are some in Britain. The **Gundestrup cauldron** shows the snake as the nature-**god Cernunnos'** companion on one plate. On another plate the ram-horned snake heads a procession. The snake is often associated with Cernunnos. In an image from Cirencester, the legs of the god appear to have turned into two snakes, whose heads rear up toward two **purses** near the god's head. In a Gaulish image from Sommerécourt (Haute Marne), Cernunnos is accompanied by a goddess who is feeding a ram-horned snake from a basket resting on her knee; the god too has a snake. A wooden sculpture found at a Celtic township at Crêt Chatelard (Loire) shows Cernunnos squatting, with a ram-horned snake sliding down his arm.

There is even a ram-horned snake in the collection of Celtic rock carvings at **Val Camonica**. There is an image of stag-horned god with two torcs, and he is accompanied by a ram-horned snake.

The associations of the ram-horned snake show that it was a symbol of prosperity and plenty. Its presence with or even held by the god Cernunnos, a fertility image, confirms that it had a fertility role. The ram was a fertility symbol in the Mediterranean world, so the ram's horns may have been a borrowing from the Mediterranean.

One significant image comes from Lypiatt Park in Gloucestershire, where a ram-horned snake coils itself around a small, stone **altar**. On the focus of the stone is a **wheel** symbol that connects the **serpent** with the sky. This links with the Jupiter columns, where negative, Earth-bound forces are represented by a creature with snake limbs. The sacred symbols of Underworld, fertility, and **healing** are fused.

RAVEN

Carrion birds are prominent in Celtic religion. Because they consume dead things, they are associated with death and the journey to the Underworld.

The Mabinogion shows ravens as beneficent beings of the **Otherworld**, associated with **Rhiannon**.

On the other hand, in Irish legend, ravens are usually connected with **warfare** and destruction. The stories constantly tell of war **goddesses** such as the Mórrígan and Badb **shapeshifting** into ravens or crows.

Raven goddesses were able to foresee the disastrous outcomes of battles. This ability to foretell the future was used by Irish **Druids** in the process of their auguries.

In relation to the hero **Cú Chulainn**, ravens were malevolent creatures of the Otherworld.

RIVER

Rivers are regarded as sacred. They are fed by **water** that **springs** mysteriously from the Underworld. They are also in continuous motion, like living things. They are a focus for religious feeling and for offerings (*see* Places: **Source de la Seine**).

ROWAN

The rowan is the emblem tree for the second letter of the **Ogham** alphabet, *Luis.* By tradition, the **sacred groves** of the **Druids** were groves of **oak** or rowan.

Rowan trees flourish in mountain country, so the rowan is sometimes called the Lady of the Mountain. It is also known as witchwood, which reflects its role as a protector against **witchcraft** and **fairies**. Witches themselves have viewed the rowan as a **magic** tree, making use of its wood, leaves, and distinctive bright vermilion berries in their **spell**-casting.

In Scotland, the rowan is seen as giving protection against

mischievous spirits, because of its red berries:

Rowan, lammer [amber] and red thread
Pits witches to their speed.

Rowan is one of the woods that may be used for making wands. Two rowan twigs tied together with red thread to make a cross may be used as a symbol of protection; this charm might be put over a door to ward off evil or over a baby's cot to prevent the child being stolen by fairies (*see* Myths: **Redeemed from Fairyland**).

Rule of Three

(triplism)

Multiplying an image was a simple way of emphasizing it. In Britain and Gaul the most common way of doing this was to multiply an image by three. This is sometimes called triplism. Three was a Celtic magic number.

Showing deities in threes is not restricted to any one **god** or goddess. Some images are described and defined by their triplism, such as the Three Mothers, the *Tres Matres* (*see* Religion: **Mother Goddess**). There was also a Triple **Mars**: a stone tablet found in a Roman well at Lower Slaughter in Gloucestershire shows three identical **war gods** in a row. They conspicuously wear tunics and boots, like Roman soldiers, and carry round shields. They also, curiously, have a great deal of hair, in a style that looks like a mid-eighteenth-century wig.

It is possible that where the three-fold image was used a great deal, as with the Three Mothers, there may have been some symbolism in the number three. Perhaps the three images stood for life, death, and re-birth, to remind us of the cycle of life. Perhaps they stood for three phases or aspects of a lifespan: childhood, adulthood, and old age.

King **Arthur** was said to have fought for three days and three nights at the Battle of **Badon**. This must have been an **exaggeration** and cannot be taken as literally true. It meant only "a long time."

Perhaps the most interesting literary use of the rule of three comes in the Welsh Triads. These are verses or summary stories in which three of a kind are described. One Triad is *The Three Very Famous Prisoners of the Island of Britain.* It lists three long-forgotten Dark Age celebrities, then adds:

...and there was one who was more famous than all three: he was three nights in the prison of Kaer Oeth and Anoeth, and three nights in the prison of Wenn Pendragon, and three nights in the magic prison beneath the flagstone of Echymeint. This famous prisoner was Arthur. And the same youth released him from each of these three prisons, Goreu vab Custennin, his cousin.

Another triad reads, "The Three Red Ravagers of the Island of Britain: Rhun, son of Beli, Lleu Skilful Hand, and Morgant the Wealthy. But there was one who was a Red Ravager greater than all three: Arthur was his name." (*See* **Arthur**.)

S

SERPENT

One of the most mysterious ancient Celtic symbols. Little understood, it seems to have stood for fertility. Because snakes emerge unpredictably from crevices in the rock, they are visitors from the Underworld (*see* **Ram-horned Snake**).

Snakes occupied a similar, and similarly mysterious, place in the Bronze Age Minoan belief system.

SHAMROCK

A modern Irish emblem of Ireland itself. The four-leafed clover, a relation of the shamrock, is said to bring good luck.

SHAPESHIFTING

Via shapeshifting, **people**, and more particularly **gods and goddesses**, were able to change into animals, and vice versa. People were also able to transform their own appearance deliberately, for example warriors pulled grotesque faces to make themselves more frightening in battle. The Celts took this to extremes. The description in the Irish folk-tale the *Táin bó Cúalnge* may exaggerate, but it gives an idea of what warriors were trying to achieve. The hero **Cú Cuchlainn** mounted his scythed battle **chariot**:

Then took place the first twisting fit and rage of the royal hero Cú Chulainn, so that he made a terrible, many-shaped, wonderful, unheard-of thing of himself. His flesh trembled about him like a pole against the torrent or like a bulrush against the stream... He made a mad whirling-feat of his body inside his hide... He gulped down one eye into his head so that it would be hard work if a wild crane succeeded in drawing it out to the middle of his cheek from the rear of his skull... The Hero's Light stood out on his forehead, so that it was as long and as thick as a warrior's whetstone, till he got furious handling the shields, thrusting out the charioteer, destroying the hosts... When now this contortion had been completed in Cú Chulainn then the hero of valour sprang into his scythed war chariot with its iron sickles.

An unusual **coin** from north-western France shows a **horse** with a gigantic human **head**, as if the horse is turning into a god. Behind the horse god is a suggestion of a chariot and a charioteer, holding onto the monster's reins. The **gold** coin was minted by the Aulerci Diablintes **tribe** in the first century BC.

There are stories that indicate that a belief in the transmigration of souls was widespread in Wales; the departing soul went into the body of an animal (*see* **Hare**).

SHEELA-NA-GIGG

This is a grotesque naked female figure with exaggerated genitalia. She seems to be the female counterpart to a whole **tribe** of male images also with hugely exaggerated genitals (*see* **Exaggeration**; Places: **Cerne Abbas**).

The sheela-na-gigg is usually carved in stone. She is invariably squatting, and reaches down with both hands to pull the lips of her vulva wide apart. The exact meaning of this is lost to us, but it is possible to speculate. The figure is sexual only in the sense that it emphasizes genitals; it is in no way erotic. No attempt is made to show the figure as attractive—just the opposite. The image is repellent, so it may be that the intention is exactly that: to frighten off. People today still use sexual language aggressively, to frighten or intimidate others; the sheela-na-gig may have been designed to ward off evil.

Curiously, the image was borrowed by early church architecture; there are gargoyles and grotesque corbels built into Norman churches in Britain with sheel-na-gigg carvings. It may be that, as in earlier centuries, the Church was acknowledging the eccentricities of local pre-Christian beliefs and customs.

SHIELD KNOT

The **triquetra** is perhaps the simplest **knot**, with just three loops; the shield knot is the next simplest, with four.

The effect is to make a design with four "ears" marking the corners of a square space in the center. It is a protecting charm, with its edge marked by a never-ending path.

The shield knot is found in many **cultures**; it is not exclusive to the Celts.

SKY FALLING DOWN

Solemn oaths might be sworn under the sanction of the **sun** or moon or some other elemental part of the cosmos (*see* **Vow**). But if such oaths were broken, terrible retribution might follow. The worst fear was that the sky might fall down.

In the Irish folk-tale *The Cattle Raid of Cuailnge*, the Ulstermen are rebuked by the severed **head** of Sualtaimh for coming too sluggishly to the aid of the hero **Cú Chulainn** as he alone defends the province. Conchobar, King of the Ulstermen, answers the head:

"A little too loud is that cry, for the sky is above us and the sea all around us, but unless the sky with its showers of stars fall upon the surface of the earth or unless the ground burst open in an earthquake, or unless the fish-abounding, blue-bordered sea come over the face of the earth, I shall bring back every cow to its byre and enclosure, every woman to her own abode and dwelling, after victory in battle and combat and contest."

This was a mighty oath the king was swearing on behalf of his **people**. If he and his people did not do as he promised, natural catastrophe would overwhelm them.

Similarly, when the inhabitants of the Adriatic coast were asked by Alexander the Great what they feared most, they said they feared no one; their only fear was that the sky might fall down on them.

SKY HORSEMAN

The **wheel god** on horseback represents a particular aspect of the god: the dominion of life over death. Where he is shown with a **wheel**, he usually holds it in his left hand as if it were a shield; his wrist passes between the spokes to hold onto the reins of his **horse.** More distinctive still are the monsters under the horse's hooves. They represent the dark forces of the Earth and Underworld, and the **sky god** is riding them down, trampling them underfoot. This is a very specific scene from Celtic myth.

The more sophisticated carvings at first sight look like classical equestrian groups, and they are found only in the western prov-inces of the Roman Empire, but they are heavy with mythic significance and symbolism. Above all, they were raised in honor of the Celtic sky god. They were well and truly raised, too, on top of lofty columns, and there were about 150 of them. These "Jupiter columns" or "Jupiter-Giant columns" were very imposing monuments. The one that stood at Hausen-an-der-Zaber near Stuttgart has been reconstructed and it looks like a miniature Nelson's Column.

The stone base was eight-sided or four-sided, displaying images of gods to do with the **sun**, moon, and planets, and inscriptions to Jupiter or Juno. On top of the plinth is a tall pillar decorated with foliage patterns to suggest that it represents a tree: the Hausen column was decorated with **oak** leaves and acorns, the oak being sacred to Jupiter in the Roman world.

The symbolism of the pillar-tree is interesting in itself. Possibly there were early, crude versions made of wood, which in turn were based on even earlier sacred trees. The column may represent a pillar to support the sky, or it may be there to hoist the sculpture of the sky god as near as possible to the celestial world. Or it could symbolize the link between the two worlds, like the beanstalk in *Jack and the Beanstalk*. On top is a Corinthian capital, which supports the sculpture of the sky horseman trampling the monster. The overall height of the monument at Merten was 49 feet (15m).

The sculpture at the top is the key to the monument's meaning. The image is a horseman riding over a humanoid monster whose legs are in the form of snakes. This may ultimately reflect depictions of a Greek myth in which the Olympian gods do battle with the earthly Titans, as the Titans are shown with snake limbs. But the classical battle never shows a horse. The horse is purely Celtic, and is intended to show that the rider is the sun god or sky god. Rider and rearing horse together show Jupiter as Celtic sky lord, the quintessence of sky, light, goodness, and the life-force. Jupiter is in a dualistic conflict with his opposite: an earthbound, dark, and probably evil monster. The dualism may incorporate ideas of good and evil, light and darkness, day and night, higher and lower aspects of mythic beings, and perhaps even life and death. Seen in this way, the set-piece drama shown on the Jupiter column is a major key to Celtic religious thought.

A Jupiter column once stood in the Roman town of Cirencester. A formal inscription has survived that records its restoration in the Roman period, but "under the old religion." It was rebuilt by a governor of the province of Britannia Prima, Lucius Septimius, a citizen of Rheims. Diocletian did not divide Britain into four provinces until AD 296, so the restoration must be later than that. The interesting reference to "the old religion" may refer to the pagan revival that happened during the reign of the Emperor Julian in the middle of the fourth century AD. The very finely carved Corinthian capital of the Cirencester column survives.

But it must be their ambitious size that strikes us most about the Jupiter columns. They must, incidentally, have been expensive to build. They now exist only in a fragmentary state, and the remains show signs of deliberate vandalism. It may well be that Christians deliberately set out to topple and deface these very conspicuous monuments to pagan beliefs.

SPEAR

The **magic** spear in Celtic lore usually has to be forged by a certain smith for a certain purpose. Lleu, for example, might be slain only with a spear that has taken a whole year to make, and that has only been worked at on a Sunday, during the time when Mass is celebrated. Because he is divine, he is magically protected in a number of ways; he cannot be killed on foot or on horseback; he may not be killed indoors or out in the open. The only way he envisages that he can be killed is in a bath on a riverbank, with a thatched, round roof above the bath; he would have to place one foot on the back of a goat and the other on the edge of the bath. Then, and only in that position, might he be killed with the spear (*see* Myths: ***The Four Branches of the* Mabinogi**).

The smith himself is invariably an uncanny figure, and it must be suspected that the character is a borrowing from Greek or Roman mythology, where the smith-god Hephaistos or Vulcan cuts a very similar figure. The ancestry of the cunning smith god probably reaches right back to the Bronze Age, where the first creations of metal objects—and **swords** and spears in particular—must have seemed pure magic.

The Irish smith-god **Gobhniu** prepares the spear that kills Balor, the Fomorian Cyclops god. It is **Lugh**, the grandson, who plunges the spear into the single eye of Balor, in revenge for the killing of his father, MacKineely.

Lugh, the **sun** god, owns a magic spear that seems to symbolize the sun's rays. His spear has a life of its own, and a thirst for blood. It can only be kept from killing by soaking its point in an infusion of poppy leaves. When the day of battle comes, the spear may be lifted from this narcotic anesthetic brew. Then it shouts and lashes itself into a frenzy, giving off flashes of flame. Once freed, it hurls itself into the enemy ranks, dealing death in an orgy of slaughter).

SPELL

The natural and spirit world can to some limited extent be controlled by chanting spells. This is the magical equivalent of prayer. Several seventeenth-century manuscripts offer **magic** spells for gaining power over **fairies**: some to call them up, and some to get rid of them—a kind of pest control:

An excellent way to get a Fayrie, but for myselfe I call Margaret Barrance but this will obtaine any one that is not already bound.

First get a broad square christall or Venus glasse in length and breadth 3 inches, then lay that glasse or christall in the bloud of a white henne 3 Wednesdays or 3 Fridays: then take it out and wash it with holy aqua and fumigate it: then take 3 hazle sticks or wands of a yeare growth, pill them fayre and white, and make so longe as you write the spiritts name, or fairies name, which you call 3 times, one every sticke being made flatt one side, then bury them under some hill whereas you suppose fairies haunt, the Wednesday before you call her, and the Friday followinge take them uppe and call hir at 8 or 3 or 10 of the clocke which be good plannetts and howres for that turne: but when you call, be in cleane Life and turne thy face towards the east, and when you have her bind her to that stone or Glasse.

Here, much easier, so long as you can speak Latin, is a call to the Queen of the Fairies:

Micol o tu micoll regina pigmeorum deus Abraham: deus Isaac: deus Jacob; tibi benedicat et omnia fausta danet et concedat Modo venias et mihi moremgem veni. Igitur o tu micol in nomine Jesus veni cito ters quatur beati in qui nomini Jesu veniunt veni Igitur O tu micol in nomine Jesu veni cito qui sit omnis honor laus et gloria in omne aeturnum. Amen Amen.

SPIRAL

An ancient symbol that was important throughout the evolution of the Celtic **culture**. The oldest spirals that exist in the British Isles are those that decorate the Boyne passage graves. Spirals were carefully and elaborately carved into the huge stone at the entrance to the **Newgrange** passage grave 5,000 years ago.

Another stone, deep in the heart of the tomb, was carved with another double-triple spiral, very like the one at the entrance. The central tomb chamber where the second double-triple spiral was placed was lit by the **sun**, just once a year, at the midwinter sunrise, when the rays of the sun were allowed in through a specially made roofbox, a slot above the blocked door.

Similar complex multiple spirals were carved into the stones forming the chamber walls of the Gavrinis passage grave in Brittany.

The spiral is a long-enduring symbol, a true archetype, and one that has many meanings. The outward-moving path, endlessly expanding as it goes out, suggests limitless possibilities. It also symbolizes a journey, inward or outward, and perhaps both. Jung saw the spiral as a symbol of psychic journeying, inward toward the center of the self, then out again in order to function in the everyday world. It became, in the twentieth century at least, a symbol of *reculer pour mieux sauter*, a favorite psychic healing technique of Jung, and of the self-discovery to which it leads.

The spiral is the simplest form of **labyrinth**, one in which no choices

are presented beyond the choice to travel. It is a single path, a path to the center and back.

Other spirals lead on from one to another. The triple spiral that is the central focus of the Newgrange passage grave is in fact a triple double-spiral: each spiral has a path to lead you in and a second path to lead you out again; that takes you by way of an S-bend to the next spiral, where the same thing happens again. This is a very highly ordered never-ending path: a maze to make you giddy. What the makers of it meant is probably unknowable. But it is at least certain that this visually powerful symbol was an intentional design, because it was repeated exactly on the huge entrance stone at the outer end of the entrance passage, and the Newgrange spirals meant journeying, perhaps the never-ending journeying of the sun and also the possibly-never-ending journeying of the human spirit (*see* **Labyrinth**, **Triskele**).

STAG

The stag symbolizes the spirit of the forest. It bears antlers that are themselves treelike, so the beast actually seems to carry the forest around on its head. It is agile, fast, and sexually vigorous, so it represents in itself the vigor of self-regenerating nature. The mysterious shedding of the antlers each autumn and their regrowth in the spring emphasize the general seasonal cycle of the forest, which sheds its foliage each autumn and grows new each spring.

Stag symbolism is to the fore on the **Gundestrup cauldron**. The stag-**horned god Cernunnos** is shown with a stag beside him. On another vessel, a **god** is shown gripping a stag in each hand.

Stag figurines in bronze are not very common, but there is no doubt that the stag cult was widespread. A stone found in Luxembourg shows a stag with a stream of **coins** coming out of its mouth. A carved stone from Rheims shows

Cernunnos with a stag and a bull, drinking from a stream of coins. The imagery is supposed to convey that stags are associated with prosperity. But in most places, the stag is firmly connected with hunting. In northern Britain, the stag was associated with the hunter-god **Cocidius.** At Colchester, the god Silvanus Callirius (**Silvanus** the woodland king) was associated with a stag at a **shrine**.

At Le Donon in the Vosges, there was a mountain shrine where a nature god or hunter god was worshiped. He was depicted in stone, clothed in an animal pelt hung with fruit; he rested his hand in a gesture of benediction on the antlers of a stag standing beside him. The images of forest and hunting come face to face with images of benign prosperity. The relationship between hunter and hunted is close, almost affectionate in nature, and like no other Celtic image it shows the Celtic mindset regarding the relationship between humanity and nature.

A sculpture of a **divine couple** made by the **Aedui tribe** shows the god and goddess presiding over the animal kingdom. They are seated side by side with their feet resting on two stags below them.

The god offers a goblet of wine to a **horse** beside him, while the goddess symmetrically offers a drink to a second horse that she is caressing. This region of Burgundy was a horse-breeding area. It was also an area where the stag-antlered Cernunnos (virtually a stag god) was worshiped. The stag was a shorthand image for nature and the world of animals.

The antlers of the stag are a reminder of the potential violence of nature, of the fact that nature can do **people** harm, but they are also attributes of mainly gentle, shy, and benign creatures who are not hostile to people. They are also symbols of the masculine fertility of the rutting stag and of the fertility of nature in general.

STANDING STONES

The practice of raising standing stones began very early in Brittany, perhaps as far back as 4000 BC, and spread rapidly to the other regions of the Atlantic Celts—and beyond. Standing stones became a widespread feature across a large area of western Europe.

The simplest type of monument is a naturally weathered stone tipped up on end into a supporting pit and held in place by some packing boulders in the pit around the base. In France these are called *menhirs*, "long stones." In Britain they are called standing stones.

Sometimes the standing stone acts as a territorial marker, and sometimes (especially in later antiquity) as a grave marker. They may be places where sacrifices were made. In some places they acted as foresights for alignments on cols or hilltops on the horizon where a particular astronomical event, such as a midwinter sunset, might be observed. Many such locations have been identified, and there were evidently used to mark and honor certain landmarks in the calendar.

The most impressive standing stone in Britain is the Rudston Monolith (monolith = single stone) in Yorkshire. It is 26 feet (8m) high and is believed to weigh more than 80 tons (70 tonnes).

Its dominance in the landscape has been destroyed by the building of the parish church right next to it. Whether this was a deliberate attempt to steal the ancient monument's thunder can never be known, but it was common for churches to be built in places that were already a focus for communal worship and ritual. Christian missionaries were explicitly advised to do this by Pope Gregory.

What is no longer visible at Rudston is the big ceremonial landscape that surrounded the tall monolith. There were no avenues of standing stones leading to it— there were too few suitable stones available in the area—but there were three avenues marked by earth banks, called cursus monuments. These huge processional ways converged on the Rudston Monolith.

The name "Rudston" comes from *rud stan*, meaning "cross-stone." It would seem that at some stage, perhaps in the early Middle Ages, some well-meaning Chris-

tians understood that the stone was a leftover from the pagan past and perched a cross or a cross-beam on top to render it harmless. Some Breton menhirs had their tops carved into crosses to Christianize them.

What we see here, and at other standing-stone sites such as Carnac in Brittany, or Stenness in Orkney, or Avebury in Wiltshire, is a profound relationship developing between **people** and landscape.

Single standing stones are often hard to interpret. By 3200 BC, the practice had developed into the laying out of stone circles, such as Avebury in Wiltshire or the Ring of Brodgar in Orkney. Lines of stones were laid out to mark a ceremonial path across the landscape. Sometimes two lines were set up to make an avenue. Two winding stone avenues led to the great stone circle at Avebury: one to the west entrance and one to the south entrance; these were evidently ceremonial ways.

This architecture of great stones was developed still further to make a whole family of stone tombs. Three stone slabs might be raised to make three sides of a square, then a fourth slab might be slid on top to make a roof. This burial chamber might then be covered by an earth mound with an entrance on one side. If the grave mound needed to be big and imposing, the tomb chamber might be given an entrance passage. This was made by raising two rows of vertical slabs and then adding a slab roof. The passage grave Maes Howe in Orkney was designed in this way, but with a variation: the four chamber slabs were erected in the corners and the sides were made of drystone walling using large, flat slabs of sandstone.

Sun

The sun is often represented by a **wheel**. The journey of the sun across the sky needed **horses** as well as a **chariot** with wheels, so the horse itself was probably seen as a sun symbol. Celtic **coins** carry horse and sun signs together.

The **goddess Nehalennia** had a solar aspect. One image of her from Domburg shows her wearing a solar amulet. An **altar** dedicated to her from the same site has a radiant sun depicted at its top. **Mother goddesses** too were sometimes accompanied by a sun wheel, so we should not be too quick to identify deities with sun symbols as sun deities. The link may be subtler.

Sucellus, the hammer god, is sometimes shown decorated with sun symbols, suggesting some kind of association with the sun. This may be a more general association with sky, as if the hammer is telling us that Sucellus is the thunder god. Thunder comes from the heavens, where the sun also is.

Sword

Celtic tales contain many references to **magic** swords. The Irish sea god, **Manannán mac Lir,** owned no fewer than three such magic weapons, named The Retaliator (or Answerer), The Great Fury, and The Little Fury.

Another Irish deity, Nuada of the Silver Hand, was the owner of a sword known as The Silver Hand, and which features in the stories about the **Tuatha dé Danann.**

Finn MacCoul, hero of *Finn MacCoul and the Bent Gray Lad*, had a notable sword, made specially for him by his grandfather. Its edge was so sharp that no second blow was ever needed. In its forging, it had been tempered with the blood "of a living thing"—a **dog** (*see* **The Grail Quest**).

According to the Arthurian romances, Lancelot's magic sword is called Arondight.

Then there is Excalibur, the ever-famous Otherworldly sword of **Arthur**, given to him by the Lady of the Lake and ultimately returned to the lake after his final battle was fought.

T

TREASURE

In the days before the Anglo-Saxons arrived and divided up the Island of Britain, and before the island was converted to Christianity, there were, it is said, "Thirteen Treasures of the Island of Britain." These are mentioned in various medieval documents included in *The Red Book of Hergest*, which was written in about 1400, and *The Black Book of Carmarthen*, which contains poetry of the ninth–twelfth centuries, much of it written in the voice of **Myrddin**.

These are the Treasures of Britain:

1 The Horn of Bran of the North. It will supply you with whatever drink you wish for.

2 Dyrnwyn, the **magic Sword** of Rhydderch the Generous. Dyrnwyn means "White Hilt." When an honorable man draws this sword, it flames from tip to hilt.

3 The Hamper of Gwyddno Long Shanks. Food for one man may be put inside it. When the hamper is reopened, there is enough food for 100 men.

4 The **Chariot** of Morgan the wealthy. Step into the chariot and it will take wherever you wish to go—instantly.

5 The Halter of Clyddno Eiddyn. If a man fixes this to the foot of his bed, whatever horse he wishes for will be there by morning.

6 The Knife of Llawfrodedd the horseman. This will serve for 24 men sitting at table.

7   The **Cauldron** of Dyrnwch the **Giant**. If meat for a coward is put into the cauldron, it will never boil, but meat for a brave man will boil immediately. So a coward may be recognized at once.

8   The Whetstone of Tudwal Tudglyd. If a brave man sharpens his blade on the whetstone and then draws blood from his enemy, the enemy will die. If a coward sharpens his blade on it, his opponent will be unharmed.

9   The **Cloak** of Padarn. A test of breeding: when a nobly born man puts on the cloak, it fits him perfectly; when a low-born man puts on the cloak, it will not fit.

10 The Crock and

11 Dish of Rhgenydd the Cleric. Whatever food you wish for is found in these bowls.

12 The Chess Board of Gwenddolau, son of Ceidio. If the pieces are set they will play by themselves. The board is made of **gold** and the chess pieces are made of silver.

13 The Mantle of **Arthur** in Cornwall. Whoever is under the mantle cannot be seen, and yet he is able to see everything.

The manuscripts say that the keepers of the Treasures met "in the North." At this meeting, Myrddin asked that the Thirteen Treasures be handed to him. The keepers were reluctant, but in the end agreed, on condition that he obtained the Horn of Bran of the North; if Myrddin could acquire the horn, they would hand over the other 12 treasures.

Myrddin took the Thirteen Treasures of the Island of Britain to the Castle of Glass, where they remain to this day. No one knows where this castle is, though it is said that the Welsh **goddess** Arianrhod lives in a castle of glass hidden in Snowdonia; that is where she spins the threads that make the web of life, so perhaps the Thirteen Treasures are in Snowdonia.

It is said that if the Thirteen Treasures can be brought back together again in this mortal world, then the Mab Darogan, the Son of Prophecy, a Celtic Messiah, will arise.

TREE OF LIFE

Trees had a major symbolic importance in the ancient Celtic mindset, being associated with the bursting forth of life. Trees in the northwest European spring look like frozen fountains of leaves; they are the clearest image of goodness drawn up out of the Earth and made available for our use.

A very primitive sculpture from Caerwent, a purely Celtic work found in a pit near the Romano-Celtic temple, shows a **mother goddess** holding in front of her a palm or conifer branch in one hand and a small fruit in the other. The palm could represent victory over death if this was a Roman artwork, but the crudity of the carving implies that it was made locally, and few Britons living in South Wales would have seen a palm tree.

Cernunnos, the nature god, is naturally shown with a tree, to symbolize his forest home and that of his **stags**. The symbolism goes one layer deeper, though, as the stag's antlers are treelike in form, and trees seem to have been the model for the form of the beast. There is an empathic bond between the animals and their environmental setting that fascinates the Celtic mind.

The god **Esus** is shown chopping down a **willow** tree in a symbolic enactment of the seasonal death of vegetation.

The symbolism of trees has been taken up and developed in neo-Celtic beliefs, in which specific human values are attributed to specific tree species. The idea is that through meditation we can be absorbed into the essence of a tree, tap into its energies, and by doing so expand our capacities as human beings. It is a way of engaging and bonding with nature (*see* **Ash Tree**, **Ogham**).

TRIPLE-HORNED BULL

The three-horned **bull**, an essentially Gaulish creature, is shown in stone or bronze. About 35 have been found in Gaul and only six in Britain. The silvered bronze bull from the **shrine** at **Maiden Castle** has traces of three female figures who were originally riding on his back. A remarkable find at Willingham was a three-horned bull decorating a scepter-terminal, together with images relating to the **sky god**.

The tripling of the horn may be explained in different ways. Triplism, or "threeness," is a powerful symbol of intensification. Horns are strong fertility symbols. Multiplying that fertility by three is a way of exaggerating the statement's power. The three horns also serve to pull the image out of the realm of everyday objects and events. (*See* **Exaggeration**, **Rule of Three**).

TRIQUETRA

The triquetra is the simplest possible **knot**. It is three intersecting lenses that connect in such a way that they are formed from a single continuous line. It is another never-ending path, like the **labyrinth** or the **spiral**.

The triquetra symbol is very common in Celtic **art**, especially in metalwork and illuminated manuscripts such as *The Book of Kells*. It was not seen in Celtic art until the seventh century, however, and is by no means unique to Celtic artwork. It is found on northern European rune stones and early Germanic coins. The symbol had a pagan religious meaning and it may be significant that it is similar to the Valknut, a symbol of the **god** Odin.

The triquetra is rarely allowed to stand on its own in medieval Celtic art, which has led some to say that it was probably never a primary symbol of belief. Its main role appears to have been to fill a space or as an ornament within more complex compositions. In knotwork panels, the triquetra often appears as a design motif. But these observations overlook the fact that the triquetra is a very simple design that incorporates both the **rule of three** and the never-ending path. In Celtic minds this must have given it a certain power.

In the Christian period, the triquetra has seen use as a symbol of the Holy Trinity, especially in and since the nineteenth-century Celtic revival.

A very common development of the triquetra is its combination with a circle. The circle emphasizes the unity of the combination of the three elements of the triquetra. As such, it makes a perfect symbol of the Holy Trinity, the Three-in-One and One-in-Three, "God in three persons." In neo-pagan beliefs, the triquetra is seen as symbolizing the three stages of the Triple Goddess: maiden, mother, and crone.

In modern times, the triquetra is often used as a pattern in jewelry, such as a necklace or ring. Here is it seen as representing three promises inherent in a relationship, such as to love, honor, and protect. The knot is commonly engraved on wedding rings. In neopagan groups, especially Celtic Reconstructionist groups, the triquetra is used to represent one of the many triplets or triads in the belief system, such as the three-fold division of the world into land, sea, and sky, or one of the Triple Goddesses (*see* **Labyrinth**, **Rule of Three**, **Spiral**).

TRISKELE

(TRIPLE SPIRAL)

The triple **spiral** occurs as a religious symbol in many early **cultures**. As far as the Atlantic Celts are concerned, it makes its appearance in around 3200 BC in the carvings on the megalithic tombs in the Boyne Valley in Ireland. The most famous example is the double-triple spiral carved into a stone right at the heart of the great megalithic passage grave of **Newgrange**.

Each of the three spirals consists of two lines. The symbolism may be simple: one path in and the other out. With any **labyrinth,** there has to be a way in and a way out, and the spiral is the simplest form of labyrinth. The triple spirals at Newgrange date from the time of the passage grave's construction, 5,000 years ago. So the triskele has been part of the Celtic culture of the Atlantic **west** for a very long time.

It is possible to manufacture all kinds of symbolism for the triple spiral. It was in use in ancient Greece. It was in use as an ancient symbol of Sicily. Pliny the Elder attributed the origin of the Sicilian triskele to the triangular shape of the island. This is possible, but it is an explanation that will not do elsewhere, for instance in Neolithic Ireland.

In the early Christian, post-Roman world, the device was easily adopted as a symbol of the Trinity. It must be suspected, though, that usually when it was used in illuminated Gospels in the eighth and ninth centuries AD it was for the convenience of its shape—a natural space-filler between the curves of the main designs and the corners of the page.

Celtic neo-pagans also use the triskele symbol to represent a range of triplisms. It is tailor-made to represent any of the many triads in the Celtic tradition (*see* **Rule of Three**).

WATER

There is a fascination among the Celts with water in all its forms: the sea, lakes, bogs, **rivers**, streams, and **springs**. Water is necessary and essential. People need to drink it and cattle need to drink it; it is essential to make crops grow and keep pastures green. But water can also cause problems. A heavy rainstorm can batter down a cereal crop and a storm at sea can sink ships and drown sailors. There are strong water-veneration and water-propitiation traditions in both Britain and Gaul.

One manifestation of this veneration is the age-old custom of dropping offerings to **gods** into water. The Battersea shield and the Waterloo Bridge **helmet** were both very valuable metal objects, high-status objects, that were dropped into the Thames River as offerings. This custom went on throughout the Bronze and Iron Ages. The practice continues even to the present day, on a very small scale, with the tradition of leaving coins in wishing wells.

The **Otherworld** was seen literally as being underground, so springs were seen as sacred portals: places where water passes from the Otherworld into this world. St. Augustine's Well at **Cerne Abbas** was probably a pagan **sacred spring** that was later Christianized. There are many superstitions surrounding the spring, and visitors still throw the occasional coin into it.

Some years ago, I met Lady Vickers when she was responsible for cleaning St. Augustine's Well and she showed me two coins that she had retrieved from the spring. One was a 1950s threepenny piece. The other looked as if it might have the bust of a Roman emperor on one side and a classical temple on the other. This was potentially an exciting discovery, as it conceivably might be evidence that the spring was visited in the Roman-British period. Initially

it was identified by Chichester Museum as a fourth-century AD Roman coin. Closer examination revealed the word "TED" on the reverse. Dr. Howgego of the Ashmolean Museum in Oxford conclusively identified the coin for me as modern American, a ten-cent piece dating from around 1960, showing Abraham Lincoln on one side and the Lincoln Memorial on the other. The corroded and lime-encrusted condition of the coin made it look much older than it actually was; the alleged healing properties of the water prematurely aging it 1,600 years in just 30. The initial excitement of the discovery gave way to disappointment. On the other hand, Roman coins have turned up in rabbit burrows within 100 yards (91m) of St. Augustine's Well, so we do after all have evidence that the site was visited during the Roman occupation.

Rivers had local cults, many involving depositing offerings in the water. In August 12 BC, Drusus set up the cult of Rome and Augustus outside Lyons (Lugdunum) at the confluence of the Saône and the Rhône. He set up a temple and an **altar**. On the altar were inscribed the names of 60 Gaulish **tribes**. The consecration ceremony was conducted by the chief **priest** of the **Aedui** tribe, and it must represent a recognition of native Celtic religious ideas.

There were many other river cults. Condatis was the god of the watersmeet. The name of the consort of **Sucellus**, **Nantosuelta**, meant "Winding River." Many of the rivers had female deities. The goddess of the Wharfe in northern England was Verbeia.

One explanation for the focus on water for offerings may lie in the simple fact that water was the ultimate resting place of the dead. Earlier, the Battersea shield was mentioned. This was found in the lower Thames along with a large quantity of other prehistoric metalwork, in the same reaches as human remains, including many skulls. So some stretches of some rivers were used for depositing the dead and the offerings to the Otherworld to accompany them. The Thames was not the only river to be treated in this way: the Witham in Lincolnshire was deluged with offerings. The Witham shield, bearing strange animal decoration, is one of many high-status objects to come out of the river not far from Lincoln. A brand-new logboat was deliberately "sacrificed" underneath a timber causeway with a large collection of tools and weapons. The timber was dated to the middle of the fifth century BC.

Springs were often associated with **healing**. Some were doubtless visited informally in the hope that a prayer or a small offering to the water deity would relieve a toothache, backache, or failing sight. Others were developed with full-scale sanctuaries. At the Giant's Springs at Duchcov in the Czech Republic there is a natural spring. In the third or second century BC a large bronze **cauldron** was dedicated to the spring. It contained more than 2,000 bronze offerings: mainly brooches and bracelets. This is interesting in itself, but doubly so since most of the offerings to water elsewhere seem to be not only male in origin but military, like the Battersea shield. Here at the Giant's Springs is what looks like a collective offering that is exclusively female. But this cannot be pressed too far, as men also wore jewelry. Presumably these offerings were deposited one by one, by individual people over a period, and then collected together to be deposited in the cauldron.

Lakes and bogs were also places people visited in the hope of divine intercession. It is likely that the locations that are now bogs were lakes in the Iron Age; they have become filled up with silt and vegetation. One attraction of lakes was that the offerings left there would rest undisturbed: there was no flow of water to move the offerings around.

The classical writers tell us about the practice. Strabo describes an incident that happened in 106 BC in the territory of the Volcae Tectosages tribe, who lived in the Toulouse area. The tribe had amassed an enormous hoard of **gold** and silver sacred **treasure** in the form of metal ingots heaped up at the Tolosa sanctuary; some in temple enclosures and some in a sacred lake. The treasure was plundered by the Romans. Strabo comments that religious treasure hoards such as this existed in many parts of the Celtic lands, "and the lakes in particular provided inviolability for their treasures, into which they let down heavy masses of silver and gold." The Tolosa sanctuary was regarded by the Gauls as especially sacred; its treasure was unusually large, partly because the place was regarded as unusually sacred and no one would have contemplating committing

sacrilege there. The Romans, of course, had no such scruple. The trauma experienced by the Volcae Tectosages when they had their lake sanctuary ransacked can only be imagined.

St. Gregory of Tours describes a three-day (pagan) religious festival that took place at Lake Gévaudan in the Cévennes. During this annual festival, the local peasants threw into the lake food, clothing, and the bodies of sacrificed animals. Depositing offerings into deep water meant that they could never be retrieved; they were gone beyond physical recovery, and were in effect sent to the Otherworld. Throwing something away so irrevocably must have added to the value of the sacrificial act.

The **Daghda**, an Irish father god, was wedded to the land by being married to the territorial goddess **Boanna** of the Boyne River. According to legend, she was detained by Nechtan when she questioned the power of his sacred spring.

Water is a regenerative force. Some of the healing springs are a source of mineral water with true medicinal qualities; others are just a source of pure clean water. Water is seen as healing in a number of ways. Devotees can apply it to infected areas of their body, wash in it, immerse themselves in it, or drink it. The evidence from all the different sanctuaries points to all methods being used. Healing and ritual cleansing always go together.

The Lady of the Lake represents the later Celtic aspect of water **magic**, the Romantic and mysterious aspect. In the fully developed Arthurian legend of the high Middle Ages, there are several **fairy** ladies who appear and disappear. By the time Sir Thomas Malory told his version of the story, the fairies (originally from the Otherworld) had been converted into enchantresses (dwelling in this world, but with magic powers). Early versions of the tales show the fairy nature of enchantresses better.

One very early version of the Lancelot story has the Lady of the Lake as a true spirit of the lake; a queen of an isle of lake maidens in the middle of an enchanted lake, where winter never comes and there is no sorrow. Later in the Middle Ages, the same queen becomes a sorceress and even the lake is an illusion. Jessie Weston argued that the original tale was about the capture of a royal child by a water-fairy. But the Lady of

the Lake is still there, just, in the final rendition of the **Arthur** story. She gives the **sword** Excalibur to him at the beginning of his reign and takes it back again at the end as a summons to **Avalon**. At the end of the story, we see only her arm sticking up out of the lake; in the process of endless re-telling, she has almost disappeared from the story.

THE WEST

To the west is the open Atlantic Ocean, and beyond that—who knows? It is an obvious location for lost lands, for fantastic adventures, and for the **Otherworld** itself. It is also the place where the sun sets, and therefore associated with death. The west becomes the destination of departed souls, the Isle of the Dead.

The west is the perilous seascape within which the voyages of St. **Brendan** took place (see People: **Barinthus**, **Brendan**; Religion: **Otherworld**).

WHEEL

The wheel had become a cult symbol by the end of the Bronze Age. Often it can be seen in Iron Age images, for example on **coins**, just floating in a corner. It may represent exactly what it seems to represent: the wheel of a wagon or a **chariot**. On some coins the wheel floats beneath a horse, and in that context it looks as if a chariot might be intended. If so, it could represent the power of trade or the military power of the warrior elite. Given that chariots and wagons were often included among the grave goods of the rich and powerful, the wheel may represent a very specific journey: the journey to the **Otherworld**.

In about 600 BC a remarkable cult wagon was built at Strettweg in Austria. It carries a group of human figures with battle trumpets (horsemen and infantry with **spears** and shields), surrounding a large central female figure who holds a shallow bronze bowl above her head. The wagon has four large eight-spoked wheels.

But the wheel could equally be a transformation of the **sun**, in which case it could take on a variety of meanings, such as life, strength, power, and sovereignty. The wheel is a natural symbol for the sun: it is round, it has spokes that radiate like the sun's rays, and it is capable of moving. Even where it is shown with a horse it could represent the sun, because a celestial horse was envisaged as necessary to draw the sun across the sky.

The solar wheel cult had been in existence for a long time. The Trundholm chariot from Denmark dates from 1300 BC. It consists of a bronze model horse pulling a bronze disk, **gold**-plated on one side and borne along on three pairs of wheels. There can be no doubt that this disc represents the sun and the horse is imagined as drawing the sun across the sky. Sometimes the wheel is paired with a crescent, making the obvious paired association between sun and moon.

The wheel is not considered to be self-running; even if it is shown on its own, there is an implication that some god must be responsible for rolling it along. Some figurines show a deity with one hand on the wheel, so in those depictions we can see who it is who rolls it. A favorite Roman goddess was **Fortuna**, who was responsible for turning the wheel of fortune. She appears on Roman coins, and the image is very familiar to Britons of an older generation, because she was adopted and adapted to become Britannia, who very similarly appeared on coins. In her new role as Britannia, Fortuna finds her wheel of fortune itself transformed—into Britannia's proudly held round shield.

Another transformation of the solar wheel to suit the values of a later age is the rose window. Several great European cathedrals have magnificent rose windows, which are huge sun-wheels made of stone and glass and sunlight. In the Middle Ages they were actually referred to as *rota*: "wheels."

In the last two centuries BC, an Iron Age celestial and mainly solar cult becomes evident, with the wheel as its symbol. The Romans had their **sky god**, Jupiter, borrowed from the Greek Zeus, and these were powerful bearded male figures, emphatically modeled on the human male. But among the Celts, representations of the gods in human form were still quite unusual. By the second century AD, however, a Romano-Celtic **wheel god** had emerged. This late shift into human form is an indication of the Celts' reluctance to think

of their gods in human form; in this case it seems only to have happened as a result of contact with the Greco-Roman civilization. But in a way we are lucky that this happened, or we might not have realized that the wheel was in fact a god.

Miniature wheels have been found at a number of Iron Age sites, from Britain across to Slovakia. Often these are only 1 inch (2.5cm) in diameter, with four spokes, but some are larger and have six or as many as 12 spokes. They were probably carried as talismans or good luck charms.

At the **La Tène** site of Villeneuve au Châtelot in France, large numbers of lead wheel models have been found at a site that is believed to be a temple. The lead wheels were presumably sold to worshippers to leave as offerings, as a kind of divine currency.

In a similar spirit, wheel models were left as grave goods. At the Dürrnberg hillfort near Hallein in Austria, the grave of a small boy dating from 400 BC contained jewelry that included a realistic wheel model. Another grave, of a young girl, contained a model wheel and a model axe. Grave goods such as these were left as a help on what was imagined to be a difficult journey. The little girl was very small for her age, to the point of disability, and this may be why her parents felt that she needed some good luck charms to help her on her way.

The wheel was also inscribed on tombstones. In the cremation cemeteries of Alsace there are some distinctive house-shaped tombstones, which have wheel symbols scratched onto them. Some have wheels and rosettes together.

Irish legend tells of a magic wheel, the Roth Fáil, made by the **Druid** Mog Ruith. This wheel is said to have carried the Druid through the heavens, but it met with an accident and broke up. Mog Ruith's daughter, Tlachtga, gathered some fragments of the wheel, and took them to Ireland, which in itself (according to Irish tradition) was a calamity. She raised one of the fragments as the pillar-stone of Cnamchoill, near Tipperary. The Roth Fáil, the Wheel of Light, was clearly not intended to be a flying-machine at all but to symbolize the sun, and some of the storytellers who passed on the story did not understand this. This has its parallel in the Greek tale about Icarus, who flew through the air with aid of a pair of wings made by his father Daedalus; he flew too close to the sun and the sun's heat melted the wax that held the feathers in place.

A Roman sarcophagus dating from AD 350 has a remarkable symbol carved on it. It combines the circular Roman laurel wreath, the wreath of victory and **immortality**, with the *chi-rho* symbol: the first two letters of the name of Christ when spelt in Greek, "X" and "P." So the symbol represents Christ Victorious. Yet these elements have been carefully put together to make a six-spoked wheel. It is the sun-wheel of the Celtic pagan god **Taranis**, but Romanized and Christianized to make it into what is sometimes called an Ichthys wheel.

The wheel with eight spokes instead of six is the Wheel of the Year, with its eight calendar festivals:

December: ***Winter Solstice***
February: ***Imbolg***
March: Spring Equinox
May: ***Beltane***
June: Summer Solstice
August: ***Lughnasad***
September: Autumn Equinox
November: ***Samhain***

The Element Encyclopedia of the Celts

WIDDERSHINS

There is a very old custom, when walking around something, to walk round it clockwise, in other words veering to the right. This is seen as conforming to the movement of the **sun** across the sky. Viewed from northern Europe, the sun is generally in the southern half of the sky, and when you look south the sun rises to your left and crosses to the right, so this clockwise processional movement is sometimes described as "sunwise." It is in keeping with the natural order of the universe.

We can imagine the ancestors of the Celts walking or dancing around their stone and earth circles "sunwise," perhaps in rituals that related directly to the movements of the sun itself. In Irish and Scottish Gaelic this movement with the sun is called *deiseal* (right-handwise).

The opposite, circling to the left hand, is called *tuathal* in Gaelic, and is regarded as unlucky. It is known in England and Lowland Scotland as "widdershins," meaning "walking against."

In the seventeenth century, if ordinary people in the Western Isles of Scotland happened to be passing a prehistoric cairn, they used to make a point of walking around it three times, always sunwise, for good luck. It made no difference whether they were Protestants or Catholics—it was understood, even then, that this was a very ancient custom handed down from the way their ancestors worshiped. On Colonsay, people walked "sunways" around the church and turned their **boats** in the same way. In the Highlands, wedding processions often went clockwise round the church. Herdsmen danced three times sunways around the Beltane fire.

To go widdershins was to go the wrong way. A Scottish witch who was refused some grain by a neighbor deliberately walked around the neighbor's stack the wrong way, "contrair to the sunis cours," in order to do damage to the grain.

The Element Encyclopedia of the Celts

WILLOW

A tree associated with mourning, because of its drooping shape, and therefore also with death. The fact that willows grow near **water** may also associate them with the **Otherworld**. Willow is supposed to assist in communicating with the Otherworld. It was sometimes used to line graves for this reason (*see* **Crane**).

WITCHCRAFT

WITCHES IN WALES

On the whole, witches and wise men were feared or respected in Wales, and generally left alone. Wise men (wizards) seem always to have flourished there. At one time, every village had its *dyn hysbys*. It was said that they maintained their numbers by persuading ignorant country-**people** to sacrifice their children to the Devil in order to turn them into wise men.

Witches put **spells** on animals belonging to neighbors who annoyed them. If a cow was the victim it would grow sick for no apparent reason, perhaps stop giving milk, and even die. "Witching" a pig would cause it to have a seizure. There was an example of an old witch living near Llangadock in Carmarthenshire. She had witched a pig and was compelled to unwitch it. She went and put her hand on its back and gave the counter-charm in Welsh, "God keep you to your owner."

Mary Lewis, the Welsh folklorist, knew a witch who lived not much more than a mile (1.6km) from her own home. The witch was called Mary Perllan Peter. The custom in Wales was to avoid using surnames as there were only a few, and far too many people going by the name of Jones or Davies or Evans, so the person's forename was used along with their address. Mary lived at a house called Perllan Peter, deep in a wooded ravine. Once she asked a neighbor to take her some corn. He agreed reluctantly, as the path down to her cottage was very steep and the sack of corn was heavy. He spilt some on the way down and Mary was very angry. She muttered threats to him as he was leaving. When he got home, he was amazed to see his little mare sitting on her haunches and staring wildly. He tried in vain to pull her to her feet. The man became frightened, and thought of the witch's threats. He set off to find Mary, to get her to remove the spell. She went to the mare and said simply, "What ails you now?" The mare jumped to her feet and was as well as ever.

Other, similar stories were told about Mary.

In Cardiganshire, as in other rural districts, it was commonly believed that when the butter would not "come" when it was being churned it had been bewitched. There were always remedies. One was to hang a branch from a **rowan** tree over the dairy door. Another was to put a knife in the churn; witches, like **fairies**, hate iron.

When Mary Lewis was staying at Aberdovey, she noticed a strangely shaped depression on the top of the hill behind the school. When she asked about it, she was told it was called the Witch's Grave, that a witch was supposed to have been burned there and her ashes were buried on the spot. The old village green used to be up on that little plateau and if there ever

was a witch-burning, that would have been the place. That was the only example Mary Lewis found of witches being ill-treated.

In about 1600, however, the Reverend Rees Prichard wrote a hymn against conjurers:

To drag children through a hoop,
Or flame of fire on All Hallows Eve,
And taking them to the mill bin to be
shaken,
Is the way of sacrificing them to the
Evil One.

The first image may refer to an old Welsh custom of passing delicate children through a split **ash** to cure them of rickets and other ailments. The intention was to effect a cure, though, not to dedicate the child to the Devil.

Some of the stories about wizards reveal them to be frauds. A wise man who lived at a farm near Borth, not far from Aberystwyth, was frequently consulted; he sometimes wrote charms for people to wear. A girl in the district was ailing and her relatives thought a spell had been put on her. They went to the wizard, who told them that the first person they met on the way home was the witch who had put the spell on the girl.

They set off and the first person they met was a harmless old man whom they knew must be innocent. Naturally they hurried back to the wise man to remonstrate, but he was as cool as could be: "It was not he, but his brother, who is dead. The girl will not be well until the brother's body is decayed." He was a poor and unconvincing wizard, to say the least.

Sometimes, surprisingly, it was the vicar who was the local wizard. There was a well-known Vicar Pritchard of Pwllheli who was well-known for being able to lay ghosts. A hundred years ago he was still remembered in Merionethshire as a useful man to bring in if people were troubled by ghosts. He went armed with book and candle and said to one ghost, "Now, will you promise me to cease troubling this house as long as this candle lasts?" The spirit gladly promised, thinking there was perhaps an hour to wait. But the vicar put out the candle, put it into a lead box, and sealed and buried the box under a tree, where it still lies. What he was doing was in a long tradition of Welsh witchcraft.

As well as witches and wizards, there were also herb doctors, who prescribed various substances—of-ten rather unpleasant substances— as cures. Dried earthworms were prescribed for fits. Oil of earthworms was prescribed for the nerves and "pain of the joints." Snail water was particularly awful.

RECIPE FOR SNAIL WATER

Of Garden Snails two pounds, the juice of ground ivy, colt's foot, scabious lungwort, purslain, ambrosia, Paul's betony, hog's blood and white wine, dried tobacco leaves, liquorice elecampane, orris, cotton seeds, annis seeds, saffron, petals of red roses, violets and borage. Steep all of this three days and then distil. Then drink. [Readers are strongly advised not to try this.]

A man called Brookes wrote *A General Dispensatory* in 1753 and in it he listed some of the odd materials currently used by medics and quacks. Various stones were recommended: Eagle-stone, Jew's stone, Blood stone, and several others. Brookes claimed, "The stones are cried up as an antidote against all manner of poisons, plagues, contagious diseases, malignant fevers, the smallpox and measles." Sometimes the stone was ground and drunk as a powder in a drink; sometimes it was applied externally by being rubbed onto the body. A particular stone, the size of a large marble, was used repeatedly in Cardiganshire to cure goitre.

In some parts of Wales a dried toad tucked into the armpit was believed to ward off fever. The unfortunate toads were put into an earthen pot and gradually dried in a moderate oven until they were dry enough to reduce to a powder. A similar powder made from bees "trimly decks a bald head being washed with it."

Some remedies were very ordinary (rubbing a potato on a joint to cure rheumatism, and nettle tea for the chest), while others were not so (crab's eyes to cure pleurisy, and snail broth to cure consumption). Amber was worn as a powerful charm against blindness, the evil eye—and witches.

WYVERN

See **Dragon**.

Y

Y DDRAIG GOCH

See **Dragon**.

YEW

The yew has always been held in awe because of its very long life. It used to be said that yews were grown in churchyards because churchyards were enclosed and penning yews in was a way of preventing livestock from being poisoned by grazing on the tree (yew berries are poisonous, which gives the tree an association with death that is apt, given that churchyard yews are surrounded by graves).

This explanation may have some truth in it, but some English churchyard yews are 1,500 years old, which means that they were growing before Christianity arrived. This supports the idea of churches being built on sites that were already held sacred: pagan sites.

The yew grows in an unusual way, with new stems growing around the outside of the tree. This makes it a symbol of self-regeneration. Because it seems, to human bystanders, to live forever, it has become a symbol of everlasting life.

The churchyard yew was doubtless reverenced in the early days because of its associations with old pagan beliefs. The later idea of growing yews in a safe place away from livestock gave the tree a new meaning and value. The yew was then tolerated because of the usefulness of its timber, for making **spears**, shields and, above all, the English longbow.

PART 6

Celtic Twilight and Revival

CELTIC TWILIGHT

THE EBBING TIDE

From the first millennium BC onward, the ancient Celtic cultures came under attack from outside. This happened both on Europe's Atlantic coast and in the center of Europe. The process of retreat was complex and the outcome was by no means inevitable.

When the tide is high, turns, and begins to fall, we cannot always see from minute to minute what is happening, with some waves higher and some lower, some breaking further up the beach, and some breaking further down. It is only after an hour passes that we can see that the tide has fallen. In the same way, with hindsight, we can see that the Celtic cultures were in retreat and decline for 2,000 years.

THE IMPACT OF ROME

That imperceptible turn in the tide began as early as the third century BC, which was when the central European Celtic world started to weaken and shrink under the impact of Roman expansion.

Celtic tribes from north of the Alps had some success in settling the North Italian Plain, but by 133 BC the Romans had retaken control of that region: it became Gallia Cisalpina. Rome also conquered most of the Iberian Peninsula, including western Galicia. Only the northern coast of Spain remained unconquered.

From 100 BC on, the power of Rome encroached remorselessly on the Celtic world, reaching out across the Alps to subdue, conquer, and annex the tribal lands.

In Gaul, the Celtic territories kept their separate existence and their distinct cultures until the first century BC, but by 58 BC a sequence of internal political crises in Gaul had precipitated the collapse of the ancient kingdoms and the development of new tribal groupings. Julius Caesar's

The Element Encyclopedia of the Celts

attack on them was cleverly timed; he caught the Gauls in disarray. He was also greatly aided by the willingness of some Celtic tribes to take his side. Although Caesar did not conquer Britain, the process of Romanization had begun, and diplomatic negotiations began with prospective British client kingdoms.

From 15 BC onward there was a steadily increasing volume of trade between Rome and the Celtic tribes of Britain. The Britons first imported fine wines for the aristocracy, but later also large quantities of cheap wines for a less discerning market. *Amphorae* arrived filled with Mediterranean products such as fish-sauce from southern Spain. New kinds of tableware, some of it elaborately decorated in relief, came in as well. These innovations were first welcomed by the rich and privileged, then, after a time-lag, by the less wealthy. Some of the imported goods were spectacular, such as the beautifully wrought silver feasting-cup from Italy that was buried with a British chief at Welwyn, but *all* of the imported goods were sought-after.

This process of Romanization enabled the Claudian invasion of Britain in the first century AD to move forward swiftly. The process of subjugating Britain went forward relentlessly, culminating in the Battle of Mons Graupius in AD 84, when Agricola's troops put the Caledonian (Scottish) Celts to flight. It happened very quickly. In one generation, Celtic Britain had become Roman Britannia.

By AD 200, Rome controlled the whole of what we now call Spain, Portugal, France, Belgium, England, Wales, Switzerland, south-west Germany, and Austria as far north as the Danube. Of all the lands of the central European Celts and the Atlantic Celts, only northern Scotland and Ireland remained free of Roman control.

Roman rule tolerated harmless local customs and many aspects of life went on as before, but it was still a weakening experience. By the time the Romans abandoned Gaul in the fifth century AD, when the Western Empire collapsed, the Gaulish language was virtually extinct, being spoken only by occultists, witches, and a few people in the backwoods. The language spoken in Brittany in later centuries comes from different stock; it was introduced from the English West Country in the fifth and sixth centuries. Outside Gaul, Celtic culture lingered on, but even there it was increasingly transformed by contact with Rome.

The situation in Ireland was completely different. The Romans were inhibited from attempting a conquest by the Irish Sea, which for them represented one sea crossing too many. The Roman general Agricola believed that Ireland could be taken relatively easily with just one legion and a few auxiliaries, but his plan was never put to the test. So, while the ancient culture of Gaul and Britain suffered the massive impact of Roman conquest, it was able to continue in Ireland uninterrupted.

CELTS UNDER ATTACK: GOTHS, VANDALS, VISIGOTHS, ANGLES, SAXONS, AND FRANKS

After occupying Britain for four centuries, the Romans abandoned it to its fate in the fifth century AD. They also abandoned Gaul.

In fact, by the time the emperor Justinian died in AD 565, the Romans had withdrawn from all the conquered Celtic lands; they had abandoned Britannia, Gaul, Hispania, and Germania.

On the face of it, after the Roman withdrawal there could have been a Celtic revival. That might have happened but for the fact that there were now new incomers—a whole host of them. Huns arrived in the lands of the central European Celts, and various Germanic peoples invaded Gaul: Goths, Huns, Vandals, and Visigoths. The central European heartland itself was invaded by Slavs.

On the English coast, the Romans had built massive shore forts to defend the coastline against the Saxons. Once they had gone to deal with barbarians threatening them closer to home, however, there was little to stop the Saxons, Angles, and Jutes from crossing the North Sea and setting up colonies. In Kent, the Jutes removed the ruling class by massacre, exile, or voluntary self-exile. The surviving British aristocracy fled to the west, some seeking refuge in Cornwall, and many crossing the Channel to Brittany to settle there. This left the ordinary Kentish working people in place, and Celtic culture may have been preserved and handed on to some extent by the peasant class. The genes certainly were.

THE MIRACLE BOOKS

In the Dark Ages that followed the Germanic occupation of Britain, the Celtic cultures struggled to continue, suffering further blows from the Christian Church and from repeated plagues.

But, even then, some aspects of the ancient culture flourished: the art of storytelling, including poetry about the pagan paradise, and the art of illuminated manuscripts. Even during the long period of political eclipse, Celtic artwork was taking on new and wonderful forms. Startlingly, in the midst of this adversity, there was a Celtic renaissance.

This was the age of *The Book of Kells* (eighth century), *The Book of Durrow* (late seventh century), and the Lindisfarne Gospels (early eighth century).

The intricate interlacing lines of the decorative borders were made to be gazed at and marveled at; the labyrinthine knotlike wanderings of the continuous and endless lines have an almost hypnotic effect. It is possible, still, to go on and on gazing at great artwork like this. In times when there were few other distractions, we can imagine readers falling into a meditative trance-like state as they contemplated, rather than read, just one page.

The Book of Kells has the knot of eternity as a recurring image. It is the most elaborately decorated of all these gospels. One page, called the Chi-Rho page, is given over almost entirely to those two letters, the Greek initials "X," "P," the first two letters of the Greek word *Christos*, Christ. They are almost entirely consumed in minutely swirling decorative lines, eddying like a flowing river. A several points there are triskeles, each formed out of smaller triskeles. The design is completely abstract—or almost completely. If you look very carefully, you can find tiny heads and animals—moths, two cats and four mice, and an otter swallowing a fish—perhaps symbolic, perhaps just a sign of a master-artist enjoying himself.

The Book of Kells is thought to be the work of three scribes and three illustrators, who may have been the same men as the scribes. One painter was responsible for the portraits of the Evangelists, another for dramatic scenes such as the Temptation of Christ, and another, nicknamed the Goldsmith, was responsible for fantastically ornamented pages such as the Chi-Rho page. It is an astonishing achievement for six or possibly as few as three artists: 680 pages of immensely fertile creativity—and we don't even know their names.

Another wonderfully intricate example of Celtic art is the bronze shrine-casket made in about 1100 to hold St. Patrick's bell. The bronze casing is decorated with silver plating and elaborate curving filigree. Even more magnificent is the Hunterston Brooch from Ayrshire in Scotland, made in about AD 700. It is decorated with gold, silver, and insets of amber, and is covered with the most refined curving Celtic tracery.

But these magnificently refined works of art were a swan-song. In the twelfth century the monastery at Kells was dissolved, though its church continued as the parish church of Kells. The great book was kept there until 1661, when the Bishop of Meath presented it to the library of Trinity College, Dublin. Where *The Book of Kells* was actually produced is still a mystery. It could have come from Lindisfarne, Durrow, or Iona, and it seems possible that it was begun on Iona, by the monks there, and then finished at Kells after the monks relocated following the Viking raid of 806.

If this is so, it makes a fitting conclusion to the Iona saga. There is a tradition that St. Columba transcribed the Cathach (or Battler) of St. Columba. This manuscript copy of the Psalms is not illuminated in the sense that *The Book of Kells* would later be, nor is it colored, but it does have initial capital letters that are quite elaborate, extending down through three lines of text. It was a starting-point for the development of illumination in the seventh and eighth centuries. There is no way of knowing whether it really was St. Columba himself who transcribed this copy of the Psalms, but there is a tradition that he clandestinely copied a gospel book that belonged to one of his colleagues. This illicit copying led to a series of violent disputes, which culminated in Columba's departure to Iona in AD 563. Perhaps he took with him the idea of elaborately decorated copies of scripture. Columba's exile to Iona started the spread of Celtic Christianity and the Irish manuscript tradition across to Britain and mainland Europe.

THE VIKINGS

This enclave of Celticism was under attack now from the Vikings, who saw the isolated monasteries as easy targets. The rich stores of treasure accumulated by the monks were exactly the kind of booty the Vikings were looking for.

The Anglo-Saxon Chronicle records the first known Viking raid on Britain, in Northumbria in 787. In 793, the Northumbrian monastery of Lindisfarne was sacked; the next year there was an attack on Bede's monastery at Jarrow. A few years later there were raids on the monastery of Iona. These raids targeted the very establishments where the finest Celtic artwork was being produced; it was a blow that seemed to be aimed right at the reviving heart of Celticism.

At the same time as these destructive raids, the Vikings were colonizing parts of Britain and the islands around it—the Western Isles, the Shetland Islands, and the Orkney Islands. The Isle of Man was another colony, and from there the Vikings could reach out and set up colonies on the shores of the Irish Sea. Wales was attacked, though never successfully colonized.

Generally the numbers of Vikings seem to have been small, and they were assimilated, but their impact on Orkney and Shetland was considerable. There are aspects of Shetland custom today that reflect an inheritance from Viking law.

On the Scottish mainland, the withdrawal of the Romans meant at first a return to a Celtic way of life. The Celtic royal families and their royal citadels were still there and in the fifth and sixth centuries their kingdoms were simply revived.

The fort of Dunadd in Argyllshire was a major citadel of the Scottish kings of Dalriada, who oversaw the restoration of a Celtic warrior-hero culture. The only change was that the great kingdoms of the Iron Age had been fragmented.

Something similar was happening in Wales, where the late Iron Age tribal territories were revived or continued, but under new names. North-west Wales (Snowdonia and the Isle of Anglesey) had been the lands of the Ordovices: now in the post-Roman Dark Ages it became the kingdom of Gwynedd. South-west Wales (Pembrokeshire) had been the land of the Demetii tribe: now it became the kingdom of Demetia. South Wales (Glamorgan) had been the land of the Silures: now it was the kingdoms of Brycheiniog and Glevissig. Central Wales and the Marches had been the land of the Cornovii: now they became the kingdom of Powys.

In the English West Country there had been two tribal territories in pre-Roman times: the Dumnonii and the Durotriges. Now that the Romans had gone these were combined to create the kingdom of Dumnonia. This, together with the Welsh kingdoms, had formed the Roman province of Britannia Prima. It seems that after the Romans went a loose association among these kingdoms of Britannia Prima continued, and they still fought together against the common foe, the advancing Saxons, under a common battle leader. The first battle leader, or *dux bellorum*, was Ambrosius Aurelianus, and his successor was Arthur. They were both associated with Dumnonia, so Arthur probably had two roles: one as king of Dumnonia and the other as commander-in-chief or leader of battles at the head of the armies of what had formerly been Britannia Prima.

The high-status strongholds of these powerful Dark Age kings are easy for archeologists to identify today—from the presence of expensive pottery shipped in from the Mediterranean. Only kings could afford to live like this.

THE MEDIEVAL

SUBJUGATION OF WALES

In the Middle Ages, Wales fell gradually under the sway of the English crown, partly because of steady and insistent pressure from the English kings and partly because of in-fighting among the Welsh. Gerald of Wales put these words into the mouth of an old man who came face to face with an invading English king: "This nation may be harassed now, weakened and decimated by your soldiery, but it will never be destroyed by the wrath of man."

The 1218 Treaty of Worcester recognized Llywelyn's control in Wales. Llywelyn had married the King of England's sister, Princess Joan, in 1205. This was a sensible diplomatic move, but it was not enough to prevent the two men quarreling over who ruled Wales. By this stage most of Wales had felt the mailed fist of the English kings and large areas had been uneasily settled under the rule of Anglo-Norman barons. Only the principality of Gwynedd held onto its nominal independence.

By 1255 Gwynedd was ruled by Llywelyn's grandson, Llywelyn ap Gruffudd. He allied himself with Simon de Montfort. At first this seemed to work in his favor. De Montfort defeated the English king, Henry III, at the Battle of Lewes in 1264 and agreed to recognize Llywelyn as Prince of Wales, although in return for a promise of £20,000. The Treaty of Montgomery three years later ratified this agreement and it was signed by the restored Henry III. It was the pinnacle of Llywelyn's power. But he had two insoluble problems: he had no son and heir; and, equally seriously, he could not pay the £20,000. He was forced to levy oppressively high taxes, which put him at extreme risk of civil war in Wales, which may have been what Henry III secretly hoped for.

Worse was to follow, when Edward I came to the English throne in 1274. As the new king he was entitled to expect Llywelyn to pay him homage. Llywelyn was summoned five times to do so, but he refused to go. Finally, in exasperation, Edward I led an army into Wales and forced Llywelyn's submission.

On the back of the invasion, Llywelyn was able to lead a Welsh rising against Edward I, as the Welsh council complained that he had broken his word: "The people of Snowdon [i.e. Gwynedd] say that even if the prince were willing to give their land to the king, they would nevertheless be unwilling to do homage to a stranger whose language, customs and laws are totally unknown to them."

The people of Wales were persuaded that they had been provoked into fighting a war of national liberation. They were fairly successful in making guerrilla attacks, but then Llywelyn was killed, almost by chance, in a minor skirmish with an English infantryman. In an echo of an ancient Celtic custom, his severed head was sent to London as

a trophy; it was to prove that he was dead. With its leader gone, the revolt petered out and the Welsh submitted.

Edward I confirmed his hold on Wales by setting up colony towns and building more castles. It was a turning-point. Wales had become an English colony, a conquered land.

A 1284 statute imposed English common law on Wales. The heartland of the principality, as recognized by the Welsh claimants to the title Prince of Wales, was Gwynedd. The English pointedly carved it up into four counties. The Welsh language was left alone, but business was increasingly transacted in English. Wales's national treasures, such as the royal insignia, were removed to London as a gesture of conquest. There was a concerted attempt to eradicate Welsh national identity and to forge the two neighboring nations into one. It was a bold and savage strategy—a lesser king than Edward I would not have attempted it. Welsh soldiers were to find their place at the heart of Edward's royal armies. Ten thousand of the 12,000 foot-soldiers Edward used to defeat William Wallace at the Battle of Bannockburn in

1298 were Welshmen. Here was a piece of irony: the English king was deploying the warriors of one subject nation to subjugate another! But it was risky, as the Welsh infantrymen were unreliable, wild, and disobedient. Edward was frustrated too when they murdered rather than captured enemies with a high ransom value.

The overall cost of subjugating Wales was enormous. England crippled itself in the process. The invasion, colonization, and castle-building cost more than £240,000. The Crown had to take massive loans from foreign bankers—and raise taxation.

The most striking gesture of the English conquest came in 1301, when Edward I installed his son as Prince of Wales. This was the title most honored in an independent Wales, and here was the King of England giving it to his infant son as if it was a baby's rattle. Edward I was astute enough to have his pregnant queen brought to Caernarvon Castle so that the infant prince would be born a Welshman. It was provocative, but clever. From then on, the monarch's eldest son has always taken the title "Prince of Wales."

There were intermittent revolts after that. The last significant one was the ten-year rebellion led by Owain Glyndwr in the early fifteenth century. It failed and Glyndwr died an outlaw in the Welsh hills, refusing Henry V's offer of a pardon in 1415.

By a quirk of history, the English throne was usurped by a Welshman at the Battle of Bosworth in 1485. He was Henry Tudor.

His son, Henry VIII, thought of himself as English, however, and passed the Laws of Wales Acts (later known as Acts of Union), which aimed to incorporate Wales fully into the kingdom of England.

At the beginning of the seventeenth century, Elizabeth I was succeeded by James VI of Scotland, and so a Scot became King of England.

James strove to unify the four realms of his kingdom. Initially he issued a gold sovereign that named him King of England, Scotland, Wales, and Ireland, but within a few years he was claiming to be King of Great Britain.

So, first the *Welsh* King Henry VIII passed Acts of Union to insure the incorporation of Wales into a united kingdom. Then the *Scottish* King James I incorporated Scotland and airbrushed the names of the member kingdoms from the coinage. These were initiatives by a Welsh king and a Scottish king to integrate Wales and Scotland into a union with England.

Then, a century later, under the authority of the English Queen Anne, the *de facto* arrangements originated by the Welsh king and the Scottish king were formally ratified. In 1707, Wales became part of the United Kingdom of Great Britain.

THE MEDIEVAL SUBJUGATION OF SCOTLAND

In 1305 the Scottish rebel or freedom-fighter William Wallace suffered the same traitor's fate as the Welsh leader Dafydd ap Gruffudd about 20 years earlier and for the same reason—striving to maintain the independence of a Celtic realm. Both dared to raise armies against Edward I of England.

As in Wales, the problem lay partly in an internal power struggle. When Alexander III of Scotland died in 1286, his heir was his granddaughter Margaret, the infant daughter of the King of Norway. Edward I saw a dynastic marriage as the route to cementing England and Scotland together and proposed that Margaret should marry his own son, who would become Edward II. But the princess died and the succession was open to several claimants. The strongest of these were John Balliol and Robert Bruce. Balliol was chosen, but he declared he would be answerable only to the Scots people and he refused to offer military service to Edward, even though Edward had supported his election. He then rashly made a treaty with France and invaded England.

Edward I went north to receive homage from the Scottish nobles, who were ready to acknowledge him as their feudal lord. Among these was Robert Bruce, who had estates in England and therefore had little choice but to acknowledge Edward as his lord. Balliol punished Bruce by seizing his lands in Scotland and giving them to his own brother-in-law, John Comyn.

At Dunbar in 1296 Edward defeated John Balliol, who surrendered the Scottish throne to the English king. In a theatrical symbolic gesture, Edward removed the stone of Scone, the coronation stone of the Scottish kings, and took it to Westminster Abbey, where it sat beneath the Coronation Chair for 700 years.

Edward summoned a Parliament at Berwick, where he received an oath of fealty from more than 2,000 Scots.

But the arrival of English armies provoked and fueled Scottish nationalism. A Scottish nobleman, William Wallace, led a resistance movement. He had a major success at Stirling Bridge, where he defeated a much larger and better-equipped English army. But this was followed by defeat at Falkirk by an even larger English force. Wallace went into hiding for several years, until his capture and execution in 1305. At his trial he declared he was no traitor, because Edward was not his king.

Just as a Welshman, Henry Tudor, almost by chance became King of England in 1485, so a Scot, by an accident of succession, became King of England in 1603. James VI of Scotland became the heir to the joint throne because his mother's cousin, Elizabeth I, refused to marry and have children. So it was that from 1603 the two kingdoms became one, and James I was keen to merge the various systems, including the laws. It was a natural step a century later to proclaim a United Kingdom.

The sense of a loss of Scottish identity has been reawakened intermittently. In the mid-twentieth century, Scotland's great heavy industries folded, one after another, and many Scots felt that Scotland had been emasculated, that something vital had been taken away from it. It happened again at the time of the coronation of Queen Elizabeth II in 1953. Some Scots felt that this title was a slight to Scotland's identity, in turning a blind eye to Scotland's history. The present Queen of the United Kingdom is the second Queen Elizabeth of England, but only the *first* Queen Elizabeth of Scotland. So, just as James VI of Scotland became James I of England, on accession Elizabeth II of England became Elizabeth I of Scotland. This was never satisfactorily recognized.

THE SUBJUGATION OF
BRITTANY

The conquest of Brittany by Julius Caesar began in 57 BC. The Seventh Legion under Crassus Publius defeated one tribe after another with minimal resistance, taking hostages from each as a precaution against rebellion.

Then the legion went to overwinter near Angers, but poor harvests there caused Publius to requisition food from the Breton tribes. The Veneti were outraged at this imposition and won support from neighboring tribes to the east and even from across the Channel in Britain. Caesar decided to move heavily against them and ordered warships to be built on the Loire. The Veneti were seafarers, with 220 warships of their own.

In the post-Roman period, Brittany recovered its identity, though it was under threat from the sixth century AD onward, from the Franks. Even so, at that time the whole of Brittany as far east as Rennes was Breton-speaking. The earliest known text in the Breton language was a book about botany, written in 590: the earliest book in French dates from significantly later—843.

In the fifth and sixth centuries AD, British refugees crossed to Brittany to escape the westward advance of the Anglo-Saxons across what was soon to be England. So many British refugees arrived that Brittany became known as "Little Britain," but they quickly assimilated to make a strong Celtic Breton kingdom. Then it too came under pressure from the east as the Franks expanded their dominion across Gaul. In AD 845 a Breton army under King Nominoe defeated the Frankish army at Ballon and the Franks were forced to recognize the independence of Brittany.

The Bretons were also under attack from the Vikings. The year 799 saw the first Viking raid on Gaul. The Vikings were particularly interested in establishing themselves in two great estuaries: the Seine and the Loire. The Loire estuary formed the southern boundary of Brittany. For the next century, the Bretons were continually fending off Viking raiders.

The death of Alain the Great of Brittany in 907 left the duchy with no strong leader. The Norsemen chose this moment to divert their attentions westward from the Seine: now Brittany was their focus. In 919 there was a massive attack under the Viking leader Rognvaldr, who devastated the region and had complete control of it by 920.

In the Middle Ages, Brittany was weakened by power struggles between factions among the nobles of Brittany and France. At the same time the French kings sought to annex Brittany. Even so, Breton independence lasted 600 years, until 1488, when the armies of Francis II were defeated by the French (i.e. Frankish) armies of Charles VIII. Then there was a Union of Crowns, when Anne of Brittany was forced to marry Charles VIII of France in 1491. When Charles died seven years later, Anne was forced to marry his successor, Louis XII.

This led to the incorporation of the Duchy of Brittany into France in 1532, by an Edict of Union between Brittany and France. Under this arrangement, Brittany was to be a self-governing province within France.

But the Celtic spirit of rebellion simmered on and it was no coincidence that several Bretons joined in the American War of Independence—Lafayette conspicuous among them—and the Bretons fitted out 16 warships for the American rebels. Triumphantly victorious, the Breton rebels returned home full of republicanism, but their support for the French Revolution misfired: the Breton Parliament was abolished in 1790 on the grounds that everyone in France must be equal. There were going to be no special rights for the Bretons.

That might have been the end of the matter, except that the Bretons continued to feel that they were Celts, not Franks, and therefore *not French*. This conflict drove many Bretons back toward royalism. Central government in Paris was unrelenting, yet Brittany remained a predominantly Celtic-speaking region. As late as 1914, 1.5 million of its 2.5 million people spoke Breton. Today that has declined to about 800,000 Breton-speakers, but the desire for self-government is still strong in Brittany.

THE SUBTLE TRANSFORMATION OF GALICIA

Galicia's history has been very different than that of the other realms of the Atlantic West.

Roman legions arrived in Galicia in 137 BC, and the area became part of the Roman Empire in the reign of Augustus. The Romans were mainly interested in extracting Galicia's mineral resources, but there was a considerable impact on the Galician way of life, to judge from the abandonment of the *castros*. On the other hand, the area was remote and there was less Romanization there compared with other areas that were conquered. This left the Celtic culture more intact and it slowed down the introduction of Christianity. In the third century, north-west Spain became a province of the Roman Empire, Gallaecia.

In the fifth century, the Suevi took over, forming the first medieval kingdom in Europe, the kingdom of the Suevi, in 411, even before the Roman Empire had collapsed. Then in 585 the kingdom was conquered and taken over by the Visigothic King Leovigild. After the Moors invaded Spain in 711, Gallaecia managed to escape Moorish control, but it was absorbed instead into the neighboring (Christian) kingdom of Asturias.

Then something happened that was quite different than anything that happened in any of the other Celtic provinces: Galicia became the focus of an international religious cult, which gave it a special status in the international community, and with that a special identity. The ninth century saw the rise of the pilgrimage cult of St. James at the city of Santiago de Compostela. This put Galicia on the European map in a special way that helped it to retain its independent identity through the rest of the Middle Ages. In fact it was not until as late as 1833 that it ceased to be an independent kingdom; only then did it become part of Spain.

The Element Encyclopedia of the Celts

CELTIC REVIVAL

THE FIRST RIPPLES OF THE TURNING TIDE

In the sixteenth century a new kind of Celtic art appeared in Scotland and Ireland. It is hard to be sure where this renewed interest in the ancient interlace designs came from. It could have arisen from a continuation of old Celtic designs, which were still plainly visible on sculpted stones, for example on Iona, or it could have been inspired by newly arriving imported goods from Renaissance Italy, and therefore not Celtic in origin at all. Possibly it was both: Scottish and Irish artists were inspired by the new because it reminded them of the old. Whatever the reason, the Renaissance Celtic artists quickly took up geometric interlace designs and used them to decorate a range of decorative objects.

Then came one of those moments in history that changes everything. As far as the Atlantic West was concerned, it was a turning of the tide. In the early eighteenth century, the Celts of the past and present were given an identity by some obscure scholars who saw a kinship among their languages.

The first person in modern times to use the phrase "the Celts" seems to have been a sixteenth-century Scot called George Buchanan; he saw the Celts as a people who had once lived in southern Gaul. Some of them, he thought, had migrated to Spain and from there to Ireland, then to Scotland. In this he showed astonishing insight: this northward migration is, in outline, what actually happened thousands of years ago, but it has only recently been confirmed scientifically.

George Buchanan thought this northward migration was the origin of the Gaelic language. He saw similarities between the languages of ancient Gaul, modern Welsh, Cornish, and Breton, and grouped them together as Gallic. But they were distinct and separate, he thought, from the languages of the Irish and Scots, which he called Celtic.

The Element Encyclopedia of the Celts

In 1703 a Breton scholar called Paul-Yves Pezron published *Antiquity of the Nation and Language of the Celts* (written in French, not Breton). This was read with great enthusiasm by the Welsh scholar Edward Lhuyd (1660–1709), who had the book hastily translated (into English, not Welsh). For publication in Britain, Lhuyd changed the title significantly, adding "… the Celtae or Gauls, taken to be originally the same people as our Ancient Britains." By this he meant "Britons," not "Britains," but perhaps the mistake is a sign of his haste and enthusiasm.

Lhuyd jumped to false conclusions about what Pezron was saying but, even so, the influence of his subsequent writings was enormous. By 1723 his friends were writing as "we Celts." A very important idea had been launched: the peoples of the Atlantic West were one people united by a common Celtic language.

An unintentional spur to the acceptance of this idea was the passing of the Act of Union in 1707, which came just three weeks after the publication of Lhuyd's *Archaeologia Britannica*. The Act in effect announced a drive toward a uniform Britishness; that Britishness would be fundamentally English in texture, and applied to all parts of the new United Kingdom. This was unwelcome and indeed felt as a cultural threat: an imposition of Englishness on the non-English or less-English provinces of the kingdom and, as we know from other times and other places, nationhood is often inspired or even forged by a sense of shared difference and perceived threat from outside.

In Wales, the takeover by England had already happened under Henry VIII. It had been reinforced under James I, when he switched from calling himself "King of England, Scotland, and Ireland" to calling himself "King of Great Britain." But that was slipped through on the coinage, abbreviated and in Latin: "*MAG. BRIT.*" In April 1604, the English Parliament had refused his request to call himself King of Great Britain and six months later, when James assumed the title anyway, by proclamation, not by statute, Sir Francis Bacon warned him that he would not be able to use it in any legal context. But the king went on proclaiming his political union message on his coins. His 1613 Gold Laurel declared: "I Have United Them Into One Nation."

The prior claim of the Welsh to the land they occupied went on being important to them in maintaining their non-English identity. This newly imposed Jacobean British identity was a problem; it felt like a usurpation. The Welsh needed a new way to assert their non-English identity and their prior claim to Britain. Lhuyd's Celts exactly matched their current need. Within a few years, educated Welsh people were describing themselves as Celts and exploring their own language and literature.

The induction of the Welsh into Celticness spread through the rest of Lhuyd's Celtic language-speakers, all of whom were facing political and cultural challenges from dominant neighbors. The rediscovery of Celticness gave stressed marginal groups the identity they were looking for. The result was Celtomania—an explosion of interest in things Celtic in art and literature, and an explosion of political activism.

In the eighteenth century, the most obvious manifestation of the resistance to being forced to be English was the Jacobite Rebellion, which surfaced in 1715 and again in 1745. After each of these risings, the English treason law was applied in Scotland and prisoners were removed to England for trial. The imposition of English law on the Scots was blatant. At the same time, it must be owned that James I, himself a Scot, had 100 years before wanted to see one law for England and Scotland, though he never achieved it. He had been ambitious to build on the personal union of the Crowns of England and Scotland to establish a single united country under one monarch, one parliament, and one law. But there had been opposition to this in *both* countries. Exasperated, James had asked the English Parliament the question: "Hath He not made us all one island, compassed with one sea and of itself by nature indivisible?"

Not long after the idea of a common language came the idea of a common ethnicity, a common race, with assumed large-scale movements of ancient peoples. Yet in the popular mind in the eighteenth century there was something far more distinctive than language to give the Celts an identity. It was the Druids, and the Druids as popularized by the English antiquarian William Stukeley in particular, that caught the popular imagination. Stukeley linked the Druids with the stone circles and ancient stone tombs, and this in turn gave the Celts a presence in the visible landscape; they were no longer merely archeological. And they had ancient squatters' rights.

The nineteenth-century Celtic revival continued this Stukeley-led vision of Druids. It too had a strong Romantic emphasis and an interest in recording folklore and reviving old customs.

Two Welsh teachers, father and son, T. C. Evans and Christopher Evans, designed a pictorial wall-chart for Sunday-school children. It was based on the standard alphabet chart, in which "A" is for Apple and there is a picture of an apple. What the Evanses did was simply to add the Welsh equivalent: *Afal* (Apple), *Bardd* (Bard), *Cath* (Cat), etc. *Y Wyddor* (The Alphabet) was a small but significant step forward, taken at a time when the Welsh language was in retreat.

A FRENCH CELTIC REVIVAL?

When nineteenth-century French nationalists wanted to gather support for their cause, they fell back on an episode a long way back in French history. They pointed to the attack on "French" identity by Julius Caesar and the Gauls' resistance under the heroic leadership of Vercingetorix. The Gallic commander-in-chief was compared with Napoleon, while the French themselves were portrayed as the direct descendants of the Gauls. There was an attempt to encourage modern French people to look back and see the late Iron Age Gauls as their ancestors, in much the same way that Victorian historians across the Channel in England made it their business to encourage English people to look back and see the Angles and Saxons as *their* ancestors. Neither of these scenarios was really true, for England or for France, but revisionist history is often made to serve a socio-political purpose in helping to create a sense of nationhood.

There has been a tendency in Britain to bring to the fore different alternative heritages at different times. In the nineteenth century, for instance, it was popular to promote Saxon and Norse pasts in both England and Scotland, though for George IV's Scottish visit it was Scotland's Highland Gaelic past that was brought out on parade.

In nineteenth-century Switzerland there was an effort similar to that in France—to develop and strengthen a sense of national identity by portraying the modern Swiss as descended from ancient Celts. The ancestors of the Swiss were believed to be the Celtic tribe of the Helvetii. This is perpetuated, subliminally but very effectively, in Swiss postage stamps, which still, even in the twenty-first century, bear the archaic name *Helvetia*.

AN IRISH REVIVAL

Given that Ireland is an island, with a very distinct geographical identity, it is surprising that the Irish did not develop a sense of common national identity until relatively late. There was a High King, but the main sense of identity was more local, at least until the early Middle Ages, when the Irish adopted for themselves the name *Gaidel* (or *Gaedheal* in modern Gaelic), borrowing the Old Welsh name for them, *Guoidel*, which meant "pirates" or "raiders." It seems strange now, but the thought that they were Celts did not occur to the Irish, or indeed to anyone in the British Isles, until the beginning of the eighteenth century.

Nowhere did the Celtic revival have a bigger impact on national identity than in Ireland. It led directly on to an Irish nationalist movement, a drive toward independence, and it was supported by Protestants and Catholics alike. The first society for the preservation of the Gaelic language was set up by Ulster Protestants in 1795.

A hundred years later, the situation had changed, and the Protestants began to see the revival of Gaelic as a threat to them; the Catholic majority were seen as shaping and defining the new national identity, one that would be intolerant of the identity of the Protestants, who were the descendants of English settlers and Lowland Scots.

So, while the Catholic Celtic revivalists were heading for independence, the Protestants supported Union with Britain; because of this they were known as Unionists. So, the Irish nationalist movement unfortunately failed to create a national identity that was inclusive. Here lay the seeds of partition. This was why, when Ireland became independent in 1921, predominantly Protestant Ulster remained part of the United Kingdom.

The Easter Rising of 1916 remains the landmark moment in modern Irish history, the starting-point for Irish independence from Britain. On that fateful Easter Monday, Padraic Pearse read out a declaration: "In the name of God and of the dead generations from which she receives her old tradition of nationhood, Ireland, through us, summons her children to the flag and strikes for her freedom."

A WELSH NATIONAL COSTUME

The distinctive national costume for Welsh women consists of a cotton bedgown worn over a petticoat. Over that is worn a white apron and a red flannel shawl. On the head, a tall, black, silk "stove-pipe" hat is worn on top of a bonnetlike white cotton cap. This costume was invented in the middle of the nineteenth century and is only partly based on what Welsh women had been wearing in the previous few decades, still less on what they had worn earlier than that. The tall hat, for instance, did not appear until the late 1840s. The reality was that Welsh women wore many different outfits; there was no real national style at all.

The newly invented national costume was most actively promoted by Lady Llanover

(Augusta Hall), who was the wife of a wealthy Gwent ironmaster. She was equally keen to encourage the use of the Welsh language, and she believed that adopting national language and costume would aid the development of a stronger sense of national identity. Her promotion of the national costume was helped enormously by artists who produced prints for the growing tourist trade. By 1900, photographers were taking over from artists, producing thousands of postcards showing women wearing the distinctive costume.

Lady Llanover designed a remarkable costume for her "court harpist," who was a man, but in general she was not interested in developing a national costume for Welsh men. As a result there is no available national costume for Welsh males. Attempts have been made subsequently to rectify this omission, including a design for a Welsh kilt, but without success.

Thomas Moore

Much of the Celtic revival culture was shakily founded in terms of what the past had actually been like, but it still succeeded in capturing popular interest. Associated with it was a general Romantic nostalgia for a ruined, ivy-grown Past—for an imagined greatness that once was.

The most eloquently yearning evocation of the Celtic past was the poetry of Thomas Moore, the popular Irish poet who died in 1852. His famous lines evoking the silent harp hanging on a wall at Tara stand for a whole literature of lament:

The Harp that once through Tara's halls
The soul of music shed,
Now hangs as mute on Tara's walls
As if that soul were fled.
So sleeps the pride of former days,
So glory's thrill is o'er,
And hearts that once beat high for praise
Now feel that pulse no more.

No more to chiefs and ladies bright
The harp of Tara swells.

The Element Encyclopedia of the Celts

The chord, alone, that breaks at
night
Its tale of ruin tells.
Thus freedom now so seldom wakes,
The only throb she gives,
Is when some heart indignant breaks
To show that she still lives.

Sir Walter Scott

The cause of Celtic freedom was honed by the violent suppression of the Jacobite Rebellions of 1715 and 1745. Little empathy could be stirred in the eighteenth century among the great English majority in Britain, who believed their Anglo-Saxon culture to be vastly superior to the Celtic culture that was in retreat. And yet in the nineteenth century, the novelist Sir Walter Scott was able to elicit sympathy in Britain generally for the way the Highland Scots had been treated.

By the early nineteenth century, even the most optimistic and fervent Scots patriots had come to see Scottish independence as a lost cause. The two Jacobite risings and the savage way they had been dealt with had sapped all resistance. Sir Walter Scott held strong views about the Act of Union, which in effect abolished Scot-land as an identifiable nation. But he was clever. He did not openly espouse the cause of Scottish independence, and he did not resist the Union, he merely raised awareness of Scotland's evaporating history. Above all, he wanted the English to treat the Scots better. This gentle approach was very effective.

Sir Walter Scott's *Waverley* novels were enormously influential in building a Romantic picture of Highland Scots as noble clansmen. They showed the state of Highland society in the wake of the Jacobite risings. *Waverley* itself (published in 1814) begins symbolically in 1745, the year of the second rebellion, and shows two opposing families reconciled. *Redgauntlett* (1824) more daringly deals with a hypothetical third Jacobite rising—one that did not happen in 1765.

Scott knew that the real conflict was not between Jacobite and Hanoverian, or between Scots and English, but between Scottish Highlanders (Gaels) and Scottish Lowlanders (Lallanders). The Highlanders spoke Gaelic and wore tartan kilts; the Lowlanders did neither.

In a very peculiar but historically very important royal visit in 1821, the new king, George IV, came to Edinburgh. Sir Walter Scott was Master of Ceremonies, with Colonel David Stewart as his deputy, and the two of them had devised new tartans for the whole country, not just the Highlands. The king placed an order with his outfitters, George Hunter & Co., for a magnificent Highland outfit costing £1,355. It was in a bright red Royal Tartan, which later became known as Royal Stewart. It was ornamented with gold chains and various weapons including a dirk, sword, and pistols. Instead of going bare-legged, the king wore pink tights. David Wilkie painted a flattering portrait of him in his expensive new costume, with the legs portrayed bare; the painted king cut a fine figure, but the image was a gift to the political cartoonists of the day.

However, when George IV duly appeared in Edinburgh in his Royal Stewart kilt, it was an incredible, yet immensely successful, publicity stunt, one that at a stroke created a national tradition that unified Scotland. It was a piece of artifice, but it worked in forging a new sense of nationhood.

By the time Queen Victoria's consort, the German-born Prince Albert, arrived at Balmoral, it did not seem remotely odd that he should invent a tartan for his family to use. The Scots had in effect found a dressing-up game that made the Gaels and Lallanders put aside their differences.

The tartan kilt became a national costume, mainly because of Sir Walter Scott's enterprise. The pleated kilt, or *philibeg*, had been invented as recently as 1727 by Thomas Rawlinson; he was an English ironmaster who was trying to devise a comfortable garment for his employees to wear in the ironworks instead of their genuine traditional costume, which was the belted plaid. It may have been modern, it may have been designed by an Englishman, but it worked.

Robert Louis Stevenson commented:

In spite of the difference of blood and language, the Lowlander feels himself the sentimental countryman of the Highlander. When they meet abroad, they fall upon each other's neck in spirit; even at home there is a kind of clannish intimacy in their talk. But from his [English] compatriot in the south, the Lowlander stands consciously apart.

Sir Walter Scott's treatment of Rob Roy in the 1818 novel of the same name typifies what was happening. Rob Roy was a real-life Highlander, an eighteenth-century cattle-thief who ran a protection racket. Scott turned this dubious historical character into a Robin Hood: a Celtic hero.

James Macpherson

The reality of the past was slipping quietly into the background. The Ossian hoax of the 1760s was an indication that the British in general were ready to accept, quite knowingly, a past that was fictitious. This hoax involved a certain James MacPherson, who brought out a collection of fake poems that he claimed were written by an ancient Highland bard called Ossian. At first, many were taken in. Dr. Samuel Johnson, however, was one of those who saw through Macpherson; he was convinced that he was "a mountebank, a liar, and a fraud, and that the poems were forgeries." The poems were in fact quickly exposed as forgeries, and yet, surprisingly, they continued to be very popular. They were bestsellers. Even Goethe and Napoleon became devotees.

"Fictitious" Spelling

William Stukeley's fantasy that Druids conducted their ceremonies at Neolithic standing stones was also eagerly adopted, though he produced no evidence to support his claim. In 1802 Edward Jones published *The Bardic Museum*, which purported to represent the "musical, poetical and historical relicks of the Welsh Bards and Druids, drawn from authentic documents of remote antiquity (with great pains now rescued from oblivion) and never before published." The 'relicks' included "the ancient war-tunes of the bards" and an elegant air for the harp entitled "*Y Derwydd—The Druid*." It was a jig in 6/8 time.

Ideas about Celticness snowballed. One reason for its popularity was that it seemed to offer a contrasting and comforting alternative to industrialization. The rural idyll of the peaceful white-robed Druids in their leafy glades offered a welcome contrast to the grimness of the factories and the poor terrace housing that went with them. William Blake and William Wordsworth both brought Druids into their poems.

The Element Encyclopedia of the Celts

Societies were founded to revive the Druidic religion. This entailed a lot of imagination, but new rituals were concocted, such as the Maen Gorsedd bardic ceremony, first performed in 1792 and now a routine part of the Welsh National Eisteddfod. This well-known ceremony was devised by Edward Williams, better known now by his bardic name, Iolo Morgannwg.

In the nineteenth century, there was a preoccupation with ethnicity, and in particular with establishing a pecking order of racial types. There was a general consensus in England that the Anglo-Saxons were the top race, which meant that the Celts must be inferior. On the other hand, because the Celts had settled in Britain before the Anglo-Saxons, they could argue a prior claim to the territory.

Victorian jewelers had a try at imitating Celtic brooches, but the result was clumsy by comparison with originals such as the Hunterston brooch:

Pre-Raphaelite painters were more successful at glamorizing Celticness. Several painters specialized in fairy pictures, notably Richard Dadd, Richard Doyle, J. Simmons and John Anster Fitzgerald, but many other artists besides. These showed very much the softer side of Celticness—pure escapism. Edward Burne-Jones's final masterpiece was *The Death of Arthur*, which was a grandiose Victorian establishment version of Arthur lying in state in Avalon.

Today, in a new phase of the Celtic revival, the great Irish writer Seamus Heaney looks back to Tara to weave ancient symbols and rituals into his poetry.

THE HIGHLAND CLEARANCES

But as well as a fictious past, the British were accepting a fictitious present. In the midst of the warm glow of rediscovered tartans and revived Highland games, the Highland clearances were going on.

The Element Encyclopedia of the Celts

The roots of the clearances lay in the middle of the eighteenth century, with the suppression of the Highland clans after the 1745 Rebellion. Some of the Highland landlords wanted to clear the tenantry from their land to open it up to large-scale commercial sheep grazing and sport. Whole communities were forced out and forced to emigrate.

There were other reasons for the emigrations too. The population began to grow rapidly, too rapidly, with the introduction of the potato. In 1755, the population of the island of Barra was 1,150; by 1801 it had increased to 1,925. Faced with this scale of population growth, landlords tried to find new food sources and new ways of making a living. Fish and kelp were tried. Then a new problem appeared. In 1846 the Irish potato famine reached the Western Isles of Scotland, and starvation was imminent. For Barra's landlord, Colonel Gordon, forced shipment to Canada was the simplest and quickest solution. Four hundred islanders were cleared from Barra in 1851 and shipped to Canada, where it has to be said that many of them prospered—and they would not have prospered had they stayed on Barra.

The clearances were cruel and traumatic, but they may have been a blessing in disguise. Similar stories were told all over the Highlands. It was a far cry from the kilted revels laid on for George IV's visit a generation earlier.

THE GOLDEN DAWN

Ideas of racial supremacy fell out of favor in the twentieth century, especially once the nightmare of the Nazi genocidal persecutions began. But there had in any case, even before Hitler, been a shift toward emphasizing the poetical, mystical side of Celtic culture.

A highly Romanticized version of ancient Celtic culture was developed at the end of the nineteenth century and the beginning of the twentieth, and magic was to the fore. Three men—William Woodman, William Westcott, and Samuel Mathers—who were all Freemasons and members of the Societas Rosicruciana in Anglia, founded the Hermetic Order of the Golden Dawn. This new society was one of the greatest single influences on Western occultism in the twentieth century.

It seems to have been Westcott who was the driving force behind the founding of the Golden Dawn. Key elements in the society were hierarchy and initiation, as in the Masonic Lodges. One important difference was that the Golden Dawn admitted women, and as equals with men. There were three orders. The First Order dealt in esoteric philosophy through study and the basics of astrology, tarot divination, and geomancy. The Second Order (the Ruby Rose and Cross of Gold) had proper magic as its focus: scrying, astral travel, and alchemy. The Third Order was the order of "the Secret Chiefs." These chiefs were supposed masters of magic who oversaw the activities of the two lower orders—by spirit communication with Chiefs of the Second Order.

The initiation grades give an idea of the elaborate structure of the Golden Dawn.

First Order
Introduction—Neophyte 0=0
Zelator 1=10

Theoricus 2=9
Practicus 3=8
Philosophus 4=7
Intermediate—Portal Grade

Second Order
Adeptus Minor 5=6
Adeptus Major 6=5
Adeptus Exemptus 7=4

Third Order
Magister Templi 8=3
Magus 9=2
Ipsissimus 10=1

The paired numbers beside each grade relate to positions on the Tree of Life. The Neophyte Grade of "0=0" indicates that there is no position on the Tree. In the other pairs, the first number is the number of steps up from the bottom (Malkuth), and the second numeral is the number of steps down from the top (Kether).

The Golden Dawn had its own foundation myth. The story goes that Westcott found a manuscript in cipher in a London bookshop. It contained details of rituals for a secret society devoted to magic, along with the address of a German adept. Westcott duly wrote to the adept and received the charter for the Hermetic Order of the Golden Dawn. The story was not true. The letters from the German adept, Frau Sprengel, were fakes composed by a non-German speaker. It is thought that the manuscript was most likely written by Kenneth Mackenzie (a Masonic scholar); he passed them to the Reverend A. Woodford, who died shortly after the Golden Dawn was founded, and who was unimpressed by them anyway. In 1886 he passed them to William Westcott, who decoded them and called on a couple of other Masons to develop them into a system.

The Cipher Manuscripts are the bible of the Golden Dawn. They were real enough, and they prescribe the grade rituals for the order, laying down a curriculum.

There seems to be no single inspiration for the Golden Dawn. It draws on Christian mysticism, the Qabalah, Hermeticism, ancient Egypt, Freemasonry, Alchemy, Theosophy, Eliphas Levi, Enochian magic, and Renaissance grimoires. It would be hard to see any element here that had been plucked from any Celtic tradition, whether ancient or more recent. Yet the Golden Dawn and the sheer mystery of its occultism were somehow to become a part of the fabric of the Celtic revival. If one wanted to prick the bubble of neo-Celtic mysticism, one could point to the Golden Dawn as responsible for supplying a richly textured backdrop of occultism—an all-important mystery element.

The first temple, the Isis-Urania Temple, was founded in London in 1888. This had First Order activities only as its business for the first four years. The Inner Order became active in 1892, when a circle of adepts was equipped to move on. Further temples were set up in Weston-super-Mare, Bradford, and Edinburgh. By the middle of the 1890s, the Golden Dawn was well-established in Britain. A significant number of well-known people belonged to it, notably the prominent Irish poet William Butler Yeats, the Irish revolutionary Maud Gonne, the Irish writer and creator of *Dracula* Bram Stoker, the Welsh writer Arthur Machen, the English writers Evelyn Underhill and E. Nesbit and, most notoriously, the magician Aleister Crowley.

In 1897, Westcott abruptly broke his connection with the Golden Dawn. This is thought to be because some papers relating to magic were left in a hansom cab and his connection with the Golden Dawn became known to his employers. He may have been told that he would have to resign as coroner if he continued with the Golden Dawn. Mather was left in control and he appointed the actress Florence Farr to be chief Adept in Anglia (England). But rebellion simmered, as members became dissatisfied with Mathers' leadership and uneasy about his growing friendship with Crowley. Mathers was forced out as far as the London temple was concerned, though he was active elsewhere; by the outbreak of the First World War, he had founded two temples in America.

In 1901, W. B. Yeats resigned as a result of internal politics. Most of the temples had closed by the end of the 1930s, though one in New Zealand remained in action until 1978.

It should be emphasized that the philosophical and magical teachings of the Golden Dawn bear no relation to any earlier Celtic beliefs but, because the Golden

Dawn erupted into being at a time when the Celtic revival was underway, it provided the revival movement with a kind of spiritual fuel. This was given extra potency by the participation in the movement of a considerable number of a high-profile "Celts," that is to say, celebrity members with a Scottish, Irish, or Welsh background.

CELTIC MUSIC: "HOW BEAUTIFUL THEY, THE LORDLY ONES"

In music, the Celtic revival was marked by the composition in 1911–12 of Rutland Boughton's opera *The Immortal Hour.* This was performed at the Birmingham Repertory Theatre in 1921, where it was so well received that it was taken to London. At the Regent Theatre, King's Cross, it ran and ran, for 216 consecutive performances starting in October 1923. It was revived in 1926 and 1932, again with great success. People went to see it again and again and were spellbound by it.

Rutland Boughton developed the libretto from a verse drama by Fiona MacLeod published in 1900. The piece thoroughly inhabits the remote, haunting, and enchanted world of Celtic legend. One of the characters, Dalua, sings:

I have come hither, led by dreams and visions,
And I know not why I come, and to what end,
And wherefore 'mid the noise of chariot wheels,
Where the swung world roars down the starry ways.

There, at least, are the chariots of the Iron Age Celtic warriors of old.

Boughton originally intended the work to be performed in the open air, with the opening chorus performed by singers winding their way through the trees. This is consistent with the Iron Age approach to religious ceremonies, which took place mostly in the open air.

There is a particular magic in the chorus of Unseen Voices, which seem to be the archaic spirits of place. We might call them sprites or fairies. They sing:

How beautiful they are,
The lordly ones
Who dwell in the hollow hills.

They have faces like flowers,
And their breath is a wind
That blows over summer meadows,
Filled with dewy clover...

The wonderful neo-Celtic atmosphere of *The Immortal Hour* was carried over into another opera, *The Midsummer Marriage*, composed by the Cornishman Sir Michael Tippett in 1955. He too opens his opera in a woodland clearing. His magic wood too is peopled by unseen presences: ancient spirits, who have become visible at midsummer. At the end, Tippett has his chorus of nature spirits sing:

We are the laughing children.
Fresh, free, fine,
Strong, straight, stark,
Rough, raw, rude,
Gallant, grim and gay.

There is a kinship between this and the final chorus of *The Immortal Hour*:

They play with lances,
And are proud and terrible,
Marching in the moonlight
With fierce blue eyes.

Michael Tippett wrote a detailed essay about the writing of *The Midsummer Marriage*, without acknowledging that it had its roots in *The Immortal Hour*. I wrote in my book *The Stonehenge People* that "Tippett showed a rare insight into the personality of the [Neolithic] Avebury people in *The Midsummer Marriage*, where they appear as volatile, instinctual, profoundly attuned to the forces of nature." Tippett came in time to see himself less as a Cornishman, more as a descendant of those ancient people of the stones, but the last time I saw him he was keen to explain that he thought I was wrong: when he wrote *The Midsummer Marriage* he had been thinking of the laughing children as ancient Greeks. He had come to see the people of the stones as his ancestors only later, and partly because of what I had written. I understood that, but believed, and still believe, that he was unconscious of the real force behind the opera, though he did in fact sense that the writing of it was powered from outside himself. He seemed, to the end, to have been unaware of the (neo-Celtic) influence of *The Immortal Hour*, but all of us are profoundly influenced by events we have long forgotten. And *this* is how the Celtic revival has worked, subtly reinvigorating the arts in the twentieth century.

A New Ethnicity? Celtic by Choice?

In the early twentieth century there was increasing awareness that the old Celtic languages were in danger of dying out and in need of rescue. There was a movement to regenerate them. The attempts at language revival made a new focus. Nothing gives a community a stronger sense of unity and common purpose than a threat from outside. It has been said that the sense of an English nation emerged as a direct result of the threat of military and cultural annihilation by the Vikings in the ninth and tenth centuries AD. The disruption of a multiplicity of small Anglo-Saxon kingdoms by the fierce Viking onslaught directly resulted in the emergence of a unified English state. The coalescence of Anglo-Saxon kingdoms in England and Scotland might have happened anyway, but more slowly; the Viking attack was the great catalyst in making it happen rapidly.

In a similar way, Celtic self-consciousness in the twentieth century was pushed along by the awareness that the old languages were being spoken by fewer and fewer people. This time the enemy was not the Vikings, but the English or, in the case of the Breton language, the French. The decline of the Welsh language in particular became a focus for those, such as Lady Llanover, who wanted to see Wales strengthened and revived. But this was a new sense of identity, different than the ancient sense of identity. In the sixth century, loyalties were to the kingdoms of Gwynedd, or Powys, or Ceretigan, or Demetia, not to Wales ... and in the time before the Romans invaded, the local loyalties would have been tribal—loyalties to the chiefs of the Ordovices, Deceangli, Silures, Demetae, Cornovii: again, not to Wales...

Nineteenth-century ideas on race were unsatisfactory for other reasons. More was discovered about people's origins, partly through explorations of family history, partly through archeological research, and partly through DNA evidence. Ethnicity is, after all, not straightforward. It turns out not to be the case that everyone living in Scotland is Scottish. This is not surprising.

The complications arising from the new evidence of mixed or "conflicted" ethnicity prompted a movement in the 1990s toward a new definition of ethnicity, which might be summed up as "how I think of myself." According to this approach, a person's ethnicity is their "self-conceptualization, resulting from identification with a group, in opposition to others, on the basis of perceived cultural difference and/or perceived common descent." So, according to this new approach, if I think I am English, because I have been brought up to think so, I am English. Even if my DNA and my bone structure clearly indicate that I am Celtic-British, native stock, and that my ancestors were established in south-east England long before the Angles, Saxons, and Jutes arrived there—in spite of that, I am English.

Can my ethnicity really be allowed to become a matter of choice, like religion, political allegiance, leisure pursuits, or the way I decorate my house?

There must be a suspicion that the New Ethnicity has been engi-neered largely to get around some uncomfortable truths. One is that large numbers of people with a Scottish address are actually of non-Celtic, mainly Anglo-Saxon, origin. The Scottish Lowlands, where the costly new Scottish Parliament building now stands, were colonized by Anglo-Saxon incomers as early as the sixth century, before some parts of southern England. Both Cornwall and Devon were Anglicized *after* the Scottish Lowlands, which means that the Scottish Lowlanders (even those who are Lowlanders by deep descent) are more English than the English living in Devon.

The Englishness of Scotland is often overlooked. A wave of English migrants moved to Scotland at the very beginning of the Industrial Revolution. It began in the late seventeenth century, when Sir James Stanfield took a group of English workers to set up the first framework knitting factory in Edinburgh. As industrialization developed during the eighteenth century, skilled iron workers were attracted from England to the Carron Iron foundries. Hosiery workers from Nottingham went to work in the mills at Hawick. The flow of English migrants into

Scotland continued through the nineteenth century. By the time of the 1921 census, the English had replaced the Irish as the largest group of immigrants in Scotland.

From then on, there was a massive acceleration in the rate of English immigration into Scotland until, by the 2001 census, more than 8 percent of the people living in Scotland had been born in England.

In the 1970s, the media highlighted middle-class refugees from the urban rat-race in England: people who were casting aside urban stress for the delights of rural life in the Scottish Highlands and Islands. But the reality is that most of the England-to-Scotland migration was then and still is to the Lowlands, and to urban jobs in the Lowland cities. One urban rat-race was swapped for another. Now, 20 percent of "Lowland Scots" are English-born.

The odd thing is that many of these English-born immigrants think of themselves as Scots, even though they know they have come from England. Sir Bernard Crick, an English-born political writer who moved to Scotland in 1977, has commented that the English are insecure in their identity. It seems that a Scottish identity is perceived as *stronger* and therefore more desirable. Perhaps part of the attraction is the pervasive sense of deprivation, of maltreatment across hundreds of years, like the Highland clearances in the nineteenth century, or the hammering of the Highland clans in the eighteenth. Perhaps it is rooted in a general dissatisfaction with Westminster and the way things happen there.

Whatever the reason, whatever it is that people are buying into or buying out of, it is disconcerting that so many people can so easily switch their national identity.

TWENTY-FIRST CENTURY CELTICNESS

The word "Celtic" continues to be used in academic circles to label a group of Indo-European languages. It has also, because of the Celtic revival we have been discussing, become associated—for the purposes of literary criticism—with a certain body of literature written in the late nineteenth and early twentieth centuries.

An increasing generic use of the word in a variety of contexts has given the world a label for a type of music, a type of storytelling, and a type of spirituality. These in truth have little grounding in the past but are, again increasingly, used to market products and activities that people from Scotland, Wales, and Ireland, or of descent from those places, may feel obliged to subscribe to. The Celtic worldview that is represented here—Celticity—is sometimes little more than a marketing vehicle: an antidote to the contemporary urban rat-race represented by day-to-day life in the English cities. Above all it represents an escape to an idyllic emerald-green countryside teeming with ruined castles soaring above wave-washed rocks, and caves and forests where the spirits of nature abound. It even incorporates an undemanding religion that requires only a passive submission to nature and a generalized appreciation of the magical and mystical. The misty evocations of music such as the re-cordings of Enya waft us away to a neo-Celtic neverland.

Side by side with this, Welshness has been conspicuously re-invented, with the highlighting of rugby football and male voice choirs. It is doubtful whether either of these activities is traceable back to the Celticness of the Iron Age, though maybe there is a link through their masculinity, their *machismo.*

The more "feminine," spiritual, aspect of the new Celticity has a broad appeal to the Greens and the planet-savers: all who feel the strain of modern civilization and who yearn for some sort of return to a pre-industrial age. At the moment of checking, there were 44,000 websites advertising Celtic storytellers.

I do not intend to convey that there is anything wrong with any of this, but it will be clear from the contents of this book that modern Celticness has little to do with the long-unfolding story of the Atlantic Celts. Nor does it have much to do with the socio-political status of Scotland, Wales, and Ireland, or indeed with the situations in Cornwall, Brittany, or Galicia.

CELTICNESS AND
DEVOLUTION

During the twentieth century a seriously political phase emerged in which Celticness became a platform for demanding devolution and independence. This went alongside the evolution of the European Union. In Britain the major landmark was the inauguration in May 1999 of the Scottish Parliament and the Welsh Assembly.

This development was part of a wider European phenomenon: the reawakening of dormant nationalism, which happened most disruptively in Eastern Europe following the collapse of the Soviet bloc. But it was also evident in Western Europe, where a number of composite nation-states—Britain, Ireland, Belgium, Italy, and Spain—experienced a wave of self-consciousness and political aspiration.

Another significant new factor is the existence of a European Union: an umbrella under which aspiring, new, small nations imagine they might seek shelter. The EU is seen by some as a kind of safe super-state, within which it would be possible for a multiplicity of small states to exist. In this context it is worth pointing out that Cornwall is 50 percent larger in area than Luxembourg.

Much of this aspiring to independence is driven by passionate beliefs about identity, history, and origins. Now that we are in an age where new parliaments and assemblies are being (expensively) inaugurated, and the clamor for more independence continues, is it time to examine the historical truth of the assumptions that lie behind all this?

If the "Ancient Celts of Britain and Ireland" are in effect a recent invention, what does this mean for modern people who think of themselves as Celts? There is the possibility that the Celticness of Scotland, Wales, and Ireland, as distinct from England, may be an illusion; if an illusory Celticness is being used for political leverage and advantage, then is some kind of fraud being perpetrated? Michael

Morse, writing in 2005 about the appearance of the Celts in Britain, came to the conclusion that "the Celts are, and always were, a creation of the human mind."

These are views that have been put forward recently, by a number of writers, in the wake of recent findings by archeologists about the ethnic (i.e. genetic) identity of people living in the Isles.

The Celtic revival in Brittany began in 1867, when the Breton folklorist La Villemarque called the first Inter-Celtic Congress in Brittany. His carefully worded invitation summoned his "compatriots" from Wales, his "cousins" from Scotland and Ireland, and his "brothers" from Cornwall. It was an attempt to forge a political alliance among the Celtic nations of Atlantic Europe, to counter the power of England and France.

More than a century later another conference was convened: a general assembly of the Conférence des Régions Périphériques Maritimes. It decided to set up a commission called the Atlantic Arc, which would bring together all the regions of the Atlantic façade of Europe. The purpose was to create a political and economic force that would counteract the power of the industrial regions stretching in another arc from Birmingham to Milan. Whether we are seeing the revival of a timeless geopolitical reality or the creation of another Celtic myth is unclear. One unsettling aspect of the Atlantic Arc is that it leaves out the Highlands and Islands of Scotland, the Central Lowlands of Scotland, the English shore of the Irish Sea, the head of the Bristol Channel, Northern Ireland, and the southern and western coasts of Ireland—all of which have Atlantic shores. So, selected areas of the Atlantic façade of Europe are strategically left out of the Atlantic Arc, while by contrast Andalucia is included, even though two-thirds of its coastline is in the Mediterranean.

THE LANGUAGE PROBLEM

The Celtic revival in Wales might be seen as beginning in 1886, when Cymru Fydd (Young Wales) was founded—in London.

It was not until 1925 that Plaid Cymru (the Party of Wales) was formed, its primary mandate being the promotion of the Welsh language. The 1911 census had revealed that 43.5 percent of the population of Wales could speak Welsh, compared with 54 percent 20 years earlier; by 1931 that had fallen to 36.8 percent. The Welsh language was in retreat.

A turning-point in awareness came in the 1960s, when John Saunders Lewis gave a speech on *The Future of the Welsh Language.* It was broadcast in 1962, following the revelation in the 1961 census that the percentage of Welsh speakers had fallen again, to 26 percent. After that, several measures were taken to halt the decline and promote the teaching of Welsh; the Welsh Language Society was set up during a summer school of Plaid Cymru. But, in spite of these efforts, the percentage of those able to speak Welsh has fallen even further, to 20 percent.

Perhaps the state of the language should not be seen as the "temperature" of Welshness. In Ireland the percentage of Irish speakers has fallen from 5 percent in 1891 to only 1.2 percent today and this is in spite of 80 years of compulsory teaching of Gaelic in schools in the Irish Republic. In Scotland the percentage of Gaelic speakers has fallen to 1 percent. Yet no one doubts that Scotland or Ireland have characteristic identities. It may be sad that the old languages are in retreat, but who today speaks the Linear B Greek spoken by Achilles, the Latin spoken by Julius Caesar, the Norman French of Duke William, or the English of Geoffrey Chaucer? Only a handful of language specialists.

The fact that the number of Irish speakers in Ireland has fallen to a very low level has done nothing to impair the Irish sense of identity. It may be that, for the Irish at least, language has become less important as an index of success: economic development matters more. In the 1990s, Ireland for the first time outperformed the United Kingdom in terms of per capita GDP and won a new reputation as the "Celtic tiger."

The Breton language is in a healthier state than Irish or Scottish Gaelic: about 5 percent of Bretons speak it as their everyday language. Efforts are being made to boost the language by making bilingual primary

The Element Encyclopedia of the Celts

education available, but there is little encouragement from Paris, and this approach has not been very fruitful in Wales or Ireland. An article was added to the French Constitution in 1994, declaring that "the language of the Republic is French." This was moderated in 2008 when another article was added stating that "the regional languages belong to the heritage of France."

The sixth of the "Six Celtic Nations" to be recognized is Cornwall, but there the Cornish language had all but died out by 2000. It is said that only 0.3 percent of the people living in Cornwall are able to speak Cornish. Attempts to revive it began in 1904, with the publication of Henry Jenner's *Handbook of the Cornish Language.* But disagreement followed immediately about the version of Cornish that was to be revived. Should it be Cornish as spoken in the *eighteenth* century, by which time it had become corrupted by the incursion of English? Or was uncorrupted *sixteenth-* century Cornish to be preferred? Disagreements of this kind can hopelessly weaken a cause.

The focus on language survival seems unfortunate, given the low percentages of people who are keeping the old languages going. The Celtic Congress and the Celtic League, two influential pan-Celtic organizations, use Celtic language as the defining mark of Celtic nationhood, and this is why only Six Nations are considered. This "membership" is not universally accepted; for example, Northern Ireland's Unionists do not usually consider themselves to be Celtic, nor do all the Lowland Scots.

Galicia is not now considered eligible as a seventh Celtic nation (by pan-Celtic organizations), because its language has become extinct. This seems less than fair, as the Manx language has been extinct since 1974 and yet the Isle of Man has been given Celtic nation status. Activists in Galicia, Asturias, and Cantabria (among other places) have tried to win official recognition as modern Celts, so far without success.

Galicia and the adjacent region of northern Portugal, ancient Gallaecia, lost its independence only in the 1830s, but separatists began campaigning straightaway. General Miguel Solis Cuetos led an attempt at a separatist coup in 1846, but he and his forces were defeated at the Battle of Cacheiras, and the survivors, including General Solis himself, were shot. They are remembered in Galicia as the Martyrs of Liberty. The Galicians turned to asserting their cultural independence, while the Rexurdimento movement focused on recovering the Galician language.

Galicia has lost its ancient language. But there are many who see that there are other aspects of Galician cultural life that qualify for its recognition as Celtic. In 2009, in an attempt to win formal recognition, a Gallaic Revival Movement sponsored by the Galician Celtic League announced that it was reconstructing the Gallaic language (a Q-Celtic language). It seems that this reconstructed language is being based on Vincent Pintado's *Old Celtic Dictionary* and the *Atebivota Dictionary*.

A similar attempt is being made to advance the view that north-eastern England is really Celtic. Cumbria and Lancashire together made up the Dark Age Celtic (i.e. non-Anglo-Saxon) kingdom of Rheged. It is said that there were still speakers of the Cumbric language in this area until the eleventh century, but that is 1,000 years ago. In recent years, Celtic activists have been working toward reconstructing the extinct Cumbric language, apparently basing it on Old Welsh, but it is by no means universally agreed among language scholars that Old Welsh was once spoken all over England. Some sympathizers have suggested that adopting Modern Welsh might be a better idea, rather than "reinventing the wheel." There have been parallel moves in Devon to revive whatever pre-Anglo-Saxon language was spoken there, and the idea of simply adopting Cornish has been floated.

Iolo Morgannwg claimed to have transcribed *The Principal Territories of Britain* from an old manuscript. Of the 16 listed, all but one are known to historians. The one that remains obscure is *Arllechwedd Galedin*. But the location is clear enough. Caint (Kent) is described as extending from the Tain (Thames) River and *Mor Tawch* (the Misty Sea) to the borders of Arllechwedd Galedin, which in turn extends from the borders of Kent to *Dyvnaint* (Devon) and *Gwlad yr Hav* (Somerset). Arllechwedd Galedin must therefore be the old Celtic name of Wessex and Sussex, "the hill slopes belonging to the people who came from the land which was flooded," so even this supposedly Anglo-Saxon heartland was a Celtic land and its Celtic name can be retrieved—if Iolo is to be believed, which is another story.

It is good to cherish the past and try to conserve what is left of it, but the strenuous and valiant efforts to revive old (and in some cases extinct) languages seem to be efforts poorly rewarded. Even with heavy financial investment and strenuous promotion by the authorities, as in Ireland and Wales, the take-up for the old languages has not so far been very great. It may be that conserving other aspects of the cultural traditions will in the longer term be more fruitful. History, politics, myth, religion, archeology, folklore, customs, dance, art, and music—all of these are key elements in Celtic cultures, and propagating them would be an enormously worthwhile alternative.

To some extent, the political nationalists are already leaving the language issue to one side. Language played a part in the early development of nationalist movements in Wales and Scotland. It is, significantly, no longer central to the Scottish National Party, which has civic nationalism as its focus. Even Plaid Cymru, the Party of Wales, is working to broaden its appeal in English-speaking areas.

PRESENT AND FUTURE

The influence of the Celtic past is hard to assess, because it is pervasive. We take for granted the delightful comic-book stories about *Asterix the Gaul* by René Goscinny (the author) and Albert Uderzo (the equally brilliant illustrator). But they bring elements from a quite exotic past into the present and make them familiar. Uderzo

The Element Encyclopedia of the Celts

believes the French love of fashion, talk, drink, and freedom owes much to the Celtic character.

What of today's Celticness? Local groups within the Six Nations continue to work at maintaining and reinvigorating the individual national traditions, while activists in currently marginalized "nations" such as Galicia do the same and try to gain acceptance in the wider community. Increasingly, that wider community takes over.

There is an international Celtic movement: a pan-Celtic movement that transcends political boundaries. During the nineteenth century, many Scottish and Irish people emigrated to the New World in search of a better life. On a smaller scale, the Cornish and Welsh too emigrated, and not just to North America. The descendants of this Celtic diaspora look back to Europe for their cultural roots, and naturally feel themselves to be on some level Celtic. A recent book advanced the view that it was the Scots-Irish settlers who were mainly responsible for shaping America—not the Anglo-Saxon settlers. That may not be true, but it is an indication of the value that is being placed on Celticness outside Europe. The existence of Celtic Studies departments at many universities, studying ancient and modern Celtic languages, Celtic history, and Celtic folklore, shows how this movement is being promoted.

Traditional Celtic music is alive and well. There are many individual musicians and groups keeping the Irish old style going, and the Welsh voice and harp, and the Scottish working songs. As with English folk music, collectors have been actively recording old performers singing and playing in traditional style, and new generations of performers assiduously imitate these authentic "folk" performances. This tradition dates from the nineteenth century, and what we cannot know is how far the music of that time reflects the folk music of earlier times. To some extent the claim that there are distinct Celtic music styles is a nineteenth-century assertion. At that time, folklorists were busy, in non-Celtic areas of Europe too, gathering stories, legends, myths, and music, and the presumption was that this collection represented a reservoir of ancient culture. Maybe it was.

However arrived at, the Irish and Scots Gaelic styles are compelling, convincing, and full of character: worth conserving and perpetuating for their own sake. Different traditions and styles existed in Brittany and Wales. Even so, the Breton revival has borrowed from Gaelic styles. The harp is seen as the national instrument of Wales and is used in what is called penillion singing—the harpist plays a melody and the singer sings a different melody in counterpoint. The pan-Celtic movement has led to a certain amount of cross-fertilization. Pan-Celtic music festivals, such as the annual Festival Interceltique de Lorient that began in 1971,

have played their part. Welsh instrumentalists have revived the bagpipe featuring in traditional Breton, Irish, and Scottish music. The bagpipe was in use in the Middle Ages in Wales—in fact, it was in use everywhere in Europe in the Middle Ages. Breton musicians have even borrowed the Scottish Highland pipes.

Unaccompanied singing has become popular as a folk style, though this is not uniquely Celtic, but a style shared across a wider area.

The Scottish New Year festival, Hogmanay, has its roots in an ancient midwinter festival to mark the winter solstice. The word "Hogmanay" is of unknown origin. It was first written down in 1604, but the celebration may date back to the Viking colonists. It is marked today by dancing and the singing of *Auld Lang Syne* as midnight chimes for the ending of the old year. Singing *Auld Lang Syne* has become a tradition in many other countries too. The words of the song were written by Robert Burns in 1788, revamping a poem written by James Watson in 1711; this was later sung to an existing folk tune, a strathspey called *The Miller's Daughter.*

Hogmanay was popularized both in Scotland and across Britain by the New Year's Eve television programme *The White Heather Club*, which ran from 1957 to 1968. This was presented by the traditional Scottish singer Andy Stewart, with dance music performed by Jimmy Shand and his band. As a result of this exposure, Hogmanay became an integral part of the Scottish national identity, as perceived outside Scotland.

Celtic dancing can be conscientiously traditional, or it can be reinvented and energized, and by doing this its appeal can be greatly extended. Irish stepdancing had a strong and established following within the Irish community, but the first performance of *Riverdance* in 1994 widened its appeal enormously. *Riverdance* was devised by Bill Whelan of the Irish folkband Planxty, as a seven-minute set-piece interval performance for the 1994 Eurovision Song Contest. The spectacle of precision-coordination among a large group of dancers changed world perception of Irish culture. The first performance featured Irish dancing champions Jean Butler and Michael Flatley, and it was Flatley who was responsible for most of the choreography. Michael Flatley later left *Riverdance* and put up his own show, *Lord of the Dance*. These two spectacular displays of Irish stepdancing did much to fuel the Celtomania of the 1990s.

Celtic music can be a lament, or it can rock. The Chieftains have taken the tradition and invigorated it by adding something new. This may be seen as inauthentic folk music but, as we have seen, the Celts have changed over the course of hundreds, even thousands, of years—changed, adapted, and reinvented. There was a period of accommodation during the Roman occupation; there was another when Christianity arrived, and another when the Jutes, Angles, Saxons, Franks, and Norsemen arrived. The old cultures were forced to adapt and absorb or be absorbed.

In popular music, perhaps Enya best represents the spirit of Celticness. Born in 1961 in County Donegal in Ireland, Enya Brennan gained wide recognition with her music for the 1986 BBC TV series *The Celts*. The distinctive, echoing, outdoor sound is made by layering her voice as many as 80 times to make a virtual choir. Much of the instrumental backing is produced electronically. The overall effect is disembodied and otherworldly.

James Cameron's film *Titanic* is an American take on the tragic fate of a Celtic ship, built in a Northern Irish shipyard by the Belfast firm Harland & Wolff. Some of the ill-fated steerage passengers are Irish and the film shows their high-spirited dancing below decks. What heightens the sense that this is overwhelmingly a Celtic tragedy is the highly atmospheric soundtrack. James Cameron originally planned to commission Enya to write the music, and even made a rough edit of some of her existing music

to make a temporary soundtrack. But Enya declined and Cameron then approached James Horner, who had written the soundtrack for *Braveheart*. Horner agreed and composed and orchestrated the 1997 score for *Titanic* with Enya's soundworld in mind. The wordless keening vocals were sung by the Norwegian singer Sissel Kyrkjebo (James Horner's choice). The effect is of a Celtic lament sung from a Donegal clifftop, perhaps for a Brendan-like epic voyage across the ocean toward the Blessed Isles, a voyage of discovery and self-discovery that is doomed to a tragic end.

James Cameron is Canadian (his great-great-great-grandfather emigrated to the New World from Scotland). The composer, James Horner, is American with Austrian parents. The singer is Norwegian. Of the two leading actors, Leonardo DiCaprio is American (with German-born mother and part-Italian, part-German father) and Kate Winslet is English. The strange hybrid origin of the work is typical of today's neo-Celtic world.

Thoughts about *Titanic*'s fateful Atlantic voyage bring us back to the idea of a powerful bond between Celticness and the ocean. It is a curiously sad and fatalistic dependence, "but we do only be drownded now and again."

Celticness is as distinct, but also as variable and as changeable, as the sea. Sometimes it seems to be on the rise, on the offensive, aggressively extending and engulfing large areas; sometimes it seems to be in submissive retreat, beaten back by cultural forces from elsewhere. It is a tidal culture that rises and falls, flows and ebbs and then flows again, much like the huge and notoriously powerful tides that wash the rocky cliffs of Europe's Atlantic shore.

BRIEF BIBLIOGRAPHY

Branigan, K. 2005. *From Clan to Clearance*. Oxford: Oxbow.

Brunaux, J. L. 1988. *The Celtic Gauls*. London: Seaby.

Carr-Gomm, P. 1993. *The Druid Way*. Shaftesbury: Element.

Castleden, R. 1983 *The Wilmington Giant*. Wellingborough: Turnstone Press (republished 2012. Seaford: Blatchington Press)

— 1987. *The Stonehenge People*. London and New York: Routledge.

— 1990. *Minoans*. London and New York: Routledge.

— 1993. *The Making of Stonehenge*. London and New York: Routledge.

— 1996. *The Cerne Giant*. Wincanton: Dorset Publishing Company.

— 2000. *King Arthur: The truth behind the legend*. London and New York: Routledge.

— 2000. *Ancient British Hill Figures*. Seaford: S. B. Publications.

— 2005. *Mycenaeans*. London & New York: Routledge.

— *The Apple of Discord: The ancient prequel to the* Iliad. (Forthcoming.)

Chapman, M. 1992. *The Celts: The construction of a myth*. London: St Martin's Press.

Clyde, R. 1995. *From Rebel to Hero: The image of the Highlander*. East Linton: Tuckwell Press.

Coates, R., Breeze, A., and Horovitz, D. 2000. *Celtic Voices, English Places*. Stamford: Shaun Tyas.

Collis, J. 2003. *The Celts: Origins, myths, inventions*. Stroud: Tempus.

Cunliffe, B. 1999. *The Ancient Celts*. Oxford: Oxford University Press.

— 2001. *The Extraordinary Voyage of Pytheas the Greek*. London: Penguin Books.

— 2001. *Facing the Ocean: The Atlantic and its people*. Oxford: Oxford University Press.

Davies, J. 1994. *Wales*. London: Penguin.

— 2000. *The Celts*. London: Cassell.

Davies, N. 1999. *The Isles: A history*. London: Macmillan.

Davies, R.R. 1987. *The Age of Conquest, Wales 1063–1415*. Oxford: Oxford University Press.

— 2000. *The First English Empire: Power and identity in the British*

Isles. Oxford: Oxford University Press.

Esmonde-Cleary, S. 2008. *Rome in the Pyrenees.* Abingdon and New York: Routledge.

Fouet, G., and Soutou, A. 1963. Une cime pyrénéenne consacré a Jupiter: le Mont Sacon. *Gallia* 21, 275–94.

Green, M. 1986. *The Gods of the Celts.* Gloucester: Alan Sutton.

— 1989. *Symbol and Image in Celtic Religious Art.* London: Routledge.

— 1992. *Animals in Celtic Life and Myth.* London and New York: Routledge.

— 1997. *Exploring the World of the Druids.* London: Thames & Hudson.

Green, M. A. 2001. *Dying for the Gods.* Stroud: Tempus.

Harding, D. A. 2007. *The Archaeology of Celtic Art.* Abingdon: Routledge.

Harding, D. W. 1974. *The Iron Age in Lowland Britain.* London: Routledge and Kegan Paul.

Hole, C. 1976. *A Dictionary of British Folk Customs.* London: Hutchinson.

Jackson, P. 1995. *Footloose in archaeology.* Current Archaeology 144.

James, S. 1999. *The Atlantic Celts: Ancient people or modern invention?* London: British Museum Press.

Konstam, A., and Bull. P. 2006. *The Forts of Celtic Britain.* Oxford: Osprey Publishing.

Laing, L. 1979. *Celtic Britain.* London: Routledge & Kegan Paul.

Lewis, M. 1923. *The Queer Side of Things.* London: Selwyn and Blount.

Loomis, R. S. 1993. *Celtic Myth and Arthurian Romance.* London: Constable.

MacCana, P. 1970. *Celtic Mythology.* London: Hamlyn.

McCrone, D. 1994. 'Who do we think we are?' *Scottish Affairs*, 6, 1

Malim, T., and Hayes, L. 2011. The road. *British Archaeology* Sep/Oct, 14–20.

Megaw, R., and Megaw, V. 1989. *Celtic Art.* London: Thames & Hudson.

Miles, D. 2005. *The Tribes of Britain.* London: Weidenfeld & Nicolson.

Miles, D., Palmer, S., Lock, G., Gosden, C., and Cromarty, A. 2003. *Uffington White Horse and its Landscape.* Oxford Archaeology Monograph No. 18.

Morris, J. 1995. *Arthurian Period Sources, Vol 3*: Persons. Chichester: Phillimore.

The Element Encyclopedia of the Celts

Morse, M. A. 2005. *How the Celts came to Britain: Druids, skulls and the birth of archaeology.* Stroud: Tempus.

Newman, P. 1997. *Lost Gods of Albion: The chalk hill-figures of Britain.* Stroud: Sutton Publishing.

Paxman, J. 1999. *The English.* London: Penguin.

Piggott, S. 1974. *The Druids.* Harmondsworth: Penguin Books.

Potter, T. W. and Johns, C. 1992. *Roman Britain.* London: British Museum Press.

Pryor, F. 2004. *Britain BC: Life in Britain and Ireland before the Romans.* London: HarperCollins.

— 2004. *Britain AD: A quest for Arthur, England and the Anglo-Saxons.* London: HarperCollins.

Raftery, B. 1994. *Pagan Celtic Ireland.* London: Thames & Hudson.

Ross, A. 1970. *The Pagan Celts.* London: Batsford.

— 1992. *Pagan Celtic Britain.* London: Constable.

—, and Robins, D. 1989. *The Life and Death of a Druid Prince.* London: Guild Publishing.

Salway. P. 1981. *Roman Britain.* Oxford: Clarendon Press.

Sharkey, J. 1975. *Celtic Mysteries.* London: Book Club Associates.

Spence, L. 1920. *An Encyclopaedia of Occultism.* London: Routledge.

— 1949. *The Magic Arts in Celtic Britain.* London: Constable.

Tanner, M. 2004. *The Last of the Celts.* New Haven & London: Yale University Press.

Waddington, C. 2011. Massacre at Fin Cop. *Current Archaeology* 255, 20–27.

Watson, M. 2004. *Being English in Edinburgh.* Edinburgh University Press.

Webster, G. 1986. *The British Celts and their Gods under Rome.* London: Batsford.

Williams, G. A. 1985. *When was Wales?* London: Penguin.

Woodward, A. 1992. *Shrines and Sacrifice.* London: Batsford/ English Heritage.